Cambridge Studies in Early Modern British History

LONDON CROWDS IN THE
REIGN OF CHARLES II

Cambridge Studies in Early Modern British History

Series editors

ANTHONY FLETCHER
Professor of Modern History, University of Durham

JOHN GUY
Reader in British History, University of Bristol

and JOHN MORRILL
*Lecturer in History, University of Cambridge, and
Fellow and Tutor of Selwyn College*

This is a new series of monographs and studies covering many aspects of the history of the British Isles between the late fifteenth century and the early eighteenth century. It will include the work of established scholars and pioneering work by a new generation of scholars. It will include both reviews and revisions of major topics and books which open up new historical terrain or which reveal startling new perspectives on familiar subjects. It is envisaged that all the volumes will set detailed research into broader perspectives and the books are intended for the use of students as well as of their teachers.

Titles in the series

*The Common Peace: Participation and the Criminal Law in
Seventeenth-Century England*
 CYNTHIA B. HERRUP
Politics, Society and Civil War in Warwickshire
 ANN HUGHES
*London Crowds in the Reign of Charles II: Propaganda and Politics
from the Restoration until the Exclusion Crisis*
 TIM HARRIS
*Criticism and Compliment: The Politics of Literature in the
England of Charles I*
 KEVIN SHARPE
Central Government and the Localities : Hampshire 1649–1689
 ANDREW COLEBY

LONDON CROWDS IN THE REIGN OF CHARLES II

Propaganda and politics from the Restoration until the exclusion crisis

TIM HARRIS

Assistant Professor, Brown University,
Providence, Rhode Island

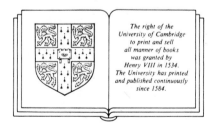

The right of the
University of Cambridge
to print and sell
all manner of books
was granted by
Henry VIII in 1534.
The University has printed
and published continuously
since 1584.

CAMBRIDGE UNIVERSITY PRESS

Cambridge
London   New York   New Rochelle
Melbourne   Sydney

Published by the Press Syndicate of the University of Cambridge
The Pitt Building, Trumpington Street, Cambridge CB2 1RP
32 East 57th Street, New York, NY 10022, USA
10 Stamford Road, Oakleigh, Melbourne 3166, Australia

First published 1987

Printed in Great Britain at The Bath Press, Avon

British Library cataloguing in publication data
Harris, Tim
London crowds in the reign of Charles II:
propaganda and politics from the Restoration
until the exclusion crisis.—(Cambridge
studies in early modern British history; 2).
1. Public opinion—England—London—
History—17th century   2. London (England)
—History—17th century   3. London
(England)—Politics and government
I. Title
942.106'6   DA681

Library of Congress cataloguing in publication data
Harris, Tim
London crowds in the reign of Charles II.
(Cambridge studies in early modern British history)
Bibliography: p.
Includes index.
1. Great Britain—History—Charles II, 1660–1685.
2. Great Britain—Politics and government—1660–1688.
3. London (England)—History—17th century.   4. Propaganda, British—History—17th century.   5. Crowds.
6. Political participation—England—London—History—
17th century. I. Title. II. Series.
DA445.H24   1987   941.06'6   87–14651

ISBN 0 521 32623 0

For Beth, Victoria and James

CONTENTS

List of illustrations   *page* ix
Acknowledgements   xi
List of abbreviations   xiii

1   APPROACHES TO THE CROWD   1
    Conceptual framework   6

2   RECONSTRUCTING THE POLITICAL CULTURE OF THE
    PEOPLE   14
    The problem of 'popular' politics   15
    The capacity for collective agitation   22
    Political consciousness   27
    Conclusion   35

3   THE PEOPLE AND THE RESTORATION   36
    Attitudes towards the monarchy, 1659–60   38
    Expectations of the Restoration   52
    Conclusion   60

4   THE PROBLEM OF RELIGION   62
    The effects of persecution   63
    The nonconformist critique   73
    The bawdy house riots of 1668   82
    The backdrop to exclusion   91
    Conclusion   94

5   WHIG MASS PROPAGANDA DURING THE EXCLUSION
    CRISIS   96
    The whig mass propaganda campaign   98
    The whig message   108
    Slanting towards a nonconformist audience   118
    Conclusion   129

6 THE TORY RESPONSE   130
   The tory counter-attack   131
   Tyranny and popery   133
   The attack on whig heroes   145
   The tory alternative   150
   The propaganda war   153
   Conclusion   155

7 CROWD POLITICS AND EXCLUSION   156
   Hostility towards the Duke of York's succession   157
   The emergence of an anti-exclusionist position   164
   Rivalry between whig and tory groups   172
   The whigs on the defensive   180
   Conclusion   188

8 THE ECONOMICS OF CROWD POLITICS   189
   The weavers' disputes   191
   Other economic grievances and their political implications   204
   Conclusion   215

9 A DIVIDED SOCIETY   217

   Bibliography   229
   Index   257

ILLUSTRATIONS

1 *Portrait of Hugh Peters* (1660)   *page 56*
2 *The Solemn Mock Procession of the Pope, Cardinals, Jesuits,*
   Fryers, Nuns, etc. . . . November the 17th, 1680, for I. Oliver
   (1680)   105
3 *The Contents (Hats for Caps) Contented* (1680)   116
4 *A Prospect of a Popish Successor, Displayed by Hell-Bred*
   Cruelty (1681)   126
5 *Strange's Case, Strangly Altered* (1680)   127
6 [Sir R. L'Estrange], *The Committee; Or, Popery in Masquerade*
   (1680)   137
7 'Visions of Thorough Reformation', frontispiece to E. Pettit,
   Visions of the Reformation (1683)   142
8 'Britannia Mourning the Execution of Charles I', frontispiece to
   J. Nalson, *An Impartial Collection of the Great Affairs of State,*
   I (1682)   143

Acknowledgement: These photographs are reproduced by
permission of the Trustees of the British Library.

Map: London in the late seventeenth century. (Based on a map in
John Stevenson, *Popular Disturbances in England, 1700–1870,*
1979.)   xv

ACKNOWLEDGEMENTS

This book grew out of a PhD thesis which was funded by a grant from the Department of Education and Science. The thesis was completed and then converted into this book whilst I was a research fellow at Emmanuel College, Cambridge. I should particularly like to thank the fellows of Emmanuel for their intellectual, moral and financial support over the years. I am also extremely grateful to the British Academy for providing me with a grant to finance much of the additional research needed for the book. The staff of the various record offices and libraries I visited when conducting my research deserve a special mention for their help and patience: the Bodleian Library, the Corporation of London Record Office, the Greater London Record Office, the Guildhall Library, the House of Lords Office, Dr Williams's Library, the Pepysian Library and the University Library, Cambridge.

In writing this book I have been assisted by a great many friends and colleagues. My approach to this topic has been influenced by the advice and criticisms I received from Jeremy Boulton, Colin Brooks, Peter Burke, Gary De Krey, Dagmar Freist, Chris Husbands, Ben Klein, Keith Lindley, Valerie Pearl, Bob Scribner, Bob Shoemaker, Bill Speck and John Walter. The greatest intellectual debt I owe to Mark Goldie, who supervised the initial research project, who patiently read all my drafts, and who continued to be a source of direction, criticism and encouragement throughout. Without his stamina, tolerance and inspiration, this work would have been vastly inferior. Special thanks also should go to John Morrill, who read the completed manuscript, and who was always ready with helpful advice at the end of the phone. Various sections of this book were tried out as seminars delivered in Cambridge, Oxford, London, Brighton, Hull and Providence, Rhode Island, and I am grateful to all who participated in those discussions and helped me clarify my arguments. Of course, the responsibility for the final form this book takes is entirely my own.

Several people have aided me in personal ways of which they might not be entirely aware. Alan Jenkins, Geoff Eley and Gwyn Prins helped nurture my early interest in history and stimulated my desire to do historical research. Peter Clemoes, Henry Phillips and John Thoday taught me more about cultural traditions than they might realize. I also owe a special debt to my family – Ron, Audrey, Kevin, Sarah and Tina – for their support over the years. I owe most to Beth, Victoria and James, my wife and children, who suffered from having to live with a moody, and all too often absent, researcher. This book is dedicated to them with thanks and joy.

ABBREVIATIONS

BIHR	*Bulletin of the Institute of Historical Research*
BL	British Library
BM Prints	F. G. Stephens and M. D. George, eds., *Catalogue of Prints and Drawings in the British Museum*, 11 vols. (1870–1954)
Bodl. Lib.	Bodleian Library
Burnet	G. Burnet, *History of My Own Time: Part One, From the Reign of Charles II*, ed. O. Airey, 2 vols. (Oxford, 1897–1900)
CClarSP	*Calendar of Clarendon State Papers Preserved in the Bodleian Library*, ed. F. J. Routledge, 5 vols. (Oxford, 1872–1932)
CHJ	*Cambridge Historical Journal*
CJ	*Journals of the House of Commons*
Clarke Papers	*The Clarke Papers: Selections from the Papers of William Clarke*, ed. C. H. Firth, 4 vols. (1899–1901)
CLRO	Corporation of London Record Office
CSPD	*Calendar of State Papers, Domestic*
CSPVen	*Calendar of State Papers, Venetian*
DNB	*Dictionary of National Biography*
EcHR	*Economic History Review*
EHR	*English Historical Review*
Evelyn, *Diary*	J. Evelyn, *Diary*, ed. E. S. De Beer, 6 vols. (Oxford, 1955)
GD	Gaol Delivery
GLRO	Greater London Record Office
Hatt. Corr.	Hatton Family, *Correspondence, 1601–1704. Being Chiefly Letters Addressed to Christopher, First Viscount Hatton*, ed. E. M. Thompson, 2 vols. (1873)
HJ	*Historical Journal*
HLRO	House of Lords Record Office
HMC	*Historical Manuscripts Commission*
ign.	ignoramus

ind.	indictment
JBS	*Journal of British Studies*
Jeaff.	*Middlesex County Records*, ed. J. C. Jeaffreson, 4 vols. (1888–92)
JMH	*Journal of Modern History*
Journal	Journal of the Common Council
LC	Library of Congress
LJ	*Journals of the House of Lords*
Luttrell	N. Luttrell, *A Brief Historical Relation of State of Affairs from September, 1678, to April, 1714*, 6 vols. (Oxford, 1857)
Morrice	Dr Williams's Library, Roger Morrice Entring Book
O + T	Oyer and Terminer
PC	Privy Council Register
Pepys, *Diary*	S. Pepys, *Diary*, ed. R. C. Latham and W. Matthews, 11 vols. (1970–83)
POAS	*Poems on Affairs of State*, ed. G. de F. Lord *et al.*, vols. I–III (Yale, 1963–8)
PP	*Past and Present*
PRO	Public Record Office
rec.	recognizance
Rep.	Repertory of the Court of Aldermen
Rugge	T. Rugge, *Diurnal*, ed. W. L. Sachse (1961)
SP	State Papers
SRO	Surrey Record Office
State Trials	*State Trials*, ed. T. B. Howell, 33 vols. (1809–26)
TBHS	*Transactions of the Baptist Historical Society*
TCHS	*Transactions of the Congregational History Society*
TRHS	*Transactions of the Royal Historical Society*

Note: In quoting from seventeenth-century sources I have retained the original spelling, although I have extended contemporary contractions and occasionally supplied punctuation necessary to the sense of the passage. Dates are given in the Old Style, but with the year regarded as beginning on 1 January. All works cited were published in London, unless otherwise stated.

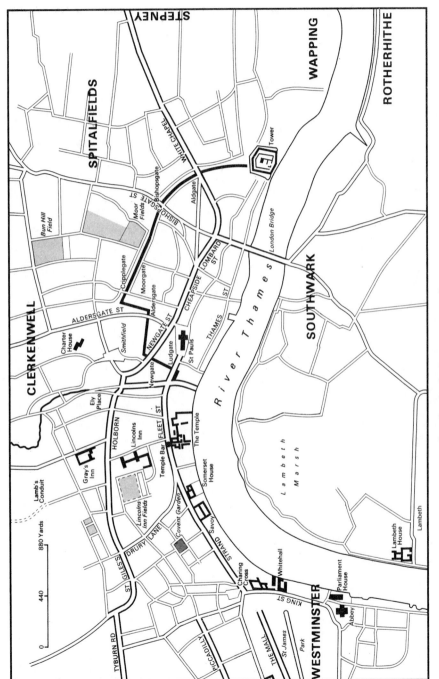

London in the late seventeenth century.

Approaches to the crowd

Interest in crowd unrest, whether in London or in the country in general, has burgeoned enormously in the past few decades. It was as long ago as 1938 that Max Beloff first published his pioneer study of popular disturbances in England in the period 1660–1714.[1] Since then, the study of the crowd has been completely transformed by a number of scholars working mainly on Hanoverian England, Eric Hobsbawm, George Rudé, and Edward Thompson being the best known.[2] Several case studies of riots in London during the eighteenth century have greatly increased our knowledge of popular political attitudes in the metropolis.[3] The work of Christopher Hill and Brian Manning, who sought to recapture the attitudes and outlooks of those below the level of society's elite in the first half of the seventeenth century,[4] has stimulated further investigation into popular political agitation for the period up to 1660.[5] Political unrest in London in the late 1630s and 1640s

---

[1] M. Beloff, *Public Order and Popular Disturbances, 1660–1714* (1938).

[2] E. J. Hobsbawm, 'The Machine-Breakers', *PP*, 1 (1952), 57–70; G. Rudé, *The Crowd in History: A Study of Popular Disturbances in France and England, 1730–1848* (New York, 1964); E. P. Thompson, 'The Moral Economy of the English Crowd in the Eighteenth Century', *PP*, 50 (1971), 76–136. A useful overview of popular disturbances in England in the eighteenth and nineteenth centuries is provided by J. Stevenson, *Popular Disturbances in England, 1700–1870* (1979).

[3] G. Rudé, *Wilkes and Liberty: A Social Study of 1763–1774* (Oxford, 1962); G. Rudé, *Paris and London in the Eighteenth Century: Studies in Popular Protest* (1970), part 3; N. Rogers, 'Popular Disaffection in London during the Forty-Five', *London Journal*, 1 (1975), 5–27; G. Holmes, 'The Sacheverell Riots: The Crowd and the Church in Early Eighteenth-Century London', in P. Slack, ed., *Rebellion, Popular Protest and the Social Order in Early Modern England* (Cambridge, 1984), pp. 232–62; N. Rogers, 'Popular Protest in Early Hanoverian London', in ibid., pp. 263–93; J. L. Fitts, 'Newcastle's Mob', *Albion*, 5 (1973), 41–9.

[4] C. Hill, *The World Turned Upside Down: Radical Ideas During the English Revolution* (Harmondsworth, 1975); B. S. Manning, *The English People and the English Revolution* (Harmondsworth, 1978); B. S. Manning, 'The Nobles, the People, and the Constitution', *PP*, 9 (1956), 42–64; B. S. Manning, 'Religion and Politics: The Godly People', in B. S. Manning, ed., *Politics, Religion, and the English Civil War* (1973), pp. 81–123; B. S. Manning, 'The Peasantry and the English Revolution', *Journal of Peasant Studies*, 2 (1975), 133–58.

[5] B. S. Capp, *The Fifth Monarchy Men: A Study of Seventeenth-Century English Millenarianism* (1972); K. J. Lindley, *Fenland Riots and the English Revolution* (1982); B. Sharp,

has received considerable recent attention.[6] As a result, the later seventeenth century has now become the historiographical poor relation to both the earlier and later periods.[7]

This neglect of interest in Charles II's reign is surprising, considering the significant part crowd agitation seems to have played in the politics of the period. In 1926 Sir Charles Firth argued that popular unrest in the City in late 1659 and early 1660 played a crucial role in bringing about the restoration of monarchy, and he drew a contrast with the 1640s, when the opposition of the City had led to the 'vanquishing' of Charles I.[8] The cause of this apparent change in the political sympathies of the London populace, and the extent to which they had shed their previous radicalism (if radical they had been) by 1660, is a question which has still to be fully investigated.[9] If Firth is correct in arguing that the restoration of the Stuarts was genuinely popular, this popularity does not appear to have lasted long. However, little is as yet known as to when and why disillusionment with the new regime began to creep in.[10]

The 1670s and 1680s were dominated by anxieties about popery: a catholic presence at Court, a foreign policy pursued in alliance with the catholic French against the protestant Dutch, the prospect of a catholic succession, were all cause for concern. Fears of what catholic rule would mean were intensified by Louis XIV's style of government in France, whilst the techniques employed at home by Danby in his attempt to 'manage' parliament, caused many to believe there was already a drift to a more absolute form of government in England.[11] It has been acknowledged that these fears of

In Contempt of All Authority: Rural Artisans and Riot in the West of England, 1586–1660 (1980); D. Underdown, *Revel, Riot and Rebellion: Popular Politics and Culture in England, 1603–1660* (Oxford, 1985); A. Fletcher and J. Stevenson, eds., *Order and Disorder in Early Modern England* (Cambridge, 1985).

[6] Manning, *English People*, esp. chs. 3, 4; S. R. Smith, 'The Apprentices' Parliament of 1647', *History Today*, 22 (1972), 576–82; S. R. Smith, 'The London Apprentices as Seventeenth-Century Adolescents', in Slack, ed., *Rebellion*, pp. 219–31; S. R. Smith, 'Almost Revolutionaries: The London Apprentices during the Civil Wars', *Huntington Library Quarterly*, 42 (1978–9), 313–28; I. Gentles, 'The Struggle for London in the Second Civil War', *HJ*, 26 (1983), 277–305; K. J. Lindley, 'Riot Prevention and Control in Early Stuart London', *TRHS*, 5th Series, 33 (1983), 109–26

[7] Excluding my work, there is only one article specifically on crowd unrest in London in Charles II's reign, and this focuses on the 'trade' disputes of the weavers in 1675. See R. M. Dunn, 'The London Weavers' Riot of 1675', *Guildhall Studies in London History*, I, no. 1 (October, 1973), 13–23.

[8] Sir C. Firth, 'London during the Civil War', *History*, 11 (1926–7), 25–36.

[9] But see the remarks on this in: Hill, *World Turned Upside Down*, chs. 17, 18; C. Hill, *Some Intellectual Consequences of the English Revolution* (1980); C. Hill, *The Experience of Defeat: Milton and Some Contemporaries* (1984).

[10] But see T. J. G. Harris, 'The Bawdy House Riots of 1668', *HJ*, 29 (1986), 537–56.

[11] J. R. Jones, *Country and Court: England 1658–1714* (1978), ch. 9.

popery and arbitrary government permeated all levels of society,[12] and that the popular anti-catholic agitation of 1688 is important to our understanding of the Glorious Revolution.[13] Much is known about the conflicts within the political elite in the second half of Charles II's reign. Historians have examined the rise of parties in the 1670s, the Popish Plot of 1678 and its subsequent political exploitation, the demand for the exclusion of the catholic heir and the strife between the whigs and tories in the three exclusion parliaments of 1679–81; and also the extra-parliamentary activity of the whigs after 1681 and the consequent tory reaction.[14] Party tensions within the City of London have been investigated; in particular, the political struggles of the whigs and tories in the common council and the court of aldermen, and also the battles for control of the important political offices of lord mayor and sheriff.[15] The 'London crowd' is known to have played an important part in the drama of these years: important enough, indeed, to lead to the coining of a new word. According to Sir Roger North, it was during the exclusion crisis that 'the Rabble first changed their Title, and were called the Mob', being a contraction of the Latin *mobile vulgus*.[16] We know that the whigs sought to apply pressure for exclusion by mobilizing mass support, especially in London, by using techniques of agitation and propaganda, the most famous being their petitioning campaigns and the pope-burning rituals held on 17 November.[17] Yet the crowd agitation of the period

---

[12] R. Clifton, 'The Popular Fear of Catholics during the English Revolution', in Slack, ed., *Rebellion*, pp. 129–61; R. Clifton, 'Fear of Popery', in C. Russell, ed., *The Origins of the English Civil War* (1973), pp. 144–67; K. H. D. Haley, '"No Popery" in the Reign of Charles II', in J. S. Bromley and E. H. Kossman, eds., *Britain and the Netherlands*, V (The Hague, 1975), 102–19.

[13] W. L. Sachse, 'The Mob and the Revolution of 1688', *JBS*, 4 (1964), 23–41.

[14] K. G. Feiling, *A History of the Tory Party, 1640–1714* (Oxford, 1924); J. R. Jones, *The First Whigs: The Politics of the Exclusion Crisis, 1678–83* (Oxford, 1961); K. H. D. Haley, *The First Earl of Shaftesbury* (Oxford, 1968); J. P. Kenyon, *The Popish Plot* (1972); J. Miller, *Popery and Politics in England, 1660–1688* (Cambridge, 1973); J. R. Western, *Monarchy and Revolution: The English State in the 1680s* (1972); J. H. M. Salmon, 'Algernon Sydney and the Rye House Plot', *History Today*, 4 (1954), 698–705; D. J. Milne, 'The Results of the Rye House Plot and their Influences upon the Revolution of 1688', *TRHS*, 5th Series, 1 (1951), 91–108; R. E. Pickavance, 'The English Boroughs and the King's Government: A Study of the Tory Reaction, 1681–85', unpub. Oxford DPhil thesis (1976).

[15] D. F. Allen, 'The Crown and the Corporation of London in the Exclusion Crisis', unpub. Cambridge PhD thesis (1977); A. G. Smith, 'London and the Crown, 1681–1685', unpub. Wisconsin PhD thesis (1967).

[16] R. North, *Examen; Or, An Enquiry into the Credit and Veracity of a Pretended Complete History* (1740), p. 574. The *OED* dates the first use of '*mobile vulgus*' in England to 1600, of 'mobile' to 1676, and of 'mob' to 1688.

[17] Haley, *Shaftesbury*, pp. 559–64, 627–8, 641; Allen, 'Crown and Corporation', pp. 137–59; O. W. Furley, 'The Pope-Burning Processions of the Late Seventeenth Century', *History*, 44 (1959), 16–23; S. Williams, 'The Pope-Burning Processions of 1679–81', *Journal of the Warburg and Courtauld Institutes*, 21 (1958), 104–18.

has usually only been considered as a footnote to the history of the elite, and not seriously studied in its own right.[18]

Our understanding of the political conflicts of this time could be enhanced by a detailed study of the London crowd. Some historians have argued that the parliamentary struggles of the Stuart century can only be fully understood if we acknowledge that the 'political nation' was, in fact, far broader than usually believed.[19] Work on parties in the reign of Queen Anne has shown that the bitter party strife of this period was fed by political divisions that existed at all levels of society, and not just at the level of parliament and the electorate.[20] Although Geoffrey Holmes has recently warned against exaggerating these tensions, he still believes that the split within the elite in Charles II's reign, and the willingness of part of that elite to countenance popular agitation, especially in London, was a major cause of continuing political instability at this time.[21] Originally, historians saw the whig/tory divide of the exclusion period very much in constitutional terms, between monarchists, parliamentarians, and republicans.[22] Yet party tensions of William's and Anne's reigns have been shown to have had an important religious dimension,[23] and it has been recently recognized that religion was perhaps a more important factor in defining elite attitudes towards power within the state in the 1670s and 1680s than pure constitutional principle.[24] The crucial factor here was the question of religious persecution, a persecution which, arguably, affected the lower orders much more severely than it did members of the elite. In short, our full understanding of politics in Charles II's reign has been limited by an over-concentration on the elite, something which a study of crowd politics in London could go some way towards rectifying.[25]

[18] The only person to examine the activities of the London crowd in Charles's reign in any depth is Arthur Smith, although he focuses on the period 1681–5. See Smith, 'London and the Crown', chs. 5, 6. Useful insights into popular agitation can be found in Haley, *Shaftesbury.*

[19] J. H. Plumb, 'Political Man', in J. L. Clifford, ed., *Man Versus Society in Eighteenth-Century Britain: Six Points of View* (Cambridge, 1968), pp. 1–21; J. H. Plumb, 'The Growth of the Electorate in England, 1600–1715', *PP*, 45 (1969), 90–116; D. Hirst, *The Representative of the People? Voters and Voting in England under the Early Stuarts* (Cambridge, 1975).

[20] G. Holmes and W. A. Speck, eds., *The Divided Society: Party Politics in England, 1694–1716* (1967).

[21] G. Holmes, 'The Achievement of Stability: The Social Context of Politics from the 1680s to the Age of Walpole', in J. Cannon, ed., *The Whig Ascendancy: Colloquies on Hanoverian England* (1981), pp. 1–27.

[22] B. Behrens, 'The Whig Theory of the Constitution in the Reign of Charles II', *CHJ*, 7 (1941), 42–71; O. W. Furley, 'The Whig Exclusionists: Pamphlet Literature in the Exclusion Campaign', *CHJ*, 13 (1957), 19–36; Jones, *First Whigs*; D. F. Allen, 'Political Clubs in Restoration London', *HJ*, 19 (1976), 561–80; Allen, 'Crown and Corporation'.

[23] G. Holmes, *Religion and Party in Late Stuart England* (1975); G. S. De Krey, *A Fractured Society: The Politics of London in the First Age of Party, 1688–1715* (Oxford, 1985).

[24] M. A. Goldie, 'John Locke and Anglican Royalism', *Political Studies*, 31 (1983), 61–85.

[25] Cf. J. S. Morrill, *Seventeenth-Century Britain, 1603–1714* (1980), p. 126.

It is necessary to say at the outset something about what I mean by crowd politics. To maintain a certain flexibility, it might be more helpful to start with some negative definitions. Unlike Rudé, who chose to focus on the 'aggressive mob' and the 'hostile outburst', I shall not limit my study to riots and social protest. Many of the crowd scenes of Charles II's reign are more appropriately described as demonstrations, which were often of a peaceful kind.[26] Indeed, the best-known crowds of that period are the ones which witnessed the pope-burning processions of the exclusion period, and these more properly come within Rudé's category of audiences, or ceremonial crowds, which he did not include in his area of study.[27] Another weakness with focusing on riot is that we only look at the disaffected. If, as Rudé has shown, crowds were usually comprised of 'the inferior set of people',[28] it is nevertheless a fallacy to assume that 'the inferior set' as a whole must have shared the views expressed in the riot.[29] Yet I do not intend to offer a study of the 'crowd' in London *per se*, whether that crowd be a riotous or a celebratory one.[30] For reasons which will be explained shortly, I do not believe the concept of the crowd to be a very helpful organizational category. Moreover, this study will find it necessary to examine many types of activity, such as the speaking of seditious words, which are not crowd phenomena. Nor is my main concern the suppression of crowd activity, or the maintenance of order,[31] although aspects of this, and of riots and crowds in general, will, of course, be considered.

What I am interested in is studying the political views of those types of people whom contemporaries regarded as comprising 'the mob', the mass of ordinary Londoners below the level of the social and political elite. I shall be concerned with political activity which took a non-institutional form, or what might loosely be termed 'street politics'. Primarily my intention is to offer an investigation of the expression and significance of public opinion in London, exploring the attitudes and concerns of those below the level of the elite. Central to this book will be an examination of the proposition,

---

[26] The word demonstration was not used in this sense in English until the nineteenth century. See *OED*. However, it was fairly common for contemporary observers to refer to crowd scenes as 'demonstrations of joy' or 'demonstrations of infidelity'. See Bodl. Lib., MS Carte 30, fol. 649; BL, Add. MS 25,363, fol. 125; *HMC, Ormond*, NS IV, 580; LC, MS 18,124, VIII, fol. 174; ibid., IX, fol. 93.

[27] Rudé, *Crowd in History*, p. 4.

[28] G. Rudé, 'The London "Mob" of the Eighteenth Century', in his *Paris and London*, pp. 298–302.

[29] Rudé, *Crowd in History*, p. 210.

[30] For such a study, see J. M. Harrison, 'The Crowd in Bristol, 1790–1835', unpub. Cambridge PhD thesis (1983).

[31] D. F. Allen, 'The Political Role of the London Trained Bands in the Exclusion Crisis, 1678–1681, *EHR*, 87 (1972), 287–303; Dunn, 'Weavers' Riots'; Lindley, 'Riot Prevention'.

which has not been seriously challenged, that 'the London crowd' was in favour of a restoration of monarchy in 1659–60, but 20 years later had become alienated from the Stuarts, and was once more an instrument of radical politics. Such an examination will, in part, entail a study of popular protest after the fashion of historians like Rudé, Holmes, and Rogers, using legal records to look at riots, demonstrations, and seditious words. It will involve a consideration of celebratory crowds and public rituals. It also necessitates an investigation of how people become informed about the political controversies of their age, whether through exposure to propaganda deliberately aimed at politicizing the masses, or through everyday religious, social, and economic experience. As well as asking which people protested and why, it will also need to assess the typicality of those who protested, ask whether some people perhaps remained loyal, and investigate whether we are seeing a redefinition in the allegiances of the London crowd over time, or whether we in fact have two very different crowds in London. A study of this nature raises particular conceptual problems, which need to be considered first.

CONCEPTUAL FRAMEWORK

Studies of the crowd, and the related sphere of collective protest with which it has often been (rather confusingly) conflated, have come from a variety of academic disciplines with very different preoccupations. Nevertheless, in two crucial respects, most of the existing literature encourages us to think about the crowd in similar ways. First, there is a tendency to invest the crowd with an artificial reality of its own, or to 'reify' the crowd. Not only is the crowd ascribed a greater unity and homogeneity of feeling than is necessarily warranted, but 'it' is even said to possess a mind of its own. Secondly, most approaches are dominated by structural considerations which make it difficult to investigate the way crowds change over time.

In the late nineteenth century, Gustave Le Bon postulated the view that 'the crowd' had a 'collective mind', and that the people that comprised it thought and acted 'in a manner quite different from that in which each individual of them would feel, think, and act were he in a state of isolation'.[32] Sigmund Freud sought to underpin Le Bon's conclusions in psychoanalytic theory, reinforcing the description of the homogeneity of crowd members when he argued that individuals in the group 'behave as though they were uniform'.[33] Although their views on the irrational behaviour of crowds have

---

[32] G. Le Bon, *The Crowd: A Study of the Popular Mind* (1896), p. 6.
[33] S. Freud, *Group Psychology and the Analysis of the Ego* (1922), p. 56.

been severely criticized,[34] the concept of the collective conscience of the crowd has been acknowledged to possess some merit.[35]

A massive literature by social psychologists and sociologists exists which investigates the question of why collective unrest breaks out,[36] the aim being, in contrast to historical research, to develop analytical concepts which are both temporally and culturally non-specific; or, as one author put it, to discover 'principles common to all crowds'.[37] Despite the greater interest of historians in the unique or the individual episode, and the desire to set their work in a context which is historically specific, we can still detect a tendency towards a rather static analysis. Historians have asked important questions about the structure of a particular crowd, or the 'rules' governing a particular type of disturbance (such as the food riot), but have been less interested in looking at changes through time in the assumptions and attitudes of the types of people who comprised the crowd. The invaluable contributions of scholars like Hobsbawm, Rudé, and Thompson,[38] which have led to a complete re-thinking of the approach to the study of riot, were all preoccupied with the questions of the composition, organization, objectives and beliefs of the rioting crowd. The conclusion found for eighteenth-century England, that the crowd was not the 'rabble' or society's dregs, but was comprised of respectable (if often lowly) types, who were informed, disciplined, and in possession of broad notions of the necessity and legitimacy of their actions, has also been found to have an applicability in other countries and centuries.[39] The typical technique has been to offer case studies of particular riots, and this has even been true when a number of riots are being studied in a single area over a period of time. Thus Rudé has

---

[34] G. Lefebvre, 'Foules révolutionaires', *Annales historique de la Révolution française*, 11 (1934), 1–26; R. A. Nye, *The Origins of Crowd Psychology: Gustave LeBon and the Crisis of Mass Democracy in the Third Republic* (1975).

[35] Lefebvre, 'Foules révolutionaires', pp. 10–11.

[36] For useful surveys of this literature, see: S. Milgram and H. Toch, 'Collective Behaviour: Crowds and Social Movements', in G. Lindzey and E. Aronson, eds., *The Handbook of Social Psychology*, IV (Reading, Massachusetts, 1969), 507–610; S. Wright, *Crowds and Riots: A Study in Social Organization* (1978), ch. 1; S. Taylor, 'The Scarman Report and the Explanation of Riots', in J. Benyon, ed., *Scarman and After: Essays Reflecting on Lord Scarman's Report, the Riots, and their Aftermath* (Leicester, 1984), pp. 20–7.

[37] Milgram and Toch, 'Collective Behaviour', p. 509.

[38] See references in footnote 2 above.

[39] See, for example: D. J. V. Jones, *Before Rebecca: Popular Protests in Wales, 1793–1895* (1973), pp. 201–3; K. J. Logue, *Popular Disturbances in Scotland, 1780–1815* (Edinburgh, 1979), ch. 9; Rudé, *Crowd in History*, pp. 23–31, 38, 44; E. J. Hobsbawm, *Primitive Rebels: Studies in Archaic Forms of Social Movement in the Nineteenth and Twentieth Centuries* (Manchester, 1959), pp. 113–14; R. Pillorget, *Mouvements insurrectionnels en Provence entre 1596 et 1715* (Paris, 1975), pp. 992–5; L. Rodriguez, 'The Spanish Riots of 1766', *PP*, 59 (1973), 143–5; J. C. Scott, *The Moral Economy of the Peasant: Rebellion and Subsistence in South-East Asia* (New Haven, 1976). Of course, this is not to suggest that all the conclusions of these authors are similar.

offered a series of case studies of 'the London mob' through the eighteenth century, but he has not investigated the way the attitudes of the lower orders, as occasionally revealed in riot, changed over time.

All the above approaches concentrate on crowd conflict. This is something which has been criticized in recent years, because the focus is solely on forms of dissension within society. An historical distortion is thereby encouraged by deliberately ignoring those forms of collective behaviour which could function to generate and sustain consensus.[40] Emile Durkeim, in his work on religious rituals, showed how certain types of collective activity could function as a form of social integration.[41] E. Shils and M. Young, in their study of the coronation of Elizabeth II, developed a neo-Durkheimian analysis, seeing the coronation as the kind of ceremonial 'in which society reaffirms the moral values which constitute it as a society and renews its devotion to those values by an act of communion'.[42] This type of approach could have a pertinence for some of the public rituals of Charles II's reign, such as the coronation of 1661, the lord mayor's shows, or even the pope-burning processions of the exclusion crisis. By concentrating on the extent to which cohesion or social integration is encouraged by such rituals, however, we can blind ourselves to more fundamental tensions that still exist. Just because a crowd is willing to take to the streets to demonstrate its attachment to the monarchy, say, or to the civic authorities, or its hostility towards catholicism, this does not mean that the experience of that attachment is the same for different members of the crowd.[43] In that respect, many historians who focus explicitly on crowd protest nevertheless commit a similar error to the neo-Durkheimians. For them, the conflict exists between the crowd, often synonymous with the lower orders, and the ruling classes; but at the level of the crowd, the model is still a consensual one. The real problem with focusing on the rioting crowd, therefore, is not that it exaggerates dissension, but that it obscures it. Because the contented and the satisfied seldom have anything to protest about, such an approach cannot help us understand the extent to which dissatisfaction was not the norm amongst those whom Rudé styles 'the inferior set of people'. And yet in particular political circumstances, such as those which prevailed in London in 1647,

---

[40] R. J. Holton, 'The Crowd in History: Some Problems of Theory and Method', *Social History*, 3 (1978), 219–33; Harrison, 'Crowd in Bristol', pp. 3–4, ch. 11.

[41] E. Durkheim, *The Elementary Forms of Religious Life*, trans. by J. W. Swain (1915), esp. p. 427.

[42] E. Shils and M. Young, 'The Meaning of the Coronation', *Sociological Review*, NS I, no. 2 (December, 1953), 67.

[43] Cf. criticisms of the neo-Durkheimian approach by S. Lukes, 'Political Ritual and Social Integration', *Sociology*, 9 (1975), 292–3; E. Hammerton and D. Cannadine, 'Conflict and Consensus on a Ceremonial Occasion: The Diamond Jubilee in Cambridge in 1897', *HJ*, 24 (1981), 111–46.

it is possible to see from collective actions that there was fierce political disagreement amongst the lower orders.[44]

Although the approaches so far summarized are different in significant respects, they all encourage us to see the crowd as an homogeneous entity and as representing a consensus, at least within itself, and amongst the types of people of whom it was comprised. This tendency to 'reify' the crowd is reinforced by the static approach usually employed. No way has been suggested for examining changes in the attitudes of the crowd over time. This raises problems when 'it', 'the crowd', is seen to change its mind. Contemporaries simply believed that the masses were fickle: 'what is more fickle than the multitude?';[45] 'the multitude judg weakly', and nothing could be expected from them but 'uncertaintie'.[46] Oliver Cromwell believed that 'those very persons' who cheered him in success, 'would shout as much if [he] ... were going to be hanged'.[47]

Despite the attempts of modern historians to ascribe a certain degree of rationality to the activity of the crowd, those who have attempted a diachronic analysis by joining up the case studies have been led to similar conclusions. The London crowd was pro-Stuart in 1660, whig in 1679–81, anti-Stuart by 1688, tory by 1710, anti-Hanoverian, if not unambiguously pro-Stuart after 1714, and pro-Wilkes by the 1760s. The London crowd is therefore seen as traditionally acting in opposition to whichever government was in power.[48] For example, Dame Lucy Sutherland suggested that 'whenever political excitement ran high the London crowd could be relied on to emerge and give the added support of their clamour to the Opposition cause'.[49] Even Rudé fell into the same trap. Discussing the view that the London crowd in the late eighteenth century was still an unreliable instrument of radical politics, he cited as proof the fact that 'the same crowd that had shouted for "Wilkes and Liberty" in 1768 was, a dozen years later, directing its energies into channels that were hardly propitious for the radical cause – destroying catholic houses and chapels'.[50]

Three things need to be avoided: the reification of the crowd; the temptation of using 'it' as evidence of 'public opinion' in general; and, finally, trying to measure changes in that opinion by comparing the activities of

---

[44] Gentles, 'Struggle for London'.

[45] N. Estwicke, *A Dialogue Betwixt a Conformist and a Nonconformist Concerning the Lawfulness of Private Meetings* (1668), p. 9.

[46] Rev. J. Ward, *Diary, Extending from 1648 to 1679*, ed. C. Severn (1839), pp. 223, 291.

[47] Burnet, I, 154.

[48] Stevenson, *Popular Disturbances*, p. 315. See also the analysis in his ch. 4.

[49] L. Sutherland, 'The City of London in Eighteenth-Century Politics', in R. Pares and A. J. P. Taylor, eds., *Essays Presented to Sir Lewis Namier* (Oxford, 1956), p. 59.

[50] Rudé, *Crowd in History*, pp. 220–1.

'the London crowd' over time.[51] Although an obvious point, it perhaps needs to be stressed that a crowd is a collection of individuals, and every time a new crowd appears, the individuals are re-grouped. Some die, some become disillusioned, some change sides, some do fight again, whilst others see no need to, but each crowd is different from the last. The conceptual starting point should not, therefore, be 'the crowd', but the problem of individual political self-definition. We need to discover how different people perceived and experienced their political world: for example, through an inherited cultural apparatus, through religious practice, a direct experience of the workings of the law, exposure to propaganda, socio-economic influences, the unfolding of political events, and so forth. The ideal must be to recreate all the dimensions of the political culture of the people of London. When considering collective action, a certain crowd at a specific time might be seen as perhaps offering only a partial statement of certain aspects of that political culture. Another crowd later on might contain some similar elements to the last, although some might have been redefined, and different people might be stating different views for the first time, even though these views were held before but remained unexpressed in protest. To put it another way: whig and tory crowds at different times might not mean that 'the London crowd' changed its mind. Instead, we might be witnessing two different aspects of London political culture that were present (in some form) throughout the period, but which required different historical conjunctures for them to manifest themselves in protest and therefore become visible to the historian.

It is thus essential to begin by exploring the contours of London political culture, and then to investigate the ways in which the concerns and preoccupations of Londoners developed and were shaped over time so that we can achieve a satisfactory diachronic approach. In Chapter 2 I shall look at the potential for political activity by the masses, at their ability to take self-coordinated collective action in support of their views, and at the degree to which they were informed and concerned about the political issues of their day. What will become clear is that London political culture was not a consensual one. Instead, fundamental tensions existed which tended to divide the London populace. In particular, we shall notice that antagonism between anglicans, presbyterians and separatists worked against any form of collective identity for 'the London crowd'. The implications of this divided political culture for our understanding of crowd unrest in the capital in Charles II's reign are then explored in full in the rest of the book.

---

[51] Cf. F. H. Allport, 'Towards a Science of Public Opinion', *Public Opinion Quarterly*, 1 (1937), 7–8.

This study has chosen to focus on London, which was the capital, the economic and political centre of the country, and the area where the 'mob' got its name. But how should London be defined? The City of London proper was the area governed by the lord mayor, court of aldermen, and the court of common council. This comprised 97 parishes within the City walls, and a further 13 parishes (or extra-parochial precincts) outside the walls, which came under the jurisdiction of the Corporation.[52] By 1695, it has been estimated, the population of this area totalled some 123,000.[53]

The population had long since begun to overflow into the suburbs of the north and east, and also south of the Thames in and around the borough of Southwark, whilst the neighbouring City of Westminster to the west was increasingly becoming part of the urban metropolis. With this expansion, 'London' came to be used rather loosely to describe the whole urban area, with the part under the lord mayor's jurisdiction being distinguished as 'the City'.[54] The demographic expansion of London was particularly rapid in the seventeenth century, the population of the whole area increasing from about 200,000 in 1600 to 490,000 in 1700.[55] As residential settlement in both the west and east ends, and also south of the river, became more dense, the built-up conurbation came to form a continuous urban area.[56]

Any study of mass political agitation in London in the seventeenth century must concern itself with the whole conurbation. It was not unknown for a crowd from Stepney, in the east, to march through 'the City' to Westminster to demonstrate their grievances outside Westminster Hall.[57] A warning has recently been voiced against limiting a study of rioting in the capital to the area under the lord mayor's jurisdiction, 'for disturbances which began in the suburbs could soon cross over the City's limits or the citizens them-

---

[52] Allen, 'Crown and Corporation', ch. 1; Smith, 'London and the Crown', ch. 2. This area was also divided into 25 wards.

[53] P. E. Jones and A. V. Judges, 'London Population in the Late Seventeenth Century', *EcHR*, 6 (1935), 54. The figures are 69,581 residents within the walls, and 53,508 in the City without the walls, a total of 123,089.

[54] *Calendar of the Middlesex Sessions Records*, NS I, 1612–14, ed. W. Le Hardy (1935), i.

[55] R. Finlay and B. Shearer, 'Population Growth and Suburban Expansion', in A. L. Beier and R. Finlay, eds., *The Making of the Metropolis: London, 1500–1700* (1986), pp. 38–9, 48.

[56] N. G. Brett-James, *The Growth of Stuart London* (1935); L. Stone, 'The Residential Development of the West End of London in the Seventeenth Century', in B. C. Malament, ed., *After the Reformation: Essays in Honor of J. H. Hexter* (Manchester, 1980), pp. 167–212; M. J. Power, 'Shadwell: The Development of a London Suburban Community in the Seventeenth Century', *London Journal*, 4 (1978), 29–48; J. P. Boulton, 'The Social and Economic Structure of Southwark in the Early Seventeenth Century', unpub. Cambridge PhD thesis (1983), ch. 1.

[57] For example, this was to be the case with the Spitalfields weavers in 1697. See: Luttrell, IV, 172, 174–5; *CSPD, 1697*, p. 16.

selves could participate in disorders outside those limits'.[58] As a result, a study of this kind will inevitably cut across administrative boundaries. The urban parishes of St Giles-in-the-Fields, in the west, St James Clerkenwell and St Leonard Shoreditch in the north, through to Stepney and Whitechapel in the east, were under the jurisdiction of Middlesex, a county which also covered the then rural areas of, say, Staines and Acton. Westminster, a City in its own right, had its own courts, covering the parishes of St Margaret's, St Martin-in-the-Fields, St Clement Dane, St Mary-le-Savoy, St Paul's Covent Garden, and also the liberties of the Rolls and the Savoy. St Martin-le-Grand, geographically situated within the walls of the City, was in fact a liberty of Westminster. The position for the urban area south of the river was particularly complex, coming partly under the jurisdiction of the lord mayor, and partly under that of the county of Surrey.[59]

In defining London so broadly, it should be clear that this was a place with more than one identity. Properly speaking, it comprised two cities, one borough, and parts of two counties, each with its own political and administrative systems and institutions. As one early eighteenth-century observer noted, 'When I consider this great city in its several quarters and divisions, I look upon it as an aggregate of various nations, distinguished from each other by their respective customs, manners and interests.'[60] Research has shown that there were wide variations between the wealthiest and the poorest London inhabitants, although there were also many house-holders of middling rank, who were neither rich nor poor. The poorer par-ishes were those located around the City walls and along the riverside, and also those in the suburbs, especially to the east.[61] At the top of the social hierarchy were the gentry, increasingly becoming concentrated in the west-end, the professional and legal classes, many living in and around the ward of Farringdon without, and the mercantile elite of the City. Next to them were the wealthier members of the more prestigious livery companies, such as the grocers, merchant-tailors, and goldsmiths. At the bottom were the destitute poor, vagrants, beggars, and slum-dwellers. In between were to be found the people engaged in a huge variety of retail and manufacturing

[58] Lindley, 'Riot Prevention', p. 109.
[59] Boulton, 'Southwark', pp. 3–4; D. J. Johnson, *Southwark and the City* (Oxford, 1969), part IV.
[60] Quoted in Stone, 'Residential Development', p. 189.
[61] R. Finlay, *Population and Metropolis: The Demography of London, 1580–1650* (Cambridge, 1981), pp. 77–9; D. V. Glass, *London Inhabitants within the Walls, 1695* (1966), p. xxiii; R. W. Herlan, 'Social Articulation and the Configuration of Parochial Poverty in London on the Eve of the Restoration', *Guildhall Studies in London History*, II, no. 2 (April, 1976), 43–53; Stone, 'Residential Development'; Power, 'Shadwell'; M. J. Power, 'The Social Topography of Restoration London', in Beier and Finlay, eds., *Making of the Metropolis*, pp. 199–223.

occupations: small shopkeepers, small master craftsmen, journeymen, apprentices, labourers, and servants. It was these types whom Rudé chose to style as 'the inferior set of people', and whom he found to be the most likely to engage in crowd protest in eighteenth-century London.[62] But even within this group there were numerous gradations of social ranks. For example, a master craftsman would have ranked himself above journeymen, as would a skilled artisan above an unskilled labourer.[63]

There were also cultural distinctions which prevented this group from being a homogeneous one. London's population had increased only as a result of immigration, the growth in the period 1650–1750 demanding a net annual influx of some 8,000 people.[64] Some of those who came to London were foreigners, many of them involved in silk-textile production in the Spitalfields area.[65] A large number were youths coming to take up apprenticeships. In this way people were brought to London from all over the country, although the trend as the century progressed was towards a greater concentration from the home counties.[66] The possible significance of this for the political attitudes of post-Restoration Londoners should perhaps be considered. Coming from areas and brought up in households whose experiences of the turmoil of the 1640s and 1650s must have been so different, the preconceptions and prejudices they brought with them, especially with regard to the key issues concerning power in the state and the church, must have varied considerably, helping to give London a rich and diverse political culture.[67] It is the precise nature of this political culture that must be explored first.

[62] Rudé, 'London "Mob"', pp. 299–302.

[63] M. D. George, *London Life in the Eighteenth Century* (1925), pp. 159–60.

[64] E. A. Wrigley, 'A Simple Model of London's Importance in Changing English Society and Economy, 1650–1750', *PP*, 37 (1967), 46; Stone, 'Residential Development', p. 171; Finlay and Shearer, 'Population Growth', p. 50.

[65] Brett-James, *Growth*, ch. 19; R. Gwynn, 'The Distribution of Huguenot Refugees in England, II: London and its Environs', *Proceedings of the Huguenot Society*, 22 (1976), 509–68; C. M. Weekley, 'The Spitalfields Silkweavers', ibid., 18 (1947–52), 284–91.

[66] D. V. Glass, 'Socio-Economic Status and Occupations in the City of London at the End of the Seventeenth Century', in A. E. J. Hollaender and W. Kellaway, eds., *Studies in London History, Presented to Philip Edmund Jones* (1969), p. 386; S. R. Smith, 'The Social and Geographical Origins of the London Apprentices, 1630–60', *Guildhall Miscellany*, IV, no. 4 (April, 1973), 202–5; V. B. Elliott, 'Mobility and Marriage in Pre-Industrial England', unpub. Cambridge PhD thesis (1978), pp. 156–73.

[67] The definitive study of social structure in London is still awaited. In addition to the works already cited in these last two paragraphs, the following are useful: G. Rudé, *Hanoverian London, 1714–1808* (1971), chs. 2, 3, 5; T. R. Forbes, 'Weaver and Cordwainer: Occupations in St Giles without Cripplegate, London, in 1654–93 and 1729–43', *Guildhall Studies in London History*, IV, no. 3 (October, 1980), 119–32.

2

Reconstructing the political culture of the people

Historians of the late seventeenth century have been largely sceptical about attributing a political consciousness to the London crowd. This scepticism rests on three sets of assumptions: that politics was primarily the concern of a small political elite; that the masses were incapable of coordinating direct political action themselves; and that the 'lower orders', those who comprised the 'mob', were essentially apolitical. For example, John Miller has written that 'the [London] mob was not very important during the Exclusion crisis', and had little or no influence on a government determined to ignore them. 'The real battles were fought elsewhere, in elections, in wars of pamphlets and petitions, and above all in parliament.'[1] J. R. Jones has argued that 'the London masses were not capable of independent and sustained political action', but believes that radicals were able to mobilize popular support when 'there was a good deal of dislocation to trade, resulting in a shortage of employment and high prices for food and fuel'.[2] Even Christopher Hill, who has done more than most to stimulate interest in studying history from below, accepts this view of manipulated crowds, which he sees as a heritage of the English Revolution.[3] 'The "mob"', he has written elsewhere, 'is basically non-political'.[4]

Such views have not gone unchallenged. Nicholas Rogers, for example, has done much to reassert the integrity of popular political assumptions in his work on protest in early Hanoverian London. He sees crowd protest as reflecting a tradition of independent street politics which, although in terms of symbolism and rhetoric might be derivative of the political struggles of the elite, nevertheless embodied grievances and aspirations which were of a distinctly plebeian nature.[5] Yet neither Rogers, nor the sceptics, it seems, are prepared to allow for the possibility of any genuine participation by both the elite and the crowd in the same political struggles. In this chapter

---

[1] Miller, *Popery and Politics*, pp. 184, 187.
[2] J. R. Jones, *The Revolution of 1688 in England* (1972), p. 306.
[3] Hill, *Some Intellectual Consequences*, p. 31.
[4] Hill, *World Turned Upside Down*, p. 41.
[5] Rogers, 'Popular Protest'.

I wish to challenge the assumptions upon which such conclusions are based. I shall argue that ordinary people had a more important political role than is normally conceded; that they were capable of coordinating direct political action themselves; and that there was a high degree of political awareness amongst Londoners, even amongst quite lowly groups.

THE PROBLEM OF 'POPULAR' POLITICS

Rudé subtitled his pioneer work on the crowd 'a study of popular disturbances'. Scholars who, like Rudé, have been interested in studying history 'from below', have often employed the adjective 'popular' to describe their area of investigation. This word 'popular' is problematic. Typically, 'popular' derives its meaning by juxtaposition. As Peter Burke has said, discussing popular culture in early modern Europe, 'if everyone in a given society shared the same culture, there would be no need to use the term "popular culture" at all'.[6] The term only serves a purpose when we can identify another culture of the elite. In using this distinction between elite and popular, Burke is careful to stress that he does not wish to imply that European culture can be neatly divided into two layers. Rather, he sees the terms as representing two poles of a spectrum, and acknowledges the existence of many intermediate positions.[7] Yet as Burke realizes, the danger of using this binary terminology is that it encourages us to develop a two-tier model of society, sharply divided between two distinct social groupings.

Once we describe crowd unrest as popular protest, there is the risk of taking on board, if only unconsciously, a particular view of social and political relationships. The justification normally given for studying popular protest is that it was the only means of political expression available to people who were otherwise excluded from the political process.[8] The crowd is juxtaposed to the political elite, and popular protest is seen as the voice of the ruled as opposed to the rulers. Sometimes the term plebeian is substituted for popular, to emphasize that what is meant is not just a distinction between a narrow and a broad base of support, but also between the upper and lower classes. This language of polarities permeates most writings on collective disorder throughout the early modern period, and it conditions the way we think about crowd unrest. As soon as we use the term popular politics, we naturally assume that it must be different from elite politics – or else why use the term? And once the crowd is placed outside the political

---

[6] P. Burke, *Popular Culture in Early Modern Europe* (1978), p. 23.

[7] P. Burke, 'Popular Culture between History and Ethnology', *Ethnologia Europaea*, 14 (1984), 6–7. Cf. B. Reay, ed., *Popular Culture in Seventeenth-Century England* (1985), p. 20.

[8] A. J. Fletcher, *Tudor Rebellions* (1968), p. 9; Rudé, *Hanoverian London*, p. 183.

nation, it is easy to become sceptical about the degree of political awareness that we can justifiably attribute to members of the crowd.

Plenty of evidence can be found to suggest that contemporaries believed in a basic dichotomy between the 'official political nation', the elite, and the mass of the people below them. We need only look at the contemptuous terms the upper classes used to describe the crowd: *'mobile vulgus'*, 'the rabble', 'the rude multitude'. These types, it was often asserted, had no legitimate role to play in political society. As the duke of Albemarle wrote in 1671, 'the poorer and meaner people have no interest in the comonweal but the use of breath'.[9] 'The chief business of the People', wrote an anonymous pamphleteer ten years later, 'is to ... obey their superiors.'[10] Whenever the people dared to step out of line, they should be suppressed with the utmost speed; the 1640s and 1650s had taught prudence here. As one anglican clergyman put it: 'Sad Experience should inform us, that the Multitude is an unruly head-strong Beast: they are ever and anon for making themselves Kings ... and they must be curbed and managed by a strait Rein, or they will kick, and fling, and attempt to throw their Rider.'[11]

In fact the upper classes had a much more ambiguous attitude towards the crowd than these statements seem to suggest. In certain circumstances they were prepared to countenance or even encourage mob activity.[12] As is well known, 'opposition' politicians, such as the whigs of the exclusion period, might appeal to the people in order to put pressure on the government to change its political stance. Yet this tactic was also used by some more unlikely groups. In 1710 tory gentlemen seem to have been involved in inciting crowds to pull down nonconformist meeting houses, in protest against the whig decision to indict Dr Sacheverell for preaching up 'nonresistance'.[13] The tories were at this time in opposition, albeit temporarily, and it has been argued that they had already begun to forge an alliance with radical populist elements in the City who had formerly supported the whigs, a development which became more marked with their proscription after the Hanoverian succession.[14] Yet governmental politicians also used

---

[9] Duke of Albemarle, *Observations upon Military and Political Affairs* (1671), p. 146.

[10] *Protestant Loyalty Fairly Drawn* (1681), p. 7.

[11] J. Standish, *A Sermon Preached at the Assizes at Hertford, 9 March 1682/3* (1683), pp. 26–7.

[12] Cf. E. P. Thompson, *The Making of the English Working Class* (Harmondsworth, 1968), p. 74; M. Ingram, 'Ridings, Rough Music and the "Reform of Popular Culture" in Early Modern England', *PP*, 105 (1984), 105–6; R. B. Shoemaker, 'Crime, Courts and Community: The Prosecution of Misdemeanour in Middlesex County, 1663–1723', unpub. Stanford PhD thesis (1985), p. 532.

[13] Holmes, 'Sacheverell Riots', pp. 256–8.

[14] G. S. De Krey, 'Political Radicalism in London after the Glorious Revolution', *JMH*, 55 (1983), 585–617; L. Colley, 'Eighteenth-Century English Radicalism before Wilkes', *TRHS*, 5th series, 31 (1981), 1–19.

the tactic. For example, in 1714–17, the whig response to the anti-Hanoverian riots was not simply suppression, but they also sought to excite crowd agitation in support of their position. The duke of Newcastle, who as lord lieutenant of Middlesex played an important part in the legal proceedings against those suspected of disloyalty, deliberately encouraged pro-Hanoverian crowds, and was later to write 'I love a mob. I headed a mob once myself. We owe the Hanoverian succession to a mob.'[15] The tory response to the whig rabble-rousing tactics of the exclusion period, which they so forthrightly condemned, was, as I shall demonstrate, to try and win the people back to allegiance, to the point of stirring up crowd agitation in defence of the succession.

This paradox can be resolved if we stop discussing the crowd in terms of a polarized model of social and political relations, and instead adopt a participatory model. Those types who engaged in crowd activity often did have a legitimate and powerful role to play in the political process. They were not invariably simply 'the ruled', but could be actively involved in certain aspects of ruling. As a result effective government could be severely hampered if the elite could not carry a large section of the population with them.

It should not be assumed that crowd activity in seventeenth-century London was the preserve of plebeian elements, but was often engaged in by people who are perhaps better termed 'the middling sort'. It is clear that many of the London crowds of 1640–1, for example, were composed not just of 'mechanic people', but also of 'many citizens of good estates'.[16] The Sacheverell rioters of 1710 comprised not only gentlemen agitators, but also an appreciable 'white collar' or professional element, and a high number of self-employed artisans and tradesmen.[17] Many of the crowds in seventeenth-century London were composed predominantly of apprentices, but to describe this group as plebeian is clearly to beg many questions. For the middle of the century Steven Smith has estimated that 18 per cent of the apprentices were sons of gentlemen or esquires, and a further 23 per cent were sons of yeomen. Some 43 per cent were sons of artisans, professional men, traders, or other urban workers, but this is a broad category, and presumably includes many who came from wealthy mercantile or business backgrounds.[18] Clarendon believed that a large number of the apprentices involved in the anti-Army agitation of 1659–60 were sons of

---

[15] Fitts, 'Newcastle's Mob', p. 41; Rogers, 'Popular Protest'.
[16] A. J. Fletcher, *The Outbreak of the English Civil War* (1981), p. 15; Manning, *English People*, p. 15.
[17] Holmes, 'Sacheverell Riots', pp. 250–5.
[18] Smith, 'Social and Geographical Origins', p. 199.

gentlemen.[19] Indeed, one of them was the grandson of his kinsman, Sir Lawrence Hyde of Sarum.[20] Apprenticeship was supposed to lead eventually to being made free of the City, and although this process was perhaps breaking down, nonetheless many apprentices must have gone on to play an important part in Corporation politics and local government. Political polemicists of the exclusion crisis always distinguished the apprentices from the rabble or 'Ruffians and Beggarly Vermine'. Apprentice support was valued because these young men were often of eminent rank, with 'the greatest hopes both for Fortunes and Ingenuity in the City'.[21]

This rediscovery of the middling sort is important when we consider the nature of government in seventeenth-century London. For the City proper there were a multitude of overlapping courts and jurisdictions in which the citizens and householders were either represented or took part in person. The top layer was oligarchical, dominated by the lord mayor and his court of aldermen. There were 26 aldermen, who were elected for life, and who held supreme judicial and executive authority. The representative element was provided by the common council, elected by the freemen at the annual meeting of the wardmote, although throughout most of the seventeenth century this was a subordinate body, summoned and dissolved by the lord mayor. But at the roots of this organization, government was more diverse and pluralistic. The 89 City Companies, run by their wardens and yeomanries, continued to play an important part in economic regulation. Anyone who plied a trade in the City was supposed to be a freeman of a guild. Some 8,000 of the freemen who had been honoured with a call to the livery had a right to vote in common hall, where they elected the four MPs for the City, one of the two sheriffs, and two nominees for lord major from which the court of aldermen chose one. The 110 parishes were increasingly involved in local administration, in particular in the important area of poor relief. Although closed vestries, of 10 to 20 householders (often self-appointed), were the norm, general vestries or public meetings of the parishioners continued to be called into the eighteenth century to conduct certain types of business.

The primary units of government for police, taxation and electoral purposes were the 25 wards, which were subdivided into 242 precincts. At least three-quarters of the City's 20,000 male householders were freemen who could vote in ward elections. The institution of the wardmote enjoined attendance by all householders, and has been described by Valerie Pearl as a 'genuinely popular as well as populous assembly', which provided an

[19] Earl of Clarendon, *The History of the Rebellion and Civil Wars in England*, ed. W. D. Macray (6 vols., Oxford, 1888), VI, 57.
[20] Bodl. Lib., MS Clarendon 71, fol. 241.
[21] *Impartial Protestant Mercury*, nos. 15, 16; *Loyal Protestant Intelligence*, no. 35.

arena for public opinion and a platform from which popular views could be put before the lord mayor and aldermen. The proliferation of local offices which these institutions entailed meant that perhaps one in ten householders held annually some form of office. The 'popular' role was even greater in the period 1640–60, when the common council established its independence of the court of aldermen, and when there was a trend away from select to open vestries, both of which developments were reversed after the Restoration. Yet even discounting this exceptional period, it seems that there was, to quote Pearl, 'a remarkable degree of participation in some area of government for all but the lowest and dependent classes'.[22]

These findings apply only for the City, and it is usually argued that government in the suburbs was both less extensive and less effective. Not only was there no ward or precinct system, but it was also in the suburbs that population increased most rapidly, with the result that parishes became large and unwieldy.[23] Recent work by Jeremy Boulton, however, has discovered the vitality of the manorial and parochial system in Southwark, and his stress on the extensiveness and number of contacts householders had with local political institutions suggests a situation comparable to that in the City.[24] Moreover, the parliamentary franchise was much wider in the suburbs than in the City. In both Southwark and Westminster all those paying scot and lot were eligible to vote. From all this it is apparent that, even taking a narrow institutional perspective, politics was not the exclusive concern of a small elite.

One of the most important aspects of early modern government was law-enforcement, and here we find the scope for 'popular' participation in some process of ruling to be broader still. The carrying out of sentences was often such as to invite or necessitate crowd participation. Executions were public and usually drew a mass of spectators; as did, for example, the execution of the regicides in October 1660.[25] It was customary for copies of writings condemned by the courts as scandalous or seditious to be burnt

---

[22] V. Pearl, 'Change and Stability in Seventeenth-Century London', *London Journal*, 5 (1979), 13–18; V. Pearl, 'Social Policy in Early Modern London', in H. Lloyd-Jones, B. Worden and V. Pearl, eds., *History and Imagination: Essays in Honour of H. R. Trevor-Roper* (1981), pp. 116–19; A. E. McCampbell, 'The London Parish and the London Precinct, 1640–1660', *Guildhall Studies in London History*, II, no. 3 (October, 1976), 107–24; De Krey, *Fractured Society*, pp. 40–1. For the government of London in general, see: Allen, 'Crown and Corporation', ch. 1; Smith, 'London and the Crown', ch. 2.

[23] P. Clark and P. Slack, *English Towns in Transition, 1500–1700* (1976), p. 71.

[24] J. P. Boulton, *Neighbourhood and Society: A London Suburb in the Seventeenth Century* (Cambridge, 1987), ch. 10.

[25] Pepys, *Diary*, I, 265, 266, 268–70. See also: P. Linebaugh, 'The Tyburn Riot against the Surgeons', in D. Hay *et al.*, eds., *Albion's Fatal Tree: Crime and Society in Eighteenth-Century England* (Harmondsworth, 1977), pp. 65–117; J. A. Sharpe, '"Last Dying Speeches": Religion, Ideology and Public Execution in Seventeenth-Century England', *PP*, 107 (1985), 144–67.

by the common hangman in public places around London. This was the fate of that famous 'country party' pamphlet of 1675, the *Letter From a Person of Quality*.[26] The use of the pillory as a form of punishment effectively left execution of the sentence to the crowd. As Henri Misson observed in 1698:

> If the people think that there is nothing very odious in the action that raised him to this honour, they stand quietly by, and only look at him, but if he has been guilty of some exploit disliked by the Tribe of 'Prentices, he must expect to be regaled with a hundred thousand handfuls of mud, and as many rotten eggs.[27]

Research by legal historians has stressed just how much discretion there was available to ordinary people in influencing whether or not cases came to court. Magistrates seldom participated in the basic legal work of detection, but relied on information brought to them. Jurors and constables could present offences or offenders to the civil courts, and likewise churchwardens to the ecclesiastical courts, but most typically legal proceedings were initiated either by the person offended against, or by witnesses to the offence.[28] Of course, in the area of 'political' crime, such as the speaking of seditious words or the holding of unlawful conventicles, the government employed spies to bring such transgressions to their attention. But the fact that money was made available to encourage people to come forward with information, as under the 1670 Conventicle Act, for example, in itself testifies to the government's awareness of its dependence on 'the people' to initiate prosecutions, even in the most sensitive areas.[29]

London was policed by a collection of unpaid, part-time, local officers. These were the constables, beadles and watchmen, members of the community who served by a system of rotation. Yet because such amateurs usually had their own trades to attend to during the day, and might not be readily available when trouble threatened, a special obligation was placed on all Londoners to render assistance in maintaining order. Even when on duty, constables and watchmen had the right to call any passer-by to their assistance in making an arrest, refusal to do so being an indictable offence.[30]

[26] *LJ*, XIII, 13.

[27] H. Misson, *Memoirs and Observations in his Travels over England*, trans. by Mr Ozell (1719), p. 218.

[28] C. Herrup, 'New Shoes and Mutton Pies: Investigative Responses to Theft in Seventeenth-Century East Sussex', *HJ*, 27 (1984), 811–30; J. A. Sharpe, 'Enforcing the Law in the Seventeenth-Century English Village', in V. A. C. Gattrell *et al.*, eds., *Crime and the Law: the Social History of Crime in Western Europe since 1300* (1980), pp. 97–119; J. A. Sharpe, 'The People and the Law', in Reay, ed., *Popular Culture*, pp. 244–70; P. King, 'Decision-Makers and Decision-Making in the English Criminal Law, 1750–1800', *HJ*, 27 (1984), 25–58; Shoemaker, 'Prosecution of Misdemeanour', p. 472.

[29] For the 1670 Conventicle Act, see *Statutes of the Realm*, V, 648–51.

[30] Beloff, *Public Order*, pp. 129–33; F. F. Foster, *The Politics of Stability* (1977), pp. 29–31; Lindley, 'Riot Prevention', pp. 117–21.

Victims of crime could also raise the hue and cry. By yelling 'stop thief' or 'murder' it was usually possible to obtain the assistance of nearby pedestrians.[31]

Whenever these forces proved inadequate, recourse could be had to the militia. For the City there were six regiments of trained bands, under the control of the lieutenancy, although the king directly appointed the colonels of each regiment. There were two regiments of militia for the Tower Hamlets, commanded respectively by the constable and lieutenant of the Tower. The Westminster and Southwark trained bands were commanded by the lord lieutenant of Middlesex, whilst his counterpart in Surrey controlled the militia in that county.[32] In theory all constables, beadles, watchmen and militiamen should have been at least householders, but service was unpopular, and many wealthier inhabitants chose to hire others – often of quite lowly status – to serve in their stead. The result of this was that there was often very little difference in social status between members of the crowd and those responsible for policing them.[33]

When riots expressed grievances which were widely shared in certain communities, these peace-keeping agents, as members of those communities, would often be in sympathy with those grievances, and therefore refuse to act. We see this with regard to the weavers' riots of 1675, when some of the trained bands even seem to have taken the weavers' side, so that the army had to be called in to restore order.[34] Even those normally conscientious in the execution of their duties could be intimidated into inaction. Not only was there fear of reprisal action by the crowd, but there was also the danger of being ostracized by one's neighbours, with drastic social and economic consequences. For example, a Southwark innkeeper, who when constable in 1660 had helped hand over some regicides, found that he had his drinking establishment boycotted, to the extent that he 'quite lost his trade'.[35] One early eighteenth-century observer wrote that because constables held office normally for just one year, they were 'afraid of being strict upon the Faults of the Neighbourhood lest they should lose the good Will of their Neighbours, and expose themselves to the Revenge of those that are to succeed them'.[36]

Thus we can see why the desire to court 'the crowd' was not only an

---

[31] Shoemaker, 'Prosecution of Misdemeanour', p. 473.

[32] Allen, 'Trained Bands', pp. 290–1 and footnote 7.

[33] Lindley, 'Riot Prevention', p. 119; Allen, 'Trained Bands', p. 302; McCampbell, 'London Parish', p. 119.

[34] Dunn, 'Weavers' Riot'. This is discussed below, ch. 8.

[35] W. H. Hart, 'Further Remarks on Some of the Ancient Inns of Southwark', *Surrey Archeological Collections*, 3 (1865), 199; Hill, *World Turned Upside Down*, p. 354.

[36] J. Disney, *A Second Essay upon the Execution of the Laws against Immorality and Prophaneness* (1710), pp. 154–5.

attractive proposition for those in 'opposition', but also a necessity for the Court and their followers in parliament. For without fairly extensive support amongst the London populace, effective law-enforcement could be placed in jeopardy. The lesson of 1640–2 was there to be learnt, when constables and militia men refused to suppress the crowds who demonstrated in favour of the parliamentary cause, with the result that Charles I lost control of the streets of London.[37]

THE CAPACITY FOR COLLECTIVE AGITATION

The fact that political agitators often sought to encourage collective action in support of their cause – whether through mass petitions, demonstrations, or riots – has encouraged many historians to think of political crowds as being manipulated from above. However, most Londoners would have been familiar with the potential for self-coordinated collective protest. The multitude of representative organizations described above provided a range of bodies which Londoners could, and frequently did, petition to seek redress of particular grievances. Crowd action was also a fairly common feature of metropolitan life. This is not to suggest that London was a particularly unruly or ungovernable place, since much crowd activity was of a highly ritualistic kind, and focused on specific and rather limited objectives.

Festivals and holidays were often occasions of unrest. On Shrove Tuesday it was customary for the apprentices to rise and pull down brothels, in what James Harrington described as 'their ancient administration of justice at Shrovetide'.[38] These were fairly common in the early seventeenth century, there being 24 known Shrove Tuesday riots in the thirty-five years between 1606 and 1641.[39] The first of May was another notorious day, having taken on an especial significance since the riots of 'Evil May Day' of 1517, when the traditional carnival was supplemented with serious political unrest.[40] Holidays in general – Christmas, Easter, and Whitsun – as well as other festival times like Ascension day and St Bartholomew's day (24 August) could also be the occasion of unrest.[41] In anticipation of such unrest, it

---

[37] Lindley, 'Riot Prevention', pp. 123–4.

[38] J. Harrington, *The Commonwealth of Oceana* (1656), in J. G. A. Pocock, ed., *The Political Works of James Harrington* (Cambridge, 1977), p. 289.

[39] Lindley, 'Riot Prevention', pp. 109–10.

[40] *The Story of Ill May Day, in the Time of King Henry the Eighth* [ND], in C. Mackay, ed., *A Collection of Songs and Ballads Relative to the London Prentices and Trades* (1841), pp. 11–22; T. Allen, *The History and Antiquities of London, Westminster, Southwark, and Parts Adjacent* (4 vols., 1927–9), I, 202–6; W. Maitland, *The History of London, from its Foundation to the Present Time* (2 vols., 1756), I, 224–5.

[41] P. Burke, 'Popular Culture in Seventeenth-Century London', in Reay, ed., *Popular Culture*, pp. 36–7; Lindley, 'Riot Prevention', pp. 109–11.

was customary for the City authorities to order the doubling of the watch for holiday periods, to try and avert excessive disorder.[42]

This tradition of unrest was strongest amongst youths and apprentices.[43] Both general and specific explanations present themselves. Steven Smith sought an explanation in terms of rites of passage,[44] whilst Keith Thomas believes such rituals were an attempt by young men to assert their independence in an age when the gerontocratic ideal still prevailed.[45] Studies of modern youth unrest tend to see it in terms of the absence of meaning in most areas of a youth's life, and the need to create something 'remarkable' in everyday existence.[46] That youths featured prominently in the political disputes of Charles II's reign might just have been a question of numbers. Glass has found that in 1695, about 55 per cent of the male population of the City within the walls was under 25.[47] In addition, the young had neither the family responsibility nor the lack of physical energy which might have made older men think twice about getting involved in riotous activity.[48]

Attitudes to holiday misrule were of an ambiguous nature. Often such unrest could create considerable problems of order for the authorities. For example, on Shrove Tuesday, 1617, there was large-scale rioting in three separate centres, resulting in extensive destruction to property, and a sheriff and a justice of the peace who tried to restore order were assaulted by crowds hurling brickbats. James I was so disturbed by the extent of the

---

[42] CLRO, Journals 45–9, *passim*; CLRO, Lieutenancy Court Minute Books 1676–88, *passim*.

[43] J. Strype, ed., *John Stow's Survey of the Cities of London and Westminster* (2 vols., 1720), II, book V, 332–3; W. Besant, *London in the Time of the Stuarts, 1603–1714* (1903), p. 186; S. Brigden, 'Youth and the English Reformation', *PP*, 95 (1982), 47–8; Smith, 'Social and Geographical Origins', p. 195.

[44] Smith, 'London Apprentices', pp. 227–30. A similar explanation for youth unrest in sixteenth century France was reached by N. Z. Davis, 'The Reasons of Misrule: Youth Groups and Charivaris in Sixteenth-Century France', *PP*, 50 (1971), 41–75. See also: A. Van Gennep, *The Rites of Passage*, trans. by M. D. Vizedome and G. L. Caffee (1960); S. N. Eisenstadt, 'Archetypal Patterns of Youth', in E. H. Erikson, ed., *Youth: Change and Challenge* (New York, 1963), pp. 24–42.

[45] K. V. Thomas, 'Age and Authority in Early Modern England', *Proceedings of the British Academy*, 62 (1976), 205–48.

[46] P. Corrigan, *Schooling the Smash Street Kids* (1979); P. Marsh, E. Rosser, R. Harré, *The Rules of Disorder* (1978).

[47] Glass, 'Socio-Economic Status', p. 376. The figure is 54.6 per cent for a sample of 40 parishes.

[48] Cf. G. Wada and J. C. Davies, 'Riots and Rioters', *Western Political Quarterly*, 10 (1957), 870–1. The average age at marriage for the early modern period was about 27. See: E. A. Wrigley, 'Marriage, Fertility, and Population Growth in Eighteenth-Century England', in R. B. Outhwaite, ed., *Marriage and Society: Studies in the Social History of Marriage* (1981), p. 147; D. Grigg, *Population Growth and Agrarian Change: An Historical Perspective* (Cambridge, 1981), pp. 100, 167. The practice of certain London trades could have a debilitating effect. See: W. M. Stern, *The Porters of London* (1960), p. 7; R. Porter, *English Society in the Eighteenth Century* (Harmondsworth, 1982), p. 101; J. Rule, *The Experience of Labour in Eighteenth-Century Industry* (1981), ch. 3.

disorder that he is said to have wanted the execution of the ringleaders, although he had to be content with fines and imprisonment in irons.[49] But many people were fairly tolerant of such misrule, so long as things did not get too out of hand. On Shrove Tuesday the violence was rarely indiscriminate, but usually restricted to the brothels, which were, after all, illegal. Concerning the large-scale brothel riot of 1668, many of the apprentices' masters were reported to have been of the opinion that 'if they [the apprentices] meddle with nothing but bawdy houses, they do but the magistrates drudgery'. Consequently, they were not prepared to condemn the action of the youths, but were critical of those peace-keeping forces who tried to stop them.[50] Such feats were even acclaimed in popular literature as being a sign of the virtue of London's young men.[51]

In addition to holiday misrule, crowd unrest was common as a method of enforcing what might be termed a 'popular' perception of justice. This can be seen as an extension of the people's role in law-enforcement. As mentioned above, passers-by were expected to assist in apprehending criminals; but once a crowd had assembled and caught the suspect, it was often difficult to prevent them from inflicting their own punishment, by dunking the suspect in a pond, say, or assaulting him/her with stones or dirt.[52] The counterpart of the police crowds was the collective rescue. When, in March 1664, two apprentices were put in the pillory in Cheapside for having beaten their master, a large number of their fellow apprentices – one report estimated 4,000 – assembled together, rescued the two youths, and smashed the pillory to pieces. The two were eventually recaptured, and whipped, but this only provoked further disturbances from the apprentices on the following two days, when they threatened to pull down the houses of the aldermen and the judge who had ordered the whipping.[53] The apprentices were renowned for coming to each others' assistance in circumstances like these. As a tract of 1647 put it:

if any (either reall or supposed) wrong, or vyolence be offered to anyone, the rest (though not otherwise) knowing him to be a prentice, doe immediately (and commonly without examination of the quarrell) ingage themselves in the rescue, afrighting the adversary with this terrible sentence, knock him down, he wrongs a prentice.[54]

Crowd action was a typical way of defending local rights and customs. A classic example of this is provided by an incident that happened in March

49 Lindley, 'Riot Prevention', pp. 110, 125 footnote 78.
50 *CSPD, 1667–8*, p. 310.
51 *The Honour of London's Apprentices* (1647); *A Ballad in Praise of London Prentices and What They Did at the Cockpit Play-House, in Drury Lane* (1617), in Mackay, ed., *Songs*, pp. 94–7.
52 Shoemaker, 'Prosecution of Misdemeanour', p. 472.
53 Pepys, *Diary*, V, 99–100; *HMC, 7th Report*, p. 575; *CSPVen, 1663–5*, p. 10.
54 *Honour of London Apprentices.*

1669, when the lord mayor and his aldermen went to dine in the Inner Temple. Believing the Temple to be within his jurisdiction, the mayor ordered his sword-bearer to proceed him carrying the sword up. The students, arguing that the Temple was not included within the City's charter, ordered him to lower the sword. He refused and so the students attacked him, and the mayor and aldermen were forced to take refuge in nearby chambers until the disorder died down.[55] In September 1679, when a bailiff and his associates tried to distrain some goods in the Savoy, a liberty under the duchy of Lancaster and thus outside the jurisdiction of the City, they were attacked by a crowd seeking to defend the Savoy as 'a place priveleged from arrest'.[56]

Some forms of crowd activity were fairly elaborate affairs, and presumably required a certain amount of advance planning. An obvious example is the charivari, a ritual used to shame those who had violated sexual norms, in particular husband beaters and adulterers. In its fully ritualistic form, the charivari comprised of the offenders being ridden backwards on a horse through the neighbourhood, to the accompaniment of the rough music of shrill cries and the beating of pots and pans. Usually the victims were represented by neighbours dressed up as them, or even by effigies, and often the horse was replaced by a human stand-in.[57]

Those engaged in political unrest in Charles II's reign drew on this shared experience of crowd behaviour, as will be seen throughout this book. Carnival misrule could easily become politicized. For example, during the Easter holidays in 1668, crowds, mainly comprised of apprentices, adapted the medium of the brothel riot in order to make a protest against the religious policies of the licentious Court. Law-enforcement procedures also informed crowd protest. The two major incidents of widespread rioting in Charles II's reign – the bawdy house riots of 1668 and the weavers' riots against engine looms in 1675 – can both be described as law-enforcement riots, in the sense that the rioters were attempting to suppress activities which were illegal.[58] The organization of large-scale riots reflected public experience of law-enforcement. Rioters typically modelled themselves on the trained bands, dividing themselves into regiments, each with its captain and lieutenant, and each marching behind colours borne by an ensign.[59] Like the bands,

---

[55] *CSPVen, 1669–70*, p. 29; HMC, *12th Report*, VII, 63; Besant, *London*, p. 85; R. R. Sharpe, *London and the Kingdom* (3 vols., 1895), II, 440–2.

[56] *CSPD, 1679–80*, p. 252.

[57] Ingram, 'Ridings'; Shoemaker, 'Prosecution of Misdemeanour', pp. 481–2; E. P. Thompson, '"Rough Music": le charivari anglais', *Annales E.S.C.*, 27 (1972), 285–312.

[58] Harris, 'Bawdy House Riots'; Dunn, 'Weavers' Riots'. See also below, chs. 4, 8.

[59] G. Holmes, *The Trial of Dr Sacheverell* (1973), p. 165; Rudé, 'London "Mob"', pp. 295–6. See also below, chs. 4, 7, 8.

a crowd might be summoned by a person beating a drum.[60] On other occasions the drummer might be replaced by someone ringing a bell, and this was presumably modelled on the night watch.[61] Political demonstrators often mimicked legal procedures to make explicit their grievances, using techniques such as mock trials, hangings and public burnings (not just of human effigies, but also of 'offensive' tracts or writings). This will be seen in particular with regard to the exclusionist crowds, which are discussed in Chapter 7.[62]

In structuring their protest, then, crowds were simply drawing on procedures which would have been familiar to most Londoners. There was no need for political agitators to coordinate such activity for them. Even in the case of crowd rituals which were clearly expensive to stage, involving perhaps elaborate effigy-burnings at a large bonfire, or a plentiful supply of alcohol, it is wrong to assume *a priori* that these must have been sponsored from above. If elite sponsorship was not forthcoming, a crowd might solicit such sponsorship in a coercive manner, by stopping coaches, say, and demanding money for drink at a bonfire.[63] On 5 November 1679, for example, figures of the pope and the devil were carried about to the houses of several eminent persons by youths asking for money.[64] Even when it is clear that a particular affair must have been well-planned long in advance, the initiative could still perfectly well have come from below. In the spring of 1670 we know that a group of journeymen tailors were planning a demonstration against immigrant French artisans, whom they saw as a threat to their livelihood. The journeymen discussed the matter at work and in the alehouse, and they drew up a manifesto appealing to Londoners to join in a rising against the French on May day following. Rank was to be signified by the privates wearing one handkerchief, and the officers two. The inability of the Court to uncover elite manipulation of these tailors, despite their determination to do so, gives some credence to this account of self-organization.[65]

Yet often little formal organization was necessary for crowd activity. Because collective agitation typically followed traditional patterns, Londoners had shared expectations of each other, and so those involved in protest would know how to act even if there was no formal directing

---

[60] CLRO, Sessions File, May 1681, rec. 1; C. Tilly, 'Collective Action in England and America, 1765–1775', in R. M. Brown and D. E. Fehrenbacker, eds., *Tradition, Conflict and Modernization: Perspectives on the American Revolution* (New York, 1977), p. 55; Shoemaker, 'Prosecution of Misdemeanour', p. 467.

[61] Luttrell, IV, 174–5.

[62] Cf. De Krey, *Fractured Society*, p. 60.

[63] For example, see: BL, Add. MS 25,363, fol. 125; HMC, *7th Report*, p. 475; CSPD, 1680–1, pp. 588–9.

[64] *Domestick Intelligence*, no. 36.

[65] PRO, SP 29/274, nos. 205, 206.

agency.[66] Getting people to take to the streets might not be too difficult, especially if a traditional riot day was used. Often specific cues were devised. For example, on the 'evil' May Day of 1517, the crowd had been summoned by the cry of 'prentices, prentices, clubs, clubs'.[67] All this is not to deny that upper class politicians might often seek to coordinate collective agitation, but merely to show that such coordination was not a prerequisite for crowd action. Indeed, the knowledge that the people could take action themselves in support of their own political objectives would probably have made the elite even more determined to try and control the crowd if at all possible.

POLITICAL CONSCIOUSNESS

The seventeenth century saw the rise of mass political activity in London, the beginnings of what has been termed a 'popular political culture'.[68] The emergence of an articulate and politically aware London populace was to a large extent contingent upon the rise in literacy. Adult male literacy was probably as high as 70 per cent taking the London area as a whole, and even higher in the City alone. There were, of course, marked divergences in the literacy structures of different social groups. Labourers were predominantly illiterate (nearly 80 per cent), as were females, though there was a dramatic fall in female illiteracy in the seventeenth century (from 90 per cent to 65 per cent). On the other hand, servants and apprentices were extraordinarily literate (70–80 per cent).[69] The breakdown in censorship after 1640 saw a flood of popular political literature aimed at this newly literate market. Not that illiteracy provided a barrier to political information; those who could not read could always listen to someone reading aloud from such tracts, whilst political prints and ballads transmitted their message in a visual and aural form. Political debate was increasingly being conducted in the public arena. Political matters were discussed by societies meeting in ward-clubs and in taverns and coffee-houses, where gentry, shopkeepers and artisans mingled freely.[70] Religious developments – the proliferation of the sects, the fact that political and religious issues (which were often indistinguishable) were discussed in meeting-houses and in parish churches – were another element in this increased political sophistication of the ordinary Londoner. The period from 1640 saw the rise of political demonstrations

---

[66] Cf. W. R. Reddy, 'The Textile Trade and the Language of the Crowd at Rouen, 1752–1871', *PP*, 74 (1977), 82–4.

[67] Maitland, *London*, I, 225.

[68] Burke, 'Seventeenth-Century London', p. 43; Pearl, 'Change and Stability', p. 5.

[69] D. Cressy, *Literacy and the Social Order: Reading and Writing in Tudor and Stuart England* (Cambridge, 1980), pp. 72–5, 129, 146–7.

[70] Pearl, 'Change and Stability', p. 6.

and mass petitioning, a process which brought the people into direct involvement in politics on an unprecedented scale.

With the Restoration there was an attempt to limit this extensive involvement of the people in political discussion. Important here was the reintroduc-
tion of censorship with the Licensing Act of 1662. Hill has suggested that
censorship could exclude 'the majority of the population from being able
to take part in politics, probably even from contemplating the possibility
of participation'.[71] Yet the clamp-down was far from complete. The Licensing Act lapsed in 1679, and until it was revived in 1685 the government
was left with the difficult task of trying to control the press through the
common law of seditious libel.[72] Even at other times some unlicensed political
tracts did get printed. For example, there were many pamphlets published
in the period 1667–72 discussing the relative merits of religious toleration,
comprehension and persecution.[73] Manuscript literature, especially political
poems, certainly circulated in the underground world of the coffee-houses.
These establishments became a main focus for the dissemination of political
information. For example, in the early 1660s, the keeper of a coffee-house
in Bread Street used to meet regularly with one of the clerks of the house
of commons, who would pass on an account of what had happened that
day in both houses. This intelligence the coffee-house keeper would make
available to his clientele.[74] Throughout the 1660s and 1670s the government
feared that coffee-houses were the centres of political debates. As a royal
proclamation of 12 June 1672 put it:

there have bin of late more bold and Licentious discourses then formerly and men
have assumed to themselves a Liberty not only in Coffee houses but in other Places
and Meetings both publique and private to confuse and defame the proceedings
of State by speaking evill Things they understand not and endeavouring to create
and nourish universall jealousie and dissatisfaction in the minds of all his Majesties
good Subjects.[75]

By the end of 1675 the government had decided to try and suppress the
coffee-houses, and a proclamation to this effect was issued on new year's
day 1676. But a policy of total prohibition could hardly have been enforced,
and a week later the government announced its intention to grant special
licences for certain establishments to sell coffee. The licensee had to take
the oaths of allegiance and supremacy, and also enter into a recognizance to

[71] C. Hill, 'Censorship and English Literature', in his *Collected Essays*, I (Brighton, 1985), 32.
[72] See below, ch. 6.
[73] Hill, 'Censorship', pp. 53–4; D. R. Lacey, *Dissent and Parliamentary Politics in England, 1661–1689* (Rutgers, 1969), pp. 56–66; J. Walker, 'The Censorship of the Press during the Reign of Charles II', *History*, 35 (1950), 219–38.
[74] PRO, SP 29/99, no. 7.
[75] CLRO, Journal 47, fol. 179.

use his utmost endeavour to prevent and hinder all scandalous Papers Books or Libells concerning the Government or the publick Ministers thereof from being brought into his House or to be there read or perused or divulged and to prevent and hinder all and every Person or Persons from declaring uttering or divulging in his said House all manner of false and scandalous Reports of the Government and Ministers thereof.[76]

Who frequented such places? An order of common council of December 1675 believed that coffee-houses were the great resort not only of 'idle and disaffected persons', but also of tradesmen, who wasted of their time there which should have been spent at their work.[77] Coffee-houses seem to have been points of contact between high and low society, places where rich and poor went to learn about and discuss political issues. A tract of 1673 described the 'hodge-podge of ... Company' one might encounter there:

for each man seems a Leveller, and ranks and files himself as he lists, without regard to degrees or order; so that oft you may see a silly Fop, and a worshipful Justice, a griping Rook, and a grave Citizen, a worthy Lawyer, and an errant Pick-pocket, a Reverend Nonconformist, and a Canting Mountebank.[78]

Even if some coffee-houses tended to exclude the lowlier types, there were other places where these could go and discuss politics. In Southwark, in early May, 1660, we find a waterman, a sawyer, and the wives of an oar-maker, a waterman, and a mariner, all low status occupations, sitting in the Red Lyon Inn, discussing the imminent return of Charles Stuart.[79] During the exclusion crisis we find a number of porters, another low status group, meeting in Duke's Place to discuss the merits of the duke of Monmouth's claim to the throne.[80]

Although propaganda could undoubtedly heighten political awareness, the attitudes of Londoners were also shaped by inherited assumptions and prejudices, passed on from generation to generation, and continually rein-forced by direct experience. Three sets of assumptions stand out for their significance in informing crowd action in the seventeenth century: a strong attachment to the independence of the City government; a deep-seated hosti-lity towards catholicism; and an antipathy towards foreigners. The first clearly grew out of the widespread participation in local government and the complex system of representative institutions which has already been discussed. It was a common practice to petition the lord mayor, court of aldermen and common council to put pressure on any central government

---

[76] CLRO, Journal 48, fols. 189–91; P. Fraser, *The Intelligence of the Secretaries of State and their Monopoly of Licensed News, 1660–1688* (Cambridge, 1956), p. 119; B. Lilly-white, *London Coffee Houses* (1963), p. 19.

[77] CLRO, Journal 48, fol. 189.

[78] *The Character of a Coffee House* (1673), p. 3.

[79] HLRO, Main Papers, H.L., 28 May 1660.

[80] CLRO, Sessions Papers, July 1683, information of Hodgkinson.

which seemed to be threatening the rights and freedoms of Londoners. A desire to preserve local autonomy against outside interference is reflected in the preference for the locally selected militia over the centrally controlled army. Hill has argued that this anti-standing army position had greatest resonance amongst the men of property, especially after the experience of the New Model Army in the 1640s and 1650s.[81] But there was another important element, and this relates to the policing of crowd unrest. The type of sensitivity in dealing with riots when these expressed communal grievances was only to be expected from a local force, whereas an army, whether republican or royalist, was typically much more ruthless in its suppression of discontent.

A factor which was to play a crucial role in shaping political attitudes during this period was anti-catholicism. Jones, for example, has asserted that 'fear of, and hostility to, catholicism was to be found in every section and class' of the English population.[82] The fears associated with the reimposition of catholicism went back to the horrors of Mary's reign, captured for posterity in Foxe's *Acts and Monuments*, probably the most widely read book after the Bible.[83] Although English protestantism was saved with the accession of Elizabeth, reminders that the threat of catholicism was still not removed were provided by the Armada of 1588, Guy Fawkes's plot of 1605, the Thirty Years War, and the Irish rebellion of 1641. Because of this history, any threat to the security of England came to be associated with popish designs. Anti-catholicism, therefore, was not a hatred of catholics as individuals, but a more abstract fear that tended to grow in intensity at times of political crisis.[84]

Londoners were also renowned for their chauvinism and xenophobia.[85] It was not uncommon for foreign visitors to London to be saluted with stones, squibs and dirt.[86] Because of the threat posed to the protestant interest in Europe by the catholic powers of Spain and France, xenophobia and anti-catholicism often overlapped. On 5 November 1668, the Spanish ambassador's coach was besieged, the crowd throwing fireworks and then pursuing the ambassador to his door until the guards came to suppress them.[87] In the latter half of the seventeenth century, however, France was coming to replace Spain as the main catholic threat, and on the same day

[81] Hill, *Some Intellectual Consequences*, pp. 19–20.
[82] Jones, *Revolution of 1688*, p. 75.
[83] Clifton, 'Popular Fear', pp. 141, 144; Kenyon, *Popish Plot*, p. 3.
[84] Clifton, 'Popular Fear'; Clifton, 'Fear of Popery'; Haley, '"No Popery"'; C. Hill, 'Robinson Crusoe', *History Workshop*, 10 (1980), 11; Jones, *Revolution of 1688*, ch. 4.
[85] Lindley, 'Riot Prevention', pp. 111–12.
[86] J. Evelyn, *A Character of England, as it was Later Presented in a Letter to a Noble Man of France. With Reflections upon Gallus Castratus* (1659), pp. 7–8.
[87] *CSPVen*, 1666–8, p. 321.

in 1673 the celebrations were combined in one place with the execution of a Frenchman in effigy.[88] Because the anti-catholic tradition was associated with a threat to English security, this day from the anti-catholic calendar could be used to express hostility towards protestant enemies of England. On 5 November 1683, for example, the Dutch ambassador's coach was besieged.[89] War was clearly a crucial factor in exciting xenophobic sentiment, being the main reason for the widespread hatred of the Dutch in Charles II's reign.[90] Another crucial component of popular xenophobia was fear of economic competition from foreign immigrants.[91] This was a tradition of long-standing, and was often a central element in popular disturbances in the capital throughout the early modern period.[92]

All these assumptions were reinforced by public rituals. The legitimacy of the City's autonomous government was confirmed in the elaborate pageantry of the lord mayor's shows, which took place at the time of the annual inauguration on 29 October.[93] There was also a calendar of anti-catholic ritual. The collapse of the gunpowder plot was celebrated annually on 5 November, with the ringing of bells and sermons in the churches, and with bonfires and fireworks in the streets. Different customs emerged in different areas. In Southwark in the reign of Charles II it was customary on that day to burn as many candles as it was years since the plot, displaying them in a front window for passers-by to see.[94] The day of Elizabeth's accession, 17 November, was also commemorated in a similar fashion, although on a less regular basis. It was, however, to take on a special significance in the reign of Charles II.[95] The Court often encouraged popular patriotism by organizing firework displays and other celebrations to commemorate war victories. Sometimes this was done rather disingenuously to keep morale high when things were not going particularly well. For

---

[88] *CSPVen, 1673–5*, p. 174.

[89] PRO, PC 2/70, fol. 60; Luttrell, I, 287; Jeaff., IV, 229.

[90] See *CSPVen, 1664–6*, pp. 85–6 and *ibid., 1666–8*, pp. 320–1 for a couple of other examples of riots involving the Dutch ambassador.

[91] For a useful survey of this problem, see Brett-James, *Growth*, ch. 19.

[92] For example, the apprentice riots of May Day 1517 had its origin in hostility to foreign traders in Spitalfields, as did another apprentice riot in 1586. See: Maitland, *London*, I, 224–5, 271; Allen, *London*, I, 202–6, 298. The theme is still important in the eighteenth century. See Rudé, 'Mother Gin'. Cf. H. T. Dickinson, 'The Poor Palatines and the Parties', *EHR*, 82 (1987), 464–85.

[93] For the shows, see: F. W. Fairholt, *Lord Mayors' Pageants; Being Collections Towards a History of those Annual Celebrations* (2 vols., 1843–4); S. Williams, 'The Lord Mayor's Show in Tudor and Stuart Times', *Guildhall Miscellany*, I, no. 10 (September, 1959), 3–18; Burke, 'Seventeenth-Century London', pp. 43–5.

[94] *Loyal Protestant Intelligence*, no. 230.

[95] J. E. Neale, 'November 17th', in his *Essays in Elizabethan History* (1958), pp. 9–20; R. C. Strong, 'The Popular Celebration of the Accession Day of Queen Elizabeth I', *Journal of the Warburg and Courtauld Institutes*, 21 (1958), 86–103. See below, ch. 5.

example, in June 1666, during the second Dutch War, the receipt of news
about one battle was followed by an 'order for bonfires and bells', even
though 'it was rather a deliverance than a Triumph'.[96]

Despite the prevalence of these assumptions, they did not sustain a unified
and homogeneous political culture in London, since different sectional interests related to them in different ways. Although master craftsmen were probably as patriotic as anybody else, it was often they who had most to gain
by employing cheap immigrant labour, thus inflaming the xenophobia of
the journeymen craftsmen, who felt their livelihoods to be in jeopardy.[97]
Within the civic tradition there existed a conflict of interests between what
might be termed the oligarchic and the populist elements in City government.
In the 1640s the common council had challenged the right of the lord mayor
and aldermen to veto decisions taken in their court, and this issue flared
up again in Charles II's reign.[98] It should also be remembered that there
were large numbers of people living in the suburbs who would not have
shared the same attachment to the City's traditions, whilst there were others
who perhaps resented the authority of the City and its influence over economic regulation. This might explain the significance of a charivaresque parody
of the court of aldermen that was staged in the streets of the City in December
1664. A group of about 200, who styled themselves the Bull Feather Court,
dressed themselves up in 'scandalous habits', and 'carried about diverse
Ensignes of Government rested with hornes in abuse and derision of the
government of this City'.[99]

The most ambiguous tradition was the anti-catholic one. Anti-catholicism
gave definition to the Reformation, justifying the break with Rome, and
the struggle for the true church.[100] By extension, the puritan critique of
the Church of England was also expressed in anti-catholic terms, as had
been the case against Laud in the 1630s,[101] and as was the nonconformist
critique of anglicanism in Charles II's reign.[102] However, since catholicism
was associated with a threat to church and state, this tradition could be
invoked against protestant critics of the established church. In a parliamentary speech of 1588, Lord Keeper Puckering had argued that despite puritan

[96] Evelyn, *Diary*, III, 440. Cf. *CSP Ven, 1666–8*, pp. 29–30.

[97] See ch. 8.

[98] V. Pearl, *London and the Outbreak of the Puritan Revolution: City Government and
National Politics, 1625–43* (Oxford, 1961), pp. 149–59, 280–1. See below, ch. 7.

[99] CLRO, Rep. 70, p. 30; Sessions File, February 1665, ind. of Clocker *et al.*

[100] For a useful discussion of the distinct traditions used to justify the break with Rome,
see P. K. Christianson, *Babylon and Reformers: English Apocalyptic Visions from the
Reformation to the Eve of the Civil War* (Toronto, 1978). Cf. W. M. Lamont, *Godly
Rule: Politics and Religion, 1603–60* (1969).

[101] N. Tyacke, 'Puritanism, Arminianism, and Counter-Revolution', in Russell, ed., *Origins*,
pp. 134–5; Christianson, *Babylon and Reformers*, ch. 4.

[102] See ch. 4.

claims to be at war with the jesuits, they in effect 'do both join and concur with the Jesuits' in sowing discord at a time of threatened invasion.[103] Charles I frequently complained that jesuits and puritans were equally troublesome and seditious, since both challenged the royal supremacy. He also accused the Scottish covenanters of collaborating, if unwittingly, with the catholics in a design to weaken England that could only profit the catholic powers.[104]

The anti-catholic tradition became very ambiguous in the 1640s and 50s. It was used by virtually all the different factions in condemnation of the others. Pym tried to harness it behind the parliamentarian cause,[105] but the common front did not last long. By the mid 1640s, independents were associating presbyterian intolerance with catholicism,[106] presbyterians were condemning the independent demand for toleration as a device which would only aid the catholics,[107] whilst royalists argued that both groups could by placed alongside the catholics as the 'Three Grand Enemies of Church and State'.[108] The association of puritans with jesuits in particular became a staple of royalist polemic and historiography.[109] Yet even presbyterians, such as Prynne, argued that Charles I was put to death by those acting on the jesuits' maxims of deposing and killing kings.[110] The more radical separatists were also linked with catholicism.[111] Baxter condemned the quakers by reference to the same tradition,[112] and believed that one of the papists' 'Practical Frauds' was the attempt 'to Divide the Protestants among themselves, or to break them into Sects'.[113] The examples could be extended almost indefinitely.[114] The point to stress is that anti-catholicism was not

[103] J. Nalson, *An Impartial Collection of the Great Affairs of State* (2 vols., 1682–3), I, 1.

[104] C. Hibbard, *Charles I and the Popish Plot* (1983), p. 15.

[105] Fletcher, *Outbreak*.

[106] *Dictated Thoughts upon the Presbyterians Late Petition for Compleat and Universal Power* (1646); *BM Prints*, no. 647.

[107] *A Reply to Dictated Thoughts, by a More Proper Emblem* (1646); *BM Prints*, no. 653.

[108] [S. Shepherd], *The Times Displayed in Six Sestyads: The First a Presbyter, an Independent, etc.* (1646); *BM Prints*, no. 656.

[109] See, for example, [A. Cowley], *A Satyre. The Puritan and the Papist* (Oxford, 1643). See also Hibbard, *Charles I*, p. 15.

[110] Miller, *Popery and Politics*, p. 85.

[111] See, for example, [J. Taylor], *Religions Enemies, with a Brief and Ingenious Relation, as by Anabaptists, Brownists, Papists, Familists, Atheists, and Foolists, Sawcily Presuming to Tossse Religion in a Blanquet* [1641]; *BM Prints*, no. 245.

[112] W. M. Lamont, *Richard Baxter and the Millenium: Protestant Imperialism and the English Revolution* (1979), p. 127. But for Baxter's attitude to the sects as a whole, see ibid., ch. 3. For anti-Quaker feeling in general, see B. Reay, 'Popular Hostility towards Quakers in Mid-Seventeenth Century England', *Social History*, 5 (1980), 387–407.

[113] R. Baxter, *A Key for Catholicks, to Satisfie All whether the Cause of the Roman or Reformed Churches be of God* (1659), p. 313.

[114] See discussions in: R. Clifton, 'The Fear of Catholics in England, 1637 to 1645. Principally from Central Sources', unpub. Oxford DPhil thesis (1967), p. 352; B. G. Reay, 'Early Quaker Activity and Reactions to It, 1652–1664', unpub. Oxford DPhil thesis (1979), pp. 171–4.

a consensual tradition, but could equally well provide the justification for bitter division.[115]

These diversities within the anti-catholic tradition corresponded to political and religious differences amongst the London populace. Hill has traced what he calls a 'radical underground', a popular tradition which was anti-authoritarian, anti-aristocratic, and anti-clerical, and which survived into the Restoration period.[116] In the 1660s there was a general belief that the Commonwealth period had bequeathed the problem of a decline in reverence for the traditional hierarchical structuring of society. For example, in March 1663 the lord mayor issued a precept complaining of the 'unruely and meaner sort of people' who 'under the late usurped powers' had 'been encouraged and borne up in their undutifulnesse and contempt of their Superiours, especially of the Nobility and Gentry of the Kingdome'. Such 'insolent behaviour' caused much concern, since it was supposed to be driving 'persons of estate and quality' out of the City into the suburbs, leading to a decline in trade.[117] Ten years later a special common council committee investigated the decay of City trade, and reached similar conclusions.[118] Caution should be taken against such reports, which might just have been using the Commonwealth period as a scapegoat. These sorts of problems perhaps had deeper roots.

The extent of this lower-class radicalism should not be exaggerated. Presbyterianism was perhaps the strongest religious movement in the London parishes in the 1640s, and by the middle of that decade the presbyterians had developed a counter-revolutionary platform. Between 1646 and 1648 there was a bitter divide in London between a royalist/presbyterian coalition and an alliance of independents and levellers. Although the radicals could muster impressive numbers of signatures on their petitions, the weight of people's sympathies seems to have been with the conservatives, as evidenced by their control of the streets. Throughout the Civil War we have evidence of crowds lighting bonfires and drinking the king's health, and forcing passers-by to do the same.[119]

The existence of these tensions between presbyterians and independents should not blind us to the fact that there remained a powerful attachment to traditional forms of anglican worship. Anthony Fletcher found that the

[115] M. D. George, *English Political Caricature to 1792: A Study of Opinion and Propaganda* (Oxford, 1959), pp. 23–42; Miller, *Popery and Politics*, pp. 85–7.
[116] C. Hill, *Milton and the English Revolution* (1977), ch. 6; C. Hill, 'From Lollards to Levellers', in C. Cornforth, ed., *Rebels and their Causes: Essays in Honour of A. L. Morton* (1978), pp. 56, 63; Hill, *World Turned Upside Down*, ch. 17.
[117] CLRO, Journal 45, fol. 264; *CSPD, 1663–4*, p. 66.
[118] CLRO, Journal 47, fol. 263.
[119] V. Pearl, 'London's Counter Revolution', in G. E. Aylmer, ed., *The Interregnum: The Quest for Settlement, 1646–1660* (1974), pp. 29–56; Smith, 'Apprentices' Parliament', pp. 576–82; Smith, 'Almost Revolutionaries', pp. 317–19; Gentles, 'Struggle for London'.

order of the house of commons of September 1641, intended to undo Laud's policy of railing off church altars and to eradicate practices such as bowing at the name of Jesus, crucifixes, candles and images, met opposition in a number of London parishes. Those who opposed the order in St Giles-without-Cripplegate maintained that the altar rails had been in position for nearly eighty years and that they assisted the 'more speedy administration of the sacrament'.[120] In early seventeenth-century Southwark, Jeremy Boulton found a high level of 'popular demand for the communion service' and even for ceremonies such as churching of women after childbirth, which radical protestants regarded as a 'popish survival'.[121] Although by the 1640s this religious consensus had broken down, there was still much opposition to radical religious practices. Thus in late 1641 a petition in defence of episcopacy was circulating in Southwark which bemoaned the way some ministers were treating the prayer book.[122] John Morrill has noted the strength of anglican survivalism in the 1640s and 1650s, and has shown that even in London those who wanted to maintain the old prayer book and the old rhythms of anglicanism could easily get their way.[123]

CONCLUSION

It can be seen that there existed a rich and fairly sophisticated political culture in Stuart London. There was no sharp divide between a politically aware elite, and the unpolitical and easily manipulated masses. Ordinary Londoners were not only heavily drawn in to the processes of government, especially in the area of law-enforcement, but also the public nature of political debate meant that they could be well-informed about the major issues of the day. Most Londoners would also have been familiar with the potential for coordinating collective agitation in order to secure a redress of any grievances they might feel they had. All this means that the crowd was a much more positive force in politics, whether at the local or national level, than is usually recognized. But it is important to notice that this political culture was not an homogeneous one. The 1640s had revealed fundamental divisions, particularly in the area of religion, between anglicans, presbyterians, and separatists. These divisions are crucial for understanding the nature of crowd politics in Charles II's reign.

---

[120] Fletcher, *Outbreak*, p. 118.
[121] Boulton, 'Southwark', pp. 334–45; J. P. Boulton, 'The Limits of Formal Religion: The Administration of Holy Communion in late Elizabethan and early Stuart London', *London Journal*, 10 (1984), 148–9.
[122] Fletcher, *Outbreak*, p. 288.
[123] J. S. Morrill, 'The Church in England, 1642–9', in Morrill, ed., *Reactions to the English Civil War, 1642–1649* (1982), pp. 89–114.

3

The people and the Restoration

It is usually argued that Londoners of all ranks welcomed back the king in the spring of 1660 with positive enthusiasm. The Venetian resident remarked on the royalist mood in the capital with some amazement: 'the change in the people here is indeed miraculous', he wrote in April, 'the King's name is now as much loved, revered and acclaimed as in past years it was detested and abused, and nothing is desired with greater fervour by the people, particularly those of the lower classes... The desire for the King is universal.'[1] When Charles eventually did return the following month there was widespread celebrating throughout London. The classic explanation for this growth in royalist feeling amongst the London populace was put as early as 1926 by Sir Charles Firth. He argued that heavy direct taxation and an increase in indirect taxes such as customs and excise helped promote dissatisfaction with the Protectorate. Commercial losses caused by the war with Spain in the 1650s, and an economic crisis from 1659, swelled the rising tide of discontent. This caused rioting in London in late 1659 and early 1660, especially by the apprentices, which, combined with a petition campaign against the rule of the Army and the Rump, and in favour of a free parliament, eventually resulted in the restoration of monarchical government.[2]

Most historians agree with the view that there was extensive popular support for the return of monarchy in 1659–60.[3] Only Christopher Hill has sought to challenge what he has termed 'the accumulated legends surrounding the Restoration'. He has warned us to be sceptical about how we read the evidence of the anti-Rump and pro-Charles demonstrations of early 1660, since many of these crowds were clearly sponsored by members

[1] *CSPVen, 1659–61*, p. 136.
[2] Firth, 'London', pp. 32–6.
[3] Smith, 'Almost Revolutionaries'; J. Thirsk, ed., *The Restoration* (1976), p. xi; G. R. Cragg, 'The Collapse of Militant Puritanism', in *Essays in Modern Church History in Memory of Norman Sykes*, ed. G. V. Bennett and J. D. Walsh (1966), p. 102; R. Hutton, *The Restoration: A Political and Religious History of England and Wales, 1658–1667* (Oxford, 1985), pp. 76–80, 119, 125–6.

of the elite. Against these manipulated mobs, he has argued, should be set the many instances of seditious words spoken against the restored monarchy which can be found in the sessions records of the early 1660s.[4] Hill therefore believes that there is plenty of evidence 'to throw doubt on the universality and spontaneity of rejoicing at Charles II's return', although he would not wish to deny completely that there was a growth in royalist sentiment. He has documented how former radicals, most notably the levellers, disillusioned with the conservatism of the Protectorate, moderated some of their aims and sought to achieve them through a conditional restoration of monarchy. He has also stressed the surviving magical aura of kingship which had strong appeal to ordinary people, and which was reinforced by the deliberate propaganda of the anglican church once it had been restored to its monopoly position.[5] Nevertheless, he has argued that 'a rude and vigorous opposition to monarchy' survived, which 'was expressed in an unmistakably popular idiom'.[6]

Hill has therefore suggested a number of limitations to the orthodox view of the Restoration, especially with regard to the alleged consensus amongst the London populace and with the extent to which there was a conservative reaction amongst the masses at this time. In general terms these two criticisms have much validity. However, it is inappropriate to see the main tensions as being between those who favoured the Restoration and those who consistently opposed it. Although people's attitudes towards the Restoration were still rather ambiguous in December 1659, it is difficult to find hard evidence to deny that by the spring of 1660 most Londoners did want the return of Charles II. On the other hand, the collective agitation of this period, I believe, should be seen as an attempt by ordinary Londoners to defend what they perceived to be their rights and liberties. Support for the new king was for many conditional. Charles was welcomed in the belief that only he could solve specific grievances, and his failure to do so soon led to disillusionment. But what needs to be stressed is that different people had very different expectations of the Restoration, especially in the realm of religion. The survival of tensions between presbyterians, anglicans and separatists, rather than between committed monarchists and out-and-out republicans, is perhaps the most important legacy of the Restoration for developments in crowd politics in the capital.

---

[4] Hill, *Some Intellectual Consequences*, pp. 10–11, 31; Hill, *World Turned Upside Down*, pp. 41, 354.
[5] Hill, *Some Intellectual Consequences*, pp. 13, 27; Hill, *Experience of Defeat*, pp. 34–5. See also A. Woolrych, 'The Good Old Cause and the Fall of the Protectorate', *CHJ*, 13 (1957), 133–67.
[6] Hill, *Some Intellectual Consequences*, p. 15.

ATTITUDES TOWARDS THE MONARCHY 1659–60

There is much evidence of popular celebration at Charles's return. On 1 May 1660 both houses of parliament voted to restore the king, news that was greeted with many bonfires and the ringing of bells, people 'drinking of the King's health upon their knees in the streets'.[7] On 8 May a proclamation was read throughout the City outlining the reality of the Restoration, stating that Charles II would be regarded as having been king from January 1649. When read at Chancery Lane, the people cheered so much at the mention of Charles II, that the reader had to stop, and it was supposedly fifteen minutes before the crowd was quiet enough to let him continue. In Cheapside, this same report continues, 'the shouts of the people were so great, that though all the Bells in the City rung, Bow bells could not be heard there'.[8]

Charles did not enter the City until 29 May, which was also his birthday, landing first on the Kent coast, and making a progress westward. Thousands of 'ordinary people', we are told, 'flocked the streets as far as Rochester, so that the procession was seven hours in passing the City'. In the evening, another report tells us, there were 'an infinite number of Bonfires... as if all the houses had turned out their chimneys, into the streets', there being 'almost as many fires in the streets as houses, throughout London and Westminster'.[9] Some of the bonfires were large and elaborate, constructed several days beforehand, and presumably quite expensive. Rugge noted that there were great bonfires made at the corners of several streets in the City, 'two or three stories high, with pitch barrells, and on the tope of some a streamer with a crowne or Charles the Second pictured thereon'. In Southwark one was erected 'higher then any houses', and in Westminster 'there were many statly ones made; in the Covent Garden one made with a mast of a ship standing and a barrell one the tope of it'. An elaborate firework display put on at a bonfire in St Martin's Lane on the night of the 30th was rumoured to have cost its organizer, Mr John Alder, anything between £100 and £500. At many of these royalist celebrations wine flowed freely to encourage the crowds. Yet even if some of the bonfires were sponsored by wealthy patrons, this does not necessarily mean that those who subsequently gathered around them were any the less enthusiastic in their support for the Restoration. Rugge also remarked that although these bonfires 'stood neere a weeke before they were fired; they needed not watches to looke to them, for the

---

[7] Rugge, p. 76; Pepys, *Diary*, I, 122; *HMC, 5th Report*, pp. 145, 181; *Mercurius Publicus*, I, no. 18 (1660), 287.
[8] Bodl. Lib., MS Carte 30, fol. 649; MS Carte 214, fol. 147; Rugge, pp. 79–80; *HMC, 5th Report*, p. 167; *Mercurius Publicus*, I, no. 19 (1660), 300–2.
[9] Evelyn, *Diary*, III, 246; Pepys, *Diary*, I, 163; *Mercurius Publicus*, I, no. 22 (1660), 349–52; *HMC, 5th Report*, pp. 167, 184, 199; Besant, *London*, p. 74.

boyes of eatch street was night and day playing by them'. There were also a number of smaller bonfires on 29 May, especially in front of taverns, 'and every privett house laid in some provision or other to express their joy that day of his majesty cominge'.[10]

In early November 1660, Charles made another royal entry into London, having brought the Court back to Whitehall, including the duke of York and the queen mother. Again there were celebrations in the streets.[11] Royalist sentiment apparently stayed strong in London into 1661, and Charles's coronation on 23 April. In Axe Yard on that day, Pepys and some friends came across 'three great bonfyres and a great many great gallants, men and women; and they laid hold of us and would have us drink the king's health upon our knee, kneeling upon a fagott'.[12]

Not only was Charles acclaimed, but the symbols of the old regime were abused. On 24 May 1660 an effigy of Oliver Cromwell was burnt together with the arms of the Commonwealth at a large bonfire in Westminster.[13] On the 29th, effigies of Cromwell, his wife, and the state arms were burnt at a great bonfire in Westminster.[14] On 24 June another effigy of Cromwell, 'whose name and memory are increasingly cursed by the people', was hung from a window in the court of the palace, with a rope round its neck, abused 'by all the populace who thronged to see it and who spared no act of contempt and ignominy'.[15] In October, the republican Harrison was hanged, drawn, and quartered at Charing Cross, and when his heart and head was shown to the people, 'there were great shouts of joy'.[16] On 30 January 1661 the bodies of Cromwell, Bradshaw and Ireton were exhumed, taken to Tyburn, and hanged on the gallows, this symbolic execution being witnessed by thousands of jeering spectators, we are told, who had come to curse the architects of the republic.[17]

The celebrations at the king's return marked the climax of several months agitation in London involving tradesmen, artisans, apprentices and labourers against the republican government. To appreciate why the monarchy was welcomed back so enthusiastically, it is necessary to trace the process of alienation from the republic, and analyse the aims and aspirations of those who were disaffected. Although collective unrest did not flare up until late

---

[10] Rugge, pp. 86, 90–1.
[11] Rugge, p. 124; *CSPVen, 1659–61*, p. 215; *Mercurius Publicus*, I, no. 45 (1660), 713 (misnumbered p. 705).
[12] Pepys, *Diary*, II, 83.
[13] *Mercurius Publicus* I, no. 22 (1660), 352.
[14] Rugge, p. 90.
[15] *CSPVen, 1659–61*, p. 162; Rugge, p. 92.
[16] Pepys, *Diary*, I, 265.
[17] *Kingdome's Intelligencer*, I, no. 5 (1661), 72; Evelyn, III, 269; Rugge, p. 145; Hutton, *Restoration*, p. 134.

1659, throughout the 1650s there were many groups in London who were far from happy under the Commonwealth. Presbyterians and anglicans had never wanted the abolition of monarchy, and this royalist alliance had been the dominant force in street politics in the late 1640s.[18] So long as Cromwell kept the radicals at bay, these groups were unlikely to erupt into violent protest against the Protectorate. Although Cromwell pursued a policy of religious toleration, he neither disestablished the Church nor abolished tithes, and he proved no friend to the quakers and other radical sectarians. However, his policy of presenting independents to sequestered livings did provoke some passive resistance, in the form of tithe strikes. In March 1656 'the Ministers of this Cittie of London placed in sequestred livings' petitioned the court of aldermen 'for the recoverie and payment of their Tithes and other duties which are withheld by very manie persons'.[19] In 1657 the parishioners of St Bartholomew Exchange organized a tithe strike against their independent incumbent, John Loder, 'because hee refused to administer the Sacrament, and to christen children, except wee would be joyned in Communion with his Church'.[20]

At the other extreme were the radicals who were dissatisfied with the conservatism of the new republic. By 1656 some fifth monarchists and former levellers seem to have thought that they might stand a better chance of achieving some of their aims if they backed royalist conspirators and fought for a conditional restoration of monarchy.[21] The conditions were nevertheless some way from the leveller programme: the restoration of both houses of parliament as they existed before Pride's Purge; the confirmation of all concessions made by Charles I in the Isle of Wight treaty of 1648; legislative reform; tithe reform; and religious toleration.[22] Royalist plotting had been a continual irritant for Cromwell's government, but was probably not a serious threat to the Protectorate, as it never seems to have generated mass support.[23]

A crisis situation rapidly developed after the fall of the Protectorate in April 1659. The radicals expected great things of the restored Long Parliament, and many tracts were produced urging the revival of the 'good old cause'. Political and religious conservatives began to be alarmed by what they saw to be the increasing influence of the sects in central and local

---

[18] Pearl, 'London's Counter-Revolution'; Gentles, 'Struggle for London'.
[19] CLRO, Rep. 64, fol. 98.
[20] E. Freshfield, *The Vestry Minute Book of St Bartholomew Exchange* (1890), pp. 61, 62, 70; C. Cross, 'The Church in England, 1646–1660', in Aylmer, ed., *Interregnum*, p. 112.
[21] G. Davies, *The Restoration of Charles II, 1658–60* (San Marino, 1955), p. 22; Hill, *Experience of Defeat*, pp. 32–4; Capp, *Fifth Monarchy Men*, pp. 106–10.
[22] Hill, *Experience of Defeat*, pp. 35–6.
[23] Hutton, *Restoration*, p. 4.

government, especially in the militia.[24] This renewed challenge from the radicals prompted some who had passively, though unenthusiastically, acquiesced under the Protectorate to take a more militant stance. In August 1659 the presbyterian Sir George Booth attempted to coordinate a rebellion in order to force a return to the constitutional position reached in 1648. Although the affair is usually described as a royalist conspiracy, Booth himself never declared for Charles II, and he seems to have been thinking predominantly in terms of the restoration of proper parliamentary authority. Booth's agents had some success in enlisting support for his cause in London, especially amongst the apprentices, but the rising when it occurred was restricted to Cheshire, and it was fairly easily suppressed by the Army under Lambert.[25]

Having alienated the presbyterians, the Rump disappointed the sectaries by its lack of enthusiasm for further reforms, and Lambert forcibly dissolved it on 13 October, power reverting to the committee of safety. Fearful of the loyalty of the militia, the Army then entrusted peace-keeping in London to the sects. These events created a hornets' nest of constitutional and religious resentment in London. There was alarm at the substitution of military for civilian government, and subversion of rule by a properly constituted parliament. There was also concern at the way the Corporation's privileges had come under attack, with the City having lost control over its own militia. And, of course, there was the problem of the sects. The situation was made even more volatile by a particularly severe economic crisis. Dislocation caused by the Spanish, Dutch and Baltic Wars had led to a general deadness of trade in London. Grain prices were also rapidly increasing.[26] In the autumn of 1659 the Venetian ambassador commented upon 'the unspeakable scarcity of money' in the City.[27] On 10 November 1659 the court of aldermen ordered a special collection to be made for the 'reliefe of the honest and laborious poore Inhabitants (especially of the out parishes) of this City', on account of 'the deadness of Trade and the dearness of provisions at this season'.[28]

The Army was seen as responsible for exacerbating the economic crisis. According to Rugge, the apprentices turned against the Army because they blamed it for frightening away their customers (mainly gentlemen) from

---

[24] A. Woolrych, 'Last Quests for a Settlement, 1657–1660', in Aylmer, ed., *Interregnum*, pp. 192–5; Reay, 'Quakers, 1659, and the Restoration'; Hill, *Experience of Defeat*, pp. 34–5.

[25] J. S. Morrill, *Cheshire, 1630–1660: County Government and Society during the English Revolution* (Oxford, 1974), pp. 318–25.

[26] G. V. Chivers, 'The City of London and the State, 1658–1664: A Study in Political and Financial Relations', unpub. Manchester PhD thesis (1961), p. 17; Hutton, *Restoration*, p. 76.

[27] *CSPVen, 1659–61*, p. 94.

[28] CLRO, Rep. 67, fol. 6.

their shops.[29] Moreover, the cost of maintaining the soldiers placed a heavy burden of taxation on Londoners. The Army was partly financed by the excise, a form of indirect taxation on food, drink and other commodities in daily use, which had been bitterly resented since first established in 1643. The levellers had formerly denounced it as a burden on the poorer classes, and its collection had provoked a serious riot in 1647.[30] It came under renewed criticism in the second half of 1659.[31] Most of the cost of the Army was met by the monthly assessment, a tax on property. Poverty-stricken tradesmen and artisans, faced with demands for money they did not have, sometimes erupted into violence. In November, two soldiers were almost killed in the City attempting to levy the assessment.[32] The presence of troops without pay, however, was another cause of anxiety at this time. On 11 November there was a rumour that the soldiers would plunder the goldsmiths rather than want money, which was taken seriously enough to prompt the goldsmiths into hiding their property.[33]

It was in this context that the agitation against rule by the Army broke out. The Army leaders had a warning of the mood of the City on 8 November when, after a visit to the common council to put the case for a commonwealth before the City leaders, Whitelocke, Fleetwood and Desborough were met by 'great multitudes of people' shouting for 'a free Parliament'.[34] On 15 November the apprentices of London published a remonstrance outlining their grievances, although according to Rugge it was framed 'with the help of better heade peces'.[35] It complained of the 'decay and loss of trade' and attacked the sects for their innovations in religion. It was critical of the record of the Rump Parliament, 'such a model of Tyranny', and warned that the apprentices would 'assert with our Lives and Fortunes the Laws of this Land and the Liberty of the Subject' for 'we look upon the Laws as our Birth-right'. Having previously stated that the problems which had 'befallen these miserable and distracted Nations' had occurred 'within these twelve years', the remonstrance ended by asserting that the only 'expedient to recover and retrieve our Religion, Laws and Trade... is a returning to the Condition and State of Affairs where we begun'. This seems an implicit demand for the return of the king. However, perhaps for tactical reasons, there was no explicit mention of monarchy, but a complaint about how

---

[29] Rugge, p. 13.

[30] Davies, *Restoration*, p. 117; Pearl, 'London's Counter-Revolution', pp. 39–40, 43.

[31] See, for example, *A Dialogue betwixt an Excise-Man and Death* (1659).

[32] *Clarke Papers*, IV, 301.

[33] Bodl. Lib., MS Clarendon 66, fols. 235–6; *CSPD, 1659–60*, p. 268.

[34] Bodl. Lib., MS Clarendon 66, fol. 233; A. Woolrych, 'Historical Introduction' to *Complete Prose Works of John Milton* (8 vols., New Haven, 1953–82), VII, 143; Hutton, *Restoration*, p. 77.

[35] Rugge, p. 9.

the freedom of parliament had been 'exploded and hist, like the Members themselves, out of doors', suggests support for a full parliament.[36]

In the last week of November the apprentices started collecting signatures to a petition to the common council in which they further outlined their grievances. A house in Cannon Street was set aside where every night 'multitudes of Apprentices, Bachelors and others' flocked to subscribe their names. By 2 December it was rumoured that the petition already had nearly 20,000 subscriptions.[37] The authors stated:

we esteem and assert as our undoubted birth right, the freedome and priviledges of our Parliaments, as being the great Charter of the people of England . . . Therefore we most humbly desire that a new election may be made, or else that those worthy Gentlemen chosen to serve as members in the late free Parliament, may be restored to their priviledges, and sit without disturbance or force from the Army.[38]

The committee of safety tried to prohibit the collection of signatures to the petition, and issued a proclamation to that effect on 1 December,[39] but the apprentices defiantly presented their petition to the common council on 5 December. Early that morning units of horse and foot marched into the City to prevent the possibility of any trouble. The atmosphere was predictably very tense, with 'great multitudes of the ordinary sort of people . . . gathered together in the streets, and the shops shut up, and the Soldiery being disposed in several parts'.[40] Violence broke out when the sergeant at arms, Dendy, escorted by a troop of horse, went to post up the proclamation against petitioning at the Old Exchange. Pepys gives a vivid account of what happened:

The souldiers as they marcht were hooted at all along the streets, and where any straggled from the whole body, the boys flung stones, tiles, turnips, etc. at, with all the affronts they could give them. Some they disarmed and kickt; others abused the horse with stones and rubbish they flung at them.

Reinforcements arrived, led by Colonel Hewson, who had once been a shoemaker, and immediately the cry went up 'A Cobler, A Cobler'. In some places 'the apprentices would gett a football (it being hard frost) and drive it among the souldiers on purpose'. Many soldiers were seriously hurt, and Pepys saw one 'very neere having his brains knockt out with a brick batt

---

[36] *The Remonstrance of the Apprentices in and about London* (1659).

[37] Bodl. Lib., MS Clarendon 67, fol. 119.

[38] *To the Right Honourable . . . the Lord Mayor . . . The Most Humble Petition and Address of Divers Young Men, on Behalf of Themselves and the Apprentices, in and about this Honourable City* (1659).

[39] *By the Committee of Safety . . . A Proclamation Prohibiting the Contrivance or Subscription of any Petitions or Papers for the Promoting of Designs Dangerous to the Common-Wealth* (1659).

[40] *Mercurius Politicus*, no. 597, p. 939.

flung from the top of an house'. Eventually the soldiers lost their patience, and fired into the crowd, some reports say at Hewson's command, and about six or seven youths were killed, and several others wounded.[41]

The killings intensified antagonism towards the Army. Another petition a few days later complained to the common council how 'the Mercenary Souldiers did Murder, Slay, and Wound many of Us, only to prevent our peaceable Way of Petitioning You', voiced support for the militia, and warned that the artisans, tradesmen, apprentices, seamen and watermen were ready to 'rise as one Man' in defence of 'the Rights and Liberties of this Famous City' against the Army.[42] By the 12th the citizens had drawn up a further remonstrance, supposedly signed by 23,500 hands, warning that they had engaged themselves before God 'to defend the Rights and Liberties of the City of London; and if any person that subscribes to this Engagement, shall be molested for so doing; We will unanimously, and without delay, appear as one Man to his Rescue'. It drew attention to the fact that 'our Counsels' had been 'Affronted by Armed Troups, our Fellow Citizens knock'd on the head, like Doggs, at their own doors', and complaint was also made about 'the losse of Trade; how many Thousand Families have nothing now to do, but Begg'. The terms of the engagement were 'to defend the Rights and Liberties of the City of London', with popular force, if necessary, and included a demand for a removal of all troops which 'do not properly belong to the Guard of the City, nor receive Orders from the lawfull Magistrates thereof'.[43] A petition from the seamen and watermen of London, delivered to the lord mayor on the same day made similar points, and called for 'a free and legal Parliament' to 'be convened to sit within the City of London' to settle the government and redress grievances.[44] On 19 and 23 December a further two tracts were printed, repeating the same grievances and demands, and warning that the citizens were prepared to oppose violence with violence in order to get the soldiers out.[45]

The crisis of December 1659 proved the redundancy of the government

---

[41] Bodl. Lib., MS Carte 73, fol. 329. See also: MS Clarendon 67, fols. 178, 180–1, 186, 200–1, 222, 224–9; CLRO, Journal 41x, fol. 212; *Clarke Papers*, IV, 164–70; *CSPVen*, *1659–61*, pp. 101–2; Davies, *Restoration*, pp. 181–2; C. H. Firth, 'The Early Life of Pepys', *Macmillan's Magazine*, 69 (November, 1893), 35; Woolrych, 'Historical Introduction', pp. 145–6; Hutton, *Restoration*, pp. 78–9.

[42] *To Our Worthy and Grave Senators... the Lord Mayor, etc.... The Further Humble Petition and Remonstrance of the Free-men and Prentices of the City of London* (1659).

[43] *The Engagement and Remonstrance of the City of London, Subscribed by 23,500 Hands* (1659).

[44] *To the Right Honourable, the Lord Mayor... The Humble Petition and Address of the Sea-men and Water-men, in and about... London* (1659); H. Humpherus, *History of the Origin and Progress of the Company of Watermen and Lightermen, 1514–1859* (3 vols., 1887), I, 277–8.

[45] *The Final Protest and Sense of the Cittie* (1659); *The Resolve of the Citie* (1659).

under the Army and the committee of safety, and at the end of the month power was reassumed by the Rump. In the aftermath of the riots of 5 December a coroner's inquest had found the killing of the apprentices to be wilful murder, and the grand jury had proceeded to draw up an indictment against Hewson. One of the first acts of the restored Rump was to pardon Hewson for his alleged offence, although he did lose control of his regiment. The apprentices decided to impose their own sentence on him, in the form of ritualized mock executions which took place in January. According to Rugge,

It beeing very snowey time, the yonge men in Fleet Street and likewise in St Paules churchyeard made in snowe the effigies of Colonell Hewson, with one eye in heade and with an old face and a haulter or rope about his neck, many old shewes lying by him, a horne on his heade, a writing on his brest: This is old Hewson, the cobbler.[46]

On the 25th Pepys witnessed a similar ritual in Cheapside, a gibbet having been set up and an effigy of Hewson hung on it in the middle of the street.[47]

Clearly there was much genuine hostility towards Army rule in late 1659 amongst the tradesmen, apprentices and labourers. Although 'better head peces' might have helped frame some of the petitions, it does not seem to be the case that we have a non-political mob being manipulated by elite agitators. But this unrest should not be seen as evidence of a conservative reaction. The rhetoric employed was both libertarian and populist, the people threatening to take direct action themselves to preserve what they perceived to be their 'rights and liberties'. The explicit call was not for a restoration of monarchy, but for a return to parliamentary forms of government. We therefore need to consider the extent to which this position can fairly be described as a royalist one.

The evidence is problematic. Burnet was under no doubt that a declaration in favour of parliament was 'generally understood' as 'declaring for the King'. Yet writing, as he was, many years later, his interpretation was perhaps tainted with hindsight.[48] Spies in the employment of the exiled royal Court were naturally delighted at the anti-Army agitation, and one wrote in early December that 'as the Apprentices were a great means of ejecting the Father, they will now proove as great an instrument to bringe in the Sonn'.[49] Fleetwood believed the apprentice riots of 5 December were 'managed wholly by the Cavaleere Malignant party and those ingaged in Sir George Booth's insurrection', their cry being 'to bee revenged... for the death of theire

---

[46] Rugge, p. 27.
[47] Pepys, *Diary*, I, 28.
[48] Burnet, I, 151.
[49] Bodl. Lib., MS Clarendon 67, fol. 119.

King'.[50] Yet perhaps such statements reflect in turn the optimism and paranoia of politicians on the two extremes. A more independent guide to the
mood of the City is provided by the elections to the common council on
21 December, when many radicals were displaced in favour either of out-and-
out royalists or moderates (presbyterians).[51] But apprentices and labourers
did not vote in municipal elections.

Rugge, whose journal covers these months in some detail, gives no hint
that the anti-Army agitation of November and December 1659 was a sign
of popular desire for the restoration of monarchy. It is only by late January
and February that he makes this connection.[52] The ambiguity of the petitions
of late 1659 was doubtless deliberate, since an explicit call for the return
of the king would at this time have been an overt act of treason, and likely
to be dealt with severely by the authorities. But it is also possible that many
people might have supported a demand for a full or free parliament who
would have been suspicious of a demand for Charles II. For while the former
involved a return to the constitutional position of 1648, the latter implied
a return to the position of 1641.[53] An attempt by Hyde's agents to engage
the apprentices in a rising in favour of the king on 18 December failed
because of 'some difference in opinions among the chiefe actors in it'. The
'presbyterian party', it seems, concerned that if the king came in 'upon
the heat of a commotion', he would be 'too absolute', betrayed the plans
to 'the enemie'.[54]

When we do find statements explicitly advocating a return to monarchy,
they are critical of the demand for a free parliament. A tract of 14 December
1659 argued that to call for a free parliament was a cheat, since such could
only be called by a king, so to accept one at this point would be to 'Conclude
the Army to be Supream'.[55] A declaration from the women of London of
February 1660 showed annoyance with the ambiguity concerning the desired
political solution expressed in other petitions:

this Our Declaration is, neither for a Free Parliament, a Full Parliament, or a Piece
of a Parliament, (We leave that to the discretion of him, who onely has Power
to call a Parliament). We do therefore Declare, That the onely meanes... to bring
these Nations out of Bondage... will be, the speedy Restauration of the Banished,
we mean... that the Crown may be set upon His Head whose Right it is, C.R.[56]

---

[50] *Clarke Papers*, IV, 169.

[51] D. C. Elliot. 'Elections to the Common Council, December 21st, 1659', *Guildhall Studies in London History*, IV, no. 4 (April, 1981), 151–201; Davies, *Restoration*, p. 256.

[52] Rugge, pp. 33, 34.

[53] Morrill, *Cheshire*, p. 320.

[54] Bodl. Lib., MS Clarendon 67, fol. 270; ibid., 68, fols. 16–18, 42–3.

[55] *The Grand Cheat, Cryed up Under-Hand by Many in the Factious and Giddy Part of the Army* (1659).

[56] *The Royale Virgine; Or, The Declaration of Several Maydens in and about the once Honourable City of London* (1660).

Throughout late 1659 and early 1660 some groups, although critical of the Army, consistently opposed the monarchy, remaining loyal to the Rump. A representation from divers citizens of London to general Fleetwood on 6 December warned him that by acting against parliament he was acting against the common enemy, meaning Charles Stuart and his followers.[57] A declaration of 20 January 1660, claiming to be from many thousands of people in the London area, defended the Rump, and argued that a free parliament was impossible just now, and would only benefit the cavaliers. The cry for a free parliament was 'the Cavaliers Trojan-horse'. Strictly speaking there had never been any free parliaments in England; by that term the cavaliers wanted to include the king, popish and other lords, archbishops and bishops.[58]

Those who supported this position, however, were becoming an increasingly isolated minority. An address of the Thames watermen dated 31 January 1660 argued for a free but not a full parliament, since the return of the secluded members would lead to the return of 'our old bondage of Monarchy'. It argued that to have parliaments 'clogg'd with Kingship and Peerage', as of old, was a 'violation to the just Rights of the People... neither King nor Lords being any part of the true Parliaments of England, but an imposed power upon them from the Interest of the Old Norman Sword'.[59] This is interesting, since only six weeks earlier the watermen had petitioned in favour of a free parliament. But most of the 9–10,000 signatures had been obtained fraudulently, by telling the watermen the petition was designed to restrict the number of hackney coaches in use. The design had been carried out by a few individuals 'that have a desire to get in to be watermen to the State', and was coordinated by three overseers of the Company of Watermen and Colonel Whittan. According to Rugge, when those who had signed found out that the petition had declared for 'noe king, noe single person nor house of lords, which they disired above any thing in the world, they ware inraged and threatned to beat and kick [Whittan], and soe would neede be the death of him that ever they saw him'.[60] On 2 February, great numbers of watermen went to Westminster to disavow the petition, and to present another demanding a full and free parliament.[61]

[57] *To the General Council of Officers. The Representation of Divers Citizens of London, and Others Well-Affected to the Peace and Tranquility of the Commonwealth* (1659).

[58] *A Declaration of Many Thousand Well-Affected Persons, Inhabitants in and about the Cities of London and Westminster* (1660).

[59] *To the Supreme Authority, the Parliament of the Commonwealth. The Humble Address and Congratulation of Many Thousands of Watermen belonging to the River Thames* (1660).

[60] Pepys, *Diary*, I, 37; Rugge, pp. 32–3; CLRO, Rep. 67, fol. 82.

[61] Bodl. Lib., MS Clarendon 69, fols. 53–4; *A Declaration of all the Watermen in and about the City of London, between Gravesend and Staines; Or, A Hue and Cry after Col. Whitton and his Decoys* (1660).

They also petitioned the court of aldermen so that those who promoted the fraudulent address might be disciplined. Their statement reveals the vulnerable position of watermen as servants of the public, and indicates that they had to tailor any express statements of their political opinion so as to avoid offending potential customers. After Whittan's address, they found themselves 'much hindred and damnified in their labour and employments, the people often times reviling and sometimes assaulting them to their great danger and declining to employ them'.[62]

By February the cry for a free parliament was typically being linked with an expression of support for Charles Stuart. Events now depended on the actions of General Monck, commander of the Army in Scotland. He had fallen out with the English Army leaders over the dissolution of the Rump the previous October, and after negotiations with them had failed, he eventually decided to march south on 2 January 1660. Meeting minimal resistance from Lambert's army, within three weeks he was at St Albans, on the outskirts of London. On his way he received numerous addresses from all parts of England, including one from the City of London and another from the apprentices asking for a full and free parliament.[63]

From St Albans Monck sent a letter to the Rump Parliament asking for the units of the Army around London to be scattered into the country, a device in part designed to deprive the Rump of military protection and also to leave the way clear for Monck to enter London. However, many units refused to leave London without pay. On 1 February, when one regiment was drawn up in St James's Fields to receive orders to march the next day, scuffles broke out between soldiers and officers, which were only appeased by the promise of pay. On the next day, another regiment mutinied, seized Somerset House, and killed one of their captains. Some of them cried out for a free parliament, others, we are told, for King Charles II. Some of the apprentices sought to take advantage of the mutiny, informing the soldiers that they 'could trust that they would rise in the Citty that night, and that Generall Monk was for them and a free Parliament which would produce a Kinge and liberty'. The apprentices met in Leadenhall Street, but were set upon by a party of horse, and 38 were arrested.[64]

Monck marched into Westminster on 3 February, and as he passed many

---

[62] CLRO, Rep. 67, fol. 56.
[63] *CSPD, 1659–60*, pp. 344–5; *To His Excellency the Lord General Monck. The Unanimous Representation of the Apprentices and Young Men Inhabiting in the City of London* (1660).
[64] Rugge, p. 34; Pepys, *Diary*, I, 38–9; HMC, *5th Report*, p. 181; *CSPD, 1659–60*, pp. 344, 357; Bodl. Lib., MS Clarendon 69, fols. 53–4, 55–7, 71–3, 81–2; HMC, *Leyborne-Popham*, pp. 143–4; *CSPVen, 1659–61*, p. 115; H. M. Reece, 'The Military Presence in England, 1649–1660', unpub. Oxford PhD thesis (1981), p. 272; Hutton, *Restoration*, pp. 90–1; Davies, *Restoration*, pp. 273–4.

people cried out for a free parliament. The purged parliament had now reached its lowest point in popular esteem, Pepys recalling how 'Boys do now cry "Kiss my Parliament" instead of "Kiss my Arse", so great and general a contempt is the Rump come to among all men.'[65]

The freemen and householders of the City of London laid down an explicit challenge to the government's authority when in a petition delivered to the common council on 8 February, they said they would not submit to any laws and taxes unless they were imposed by a full and free parliament.[66] The committee of safety responded by ordering Monck to march into the City in the early hours of the 9th, arrest some of the leading citizens, take away the chains and posts in the streets and make the gates indefensible. The Rump later sent further orders for the City's gates and portcullises to be totally destroyed. On the same day the Rump received a petition from Praise-God Barebone and the radicals, asserting their loyalty to the 'good old cause' and opposition to the restoration of monarchy. Monck executed the policy reluctantly, but after a meeting with some of his officers on the 10th, did an about turn and took the City's side. In a letter sent to the House on 11 February, Monck expressed dislike of the policy of repression, and of Barebone's address, and instructed MPs to issue writs for new elections within a week, and to dissolve altogether once the house was filled.[67]

Londoners celebrated this news with bonfires, where in a ritualistic manner they roasted the hind quarters of oxen, poultry and other animals in derision of the Rump. Pepys was amazed by the number of bonfires. He counted fourteen between St Dunstan's church and Temple Bar, from Strand bridge he could see thirty-one, and in King Street, seven or eight. Some of the bonfires had sponsors, and Rugge informs us that 'Gentilemen was not backward in giving monys to buy faggotts and beere', but considering the bitter history of the campaign by apprentices and others against the Rump we can hardly describe these demonstrations as manipulated from above. According to the Venetian resident 'citizens and soldiers spent the whole night drinking together and shouting about the streets for a free parliament, for King Charles, whose name came openly from all lips without any fear, and to the confusion of the present parliament'. The Speaker of the Rump, returning home late, was affronted by a crowd, his men beaten and his windows smashed. A rump in a chair was then roasted at his gate and bonfires made there. Some apprentices also attacked Barebone's house,

[65] Pepys, *Diary*, I, 40, 45.
[66] *To the Right Honourable, the Lord Mayor . . . The Humble Petition of Divers Well-Affected Householders and Freemen* (1660).
[67] Rugge, p. 39; Davies, *Restoration*, p. 279; Hutton, *Restoration*, pp. 92–3.

smashed his windows, and pulled down his sign.[68] There were further bonfires on 21 February, when the secluded members were re-admitted.[69]

If, as the early months of 1660 passed, the demand for the return of
the king became more explicit, there were undoubtedly some who dissented
from this view. A detailed examination of charges for seditious words that
came before the London courts in the spring of 1660 shows that some
people remained hostile to bringing back Charles Stuart. On 22 May 1660
Westminster shoemaker Edward Jones, and his wife, Alice, acknowledged
'it was the King's time now to raigne, but it was upon sufferance for a
little time, and it would be theirs agine before itt be long'.[70] Some realized
that any rejection of Charles Stuart carried with it a rejection of Monck.
On 11 May 1660 Edward Medburne, a glazier from Wapping, supposedly
threatened that

if hee mett the King hee would Run his knife into him to kill him, and that hee
did not Care though he were Hanged for it himselfe, and that did wish the King
and Generall Monk were hanged togeather, and that hee did not Care if hee were
the Hangman himselfe, and that hee would Spend that day five shillings for Joy.[71]

Others simply expressed their desire to meet Charles on the gallows.[72] In
July William Fenne of St Martin-in-the-Fields was accused of saying 'that
he hoped to wash his hands in the King's blood' and would murder Charles
himself with his own rusty sword,[73] whilst Southwark man John Cowell
said he would kill the king if he 'could find a fitt opportunity'.[74] Margaret
Osmond was charged with saying on 7 June 1660 that Charles I 'was lawfully
put to death' and that Charles II 'shall not raigne one yeare'.[75] In May
1660 one William Cox apparently asserted that 'Lord Lambert deserved
the Crowne and to been King better then King Charles the Second'.[76]

The significance of this evidence is difficult to assess. All regimes experienced this type of criticism, and we only need to look at the sessions records
for the period before 1660 to find a number of individuals charged with
seditious words against the republic.[77] The problem is to know how wide-

---

[68] Pepys, *Diary*, I, 52, 54; Rugge, p. 39; *CSPVen, 1659–61*, p. 119; Bodl. Lib., MS Carte
30, fol. 537; MS Carte 213, fols. 592–3; *HMC, 7th Report*, p. 483; Verney Family, *Memoirs*,
ed. F. P. and M. M. Verney (4 vols., 1892–9), II, 153; Evelyn, *Diary*, III, 242; *CSPD,
1659–60*, p. 359.

[69] Pepys, *Diary*, I, 63; Rugge, p. 44.

[70] GLRO, WJ/SR/1216, rec. 30; Jeaff., III, 304. Cf. GLRO, WJ/SR/1261, ind. 7, recs. 16
(to prosecute), 39.

[71] GLRO, MJ/SR/1214, rec. 44 (to prosecute); Jeaff., III, 303.

[72] GLRO, MJ/SR/1214, rec. 46 (to prosecute); Jeaff., III, 304.

[73] GLRO, WJ/SR/1216, unnumbered rec. (to prosecute), fol. 27; Jeaff., III, 306.

[74] PRO, Assi 35, 101/2, fol. 24.

[75] GLRO, MJ/SR/1214, rec. 17 (to prosecute); Jeaff., III, 304–5.

[76] GLRO, MJ/SR/1214, rec. 48 (to prosecute); Jeaff., III, 304.

[77] Jeaff., III, 192–284, *passim*.

spread were the types of sentiment expressed by individuals charged with sedition. A man accused of saying in the spring of 1660 that he hoped to see the king hanged 'within syxe monthes after he came thither' claimed as an excuse that the words he stood charged with saying were pretended to have been spoken at 'a tyme when men tooke too great a Latitude in speakeing against Kingly government'.[78] No sessions files survive for the City of London for the period from late 1659 until November 1661, and so our sources probably underestimate the extent of hostility towards the restoration of monarchy. On the other hand, at a time of rapid political change, with the establishment of a new regime particularly sensitive about possible critics, we might expect an extraordinary number of sedition cases to come to court, creating an exaggerated impression of the extent of popular disaffection at this time. Moreover, in an age when authorities were very dependent upon local people coming forward to present delinquents, sedition cases can often tell us about popular hostility to the views being expressed.[79] For example, on 1 May 1660 in the Red Lyon Inn, Southwark, one Thomas Blacklocke said 'if ever the Kinge come into England, He should come in a Wheel-Barrow, and his Breach shold be stucke full of Nettles, and that he shold be hanged at the said Blacklocke's Dore, Or else he wold helpe to hange him there himselfe'. The reason why we know of this speech is because Blacklocke was speaking to a group of men and women (a sawyer, a waterman, two watermen's wives, and the wife of an oarmaker – all low-status occupations), who were 'talking of the joy of the King's coming into England', and who were only too willing to volunteer informations against Blacklocke.[80] Later that month, one Elizabeth Evans, a spinster from St Saviour's, Southwark, was out walking near her home when she saw one Lewis Powell, whom she knew by reputation to be a 'dangerous man', talking to a group of men. As she walked past, she listened carefully to what they were saying, and hearing Powell speak against the king, she eagerly reported his words to the authorities.[81]

All the evidence seems to suggest that those who continued to oppose the restoration of monarchy were a small minority. As it became increasingly obvious that Charles II would be recalled, more and more people accepted the logic of the situation, and tried to get the best out of the Restoration. As Burnet put it, in London 'all sorts of people began to cabal together, royalists, presbyterians, and republicans'. But his account implies that any alliances that were formed only partially concealed what were in fact fundamental differences between the various groups.[82] The different expectations

[78] HLRO, Main Papers, H. L., 28 May 1660.
[79] Cf. Rogers, 'Popular Disaffection', 21–2.
[80] HLRO, Main Papers, H. L., 28 May 1660.
[81] Ibid.
[82] Burnet, I, 154.

of those who, sooner or later, came to accept that monarchy must return, will now be examined.

EXPECTATIONS OF THE RESTORATION

The Restoration occurred in a climate of intense antagonism towards the sects. In addition to the anti-sectarian petitions, already examined, there were a number of collective assaults on separatist groups in late 1659 and early 1660. On 7 June 1659 the house of the quaker, William Mullins, in Vine Street, Holborn, was attacked by a crowd led by the earl of Southampton's bailiff.[83] At the beginning of October a quaker shop in Tower Street was set upon when it opened on a Sunday.[84] Shortly after Monck's arrival in Westminster in February 1660 some of his soldiers attacked the quaker meeting house of Edward Billing in New Palace Yard, saying they had come to rid England of the sectaries.[85] The month of the king's restoration saw renewed attacks on separatist groups. On 1 and 2 May William Kiffin's baptist meeting house on St Dunstan's Hill, off Thames Street in the heart of the City, was riotously defaced by a 'rude multitude' of 'the looser sort of people', with 'all the doors, seats, windows, Gallerys and floors etc. to the value of about £200 carried away'. The crowd threatened to do the same to other meeting houses around London.[86] According to the baptist, Henry Jessey, a woman from Wapping, on hearing of the attack, said 'it did her more good, than if two hundred pounds had been flung in her lap'. Also at the beginning of May, a group of baptists in Wapping, who were observing a day of fasting and prayer, were disturbed by a vintner from their neighbourhood, who asked them 'Do you see what you have gained by your fasting and Praying?... for the King is coming now, to hang you all up.' This same vintner, on the 30 May, the day after the royal entry into London, 'took a halter, and put it about the neck of one of his Consorts, and as it were hailed him along, and said to this effect, so must the Fanaticks be hanged up'.[87]

This intense anti-sectarianism is also reflected in the numerous pro-Restoration prints and ballads that were circulating at this time, propaganda forms certainly targeted at the London masses. The interesting thing about this propaganda is that anti-sectarianism was often expressed in the language

---

[83] J. Besse, *A Collection of the Sufferings of the People called Quakers* (2 vols., 1753), I, 365–6.

[84] B. Reay, 'The Quakers, 1659, and the Restoration of the Monarchy', *History*, 63 (1978), 206, 209.

[85] Besse, *Sufferings*, I, 366; Hutton, *Restoration*, p. 91.

[86] Bodl. Lib., MS Carte 214, fol. 99; T. Carte, *A Collection of Original Letters and Papers Concerning Affairs in England from the Year 1641 to 1660* (1739), p. 326; Rugge, pp. 78–9; HLRO, Main Papers, H. L., 4 May 1660; *HMC, 7th Report*, p. 80.

[87] H. J[essey], *The Lord's Loud Call to England* (1660), p. 8.

of anti-catholicism. One anti-separatist song ran: 'Let 'em cry down the Pope, till their Throats are sore, Their Design was to bring him in at the Back-Door.'[88] One anti-republican print argued that Charles I had been tried by 'Roman president [i.e. precedent]'.[89] A satirical petition purporting to be from the baptist, Praise-God Barebone, asked that

the Mystery of Jesuitism, and the Works of Ignatius Loyola may be read in Churches, in stead of what is now more commonly used, whereby the People may be instructed in all sorts of Knavery one towards another, and in all sorts of Rebellion and Disobedience to their Superiors.[90]

Much of this anti-sectarian sentiment might loosely be described as presbyterian in tone.[91] For example, the apprentice petition of 15 November 1659 combined its criticism of the sects with an expressed preference for the religion established by 'our three last Princes, with some ammendment in Discipline' as 'the only true and perfect pattern of Divine Worship'.[92] It was this petition which advocated a return to the position of 12 years previously, and this was the policy advocated by the group known as the 'Presbyterian Knot'.[93] The Cannon Street petition of December urged that 'the Ministry may be countenanced and encouraged, the Universities upheld and maintained', both of which were under threat from the sects, but defended 'the Priviledges of the Gospel which we do enjoy at this day'.[94] The watermen's petition of 12 December gave an avowed commitment to 'Parliament' and the 'Reformed Religion here established'.[95] Moreover, the 'full parliament' which met once the secluded members had been allowed to take their seats again, soon showed itself to be predominantly presbyterian in sympathy. It reaffirmed the Westminster Confession as the public profession of faith of the Church of England, and ordered the solemn league and covenant to be reprinted and read in every church in the country.[96]

[88] *A New Year's Gift for the Rump* (Oxford, 1660), in *A Collection of Loyal Songs Written against the Rump Parliament between the Years 1639 and 1661* (2 vols., 1731), II, 44. The back door was that of religious toleration, an indirect method whereby antichrist could undermine the Church of England once the direct stratagems of force and violence had failed. Cf. B. Worden, 'Toleration and the Cromwellian Protectorate', in W. J. Sheils, ed., *Persecution and Toleration* (Studies in Church History, 21, Oxford, 1984), p. 200.

[89] *The History of the Life and Death of Hugh Peters, that Arch Traytor, from his Cradell to the Gallows* (1661); BM Prints, no. 966.

[90] *To the Right Honorable, the High Court of Parliament ... The Illegal and immodest Petition of Praise God Barebone, Anabaptist and leatherseller of London* (1660).

[91] Reay, 'Quakers, 1659, and the Restoration', pp. 209–10; Smith, 'Almost Revolutionaries', p. 327.

[92] *Remonstrance of the Apprentices.*

[93] Hutton, *Restoration*, p. 105; G. R. Abernathy, *The English Presbyterians and the Stuart Restoration, 1648–1663* (Philadelphia, 1965).

[94] *To the ... Mayor ... The Most Humble Petition and Address of Divers Young Men.*

[95] *To the ... Mayor ... Humble Petition and Address of Seamen and Watermen.*

[96] *CJ*, VII, 862; T. C. Hansard, *The Parliamentary History of England* (1808), III, fols. 1582–3; Rugge, p. 51; Davies, *Restoration*, pp. 297–8; Woolrych, 'Historical Introduction', p. 194.

The revival of the position of 12 years previously meant a Restoration on the basis of the Isle of Wight terms, which would have resulted in a monarchy strictly balanced and bounded by parliament.[97] The presbyterians also wanted a comprehensive church settlement, although most were willing to compromise on the issue of episcopacy. They would have been happy with a settlement along the lines of the Worcester House Declaration of 25 October 1660, which stated that no bishop should ordain or censure without the advice and assistance of presbyters, and which also promised an effectual reformation of the liturgy, with objectionable forms made optional. Although only an interim measure adopted until a synod could meet, a number of presbyterian ministers addressed the king to express their thanks for the Declaration, in which they said that

Your Majesty hath gratified the consciences of many, who are grieved with the use of some Ceremonies, by indulging to, and dispensing with their omitting of those Ceremonies, viz. Kneeling at the Sacrament, the Crosse in Baptisme, bowing at the Name of Jesus, and wearing of the Surplice.[98]

For many, the reaction against the sects of late 1659–60 was part of a reaction against puritanism in general, and thus incorporated hostility towards presbyterians as well. There was a revival of traditional cultural and recreational activities which had come under attack during the puritan experiment in government. Maypoles, which had been prohibited by the Long Parliament, featured prominently in the public celebrations of the restoration of monarchy. At the time of the coronation in April 1661, a large maypole was erected in the Strand for the amusement of the people.[99] Christmas and other religious festivals were revived. In December 1660 John Crodacot, a presbyterian pastor in St Saviour's, Southwark, decided to conceal the lord mayor's order for observing Christmas day, but this merely prompted tumults in the streets when some people tried to open their shops.[100] The theatres, which had been closed in 1648, also came back with a vengeance. A number of anti-puritan plays were put on in London, amongst them Ben Jonson's 'Bartholomew Fair', which was staged for the first time for 40 years in 1661.[101] Although the two positions were not

[97] Hutton, *Restoration*, p. 105; Lacey, *Dissent*, pp. 4–5.
[98] *The Humble and Grateful Acknowledgment of Many Ministers of the Gospel* (1660); Hutton, *Restoration*, p. 146; Jones, *Country and Court*, p. 137.
[99] Rugge, p. 175; E. Halfpenny, '"The Citie's Loyalty Display'd": A Literary and Documentary Causerie of Charles II's Coronation Entertainment', *Guildhall Miscellany*, I, no. 10 (September, 1959), 25–6; Hutton, *Restoration*, p. 126; Underdown, *Revel, Riot and Rebellion*, pp. 274–5.
[100] PRO, PC 2/55, fol. 83; *Cal. Rev.*, p. 143.
[101] B. Jonson, *Bartholomew Fair*, ed. D. Duncan (Edinburgh, 1972); Pepys, *Diary*, II, 174; F. Bate, *The Declaration of Indulgence of 1672: A Study in the Rise of Organised Dissent* (1908), p. 7; C. E. Whiting, *Studies in English Puritanism from the Restoration to the Revolution, 1660–1688* (1931, repr. 1968), pp. 424–5.

necessarily identical, the rejection of puritanism in the general sense often involved a positive desire to see the return of traditional anglican practices. Commenting on the disastrous showing of the presbyterians in the City elections to the Convention Parliament held in late March, 1660, Barwick, one of Hyde's agents in London, expressed his opinion that 'at this instant there may be as many hands got... [to petitions] for Byshops and the Service Booke as at first there was against them'.[102]

For anglicans, the problems had started not with the failure of the Isle of Wight negotiations, but with the attack on episcopacy in the early 1640s. In the spring of 1660 some rather indiscreet sermons were preached in London, 'with such unseasonable menaces, and contempt of the Presbyterians'. Dr Matthew Griffith, who had ministered to clandestine royalist congregations according to the book of common prayer throughout the late 1640s and 1650s, gave a sermon in Mercers' Chapel on 25 March where he defended the absolute power of kings, and spoke in vengeful tones against presbyterians, independents, and sectarians alike. Around the same time, Mr Masterson of St Clement's delivered a sermon in which he spoke of revenge for Laud's and Strafford's blood, as well as the king's. Both were suspended from preaching, and locked up at the orders of the council of state. One of Hyde's agents, fearful that such 'Ranting Royalists' might be prejudicial 'to our hopeful restoration', encouraged a meeting between the leading episcopal and presbyterian clergy of the City,

that there may bee made up a good understanding between them, and that all moderation may be used on both sides in the pulpit to dispose the people for a settlement according to the true reformed religion and the laws of the nation, and not to dispute for the present the differences in Church Governmente and discipline, but for the future readily on all sides to submitte to whatsoever shall be determined by a lawful assembly of Divines.[103]

Ballads and prints often portrayed an uncompromisingly anglican vision of the Restoration. A tract of January 1660 advocated a return to 'Monarchical Government, Pious Bishops, and a Godly Ministry', and wanted 'errors, sects, [and] schismes' rooted out, under which title was explicitly included presbyterians as well as independents.[104] One song complained how in the 1640s and 50s 'The Orthodox Clergy were forc'd for to fly', 'the Common-Prayer Book was damn'd', 'the antient Order of Bishops went down', being replaced by despicable presbyterianism.[105] Hugh Peters, the independent

---

[102] Bodl. Lib., MS Clarendon 71, fol. 109.
[103] Bodl. Lib., MS Clarendon 71, fols. 150–1, 221, 230, 233, 261; Woolrych, 'Historical Introduction', pp. 201–2; Hutton, *Restoration*, pp. 110–11.
[104] *The Honest Cryer of London* (1660).
[105] *The Rump Serv'd in with a Grand Sallet* (1660), in *Collection of Loyal Songs ... Against the Rump*, II, 177.

1 *Portrait of Hugh Peters* (1660)

divine, encapsulated for anglican propagandists the religious tyranny of the interregnum. One tract condemned him for being anti-episcopal and anti-monarchical.[106] A print showed him standing on the common prayer book, next to a table on which were placed some documents inscribed 'Articles against K. C. and B. Laud'.[107]

[106] *Hugh Peters' Last Will and Testament* (1660).
[107] *Portrait of Hugh Peters* (1660); *BM Prints*, no. 968. See print 1.

The anglican image of the king was that he was semi-divine: 'the lawful Kings and Magistrates of the earth are called Gods'.[108] An attempt was made at the Restoration to play on the god-like mystique of majesty. Thus, almost immediately, Charles revived the practice of touching for the King's Evil, which was first done on 6 July 1660.[109] Majesty was supposed to be exactly that, majestic – hence the spectacle of the royal procession to the Guildhall on 5 July 1660,[110] and, more obviously, the magnificence and splendour portrayed at the coronation in April 1661.[111] An effect of overall awe was created. Note has already been made of people kneeling to celebrate the return of Charles, indicating the desire of many to see the monarch in these terms. Many who welcomed the Restoration anticipated the return of hierarchy, although this was not exclusively an anglican position, but a preoccupation of the gentry as a whole. One print from 1660 shows the tree of monarchy having been chopped down, but now three new branches are growing. Significantly, they are all of different heights, and on the highest one can be seen a crown.[112] Others saw the Restoration as a deliverance not just from the tyranny of the Rump, but also the tyranny of popular government. One song from the months immediately preceding Charles's return contained these words: 'All wise Men and Good, say it is a mischievous Fate,/ A Kingdom to turn to a popular State'.[113] Yet another looked forward to the day when 'The Cobler shall edify us no more'.[114]

Such arguments are of a very different nature to some of those we found in the City petitions of late 1659, which talked of the preservation of fundamental laws or popular birthrights, and which implied that it was legitimate for the people to take action when these had been violated. To what extent could these anglican arguments have been attractive to ordinary Londoners? To win popular support, royalist and anglican propaganda made a deliberate appeal to economic grievances. *A Dialogue Betwixt Tom and Dick*, an explicitly anti-sectarian piece, complained that in the country there was 'not a penny to be had', whilst in London people were 'broke for want of trade'.

[108] T. Marriot, *Rebellion Unmasked; A Sermon Preached at Poplar... Upon the Occasion of the Late Rebellious Insurrection in London* (1661), p. 4.

[109] Evelyn, *Diary*, III, 250; Besant, *London*, p. 163.

[110] J. Tatham, *London's Glory, Repeated by Time, Truth, and Fame* (1660).

[111] For an account of the coronation, see: J. Ogilby, *The Relation of His Majesties Entertainment Passing through the City of London to His Coronation* (1661); Halfpenny, '"Citie's Loyalty Display'd"'; G. S. J. Reedy, 'Mystical Politics: The Imagery of Charles II's Coronation', in P. J. Korshin, ed., *Studies in Change and Revolution: Aspects of English Intellectual History, 1640–1800* (Menston, 1972), pp. 20–42.

[112] A. Sadler, *The Loyall Mourner, Shewing the Murdering of King Charles the First, Fore-Shewing the Restoring of King Charles the Second* (1660).

[113] *The Rump Carbonado'd* [1659–60], in *Collection of Loyal Songs... Against the Rump*, II, 124. Cf. *Rump Serv'd in with a Grand Sallet*, in ibid., p. 180.

[114] *For General Monk's Entertainment at Cloth-Worker's Hall* (1660), in ibid., I, 263.

The resultant poverty was their slavery, as shown by this vague appeal to populist libertarian notions: 'We have been slaves since Charles his reign,/ We liv'd like lords before.'[115] *The Lamentation* argued that 'the King', if put in a position to do so, would be able to solve the problem of the City's 'emptied Chests'.[116] A poem which complained of how the Rump destroyed the Church of England, also commented on the 'robberies' committed by it, through excise, heavy taxation, and expensive wars.[117] *A City Ballad*, as well as appealing to economic grievances, also played on the tradition of civic independence, and the desire of the City to settle its own militia, in a tract which was anti-presbyterian and pro-episcopalian.[118]

The argument was that if the lower classes accepted their own lot and role in society, and left governing to their 'social superiors', they too would be better off.[119] An interesting insight into the anglican vision of the Restoration is provided by a pamphlet of 1660, set in the form of a trial of the Rump which is purported to have happened on 11 February 1660. Although claiming to be an 'arraignment' of the anabaptists' 'good old cause', the tract is in fact an attack not just on the Rump but of the whole history of the Long Parliament. Thus the charge is that 'thou didst assume unto thy self in the year 1641 the name of Supream Authority, and didst Levy a War against the chief Magistrate, and didst plot and endeavour to draw all other thy Fellow Subjects to do the same'. The tract then recalls all the horrors experienced during the civil wars, culminating eventually in the regicide and the abolition of the house of lords. A number of witnesses then appear to substantiate the charge. 'Mr Bishop' relates how 'he thrust us out of our places... branded us by the name of Popish Prelates... took away our means... [and] put us in prison'. 'Mr Duke' complains that 'whereas I had 5000 a year for all commers, and maintained good Hospitality, relieving the poor, and setting whole Towns at work... he took my Estate away, bestowed it upon some of his own friends... and hath left me nothing for myelf, but one hundred a year'. 'Mr Citizen's' complaint is that 'he imposed great Taxes upon us... quartered Soldiers upon us... hindred the trading amongst us, kept us bare of mony, and made us pay Excise for Meat and drink... He even out of meer spite, stole away the Gates and Chains of the City, and made Bonfiers of the Posts.' 'Mr Countryman' and 'Mr King' then rehearse their experiences, the latter also complaining how the Rump put out the orthodox clergy, to bring in 'all manner of prophane-

[115] *A Dialogue Betwixt Tom and Dick, the Former a Country Man, the Other a Citizen* (1660), in Mackay, ed., *Songs*, pp. 90–4 (quotations on pp. 92, 93).
[116] *The Lamentation of the Safe Committee* (1660), in *Collection of Loyal Songs... Against the Rump*, II, 167.
[117] *The Rump Ululant; Or, Penitence Per Force* [1660], in ibid., pp. 244–8.
[118] *A City Ballad* [1659–60], in ibid., pp. 80–8.
[119] Hill, *Some Intellectual Consequences*, p. 13.

ness and Poperism'.[120] Monarchy, hierarchy, the bishops, and the welfare of the City, the country, and the poor, are seen as being interdependent, and it is clearly not regarded as satisfactory simply to return to the position of 12 years previously.

Although it is impossible to assess the extent to which people accepted the whole of this anglican package, there is evidence of anti-presbyterian sentiment and a desire to return to traditional anglican practices amongst some groups. In March 1661, some apprentices and other young men addressed the king thanking him for his 'zeal in maintaining our happiness, and the wholesome discipline of the Church as it was in our glorious Martyr's day, under bishops and doctors'.[121] On 29 May that year, Charles II's birthday and day of restoration was celebrated by bonfires in many places where crowds symbolically burnt the solemn league and covenant in imitation of the official burning of the previous week by the common hangman.[122] In August 1660, 284 of the inhabitants of the parish of St Giles-without-Cripplegate either signed or put their mark to a petition to the king, asking that their presbyterian vicar, Dr Annesley, be removed, in favour of the man previously conferred by Charles I, a Dr Ryves, Dean of Chichester.[123] There were localized attempts to enforce the book of common prayer before the new religious settlement had been achieved.[124] In the autumn of 1661 several Southwark ministers were indicted at the Surrey Quarter Sessions for refusing to use the common prayer book.[125] In January, 1661 the parishioners of St Paul's, Covent Garden, successfully petitioned the bishop of London to compel the rector, the presbyterian Thomas Manton, to read the prayer book service daily at his church.[126] In early 1662 Dr Gouge, vicar of St Sepulchre's, refused to admit a churchwarden 'who would bring in Common Prayer'. The parishioners, however, petitioned the bishop of London against Gouge.[127]

Anti-sectarianism, therefore, comprised two fairly distinct positions: a presbyterian one, and an anglican, anti-presbyterian one. The sects, out-

---

[120] *The Arraignment of the Anabaptists Good Old Cause* (1660).
[121] *CSPD, 1670*, p. 658.
[122] *Kingdome's Intelligencer*, I, no. 22 (1661), 351; *Mercurius Publicus*, II, no. 22 (1661), 343. For the ceremony of 22 May, see: *Kingdome's Intelligencer*, I, no. 21 (1661), 238; *Mercurius Publicus* II, no. 20 (1661), 320; Evelyn, *Diary*, III, 288; *CJ*, VIII, 254; *LJ*, XI, 260.
[123] PRO, SP 29/12, no. 114.
[124] Cf. R. Clark, 'Why was the Re-establishment of the Church of England in 1662 Possible? Derbyshire – A Provincial Perspective', *Midland History*, 8 (1983), 100; Hutton, *Restoration*, p. 172.
[125] *Surrey Quarter Sessions Records, 1656–1666*, ed. H. Jenkinson and D. L. Powell (3 vols., 1934–8), II, 110, 149; I. M. Green, *The Re-Establishment of the Church of England, 1660–1663* (Oxford, 1978), p. 188.
[126] Rugge, p. 154; *Cal. Rev.*, p. 338.
[127] PRO, SP 29/53, no. 103.

manoeuvred, eventually came to accept the inevitability of the Restoration, putting their trust in Charles's Declaration of Breda of April in which he had promised liberty of conscience.[128] A baptist petition to the house of lords dated 4 May 1660 sheds much light on their position at this time. Complaining of the recent attacks on their meeting houses, they stated that it was their 'practice to bee obedient to Magistrates... under whom they may have protection of their Lives and Estates, and just Liberties to worshipp the Lord without Restriction, or being compelled against their Conciences', and they explicitly appealed to the king's Declaration of Breda. The petitioners then stated that they believed 'the Magistrates Authority, and the Subjects Duty, to bee Reciprocall, And that there is a stipulation betwixt them, that as Subjection is due to the one, Soe is protection to the other'. The petition was designed to show that the baptists were law-abiding people who deserved, as much as anybody else, protection under the law; but one is left wondering about the implications of this reciprocal relationship between magistrates and subjects when the former no longer protects the latter's 'liberties to worshipp the Lord without Restriction', but rather seeks to compel them 'against their Consciences'.[129]

The only group to consistently oppose the restoration of monarchy were the fifth monarchists. The leader of one of their churches, Thomas Venner, a London cooper, attempted to launch a rebellion against the government in January 1661. The affair proved disastrous, with only about 35 rising in support, and it was easily crushed. Although the government seems to have believed that Venner represented only a corner of a nation-wide conspiracy, the truth seems to have been otherwise.[130] All other separatist groups hurriedly issued declarations renouncing any associations with the rising.[131]

CONCLUSION

Most Londoners did support a restoration of monarchy by the spring of 1660. Although we have to acknowledge the survival of a 'rude opposition

---

[128] T. Ellwood, *History of His Life*, ed. S. G. Graveson (1906), p. 77; Bate, *Declaration of Indulgence*, pp. 2–6; Thirsk, *Restoration*, pp. xxii–xxiv.

[129] HLRO, Main Papers, H. L., 4 May 1660.

[130] W. G. Johnson, 'Post Restoration Nonconformity and Plotting, 1660–1675', unpub. Manchester MA thesis (1967); Capp, *Fifth Monarchy Men*, pp. 199–200; Hutton, *Restoration*, pp. 150–1; C. Burrage, 'The Fifth Monarchist Insurrections', *EHR*, 25 (1910), 739–45; W. C. Abbott, 'English Conspiracy and Dissent, 1660–74', *American Historical Review*, 14 (1908–9), 503–4; Sir W. Foster, 'Venner's Rebellion', *London Topographical Record*, 18 (1942), 27–33. For a contemporary narrative of Venner's rising, see *London's Glory; Or, The Riot and Ruine of the Fifth Monarchy Men and their Adherents* (1661).

[131] *A Renunciation and Declaration of the Ministers of Congregational Churches* (1661); *The Humble Apology of Some Commonly Called Anabaptists... With their Protestation Against the Late Wicked and Most Horrid Treasonable Insurrection and Rebellion Acted in the City of London* (1661); *A Declaration from the Harmless and Innocent People... Called Quakers* (1661).

to monarchy', it seems inappropriate to call this vigorous, since consistent republicans were a small and isolated minority. But it is wrong to assume from this that there was a political consensus amongst Londoners at this time. The value of Hill's work has been to challenge this particular myth of the Restoration, and to force us to rethink some of our conventional assumptions. Rather than seeing the important divide as being between monarchists and republicans, I have stressed the very different expectations people had of the restored monarchy. Support for the king was conditional upon his ability to solve specific economic, constitutional and religious grievances. In the area of religion, however, there was little agreement. The presbyterians wanted a comprehensive church settlement with no toleration; the separatists put their trust in Charles's promise of toleration; whilst the anglican position was antipathetic to both presbyterians and separatists.

The reality of the new regime was soon to disappoint many people's expectations. If it is arguable that the establishment of a more stable political regime facilitated a recovery from the trading slump after 1660,[132] the position with regard to taxation, and especially regressive taxation which hit the lower classes, was exacerbated. Not only was the excise not abolished, but the number of goods upon which it was levied started to grow.[133] In 1662 a tax on domestic hearths was established, payable by all but the very poorest people. In July 1663, Samuel Lewys, a merchant tailor from St Peter's, Paul's Wharfe, was charged with saying:

Wee were made to believe when the King came in That we should never pay any more taxes. If wee had thought that he would have taxed us thus, hee should never have come in. But he will never leave till he come to the same end as his father did.[134]

Yet even if Charles had been able to deliver in all other respects, the problem with regard to religion seemed intractable. Despite Charles's own wishes, it soon became clear that there would be neither comprehension nor toleration, and some people's enthusiasm for the new regime began to cool. Thus Robert Thornell was charged with saying in August 1662 'that if the King did side with the Bishopps, the Divell take King and Bishops too'.[135] It is perhaps in this context of disappointed expectations that we should understand the following words that James Barnes, a Stepney weaver, was charged with saying in December 1666: 'Here is a health to George Mounke, and the Devill take the King.'[136] In the following chapter, therefore, I shall examine the growth of disillusionment, focusing on the issue of religion.

---

[132] Chivers, 'City of London', p. 20.
[133] Beloff, *Public Order*, p. 93; W. Kennedy, *English Taxation, 1640–1799* (1913), ch. 4.
[134] CLRO, Sessions File, July 1663, ind. of Lewys.
[135] GLRO, WJ/SR/1257, rec. 5; Jeaff., III, 327.
[136] GLRO, MJ/SR/1329, ind. 20; Jeaff., III, 389.

4

The problem of religion*

The honeymoon period of the Restoration did not last long, and the rejoicing of 1660 soon gave way to disillusionment. As Ronald Hutton has recently remarked, few regimes 'have fallen in the estimation of their subjects as dramatically as the restored monarchy did'.[1] The failure to achieve a comprehensive and tolerant church settlement was a major cause of this transformation of attitudes. Many who had initially welcomed – and even actively striven for – the return of monarchy found themselves facing persecution for their religious beliefs, and they naturally felt betrayed. Religious persecution was to be the immediate cause of the first major outbreak of collective political unrest in London in Charles II's reign, namely the bawdy house riots of Easter 1668. The issue of religious dissent continued to inform the political controversies of the 1670s, and set the context for the emergence of exclusionist politics after 1678.

I shall start this chapter by looking at the nature of the laws against the nonconformists, who were affected by them, and how they were enforced. It will be seen that the vast majority of those who suffered from religious persecution were people of low social status, whilst the dependence of the central authorities on local people to enforce the laws meant that very few could escape the implications of the religious code. Socially, the enforcement of persecution tended to be divisive, making the emergence of consensus politics among the London populace extremely unlikely. It is important to stress, however, that persecution did not divide communities neatly between nonconformists and anglicans, since many of the latter were prepared to stand by their nonconformist neighbours. The divide that emerged, therefore, depended upon where an individual stood on the issue of dissent. I shall then look at the nature of nonconformist opposition to the Restoration regime. Persecution did not necessarily drive dissenters into a republican position, since Charles II's occasional championship of toleration meant

---

* Part of this chapter is derived from an earlier article on The Bawdy House Riots, published in *The Historical Journal*, Volume 29, 3, September 1986.

[1] Hutton, *Restoration*, p. 185.

that the dissenters were sometimes prepared to defend the royal prerogative against the authority of a rigidly anglican parliament. Although it is difficult to generalize for all nonconformist groups, three key elements in their critique of the Restoration regime stand out: their condemnation of the re-established church as containing too many relics of popery; their hostility to the bishops; and their criticisms of the royal Court, especially on the grounds of its moral degeneracy. These three elements informed the actions of the rioters in Easter week 1668, and help explain why a riot against persecution took the form of an attack on brothels. Finally, I shall look at the emergence of the catholic succession issue in politics in the 1670s, reflected in the pope-burning processions which started in London at this time. The beginnings of party conflict which we witness in this decade, rather than marking a completely new departure in politics, were in many respects superimposed upon these older religious tensions. This consideration is crucial for understanding the nature of exclusionist politics which will be examined later in this book.

THE EFFECTS OF PERSECUTION

There has been much debate amongst historians as to whether the re-establishment of an intolerant anglicanism was inevitable after 1660.[2] The tragic implications of the eventual religious settlement are more readily agreed upon. The failure to achieve a comprehensive national church created the nonconformist schism, whilst the failure of toleration meant that those with 'tender consciences' were to suffer heavily for their beliefs. The Act of Uniformity, passed on 19 May 1662, established the contours of acceptable religious practice. Every minister had to testify his acceptance of the new common prayer book and denounce the solemn league and covenant by St Bartholomew's Day (24 August), or face deprivation. Hundreds of clergymen throughout the country were deprived, and London lost one-third of its ministers. Many moderate presbyterians, who would have preferred to belong to a national church, found themselves unable to conform, and were forced reluctantly into separation.

A severe code was set up to penalize those who decided to worship outside of the Church of England. The Quaker Act of 1662, aimed primarily at these radical separatists, offered a series of stiff penalties (fines, imprisonment, and transportation for the third offence) for those who refused the oath of allegiance and held or attended a religious meeting. The Conventicle Act of 1664 made similar provisions, though it was intended for all

[2] R. S. Bosher, *The Making of the Restoration Settlement, 1649–1662* (1957); A. Whiteman, 'The Re-Establishment of the Church of England, 1660–1663', *TRHS*, 5th series, 5 (1955), 120–35; Abernathy, *English Presbyterians*; Green, *Re-Establishment*.

nonconformist groups. Anyone over 16 who attended an unorthodox religious meeting was to face fines of £5 (or three months imprisonment) for the first offence, £10 (or six months) for the second, and £100 (or transportation) for the third. This act was to lapse three years after the end of the parliamentary session in which it was passed, but a second Conventicle Act, with slightly different penalties, was passed in 1670. This had the more moderate fines of 5 shillings for a first offence and 10 shillings thereafter for those who merely attended a conventicle. But the preachers and those who owned the house where the conventicle was held were to be severely punished, with penalties first of £20 and then £40 for subsequent offences. There were a further two acts aimed at destroying the nonconformist influence in the boroughs. The Corporation Act of 1661 required all municipal office-holders to renounce the covenant and take the anglican sacrament, whilst the Five Mile Act of 1665 attempted to prohibit any ejected minister from residing within five miles of his old parish or of any corporate town.[3] If this were not enough, there were still other means whereby the nonconformists could be persecuted. Many of the more rigid dissenters, especially the baptists and quakers, suffered under the old Elizabethan recusancy laws, for refusing to come to church. Some conventiclers were even indicted as rioters, since technically any assembly of three or more people in order to perpetrate an unlawful act constituted a riot, and this could lead to heavier fines being imposed than under the terms of the second conventicle act.[4]

Persecution was not continuous. There was an intense period of activity against dissenters in the early years of the reign, but the disruption to normal legal and religious life caused by the plague and then the great fire, followed by the fall of Lord Chancellor Clarendon and the demise of the first conventicle act, produced a temporary respite between 1666 and 1669. Persecution was renewed briefly with the passing of the second conventicle act in 1670, but died down the following year. The final period of terror came in 1681–6, the period of the tory reaction which followed the defeat of exclusion.[5]

[3] Whiting, *Studies*, ch. 1; Hutton, *Restoration*, pp. 158–61, 169–80, 208–12, 235–6; M. R. Watts, *The Dissenters: From the Reformation to the French Revolution* (Oxford, 1978), pp. 223–7.

[4] GLRO, MJ/SBB/401, p. 41; *The Presentment of the Grand-Jury of the Hundred of Ossulston, for the County of Middlesex* (1682); Smith, 'London and the Crown', pp. 273–4, 362; P. N. Marshall, 'Protestant Dissent in England in the Reign of James II', unpub. Hull PhD thesis (1976), p. 223; Miller, *Popery and Politics*, pp. 191, 265.

[5] The records of persecution are to be found in the sessions rolls/files and conventicle certificates in the Corporation, Greater London, and Surrey Record Offices. A useful summary of the persecution can be found in *Victoria County History of London*, I, 374–82. Since the quakers were always the first to be picked on, this chronology can be gleaned from Besse, *Sufferings*, I, 366–486. Smith, 'London and the Crown', chs. 11, 15, discusses the chronology of persecution after the failure of exclusion. See also: C. F. Mullett, 'Toleration and Persecution in England, 1660–89', *Church History*, 16 (1949), 18–43; Watts, *Dissenters*, ch. 3.

The 1670s was a relatively easy time for the dissenters. In 1672 Charles attempted to fulfil the promises made in 1660 from Breda by issuing a Declaration of Indulgence, under the terms of which a large number of nonconformist congregations were given licences to worship freely. Although the indulgence was withdrawn the following year, most of these congregations continued to worship unharassed, and even the attempt under Danby in 1675 to reinforce the penal laws proved to be short-lived and in London largely ineffectual.[6] This chronology is important because it illustrates that the problems facing nonconformists were not the same at all times.

When the penal laws were being rigorously enforced, however, the effects could be devastating. In December 1681 in Southwark fines amounting to £9,680 were imposed on just 22 dissenting ministers,[7] whilst the following year Benjamin Agas was fined £840 for holding conventicles in St Giles-in-the-Fields and Arthur Barham was fined £600 for similar offences at Hackney.[8] Many had their livelihood completely ruined. Those who could not or refused to pay either had their goods estreated or were sent to prison. Conditions in some London gaols were so bad that imprisonment could seriously impair the health, and even lead to death.[9] Such penalties shaped the language of nonconformist polemic. Persecution was seen as a threat to 'lives, liberties, relations and estates',[10] responsible for 'rifling and pillaging and Spoiling' people 'of their Goods and Estates'.[11] In a tract written late in 1683, baptist preacher Thomas Delaune complained how persecution was destroying dissenters 'in their Liberties, Estates, yea Lives'. There was a bitter irony here, for Delaune was sent to Newgate for producing this tract, where he died 15 months later.[12]

The proportion of the metropolitan population who would have been susceptible to such a harsh penal code is difficult to know. The Compton census of 1676, which concluded that only one in twelve of the population of the diocese of London were nonconformists, is almost certainly a gross underestimate. Indeed, it seems to have been one of the aims of the census to prove that dissent was a spent force, so inconsequential in numerical

---

[6] G. R. Cragg, *Puritanism in the Period of the Great Persecution* (Cambridge, 1957), p. 21.
[7] *CSPD, 1680–1*, p. 613.
[8] *Cal. Rev.*, pp. 3, 28.
[9] Cragg, *Puritanism*, pp. 105–8; Watts, *Dissenters*, pp. 234–5.
[10] CLRO, Sessions File, February/March 1671, ind. of Price for printing 'An Eye-Salve for England'. Cf. Ellwood, *Life*, p. 233.
[11] SRO, Sessions File, Michaelmas 1670, ind. 2, of Penfould for printing 'A Short Warning to all Persecutors of the Innocent'.
[12] T. Delaune, *A Plea for the Non-Conformists* (1684), p. 11; CLRO, Sessions File, December 1683, ind. of Delaune; *A Narrative of the Sufferings of Thomas Delaune* (1684); *Victoria County History of London*, I, 381.

terms that it would be easy to stamp out.[13] For the early eighteenth century it has been suggested that dissenters formed some 15–20 per cent of the London populace.[14] Such a proportion does not seem inappropriate for Charles II's reign, and if anything might still be erring on the side of conservatism. It must be remembered that the City electors returned two presbyterian and two independent MPs in March 1661 so unanimously that the contrary party did not demand a poll.[15] During the persecutions of the 1680s, 425 different nonconformist meeting houses can be identified in greater London, that is, an area which covered just 130 parishes. (See Table I.) Whilst it should be said that some of the meetings were small, one-off affairs, with dissenters meeting in private houses after the larger public conventicles had been suppressed, the number is so large as to suggest that the dissenters were more than a small minority.

Persecution certainly hit large numbers of people. A study of the sessions records reveals that during the 1680s nearly 4,000 different individuals were either bound over, indicted, or summarily convicted for attendance at a conventicle.[16] This figure excludes those who suffered for non-attendance at church or refusal to take the oaths of allegiance. Moreover, many of these individuals suffered more than once, so the crude totals are much higher still. A brief summary of the geographical impact of persecution in the 1680s is offered in Table I. Once allowance is made for population size, dissent seems to have been strongest in the City parishes without the walls, where just over 1 per cent of the population suffered for attendance at conventicles in the 1680s, compared to just under 0.9 per cent for the City within, and about 0.5 per cent for the suburbs taken as a whole. This relative distribution is confirmed by an examination of where the conventiclers met. The heaviest concentration of dissenters seems to have been in the wards of Aldersgate Without, Bishopsgate Without, and Cripplegate

---

[13] G. Lyon Turner, *Original Records of Early Nonconformity under Persecution and Indulgence* (3 vols., 1911–14), III, 141–4.

[14] De Krey, *Fractured Society*, p. 75.

[15] *CSPD, 1660–1*, pp. 536–9.

[16] The sources used for identifying nonconformists and their meeting houses in the 1680s are: CLRO, Sessions Files, 1682–7; CLRO, Sessions Minute Books 52–8; CLRO, Conventicle Boxes 1 and 2; CLRO, Southwark Sessions Files, 1682–7; GLRO, M(W)J/SR/1613–97; GLRO, MJ/SBP/7; GLRO, M(W)J/SBB/392–442; GLRO, MJ/RC/3–10; PRO, KB 10/1–3; SRO, Quarter Sessions Files, 1681–6; Jeaff., IV; *A List of Conventicles or Unlawful Meetings Within the City of London and Bills of Mortality* (1683); 'London Conventicles in 1683', *TCHS*, 3 (1907–8), 364–6; W. T. Whitley, 'Thompson's List of Conventicles, 1683', *TCHS*, 4 (1909–10), 49–53; W. T. Whitley, 'London Churches in 1682', *Baptist Quarterly*, NS 1 (1922–3), 82–7; W. Wilson, *The History and Antiquities of Dissenting Churches and Meeting Houses in London, Westminster and Southwark* (4 vols., 1808–14). For a fuller discussion of the impact of religious persecution in London during Charles II's reign, see T. J. G. Harris, 'Politics of the London Crowd in the Reign of Charles II', unpub. Cambridge PhD thesis (1985), appendix one.

Table I. *Arrested conventiclers and their meeting houses, 1680s*

	Estimated population (1695)	Total NCs	M-Ho	Per 1,000 population NCs	M-Ho
City within	69,581	616	97	8.9	1.4
City without	53,508	540	106	10.1	2.0
Suburbs	236,143	1,209	221	5.1	0.9
Unidentified		1,468	1		
Total	359,232	3,833	425	10.7	1.2

KEY
NCs   = Nonconformists
M-Ho = Meeting Houses

POPULATION ESTIMATES

City within and without	Jones and Judges, 'London Population', pp. 58–62
Suburbs	
Westminster, Minories, Stepney, Wapping, Whitechapel, Shadwell, Tower, Shoreditch	D. V. Glass and D. E. C. Eversley, eds., *Population in History: Essays in Historical Demography* (1965), pp. 174–5 (Total 176, 143)
Southwark	Finlay and Shearer, 'Population Growth', p. 44 (60,000. This figure is for 1700.)

For the sources used to identify nonconformists and their conventicles, see footnote 16.

Without, all of which had about 2.5 meeting houses per 1,000 head of population in the 1680s.[17]

About 50 per cent of conventiclers who appeared in the courts can be described, rather loosely, as artisans. In particular, the trades of weaver, tailor, shoemaker, and carpenter were prominent, although these were amongst the most numerous crafts in the London area.[18] If occupations are ranked according to social status, we find that 74 per cent can be placed

---

[17] The precise figures are:

	M-Ho	Pop.	Ratio
Aldersgate without	9	3,358	2.7
Bishopsgate without	22	9,753	2.3
Cripplegate without	22	8,514	2.6

Harris, 'Politics of the London Crowd', p. 277; Jones and Judges, 'London Population', p. 62. I have found a further 16 meeting-houses in the Middlesex division of the parish of St Giles-without-Cripplegate.

[18] Cf. Ellwood, *Life*, p. 139, who says that many of the London Friends were tailors in the 1660s; Reay, 'Early Quaker Activity', p. 231, who found many quaker weavers, tailors, and shoemakers.

in status groups 3 and 4. These are Rudé's 'menu peuple', the petty shop-keepers, artisans and labourers of the metropolis.[19] Care is needed in assessing the significance of this information. Any ranking based simply on the occupational designations given in legal records is bound to be crude. For example, the term weaver could cover a whole range of socio-economic positions, from the wealthy merchant to the very poor hand-loom worker. There clearly were a significant number of wealthy nonconformists in London, as De Krey's work on the period after the Glorious Revolution has shown.[20] The fact that my own calculations show that over 25 per cent of those who suffered persecution were in high status occupations is in itself worthy of remark, and the preponderance of conventiclers amongst lower social groups probably does no more than reflect the relative occupational distribution in the London area. What can be said from this data is that religious persecution was a governmental policy which affected all social groups, including large numbers from the lowlier levels of society, and this was one very important way in which the experience of the Restoration regime touched directly on ordinary people's lives. This evidence alone should force us to challenge any view which suggests that the London masses were basically apolitical and non-ideological, unconcerned with issues of principle and only worried about their own material self-interest. Material self-interest in Charles II's reign would surely have induced the majority of dissenters to conform.

Although the issue of dissent created many tensions within the London parishes, it must not be assumed that it polarized society neatly into two groups. The dividing line between conformity and nonconformity could be rather blurred. There were a large number of occasional or partial conformists, people who refused to sever their links with the established church completely, and these were often connived at by moderate anglican clergymen. Richard Kidder, who officiated at the wealthy City parish of St Helen Bishopsgate in the mid-1670s, found that many of his communicants 'kneeled not at the Sacrament, but were otherwise very devout and regular'. This practice had been indulged by their previous minister, Dr Horton. The communions were 'very great ... and great summs of money given to the poore at those times', and considering 'the mischief of dismissing such a number of Communicants and sending them to the Non-Conformists', Kidder decided to continue to give the sacrament to those who refused to kneel, and risk being suspended for it.[21] The compilers of the 1676 census

---

[19] Harris, 'Politics of the London Crowd', appendix one, tables 1 : 4–6. The ranking of occupations is based on the hierarchies offered in Elliott, 'Mobility and Marriage', p. 79; Glass, 'Socio-Economic Status', pp. 382–3.

[20] De Krey, *Fractured Society*, ch. 3.

[21] R. Kidder, *Life*, ed. A. E. Robinson (1924), p. 19.

in the province of Canterbury noted that many dissenters came to church, and many belonged to no sect.[22] There were also a number of occasional nonconformists, people who attended the parish church in the morning, and took communion regularly, but went in the afternoon to a meeting to hear a different preacher or out of mere curiosity.[23]

The main dissenting groups in London, in descending order of numerical superiority, were the presbyterians, independents, baptists, quakers and fifth monarchists, yet even this five-fold distinction offers an inadequate description of the variety of nonconformist positions.[24] There was a fundamental split within presbyterianism, between the dons and the ducklings. The former, whose spokesmen included Baxter, Bates, and Manton, were strong believers in an established church, and therefore hostile to any proposals for toleration of the sects. What they wanted was a more comprehensive church settlement, which would incorporate people of their persuasion. The dons had more in common with moderate anglicans than with the presbyterian ducklings, many of whom after 1662 were prepared to throw in their lot with the separatists and strive for toleration outside the established church. In reality, there was little meaningful distinction between the ducklings and the independents, and indeed they often held joint meetings. Nomenclature became irrelevant. For example, under the terms of the 1672 Declaration of Indulgence, the independent divine Stephen Lobb licensed himself as a presbyterian. The baptists were another group that were divided, between the calvinist particular baptists and the arminian general baptists. All the above groups had very little in common with, and often very little sympathy for, the quakers. Even this picture becomes more complicated when allowances are made for change over time. After 1662 some of the independents were prepared to attend the established church to hear the sermon, though not to participate in the common prayer or sacraments. By the 1680s, however, it seems that some were even prepared to participate in the anglican liturgy. Such practices caused some division within the congregationalist movement, though the majority remained consistently opposed to occasional conformity. During the persecution of the 1680s even some of the baptists were prepared to go to the anglican church, and were 'most heinously censured by those that do not'.[25] From the 1670s some of the presbyterian dons seem to have been modifying their position. Although

---

[22] Western, *Monarchy and Revolution*, p. 165.
[23] M. Clapinson, ed., *Bishop Fell and Nonconformity. Visitation Documents from the Oxford Diocese, 1682–3* (Oxford, 1980), p. xviii.
[24] BL, Stowe MS 185, fols. 171–6; G. Lyon Turner, 'The Religious Condition of London in 1672, as Reported to the King and Court by an Impartial Outsider', *TCHS*, 3 (1907–8), 192–205; 'Present State of the Nonconformists, 1672', *Journal of the Friends Historical Society*, 4 (1907), 122–4.
[25] Morrice, I, fol. 623.

at first hesitant, most of the dons eventually took up licences to preach under the terms of the Declaration of Indulgence, showing that they were prepared to accept the idea of a grant of toleration without comprehension. Between 1676–84 even Richard Baxter gave up his previous attempts to achieve a comprehension for the more moderate dissenters, and recognized the need for presbyterians to unite behind the separatists' demand for toleration.[26]

Persecution did not affect all nonconformist groups equally. In the 1660s it was mainly the quakers and baptists who suffered, with very few presbyterians or independents appearing before the London courts.[27] It was not until the 1670 Conventicle Act that these latter two groups began to be affected in any serious way. Even in the 1680s, when substantial numbers of presbyterians and independents were being persecuted, the quakers continued to suffer disproportionately to their numerical strength.[28] This was partly because of the different tactics adopted in the face of persecution. Whilst most nonconformist congregations went underground, and developed sophisticated alarm systems and escape routes which would enable them to avoid arrest, the quakers refused to be compromised. They worshipped openly, and if locked out of their meeting house they would gather outside in the streets, a process which would continue week in week out until either all the members of the meeting had been arrested or the raids were abandoned.[29] The refusal of quakers and some baptists to take oaths, and of the separatists in general to indulge in occasional conformity, meant that these groups suffered under a wider range of laws than did the presbyterians. The disproportionate victimization also probably reflects a greater animosity towards the radical sects, with the local agents of law-enforcement being more willing to inform against, or less likely to shield, the quakers and baptists, than they were the more moderate dissenters.

It should not be assumed that it was only those who scrupled at total conformity with the re-established church who were affected by nonconformist persecution. The extensive involvement of the people in law-enforcement meant that many others experienced the implications of the operation of the penal laws. Not only did magistrates and juries have to decide whether to convict, but constables, churchwardens, watchmen, militiamen, and a

---

[26] Lacey, *Dissent*, pp. 15–28, 64; R. A. Beddard, 'Vincent Alsop and the Emancipation of Restoration Dissent', *Journal of Ecclesiastical History*, 24 (1973), 161–84; C. G. Bolam and J. Goring, 'The Cataclysm' in C. G. Bolam *et al.*, eds., *The English Presbyterians: From Elizabethan Puritanism to Modern Unitarianism* (1968), pp. 73–92; Marshall, 'Protestant Dissent', introduction; Western, *Monarchy and Revolution*, p. 162; Lamont, *Baxter*, ch. 4.

[27] Hutton, *Restoration*, p. 210.

[28] Harris, 'Politics of the London Crowd', appendix one, table 1 : 1.

[29] Besse, *Sufferings*, I, 408–35; Watts, *Dissenters*, p. 227; Hutton, *Restoration*, p. 211.

whole range of other local officials had to decide whether they would assist in the suppression of the conventicles. This could mean a choice between acting against one's neighbour, client, or friend, or facing a fine for non-performance of duty. Intelligence about where the meetings were being held would have been very difficult to obtain unless local inhabitants had been willing to come forward with information. This was something which the Conventicle Act of 1670 recognized, guaranteeing those who gave information leading to a successful conviction one third of the fine levied on the conventicler. They were also entitled to a fixed share of the penalties levied on those who did not act as a result of their information. Once informed against, the nonconformist might have to find friends to stand as surety for their future appearance at court, and this could draw still more people into the legal process of persecution.

The issue of dissent did not divide communities irreconcilably between conformists and nonconformists. There is much evidence to suggest that peaceful co-existence of anglicans and dissenters might have been possible. The intermittent nature of the persecution was not due to any temporary lapse in the penal laws,[30] but partly due to the fact that local magistrates were unwilling to enforce the laws unless coerced into so doing by a positive drive from the central authorities. For instance, in 1675, an order from the lord mayor acknowledged that 'complaints are frequently insinuated against the remissnesses of the Government of this Citty in not exerting against [Conventicles]'.[31] The persecution drive of the 1680s was not the result of any new legislation, but arose partly because of a tory coup in the City government,[32] and partly in response to fierce directives from the central government ordering justices to execute the religious laws.[33]

Local people often placed loyalty to their neighbours above loyalty to the strict letter of the law. Complaints were frequently made that the effec-tiveness of the legal campaign against the nonconformists was being hindered by the slackness of local officers.[34] The episcopal visitations of 1664, 1669, 1677 and 1680 reveal a general unwillingness of churchwardens to present religious delinquents. The notable exception is St Giles-in-the-Fields, which had a heavy concentration of catholics.[35] Constables could be equally

---

[30] The exception is the period 1669–70, when the Conventicle Act lapsed. Yet even at this time there were other laws under which dissenters could be prosecuted.

[31] CLRO, Journal 48, fol. 142. Cf. Smith, 'London and the Crown', pp. 263–4.

[32] Ibid., part IV.

[33] CLRO, Journal 49, fol. 384; *Domestick Intelligence ... Impartially Related*, no. 64; *Loyal Protestant Intelligence*, no. 39.

[34] *The Presentment of the Grand Jury for the City of London* (1683); LC, MS 18,124, IX, fol. 10.

[35] Guildhall Library, MS 9583/2–5. For discussions of the unwillingness of churchwardens to make presentments concerning doctrinal deviations, and the problems with episcopal

recalcitrant. Richard Hitchcocke, sub-constable of Limehouse, said in late 1681 'Hang me up, I will not inform.'[36] John Holby, constable of Stepney, said in December 1682 'The law for suppressing of conventicles is against the law of Christ.'[37] Sometimes the constables took no action because they were nonconformists themselves. For example, in May 1685 Richard Richardson, constable of Stepney, was fined for refusing to execute a warrant against a conventicle. His refusal is hardly surprising, since he had previously been convicted for attendance at a quaker conventicle.[38]

Yet the extent to which the dissenters were able to retain the sympathy of their conformist neighbours should not be exaggerated. In the previous chapter I argued that an anglican, anti-nonconformist reaction can be detected in London in 1659–60. Although perhaps not ever-present in the same intensity, hostility towards nonconformists was a latent prejudice which could become manifest at times of political crisis. This was the case in the early 1680s, as I shall demonstrate later, and partly explains the success of the persecution after the defeat of exclusion. Throughout the reign, the sessions records reveal that local men often did act against their nonconformist neighbours, and this could sometimes lead to violent clashes. Constables, headboroughs or beadles who were willing to suppress conventicles were sometimes assaulted.[39] At other times they were just chided by their incredulous neighbours. In February 1686 a Stepney weaver called a Spitalfields constable 'rogue and a rascall for executing his warrant for suppressing of Conventicles', and further threatened him by saying 'I know you, and will be even with you'.[40] In August 1682 a constable, who was a patternmaker by trade, disturbed a conventicle which turned out to be comprised mainly of women, many of whom were his customers. The women rebuked him, saying 'that except he desisted from disturbing them, they would buy no more of his Patterns'.[41] It was the informers who were particularly resented. 'An informer dare hardly owne his employment', a contemporary noted in July 1664, for fear of being stoned by the boys.[42] One Richard Boylstone, seeing an informer coming out of the Exchange in August 1670, shouted to some apprentices nearby to 'pelt him with stones'.[43] Yet those

visitations as a source in the context of the 1630s, see: M. Spufford, *Contrasting Communities: English Villagers in the Sixteenth and Seventeenth Centuries* (Cambridge, 1974), pp. 265–71; A. J. Fletcher, *A County Community in Peace and War. Sussex, 1600–1660* (1975), pp. 82–5.

[36] GLRO, MJ/SBB/394, p. 49.
[37] GLRO, MJ/SR/1622, ind. 38; Jeaff., IV, 191.
[38] GLRO, MR/RC/6, 9; CLRO, Conventicle Box 2.5.
[39] See, for example, GLRO, MJ/SR/1392, recs. 115, 134; SRO, Sessions File, Epiphany 1685, rec. 20.
[40] GLRO, MJ/SR/1682, recs. 129, 137.
[41] *Loyal London Mercury; Or, Moderate Intelligencer*, no. 17.
[42] PRO, SP 29/99, no. 9.
[43] CLRO, Sessions File, August 1670, ind. of Boylstone.

who were prepared to inform were perhaps more numerous than has usually been recognized. The trained bands, whose rank and file included people of fairly low social status, were also used very effectively to suppress conventicles. In short, persecution was made effective by turning Londoners against each other, and was beginning to divide communities between those who were sympathetic to the dissenters and those who were prepared to act against them. The point was well made in a libel addressed 'to all persecutors of the Innocent' in 1670. It asked:

O ye foolish and Blind ... Why do you not at all consider whom ye are thus rifling ... they are your own Countreymen, your own Townsmen, your own Neighbours that are your Friends.[44]

A whole code that governed behaviour between neighbours came under strain. For example, a man from St Saviour's, Southwark, decided to have a neighbour arrested for debt in June 1684, and admitted that he had no mind to arrest the man until he remembered he was an informer against conventicles.[45] This pressure working against 'neighbourliness' is important, and helps us to understand why there was no 'consensus' amongst 'the London crowd'.

THE NONCONFORMIST CRITIQUE

The religious settlement probably did more than anything to create disillusionment with the Restoration. Because of the many gradations of dissent, there was no single or coherent nonconformist critique of the Restoration regime. Exactly what was objected to in the re-established Church of England varied considerably from group to group.[46] What the various dissenting groups had in common was their opposition to the new prayer book, which they saw as reviving certain popish practices. Nonconformist criticisms of the Church of England were thus typically expressed in the rhetoric of anti-catholicism. A tory polemicist summarized the position well when he wrote in 1681 that the dissenters 'esteem the Discipline, Rites and Ceremonies of the present established Church no better than Popery and Popish innovations'.[47] Another hostile writer mocked the typical complaint against the common prayer book: 'It is Mass, 'tis Porridge, 'tis Bible babble; 'tis Will-worship; 'tis Superstition.'[48] Anglican ceremonies, priests (and what they wore), and places of worship (and how they were furnished), could all be

---

[44] SRO, Sessions File, Michaelmas 1670, ind. 2.
[45] CLRO, Southwark Box no. 17, Sessions Papers 1653–85, information of Orgall, 13 June 1684.
[46] A useful guide to the different nonconformist positions is still Whiting, *Studies*.
[47] *Weekly Discovery of the Mystery of Iniquity*, no. 3.
[48] Estwicke, *Dialogue*, p. 5.

condemned with the cry of 'no popery'.[49] Persecution was therefore important in reinforcing a particular strand of the anti-catholic tradition.

Another area of common ground shared by most dissenting groups was their hostility towards the restored bishops. Although many moderate puritans and presbyterians were prepared to concede the necessity of some form of limited episcopacy, no such 'reduction' was achieved, and the bishops returned higher than ever, with most of the influential sees going to former Laudian exiles.[50] In March 1661, one contemporary noted how 'the anti-episcopal spirit is strangely revived'. Another reported that the presbyterian teacher, Zachary Crofton, 'had 2,000 in the streets who could not get in to ... [his] meeting-house to hear him bang the bishops'.[51] At the City elections to parliament on 19 March 1661 the presbyterians, independents, and baptists united to vote in four men on an anti-episcopalian platform. Those who stood in opposition were hissed and cried down by a crowd shouting 'no bishops'.[52] A report in the state papers of that year talked of 'a generall defection in point of affection in the middle sort of people in City and Country from the Kings interest and virulent opposition to the Prelacy',[53] whilst Pepys wrote in August that the clergy were 'so high, that all people that I meet with, all do protest against their practice'.[54] Cases of seditious words reveal similar sentiments. In the spring of 1662 one Richard Major of St Paul's, Covent Garden, grumbled against the wealth of the bishops, claiming that 'the Bishop of Durham had thirtie thousand pounds more than he should have'.[55] In March 1665, William Neale of St Giles-in-the-Fields described the bishops as 'mudering rogues and the veryest rogues that live upon the earth'.[56]

An important question to ask is whether persecution turned the nonconformists against the restored monarchy. At first glance there seems to be much evidence to support the view that it did. In January 1663 Secretary Bennet was informed that the king has so many enemies in Southwark that 'any who speak in behalf of the King are in danger of their lives'. The informant claimed that a group had torn down the king's arms from his house, and defiled with dirt a loyal inscription below, which could not be removed, and he blamed the independent divine Joseph Caryll for preaching

[49] Jeaff., IV, 26–7, 'Nehuston'; W. Lawrence, *Marriage by the Moral Law of God* (2 vols., 1680–1), II, 211; Delaune, *Plea*, p. 30.
[50] C. Cross, *Church and People, 1450–1660: The Triumph of the Laity in the English Church* (1976), pp. 223–4.
[51] *CSPD, 1660–1*, pp. 538–9; *Cal. Rev.*, p. 144.
[52] *CSPD, 1660–1*, pp. 538, 540.
[53] PRO, SP 29/47, no. 71.
[54] Pepys, *Diary*, II, 167.
[55] GLRO, MJ/SR/1241, rec. 16 (to prosecute); Jeaff., III, 317.
[56] GLRO, MJ/GSR/1304, ind. 19; Jeaff., III, 368.

treason to them.[57] The following year a bizarre incident happened when a quaker entered the Bull and Mouth meeting in London with his hair cropped and wearing nothing but a loin-cloth, exclaiming god 'will cut the locks of the head, and shave the Crowne ... Woe to Charles and James, destruction draweth Nye'.[58] In November 1663 Thomas Fauster was charged with saying 'I hope ere long to trample in Kings and Bishops blood and I know five or six thousand men will join with mee in pulling downe the Bishops.'[59] In August 1670 haberdasher Josias Warne allegedly said

You Cavaleers say this King is the head of the Church, but I say hee ... is not so much as the Tayle. And wee never had good dayes since the King came in ... And if I had but sixpence in all the world I would give it to fight for the good Old Cause.[60]

It was believed that persecution was driving the nonconformists into rebellion. For example, in 1664 it was reported that dissenters were buying up horses and gunpowder, so that they would be ready should the Conventicle Bill pass.[61] When it became law, it was rumoured that 10,000 were to rise and demand liberty of conscience.[62] Tracts advocating rebellion were produced shortly after the second Conventicle Act.[63] In March 1675, at the time of Danby's anglican ascendancy, one Richard Cox, a needlemaker from Bishopsgate Street, reputedly said 'That Lawe [the Second Conventicle Act] ought not to be obeyed, And I hope there will be a Rebellion.'[64] The 1680s were another time, at least according to government sources, when nonconformists were arming themselves for an insurrection.[65] In December 1682, a paper advocating such a course was found in the churchwarden's pew in the parish church of St Giles-without-Cripplegate.[66]

---

[57] *CSPD, 1663–4*, p. 20.
[58] Friends House Library, Edmund Crosse MS, pp. 55–6. Cited in B. Reay, *The Quakers and the English Revolution* (1985), p. 109.
[59] GLRO, WJ/SR/1261, rec. 33 (to prosecute); *Surrey Quarter Sessions, 1661–3*, p. 307. This gives the name as Hauster.
[60] CLRO, Sessions File, August 1670, ind. of Warne.
[61] *CSPD, 1663–4*, p. 587.
[62] Ibid., p. 621.
[63] CLRO, Sessions File, November/December 1670, ind. of Brookes for publishing 'Ireland's Lamentation'; CLRO, Sessions File, February/March 1671, ind. of Price for publishing 'An Eye-Salve for England'. The latter can also be found in BL, Add. MS 38,856, fols. 76–80, where it has been misdated as c. 1659. Cf. Jeaff., IV, 26–7, 'Nehuston'.
[64] CLRO, Sessions File, April 1675, rec. 52 (GD), ind. of Cox.
[65] *CSPD, 1680–1*, pp. 560–1; *CSPD, 1682*, p. 538. Nonconformists were allegedly mixed up in the Rye House intrigues of 1682–3. For accounts of these, see: R. Ferguson, 'Manuscript Concerning the Rye House Plot', in J. Ferguson, *Robert Ferguson – the Plotter; Or, The Secret of the Rye House Conspiracy and the Story of a Strange Career* (Edinburgh, 1887); Ford Lord Grey of Wark, *The Secret History of the Rye House Plot and Monmouth's Rebellion* (1685); M. Ashley, *John Wildman, Plotter and Postmaster: A Study of the English Republican Movement in the Seventeenth Century* (1947), ch. 18; Salmon, 'Algernon Sydney'.
[66] PRO, SP 29/421, no. 112.

The difficulty is that much of this evidence originated from paid informers who knew how to exploit government sensibilities for financial reward. The new regime, fearful of its own security, had to treat all such reports seriously, and inevitably tended to be overcredulous. It is therefore difficult to isolate what is simply government paranoia. Towards the end of the reign, especially the periods of Danby's ascendancy of 1674–8 and the tory reaction of 1681–5, Charles II identified himself strongly with the anglican establishment, and so a criticism of the latter might more readily lead to an attack on the king. But at other times in his reign, Charles II had shown himself a supporter of religious toleration. His Declaration of Breda in 1660 promised liberty of conscience, and in 1662 and again in 1672 he tried to use his royal prerogative to suspend the laws against both protestant and catholic dissenters.

As a result, many nonconformists expressed their contempt for the intolerant anglican establishment in terms of an appeal to the king. This was true not just of the moderate dissenters, but also of the baptists, regarded by contemporaries as the sect 'most zealous for a commonwealth'.[67] In September 1661 Henry Adis produced a tract which vehemently attacked the persecutory policies of London's lord mayor, and asked him to consider 'whether thou hast not done worse things both against King Charles and also against King Jesus'.[68] During the height of the tory reaction Thomas Delaune was still stressing the fact that Charles II had on numerous occasions spoken out against religious persecution.[69] If the rhetoric of these polemicists can be dismissed as tactical, that of people charged with sedition surely cannot. In August 1661 one John Hardey drank 'a Health to the King but confusion to the Papists and Bishops'.[70] Benjamin Keeble, of Blackfriars, said of the 1664 Conventicle Act: 'The Bishops lawes are not the King's law'.[71] In March 1675 a nonconformist preacher was sent to the Gatehouse for saying at his conventicle that the king did not intend the penal laws to be enforced.[72] Often it was parliament that was condemned. In February 1662 Westminster porter, John Ascue, possibly a quaker, said 'A Plague of God confound all the Parliament.'[73] In May 1664 it was reported that nonconformists were meeting to express their dissatisfaction with parliament and adherence to the 'good old cause'.[74]

---

[67] BL, Stowe MS 185, fol. 175.

[68] CLRO, Sessions File, November/December 1661, ind. of Adis; H. Adis, *A Fanaticks Alarm, Given to the Mayor in his Quarters* (1661), p. 30.

[69] Delaune, *Plea*, pp. 51–2.

[70] GLRO, WJ/SR/1238, rec. 25 (to prosecute).

[71] CLRO, Sessions File, December 1664, ind. of Keeble. Cf. SRO, Sessions File, Trans. 1670, rec. 22, for similar words by one Benjamin Laker against the second Conventicle Act.

[72] *HMC, 5th Report*, p. 321.

[73] GLRO, WJ/SR/1247, rec. 65; Besse, *Sufferings*, I, 365.

[74] PRO, SP 29/99, no. 7.

Nonconformist hostility towards parliament can be seen most clearly in the political position adopted in the period 1670–2, from the second Conventicle Act to the second Declaration of Indulgence. Tracts written against the Conventicle Act took a fiercely anti-parliamentarian stance. *Some Seasonable and Serious Queries* argued that the Act violated both positive and natural law. It was therefore 'null and void' and ought to be 'altogether disregarded'. Significantly, it was also argued that the act was

expressly against the Kings printed Declarations and Promises for Indulgence, as well as his private frequent Conferences, wherein he hath so freely and fully expressed how much it is agreeable to his Conscience, Reason and Resolution to indulge Tender Consciences...

and asked 'whether it must not be rationally concluded That He is as well imposed upon hereby, and his Honour impaired'.[75] *The Englishman* argued that parliament had committed 'the highest treason' with the Conventicle Act, because it subverted the fundamental law, which was to preserve lives, liberties, and estates: 'Our Fundamentals were not made by our Representatives, but by the People themselves; and our Representatives themselves limited by them.'[76]

This critique was a radical populist one. A king who acted against the fundamental laws would presumably be as culpable as parliament, and the legitimacy of political authority was said to be rooted solely in the people, from below, and not from above, as it was for anglicans. Events took a different turn in 1672, however, when the king decided to relieve the dissenters through the use of his prerogative powers against the wishes of parliament. Charles's suspected desire to help the catholics, and the political implications of using the royal prerogative to overturn parliamentary statute, troubled many nonconformists, especially the presbyterians.[77] Quakers, and some baptists, refused to apply for licences, because they believed they would acknowledge the justice of the Conventicle Act by accepting dispensations from it.[78] But many presbyterians, independents, and baptists, who knew they could expect little from parliament, did avail themselves of the king's declaration.[79]

The bishop of London responded by instructing his clergy to preach against

[75] [N. Lockyer], *Some Seasonable and Serious Queries upon the Late Act against Conventicles* (1670), p. 13; CLRO, Sessions File, November/December 1670, ind. of Brookes for publishing the tract.

[76] *The Englishman; Or, A Letter from a Universal Friend ... With Some Observations Upon the Late Act Against Conventicles* (1670), pp. 8–11.

[77] Bate, *Declaration*, ch. 5. For a discussion of the presbyterian split, see Beddard, 'Vincent Alsop'.

[78] W. C. Braithwaite, *The Second Period of Quakerism* (Cambridge, 1961), p. 82; W. T. Whitley, 'The Baptist Licenses of 1672', *TBHS*, 1 (1908–9), 156. Many quakers were released from prison under the Indulgence. See Besse, *Sufferings*, I, 437.

[79] Turner, *Original Records*, II, 955–90.

popery and to magnify the authority of parliamentary laws.[80] 'Queries upon the Declaration', an anglican tract which circulated in manuscript form, argued that by accepting a licence to preach under the indulgence the nonconformists were acknowledging the king's supremacy, admitting that he had a right to suspend old laws and make new ones. An answer came in *Vindiciae Libertatis Evangelii*, which argued that the nonconformists were justified in accepting exemption from the operation of penal statutes, and explicitly acknowledged that the king did possess such suspending powers.[81] Again, distinctions between the sects still have to be drawn, and the fifth monarchists continued to be the most radical politically. For example one fifth-monarchist tract, 'An Eye-Salve for England', produced in 1671, demanded quite fundamental reforms in the nature of magisterial power. But it concluded with this remarkable sentence:

Wee stand up with our Lives and Estates to maintayne and defend a Magistracy and Ministry for the perfecting of the aforesaid Reformation whether it be Monarchical or Commonwealth.[82]

The issue of dissent was not the only factor in generating disaffection from the Restoration regime at this time. There were also anxieties concerning the nature and complexion of the royal Court. The number of catholics at Court was a cause for concern. The king's mother was the popish queen, Henrietta Maria, and according to Pepys her arrival back in England pleased 'but very few'.[83] In January 1661 one Jaine Blunstone, the wife of a leather-seller from Whitechapel, allegedly said 'the Queene is the Great Whore of Babilon and the King is the son of a whore'.[84] In 1662 Charles married a catholic, Catherine of Braganza, the daughter of the king of Portugal. There was also concern about the religion of the duke of York. As early as February 1661 Pepys expressed his anxiety over the possibility that York or his family might one day 'come to the Crowne, he being a professed friend to the Catholiques'.[85]

Another ground for complaint against the Court was on account of its moral degeneracy and debauchery. On 31 August 1661 Pepys noted the prevalence of the 'vices of swearing, drinking and whoring', and said he knew 'not what will be the end of it'. Two days later a friend informed him of the consequences, namely that 'the pox is as common there ... as

---

[80] Burnet, I, 555.
[81] *Vindiciae Libertatis Evangelii; Or, A Justification of our Present Indulgence, and the Acceptance of Licenses. By Way of Reply to ... Queries upon the Declaration* (1672); Bate, *Declaration*, p. 88.
[82] BL, Add. MS 38,856, fol. 80; CLRO, Sessions File, February/March 1671, ind. of Price.
[83] Pepys, *Diary*, I, 281.
[84] GLRO, MJ/SR/1222, rec. 4 (to prosecute); Jeaff., III, 309.
[85] Pepys, *Diary*, II, 38.

eating and swearing'.[86] The playhouses provided a source of many bedfellows for courtiers, since at the king's insistence female roles on the public stage, hitherto played by boys, were now all played by actresses. The two most distinguished rakes in this society were the king and the duke of York.[87] By late 1662 an ambassador could quote the Londoners as saying that their monarch only 'hunts and lusts'.[88] In 1664 one Anthony Derrew condemned the king for keeping none but whores about him.[89] Ten years later, one John Weedon condemned the king for keeping 'nothing but whores' and being 'a scourge to the nation'.[90]

These two grievances against the Court at Whitehall converged in the form of the royal whores, a number of whom were catholics. The king's favourite in the 1660s was Barbara Palmer, Lady Castlemaine (from 1661), later to be the duchess of Cleveland. She announced her conversion to catholicism in December 1663.[91] In the 1670s she was superseded by another catholic, Louise de la Querouaille, the duchess of Portsmouth. Throughout the 1660s and 1670s criticism of catholicism and the debauchery of the Court were linked in people's minds. For example, in April 1661 two sailors were supposed to have condemned the king, the duke of York and the nobility of England for 'their lewd living and favouring of Papists'.[92]

Two events occurred in the mid-1660s to heighten anxieties concerning catholicism and the corrupt Court. The first was the Great Fire of London, which started in Pudding Lane on 2 September 1666, and which due to freak weather conditions managed to destroy most of the City and parts of the suburbs over the next three days. The fire was blamed on the catholics, and a French watchmaker called Robert Hubert confessed to having started it as part of a conspiracy arranged in Paris, a confession which cost him his life. Because of his known catholic sympathies, the duke of York's complicity was suspected. Any group thought to be an enemy of the state was likely to come under popular suspicion for having fired the City. Thus there were rumours that the fifth monarchists had been responsible. But according to Clarendon, most people concluded that the authors were 'all the Dutch and all the French in town', understandable because at this time these two powers were at war with England.[93] The war was going disastrously, and

[86] Ibid., 167, 170.
[87] Hutton, *Restoration*, pp. 186–7.
[88] *CSPVen, 1661–4*, p. 205; Hutton, *Restoration*, p. 190.
[89] GLRO, MJ/SR/1290, rec. 4; Jeaff., III, 339.
[90] GLRO, MJ/SR/1479, ind. 5; Jeeaff., IV, 54.
[91] Pepys, *Diary*, IV, 431.
[92] *CClarSP*, V, 93.
[93] BL, Sloane 970, fols. 35–6; BL. Add. MS 15,057, fols. 44–45; *State Trials*, VI, fols. 807–66; Burnet, I, 416; Bodl. Lib., MS Rawlinson D 842, fols. 72–3; Earl of Clarendon, *Life. In which is Included, A Continuation of his History of the Great Rebellion* (2 vols., Oxford,

this was the second cause of anxiety. In June 1667 the Dutch launched an attack on Chatham, burning the dockyard and many ships, and established a blockade of much of the English coast. One critic argued that the mismanagement of the Dutch war was a direct consequence of the 'debauchery and drunkenness at Court', saying that 'no better could be expected when the Popish and profane party are in such credit'.[94] In June there were demonstrations in the capital, and Pepys recorded 'how people do cry out in the streets … that we are bought and sold and governed by papists and that we are betrayed by people about the king and shall be delivered up to the French'.[95]

Criticism of the Court was not necessarily tied up with the issue of dissent. In fact, some of the most outspoken critics were the anglican bishops. On Christmas day 1662 George Morley, Bishop of Winchester and dean of the Chapel Royal, preached a sermon at Whitehall in which he condemned the sins of the Court, though only to be laughed at by his congregation.[96] The archbishop of Canterbury, Gilbert Sheldon, was another who reproved the king for his adultery, and even refused him holy communion on that account. In October 1667 Sheldon went so far as to advise Charles to 'put away this woman that you keep', meaning Castlemaine, an incident which cost Sheldon favour at Court. He was never able to recover the king's confidence.[97]

Having said that, there certainly was a powerful nonconformist contribution to the attack on libertinism. For nonconformists, what was happening at Court was just symptomatic of a more widespread decline in public morals affecting society as a whole. There was an increase in brothels, in playhouses, in drunkenness and in debauchery in general. In their eyes, all sorts of sins were being tolerated and even openly encouraged, whilst the godly, who merely wanted to worship God peacefully in their own way, were being victimized by harsh laws. After the second Conventicle Act, which established rewards for informers, nonconformists frequently condemned the double-standard they thought was being adopted by those who broke up their meetings. As one writer put it:

Just as he [the Informer] gets his Money he spends it, for as he takes Wages to Fight against God, so he lays it out again in the Service of the Devil, Consuming in Bawdy-Houses, what he gets by Surprising Meeting-Houses.[98]

1857), I, 348; D. Jones, *The Secret History of White-Hall from the Restoration of Charles II Down to the Abdication of the Late K. James* (1697), pp. 25–6; J. Bedford, *London's Burning* (1966), pp. 149–76; Hutton, *Restoration*, pp. 247–50.
[94] *CSPD*, 1667, p. 196.
[95] Pepys, *Diary*, VIII, 269–70; *CSPD*, 1667, p. 189; *CSPVen*, 1666–8, p. 171; M. Gilmour, *The Great Lady. A Biography of Barbara Villiers, Mistress of Charles II* (1944), pp. 118–19.
[96] Pepys, *Diary*, III, 292–3.
[97] Burnet, I, 453 and footnote 3; Pepys, *Diary*, VIII, 584–5, 593.
[98] *The Character of an Informer* (1675), p. 5.

A tract of 1682 claimed that 'Meetings have been disturb'd too oft by those, That to a Bawdy-house were never foes', and suggested that these people would be better advised to 'inform against the Vices of the Age', rather than against those who 'preach down sin, and pray for Reformation'.[99] Despite their rather circumspect attitude towards the monarchy, nonconformists had little hesitation in condemning the sins of the Court. When, with the relaxation of the penal laws after the plague and the Great Fire, dissenting ministers emerged to preach in the open in the mid-1660s, they passed heavy censure on the sins of the Court in their sermons.[100]

When talking about public disaffection from the Restoration regime, Pepys typically isolated two factors, hostility to the bishops and hostility to the Court. For example, in November 1662 he wrote

Public matters in an ill condition of discontent against the height and vanity of the Court ... but that which troubles most is the Clergy, which will never content the City, which is not to be reconciled to Bishopps.[101]

Although not identical, these two factors clearly reinforced each other. By August 1662 it was a proverb in London that 'the Bishops get all, the Courtiers spend all, the Citizens pay for all, the King neglects all, and the Divills take all'.[102] And despite the fact that some of the bishops risked disfavour in order to reprehend the Court for its licentiousness, with time the two objects of hatred became inextricably linked, and exposed to the same type of criticism. In July 1667 Pepys recorded how his cousin, Roger, 'told us a thing certain, that the Archbishop of Canterbury that now is doth keep a wench, and that he is as very a wencher as can be. And tells us it as a thing publickly known.'[103] Marvell relished these scandals, and in his *Last Instructions*, a poem which also lampooned Castlemaine, he accused Sheldon of having affairs with two Court ladies, Katherine Boynton and Mrs Charles Myddleton.[104] Such scandals were rife after the fall of Clarendon, many of them having been put about deliberately in an attempt to discredit the bishops for their opposition to the chancellor's impeachment. The bishop of Rochester, for example, was accused of being 'given to boys' and 'putting his hand into a gentleman (who now comes to bear evidence against him) his codpiece while they were at table'. In December 1667 Pepys noted that 'everybody is encouraged nowadays to speak and even print

---

[99] *A Word of Advice to the Two New Sheriffs of London* (1682).
[100] Burnet, I, 400–1.
[101] Pepys, *Diary*, III, 271. Cf. ibid., II, 167.
[102] A. Wood, *Life and Times, 1632–1695. Collected from his Diaries, etc.*, ed. A. Clark (5 vols., Oxford, 1891–1900), I, 465–6; Hutton, *Restoration*, p. 196.
[103] Pepys, *Diary*, VIII, 364.
[104] A. Marvell, *The Last Instructions to a Painter* (dated 4 Sept. 1667, first published 1689), reprinted in *POAS*, I, 133.

... as bad things against them [the bishops] as ever in the year 1640, which is a strange change'.[105]

THE BAWDY HOUSE RIOTS OF 1668

The issues of dissent and the licentious Court combined to produce the first major outbreak of political rioting in Charles II's reign. The protest took the form of an attack on brothels. Trouble started on Easter Monday, 23 March 1668, when a group attacked bawdy houses in Poplar.[106] The next day crowds of about 500 pulled down similar establishments in Moor-fields, East Smithfield, Shoreditch and Holborn, the main bawdy house dis-tricts of London.[107] The final assaults came on Wednesday, mainly in the Moorfields area, one report claiming there were now 40,000 rioters – surely an exaggeration, but indicating that abnormally large numbers of people were involved. Most accounts agree in describing the bulk of the rioters as apprentices. The riots attracted people from further afield than the imme-diate vicinity of the bawdy houses under attack. On the Wednesday the apprentices in Moorfields were assisted by a large contingent that came up from Southwark. On all days the crowds were supposedly armed with 'iron bars, polaxes, long staves, and other weapons', presumably the sort of tools necessary for house demolition. The rioters organized themselves into regiments, headed by a captain, and marching behind colours. Some people seemed to have joined in the disturbances on all three days, notably one Peter Messenger, who was accused of heading a troop on Easter Monday, Tuesday and Wednesday. For this reason, the riots have come to be known as the Messenger riots.

The Court responded to the disturbances on Tuesday 24th, when a letter was sent in the king's name to the lord mayor and lieutenancy of the City, asking them to order the immediate doubling of the watch and to draw up two companies of the militia.[108] But an order was also given for 'all the soldiers, horse and foot, to be in armes', and the king's life-guards, under Lord Craven, played a prominent part in the suppression of the riot.[109] When some of the participants were captured by the peace-keeping agencies, the rioters became concerned with how to rescue their arrested associates.

[105] Pepys, *Diary*, VIII, 585, 596.
[106] The following outline is taken from these sources, unless otherwise stated: GLRO, WJ/SR/1349; GLRO, MJ/SR/1350, 1352, 1353; GLRO, MJ/GSR/1351; CLRO, Sessions Files, Mar./Apr. and May 1668; PRO, SP 29/237, no. 59; Jeaff., IV, xiii–xvii, 8–12; *State Trials*, VI, fols. 879–914; Pepys, *Diary*, IX, 129–32; LC, MS 18,124, I, fol. 284; *CSPD, 1667–8*, p. 306.
[107] R. Ashton, 'Popular Entertainment and Social Control in Later Elizabethan and Early Stuart London', *London Journal*, 9 (1983), 13–14.
[108] PRO, PC 2/60, p. 237.
[109] Pepys, *Diary*, IX, 129–30.

On Tuesday 24th, Finsbury gaol was besieged, the crowd leaving when they found none of their companions there, although four other prisoners apparently managed to escape. On the same day New Prison at Clerkenwell was also attacked, and here some of the arrested rioters were successfully released. On Wednesday 25th, when the lord mayor and some of his officers dispersed the rioters, arresting some of them, the others regrouped and managed to rescue their comrades. On Friday 27th New Prison was again besieged.

When so many people cause this amount of disorder over a period of several days it is clearly unwise to try and impose a single interpretation on events. There are hints that the disturbances may have been triggered off by sailors recently demobilized after the Dutch War, perhaps because one or more of their number had been cheated of money at such an establishment. The riots started in the east end, where there was a heavy concentration of sailors, and the first house to be attacked was that of Damaris Page, whom Pepys described as 'the great bawd of the seamen'.[110] From the little that is known about other brothel riots we find that they could sometimes start in this way.[111] Once the cue had been given, the apprentices might have been prompted into re-enacting their traditional carnival of misrule. After all, it was the holidays, even if it was not Shrove Tuesday. But these explanations, by themselves, are not sufficient, for the affair was no ordinary brothel riot. Not only was the unrest on an unprecedented scale, but the government also responded to it in an unprecedented way, by having the ringleaders indicted for high treason.

What worried the government were the political slogans which the rioters adopted. On Easter Tuesday, crowds shouted 'Down with the Red Coats' and threatened 'that if the King did not give them liberty of conscience, that May-day must be a bloody day'. They also threatened that 'ere long they would come and pull White-hall down', presumably, in their eyes, the biggest bawdy house of the lot. The group that besieged Finsbury prison warned the gaoler 'we have been servants, but we will be masters now'. On Wednesday the slogans were 'Down with the Red-Coats' and 'Reformation and Reducement'.[112] There is evidence to suggest that the rioters might not have been attacking all bawdy houses indiscriminately, but had specific targets in mind. The duke of York later complained that he lost 'two tenants by their houses being pulled down, who paid him for their wine licenses

---

[110] Pepys, *Diary*, IX, 132; GLRO, MJ/SR/1350, rec. 13 (to prosecute); Jeaff., IV, 8.

[111] Linebaugh, 'Tyburn Riot', pp. 89–91; N. Rogers, 'Aristocratic Clientage, Trade and Independency: Popular Politics in Pre-Radical Westminster, *PP*, 61 (1973), 98–100; Rudé, *Hanoverian London*, p. 184; Lindley, 'Riot Prevention', pp. 112–13.

[112] PRO, SP29/237, no. 59; GLRO, MJ/GSR/1351, inds. 3, 38, 40, 43; *State Trials*, VI, fols. 880–8; Jeaff., IV, 8–11; Pepys, *Diary*, IX, 132.

15 pounds per year'.[113] York certainly seems to have been a target for the
rioters. A crowd attacked a group of troops that came to suppress the disturbances on the Tuesday specifically because they believed them led by the
duke.[114] The political overtones of the riots seemed to be confirmed by
the colours that were adopted, crowds marching behind green banners, the
colour associated with the levellers.[115] All this evidence suggests that the
riots were an explicitly political protest, motivated by grievances both against
the Court and against the policy of religious persecution.

Nothing that was said at the trials of the suspected ringleaders provides
any clue as to why the particular slogans were adopted. However, three
satires were produced at the time of the disturbances, and although we
should not necessarily assume that they served as manifestoes for the rioters,
they nevertheless offer interesting suggestions as to why the riots occurred.
All three connect the attacks on bawdy houses with grievances against the
Court. The first appeared on 25 March, and took the form of a petition
from the 'undone company of poor distressed whores, bawds, pimps, and
panders', including Damaris Page, to the infamous Court whore, Lady Castlemaine. Pepys thought it 'not very witty; but devilish sincere against her
and the king', and commented on how widely it had been 'spread abroad'.[116]
After first lampooning the way Castlemaine had risen to power, the petitioners then appealed to her for protection against the London apprentices,
by whose action the whores had lost both habitation and employment:

We humbly judge it meet, that you procure the French, Irish and English Hectors,
being our approved Friends, to be our Guard, Aid, and Protectors, and to free
us from these ill home-bread slaves, that threaten your destruction as well as ours
... should Your Eminency but once fall into these Rough Hands, you may expect
no more favour than they have shown unto us poor Inferior Whores.

They concluded by promising to contribute 'to Your Ladyship, as our Sisters
do at Rome and Venice to his Holiness the Pope'.[117] The reference to the
pope alludes to the fact that the head of the roman catholic church did
obtain some income from a tax on brothels. Yet this was also an allusion
to the number of catholics at Court, Castlemaine, of course, being one of
them.

The other two satires are both alleged replies from Lady Castlemaine
to the *Poor Whores' Petition*, one a manuscript version, the other being
printed, but they are different from each other except for their first para-

---

[113] Pepys, *Diary*, IX, 132.
[114] *State Trials*, VI, fol. 887. In fact the troops were led by Sir Philip Howard.
[115] Ibid., fol. 880.
[116] Pepys, *Diary*, IX, 154.
[117] *The Poor-Whores Petition. To the Most Splendid, Illustrious, Serene and Eminent Lady of Pleasure, the Countess of Castlemayne* (1668).

graphs. These two letters combine the lampoon of Castlemaine with an attack on the Church of England and the anglican clergy. The manuscript one, which is dated 1 April, outlines the 'real' aims of the rioters: 'wee [i.e. Lady Castlemaine] cannot otherwise beleave, but that the rude, and ill bred company of Scoundrells ... by depauperizing you [the poor whores], and pulling down your habitations aymed at us the soveraigne of your Order'. Castlemaine, after acknowledging her conversion to catholicism, is then made to condemn the Church of England as resembling 'a Brazen Bason tyed to a Barbours wooden pole [vizt.] Protestant Doctrine, and order tyed by Parliamentary power to Roman Catholique foundations, Constitutions, and Rights'. The countess also condemns the archbishop of Canterbury, Gilbert Sheldon, for his 'cowardice' in 'fearing to declare the Church of Rome to be the Ancient, Uniforme, Universall, and Most Holy Mother Church'. However, she justifies her indulgence in 'all Venereall delights' by arguing that her 'practice hath Episcopall allowance also according to the principles of Seer Sheldon'. And it was because all privy councillors were pimps, and because 'the most exquisite Whoores are the onely persons qualified for the bosome freinds of Kings and Archbishops', that the riot was 'an Act of the highest Treason', which levelled 'at the roote of the Government as now-established'.[118] The printed version of Castlemaine's answer, which is dated 24 April, is more explicit about the 'allowance' which anglican clergy gave to whores: 'we charge that none of the sisterhood take any more Circingles or Cassocks to pawn, of any churchmen either Romish or English, when they reel into their Quarters, because they turn not to Account'.[119]

The three satires, then, rehearse the grievances against the licentious Court and the bishops which were particularly strong in London in the latter months of 1667. But the existence of such grievances was not enough by itself to prompt such widescale rioting in London in the spring of 1668. The timing seems wrong, for why postpone the protest until Easter if a more obvious day to pull down brothels is Shrove Tuesday? The answer is provided by the rioters' demand for 'liberty of conscience', and the fact that the disturbances were to a large extent a protest from groups who had experienced religious persecution in the first few years of Charles II's reign. However, the riots occurred not during the fiercest persecution of the 1660s, but at a time when the nonconformists seemed to be enjoying a *de facto* toleration. Moreover, the change in the complexion of the government after the fall of Clarendon in 1667, which saw the lord chancellor being replaced by Sir Orlando Bridgeman as lord keeper, led many to believe

---

[118] Bodl. Lib., MS Don b.8, pp. 190–3.
[119] *The Gracious Answer of the Most Illustrious Lady of Pleasure, the Countess of Castlem ... To the Poor-Whoores Petition* (1668).

that this would be a signal for reversing penal measures against dissenters.[120] This period also saw the emergence of Charles's 'Cabal', one of the most important figures here being the duke of Buckingham, a declared friend to the nonconformists. By December 1667 Pepys was writing that 'the nonconformists are mighty high and their meetings frequented and connived at; and they do expect to have their day now soon'.[121]

The nonconformists had every right to be optimistic. There had already been moves towards some relief in the autumn of 1667, when a bill for the comprehension of presbyterians was drawn up, although lacking sufficient political backing, it was never formally introduced. In January 1668 more promising moves were initiated by Bridgeman. He consulted with moderate anglicans such as Dr John Wilkins (soon to be bishop of Chester) and presbyterians such as Baxter, Manton, and Bates, about the possibility of introducing a scheme for comprehension of the presbyterians and a toleration for the rest, excluding the catholics. Sir Matthew Hale, lord chief baron of the exchequer, drafted a comprehension bill, whilst the leading independent divine, Dr John Owen, probably with the backing of Buckingham, was preparing to promote a toleration bill which would have the effect of turning Charles's Declaration of Breda into an act. These schemes were to be introduced into parliament when it reassembled in February, and the king even agreed to back them in his speech.[122]

However, many anglican squires and clergymen proved to be unalterably opposed to such concessions, one of the most active opponents of the scheme being Gilbert Sheldon, the archbishop of Canterbury. When parliament reassembled, he spoke fiercely against the concessions in the house of lords.[123] The commons proved equally hostile. When Charles opened the session, on 10 February, he recommended that the house 'find some way to unite his subjects in matter of Religion'. The commons, on the other hand, having met before the king came to the house to discuss the 'insolent carriage and conventicles of nonconformists and sectarians' in recent months, voted 'that his Majesty be humbly desired to issue his Proclamation, to enforce

---

[120] R. Thomas, 'Comprehension and Indulgence', in G. F. Nuttall and O. Chadwick, eds., *From Uniformity to Unity, 1662–1962* (1962), p. 196.

[121] Pepys, *Diary*, VIII, 584–5.

[122] Burnet, I, 465–6; H. Thorndike, *Theological Works* (6 vols., Oxford, 1844–56), V, 301–8; Dr J. Stoughton, *History of Religion in England from the Opening of the Long Parliament to the End of the Eighteenth Century* (6 vols., 1881), III, 371–8; J. B. Williams, *Memoirs of the Life, Character and Writings of Sir Matthew Hale* (1835), pp. 115–19; W. G. Simon, 'Comprehension in the Age of Charles II', *Church History*, 31 (1962), 440–8; Lacey, *Dissent*, pp. 56–8; Thomas, 'Comprehension and Indulgence', pp. 197–201; N. Sykes, *From Sheldon to Secker: Aspects of English Church History, 1660–1768* (Cambridge, 1959), pp. 71–3; P. Toon, *God's Statesman: The Life and Work of John Owen, Pastor, Educator, Theologian* (Exeter, 1971), pp. 131–4.

[123] Lacey, *Dissent*, p. 58; Simon, 'Comprehension', p. 445.

Obedience to the Laws in Force, concerning Religion and Church Government, as it is now established, according to the Act of Uniformity'.[124] Charles issued his proclamation to this effect on 10 March,[125] too late to provoke trouble on Shrove Tuesday, but in time for the next public holiday, Easter.

The two satirical letters purporting to be Castlemaine's reply to the 'poor undone whores' linked the riots with the failure of the plans for comprehension and toleration. The manuscript letter, as already mentioned, lampooned Sheldon, who had played a prominent part in defeating the project. This letter also made an implicit reference to the decision to reimpose the laws against dissenters, Castlemaine promising that Charles would

commande all ArchBishops, Bishops, Archdeacons ... [to] give in charge in their respective Visitations throughout the Realme of England, that strict inquiry be made after all those sacrilegious Robbers, and despoylers of the Temples, and Synagogues of Venus, and to proceede by way of Excommunication against all.[126]

The printed versions made similar points with regard to the bishops and the failure of comprehension/toleration. A committee was to be set up to consider the grievances of the whores, it said, which would include the archbishop of Canterbury and other bishops, whilst a bill was to be introduced into parliament 'for a full Toleration of all Bawdy-houses, Play-houses, Whore-houses, etc.', with the proviso 'that all Preaching, Printing, Private Meetings, Conventicles, etc., may be forthwith suppress'd; except those that are connived at, as Members of Holy Mother Church'.[127]

Set in this context, the timing of the riots and the slogans of the rioters become intelligible. So too do their tactics. In the months up until 10 March 1668, both brothels and conventicles had been connived at. In Easter week the rioters seem to have been telling the Court that if they were going to demand the enforcement of the laws against nonconformists, they in turn would put into execution the laws against bawdy houses. This may seem ironic, seeing that Charles II had supported the attempts to secure some form of religious toleration. However, it must be remembered that the proclamation ordering that the penal laws be reimposed was issued from the Court and in the king's name. In addition, it seems that Bridgeman's initiative had been vigorously opposed not only by 'some zealous clergymen', but also by 'some concealed Papists, then in great power' (presumably at Court). As mentioned, the scheme had explicitly excluded catholics from any form of relief. According to Burnet, the catholics realized that the nation would never 'tolerate popery barefaced', and thought it best to prevent a union of nonconformists and anglicans, which would leave them isolated, and

[124] *CJ*, IX, 44.
[125] *London Gazette*, no. 242.
[126] Bodl. Lib., MS Don b.8, pp. 192–3.
[127] *The Gracious Answer*.

hope that the laws against dissenters (both protestant and catholic) would continue to be slackly enforced.[128]

The government was worried about the political overtones of the rioting, and 15 of the ringleaders were indicted for high treason, for levying war against the king. The presiding judge, Lord Chief Justice Keeling, argued that because the rioters had intended to pull down all bawdy houses, they were intent upon a public reformation, and this was tantamount to 'levying of war' and therefore was high treason, 'for they take upon them regal authority'.[129] This was a rather controversial reading of the law, however, and although it had been construed in this way in the sixteenth century to deal with those whose 'public reformation' had been the destruction of all enclosures, never once had it been used against brothel rioters.[130] Keeling therefore asked the jury to return a special verdict, so that a meeting of all the judges could be held to settle the question of the law. At this meeting, ten of the judges supported Keeling's view that it was high treason. Only one judge dissented, and this was Sir Matthew Hale, the man who had drawn up the comprehension bill in January. He argued that 'it seemed but an unruly company of apprentices, among whom that custom of pulling down bawdy-houses had long obtained, and therefore was usually repressed by officers, and not punished as traitors'.[131]

It is clear that there was some discretion available to the judges on how to act, but instead of following the usual course for those who attacked brothels, they decided on the severest interpretation of the law possible. The reasons are not hard to find. Ever since 1660, the Restoration regime had been plagued by anxieties that radical sectarians and ex-Cromwellian soldiers were plotting to overthrow the monarchy. Venner's rising of January 1661 fuelled such fears, as did a number of other rumoured plots of the 1660s.[132] Keeling was explicit about the fact that political factors had shaped the decision to proceed for high treason. As he said in court:

We are but newly delivered from rebellion, and we know that that rebellion first begun under the pretence of religion and the law ... we know that, that rebellion begun thus, therefore we have great reason to be very wary that we fall not into the same error.[133]

He later wrote in his report that capital punishment was 'at this time absolutely necessary, because we ourselves have seen a rebellion raised by gather-

---

[128] G. Burnet, *The Life and Death of Sir Matthew Hale, Kt.* (1682), pp. 43–4.

[129] *State Trials*, VI, fol. 884. Only 4 of the 15 were eventually executed.

[130] J. Walter, 'A "Rising of the People"? The Oxfordshire Rising of 1596', *PP*, 107 (1985), 129–30; *State Trials*, VI, fols. 892–911, footnotes.

[131] Sir M. Hale, *Historia Placitorum Coronae: the History of the Pleas of the Crown*, facsimile of the 1736 edition, with an introduction by P. R. Glazebrook (2 vols., 1971), I, 134.

[132] Johnson, 'Post Restoration Plotting'.

[133] *State Trials*, VI, fol. 884.

ing people together upon fairer pretences than this was'.[134] We do not know if there was pressure placed upon Keeling to proceed in the manner he did. We do know, however, that 'the courtiers [were] ill at ease to see this spirit among people' and that the duke of York was particularly upset at the affair.[135]

The government feared that the riots were part of a wider design, involving ex-Cromwellian soldiers and other 'idle persons ... nursed in the late rebellion'.[136] Circumstantial evidence seems to support the connexion with civil war radicalism. As already mentioned, the rioters organized in military fashion, with regiments headed by captains, and marched behind banners of leveller green.[137] On Tuesday 24 March, the crowd that besieged Finsbury prison told the gaoler 'We have been servants, but we will be masters now',[138] perhaps representing a challenge to the traditional hierarchy. The rioters themselves suggested the existence of a wider design when they said there would be further trouble on May Day if they did not get their way.[139] In April, one John Lilley, a Southwark waterman, was taken in Warwickshire for talking about his involvement in the bawdy riots, and claiming that he and 40,000 others were ready to rise on 1 May.[140]

The significance of this evidence may be questioned. Military organization was traditionally adopted by crowds engaged in protest in pre-industrial London, the model copied possibly being that of the City's trained bands.[141] There are reasons to doubt whether the colour green was chosen to express affinity with leveller ideals. This colour was also self-consciously chosen by the weavers in their riot of 1675, although the government here seemed happy that this did not imply political radicalism.[142] One of the rioters who carried a green apron as colours maintained that he did not willingly join the riot, but that the crowd tore off his apron, and forced him to carry it on a pole. It seems that aprons were usually chosen for colours, and that many workers commonly wore green aprons, an interpretation reinforced by what we know about the weavers' riot of 1675. In 1675 alternative colours of red and blue were employed, probably representing the different regiments into which the rioters divided.[143] For 1668 we do know that

---

[134] Ibid., fol. 897.
[135] Pepys, *Diary*, IX, 132.
[136] *CSPD, 1667–8*, p. 310; *London Gazette*, no. 249.
[137] *State Trials*, VI, fols. 880, 882, 883.
[138] Ibid., fol. 885.
[139] PRO, SP 29/237, no. 82.
[140] PRO, SP 29/239, no. 167.
[141] See above, p. 25.
[142] B.L. Add. MS 25,124, fols. 39, 43; *CSPD, 1675–6*, p. 255; Dunn, 'Weavers' Riot', pp. 17, 19.
[143] See ch. 8.

all the regiments marched behind colours, but only one, are we explicitly told, marched behind the colour green.[144]

The statement about being 'masters now' can be explained in terms of the logic of the riot. Servants, that is apprentices, were recalling the elite to the full observance of the laws against bawdy houses, as well as freeing their associates who had been arrested for taking the law into their own hands. They were, therefore, temporarily making themselves 'masters' of the situation, although this does not necessarily mean a permanent inversion of the traditional hierarchy was sought. As for Lilley, it seems that he was 'horribly overladen with drink' when he uttered the words, and his mistress produced witnesses to testify that he was working on the Thames on the days of the riots.[145] A government spy reported that the rumour that there was a general design for May Day was widespread gossip in London,[146] and so Lilley need not have had any inside information when he spoke of such a plot. There is no evidence to suggest that he went to Warwickshire to enlist support for an insurrection. It is plausible to imagine, however, that Lilley, drunk, and romanticizing about the exploits of City apprentices to 'mere country folk', might wish to boast of (not to say invent) his own involvement in the riots, repeating various rumours which made the tale sound more dramatic. The talk of May Day as the next date of unrest is equally understandable, as it was a traditional day of apprentice unrest.[147] If, as Hobsbawm says, unrest was often symptomatic of collective bargaining by riot,[148] the threat of further trouble on the next public holiday should concessions not be granted makes sense. In short, the circumstantial evidence which led the government to fear that the riots might have been a prelude to a bigger, republican design, is ambiguous, and other equally plausible interpretations present themselves.

It is difficult to discover much about those people who took part in the disturbances of Easter week 1668, but the available evidence seems to suggest gest that the majority of the rioters were employed in low status artisanal occupations, with the most prominent occupation being that of tailor.[149] As we have already seen, the persecution of the 1660s had hit mainly those involved in low status or artisanal trades, with the most common occupation for those charged with attendance at conventicles being that of tailor.[150] Such evidence seems to confirm the argument being advanced here. Of course, we must be careful not to be over-schematic and adopt a simple

144 *State Trials*, VI, fol. 882.
145 PRO, SP 29/239, no. 167.
146 PRO, SP 29/237, no. 82.
147 See above, p. 22.
148 Hobsbawm, 'Machine-Breakers', p. 59.
149 Harris, 'Bawdy House Riots', pp. 552–4.
150 See Harris, 'Politics of the London Crowd', appendix one, table 1 : 6.

monocausal explanation of the rioting of Easter week 1668. Probably many of the participants believed they were doing no more than acting out a ritual that normally occurred on Shrove Tuesday. Yet within this traditional form we have some powerful political themes being expressed. Opposition to the Court, and to catholicism in general, standpoints later to be associated with the 'country' position of the 1670s, were clearly manifest in crowd politics in 1668, although at this time firmly identified with the nonconformist and anti-episcopalian positions.

THE BACKDROP TO EXCLUSION

In this examination of the growth of disillusionment with the Restoration regime, I have been concentrating mainly on the first dozen or so years of Charles II's reign. Most historians would argue that from the mid-1670s there appeared a new dimension in politics, with the beginnings of party strife, between court and country factions. Although too subtle an historian to argue for a distinct watershed, it is significant that J. H. Plumb chose to start his account of the emergence of political stability in 1675.[151] For John Pocock, 1675 saw the first expression in print of a new country party ideology, formulated in terms of a neo-Harringtonian critique of the government.[152]

There were a number of interlocking anxieties which led to this new shape to politics, centring around what was perceived to be a drift towards a more arbitrary style of government. The earl of Danby, who had risen to power after the fall of the Cabal, developed a policy of trying to 'manage' parliament through a system of placemen and bribery, and this was feared to be upsetting the balance in the constitution and unduly increasing the power of the executive. There was also concern over foreign policy, and especially Charles's close relationship with France, in alliance with whom England had fought against the Dutch. According to some critics, not only were national interests being sold out to those of a foreign power, but to a catholic, absolutist monarchy at that. Danby was also concerned about this, and during his period of influence he tried to persuade Charles to pursue a more anti-French foreign policy. Finally, there began to be the first signs of serious concern over the succession. Although the heir, the duke of York, had long been suspected of his catholicism, his marriage to Anne Hyde, the daughter of the earl of Clarendon, had produced two daughters as heirs, both of whom had been brought up as protestants. How-

---

[151] J. H. Plumb, *The Growth of Political Stability in England, 1675–1725* (1967).
[152] Pocock, ed., *Political Works of James Harrington*, pp. 129–33; J. G. A. Pocock, *The Machiavellian Moment: Florentine Political Thought and the Atlantic Republic Tradition* (Princeton, 1975), pp. 406, 415–16.

ever, Anne died in 1671, and two years later York married a catholic princess, Mary of Modena. This, coupled with York's public non-compliance with the Test Act in the same year, brought the issue of the heir's catholicism out into the open. There was now the prospect of a continuous succession of catholic kings in England, should James have a son by his second marriage, and catholic rulers were, by definition, believed to be cruel and despotic.

From the mid-1670s, then, we see the rise of a court/country conflict, centring around, or so it is usually argued, what were essentially constitutional issues, concerning fears of a growth in arbitrary government and the prospect of a popish successor. As Andrew Marvell put it in his famous country party tract of 1677, 'there has now for diverse Years a design been carried on, to change the Lawfull Government of England into an Absolute Tyranny, and to convert the established Protestant Religion into down-right Popery'.[153] The issue of dissent is normally seen as becoming less contentious in this new political climate. Despite the failure of the second Declaration of Indulgence in 1673, the nonconformists seem to have been given a new lease of life at this time, and the penal laws against them remained largely unenforced. As anglicans became increasingly concerned with the catholic threat, their hostility towards protestant dissent abated. In 1674 the house of commons even passed a bill for the ease of protestant dissenters, although it failed to get through the house of lords.[154]

The mid-1670s also saw the emergence of a pattern of street politics which was to become typical during the exclusion crisis. There was a dramatic rise in the output of inflammatory political literature, designed to arouse the political awareness of the London populace. Because of the censorship laws, this literature circulated mainly in manuscript form, particularly through the coffee-houses. Some of it was of an explicitly republican nature. One poem of 1674 by Marvell listed grievances over foreign policy, religion, and the king's ministers, and concluded thus: 'Of Kings curs'd be the power and name,/Let all the earth henceforth abhor 'em'.[155] A poem of 1676, probably by John Ayloffe, expressed concern over the drift towards more arbitrary government and the catholicism of the heir, and concluded 'I freely declare, I am for old Noll ... A Commonwealth! a Commonwealth! we proclaim to the nation,/For the gods have repented the King's Restoration'.[156] It was because of the increase in this type of literature that the government tried to clamp down on coffee-houses in the winter of 1675–6.

The whig Green Ribbon Club, which met at the King's Head Tavern

---

[153] A. Marvell, *An Account of the Growth of Popery and Arbitrary Government in England* (1677), p. 1.
[154] Watts, *Dissenters*, pp. 249–50.
[155] A. Marvell, *The History of Insipids* (1674), in *POAS*, I, 243–51.
[156] [J. Ayloffe], *A Dialogue Between the Two Horses* (1676), in *POAS*, I, 281–2.

in Chancery Lane, and which during the exclusion crisis was responsible for organizing the famous pope-burning processions, was already meeting by 1674.[157] We cannot tell from the club's records whether it was from its inception an instrument for co-ordinating mass propaganda. We do know that one of its earliest members was John Ayloffe, the probable author of much of the coffee-house doggerel.[158] Pope-burning processions began in London at about the same time. The first we know of occurred on 5 November 1673 when youths of the City burnt effigies of the pope and his cardinals. One report told of 200 bonfires between Temple Bar and Aldgate. The reason for this display was partly displeasure at the duke of York 'for altering his religion, and now marrying an Italian lady'. Anti-French sentiment was also in evidence. One group made an effigy of a French man, and shot him, presumably in some sort of mock court martial, because they felt the French had shirked in the sea fights against the Dutch.[159] A pope worth £50 was burnt in Southwark on 26 November, the day that the new duchess of York arrived.[160] Popes were burnt at Temple Bar on 17 November in 1675, 1676, and 1677, and on 5 November 1677 at the Monument. On all occasions alcohol was provided for the 'common people' by persons of quality.[161]

Too much can be made of what was new in the mid-1670s. This emergent country position was also built upon grievances which dated back to the Restoration religious settlement. The *Letter from a Person of Quality* of 1675, a tract probably written by Shaftesbury, and which Pocock has argued is the first statement in print of the new neo-Harringtonian ideology, is in fact a violent attack on the intolerant anglican establishment, and the pretensions of the bishops.[162] The same religious priorities can be seen amongst other leading country party spokesmen. The duke of Buckingham was also launching a tirade against the bishops at this time.[163] Marvell's *Account of the Growth of Popery* of 1677 was a pointed assault on the politics of Danby and the high-church party.

Although our sources do not reveal much about crowd politics at this

---

[157] J. R. Jones, 'The Green Ribbon Club', *Durham University Journal*, 49, NS 18 (1956), 17.
[158] Pepysian Library, Pepys Misc. VII, 475–6.
[159] Evelyn, *Diary*, IV, 26; *Hatt. Corr.*, I, 119; *CSPVen, 1673–5*, pp. 85–6; *The Burning of the Whore of Babylon, as it was Acted, with Great Applause, in the Poultrey* (1673).
[160] *CSPD, 1673–5*, pp. 40, 44.
[161] *The Pope Burnt to Ashes* (1676), pp. 2–6; *Hatt. Corr.*, I, 157; *CSPD, 1677–8*, p. 446; Miller, *Popery and Politics*, p. 184.
[162] *A Letter from a Person of Quality to His Friend in the Country* (1675). Two women were indicted for publishing this seditious tract, and the passages cited in the indictment show that it was the attack on episcopacy that most concerned the authorities. See GLRO, MJ/SR/1500, inds. 40, 41; Jeaff., IV, 66–9.
[163] A. Marvell, *Poems and Letters*, ed. H. M. Margouliouth (2 vols., Oxford, 1971), II, 343.

time, those who sought to appeal to the London masses certainly thought that the old issues of the 1660s continued to be of fundamental importance. The majority of the members of the Green Ribbon Club who can be identified appear to be nonconformists, and the rest either actively supported or promoted the interests of dissenters.[164] The verse satires of the mid-1670s which were circulating in the London underground were less concerned with new country issues than they were with the familiar complaints against the bishops and the debauched royal Court. One manuscript poem, probably by the earl of Rochester, complained that Charles II had become 'a Slave to every little Whore' and also asked 'Where are the Bishops now? Where are their bawdy Court? Instead of Penance, they indulge the Sport.'[165] Another crude verse, again probably by Rochester, alleged that 'The Parsons all Keep Whores' and 'The Bishops bugger up and down.'[166] The catholicism of the Court whores continued to provoke criticism similar to what it had in the past, since Charles's favourite was now that 'whore of Babylon', the duchess of Portsmouth.[167]

CONCLUSION

In accounting for the growth of opposition to Charles II's regime it is obviously wrong to place too much stress on one factor. Many from the lower orders clearly became disillusioned when it became apparent that the much hoped for relief from their economic burdens would not materialize, and this is something I examine fully in chapter eight. Others grew disappointed because of the new king's personal failings. Charles could not live up to his image of 1660 – a majestic and semi-divine monarch; in reality, he proved to be a rather debauched, worldly man, preoccupied with venereal delights. There were also grievances over foreign policy and increasing fears, from the 1670s, that England might be drifting into a catholic-style absolutism similar to that of Louis XIV in France. All of these anxieties are important for understanding why such an explosive situation was unleashed by the revelations of the Popish Plot in the autumn of 1678.

Nevertheless, much of the growth of opposition can be traced back to dissatisfaction with the Restoration religious settlement. The issue of dissent, and especially hostility towards the restored bishops, seems to have been the prime cause of political disaffection in the 1660s, and helps account

---

[164] See below, p. 119.
[165] Bodl. Lib., MS Rawlinson Poet 173, fol. 114.
[166] BL, Harleian MS 6914, fol. 1.
[167] BL, Harleian MS 7319, fols. 33–5, 'The Whore of Babylon'. For attacks on whores in general, see: BL, Add. MS 27,407; BL, Harleian MSS 6914, 7317, 7319; Bodl. Lib., Douce 357; Bodl. Lib., Firth c. 15 – *passim*; J. H. Wilson, *The Court Wits of the Restoration* (1948), pp. 120–3.

for the nature of the widespread rioting of 1668. The problem with focusing on protest, however, is that it is easy to lose sight of those who were not disaffected. In the previous chapter I argued that there is much evidence of popular support for the return of traditional anglican practices, including the return of the bishops, and also hostility towards those who desired either toleration or comprehension. It is difficult to see how such people could have been in sympathy with the demands of the rioters of 1668 for 'liberty of conscience' or 'reformation and reducement'. What I have been tracing, therefore, is only a partial alienation of those who had welcomed the return of monarchy in 1660. Indeed, so long as hostility to the Restoration regime was associated with the issue of dissent, it is plausible that there must have been large numbers of people who remained loyal. There is some evidence to suggest that in the 1670s anglicans and nonconformists were coming to share common political anxieties over the growth of popery and arbitrary government, though even here it is important to recognize that the issue of dissent continued to be an underlying theme. And even if these domestic religious tensions were to be temporarily subsumed in the 1670s, they were to emerge again with a vengeance during the exclusion crisis, as I shall demonstrate in the rest of this book.

——— ⋘ *5* ⋙ ———

Whig mass propaganda during the
exclusion crisis

In the autumn of 1678 Titus Oates made his revelations of a Popish Plot: the king was to be killed, London burnt again, and 20,000 papists were to rise to cut the throats of 100,000 protestants.[1] Oates's story brought a new and terrifying immediacy to the problem of the catholic succession. Although there had been growing concern over the duke of York's catholicism in the 1670s, there had been no immediate problem, since Charles was only three years older than his heir, was in excellent health, and seemed likely to outlive his younger brother. The next in line to the throne was York's daughter Mary, who in October 1677 had been married to the staunchly protestant Dutch stadtholder, William of Orange. But if Charles were to be murdered, James would automatically succeed, and a catholic would occupy the throne of England.

It was this crisis that led to the demand, from those soon to be known as the whigs, that the duke of York should be barred from the succession. In January 1679 the cavalier parliament was dissolved, and over the next two years there were three parliaments elected which were much more sympathetic to the opposition cause. The whigs concentrated their efforts on trying to get parliament to enact a bill to exclude the duke of York from the throne. With the breakdown of censorship following the lapsing of the Licensing Act in June 1679 there appeared a flood of lengthy and elaborate tracts in which the whigs sought to defend their policy by outlining the legal and historical precedents for exclusion.[2] But they also sought to win mass support for their cause through propaganda which was aimed at the popular market: broadsides, newspapers, prints, ballads, plays, sermons, and public spectacles, such as the famous pope-burning processions of 17 November. Contemporaries were convinced that this played an important part in politicizing the masses. As one tory paper put it, 'Tis the Press that has made 'um Mad.'[3] An examination of the nature and effect of this whig

---

[1] Miller, *Popery and Politics*, p. 156. For the Plot in general, see Kenyon, *Popish Plot*.
[2] Behrens, 'Whig Theory'; Furley, 'Whig Exclusionists'; F. S. Ronalds, *The Attempted Whig Revolution of 1678–81* (Urbana, 1937), bibliography.
[3] Sir R. L'Estrange, *Observator in Question and Answer*, no. 1.

propaganda campaign is therefore crucial to our understanding of the collective agitation against a catholic succession.

The major emphasis in whig mass propaganda was the threat to lives,
liberties, and properties that the Popish Plot entailed. Rarely was a specific
alternative advocated; the whigs were vague about who should be the successor, and about their own views on the constitution. Instead their argument
worked largely by negative inference; that is, their propaganda continually
stressed the horrors that could be expected should a catholic be king, and
their positive ideal was left to be inferred, being what it was necessary to
do in order to avoid such a danger. I shall argue that this meant that the
whig message had a potential for being interpreted in a more radical way
than perhaps its authors desired. Most importantly, I shall show that the
whig propaganda failed to meet the Popish Plot head on. When Oates's
story was printed in April 1679, it was embellished with earlier examples
of the catholic plots, in an attempt to exploit the sensibilities of the Court.
It rehearsed the Prynne theory that the jesuits had contrived the Civil War
and the murder of Charles I, and condemned Lambert's Instrument of Government as being papist in inspiration. Jesuits, in the guise of fifth monarchy
men, were blamed for the firing of the City in 1666. The new plot was
to be similar; again jesuits, disguised this time as presbyterians, were to
be sent to stir the Scots to revolt.[4] This use of the anti-nonconformist side
of the anti-catholic argument was largely ignored by the whigs. Instead,
a clear bias towards a nonconformist audience can be found in whig propaganda, a bias which was to be exploited against them by the tories.

Propaganda sources, if correctly studied, can throw much light on the
political assumptions of the populace at this time. Such material can reveal
how those people who succumbed to whig arguments, and who demonstrated their anti-catholicism in the streets, perceived the popish threat.[5]
Yet it is wrong to assume too simple a causal relationship between the
propagandist and those he is seeking to convert. A propagandist cannot
run counter to the assumptions and prejudices of the audience he is trying
to reach. Research has shown that a person exposed to views hostile to
the ones he already holds is likely to subconsciously misunderstand them,
or interpret them in a way which confirms his existing prejudices.[6] To be

---

[4] Miller, *Popery and Politics*, pp. 155–6. There are three versions of the narratives, each
with slight differences in wording: *LJ*, XIII, 313–30; *The Discovery of the Popish Plot,
Being the Several Examinations of Titus Oates, D. D., Before the High Court of Parliament*
(1679); *A True Narrative of the Horrid Plot and Conspiracy of the Popish Party against
the Life of His Sacred Majesty, the Government, and the Protestant Religion* (1679), repr.
in *State Trials*, VI, fols. 1429–72.

[5] For the exclusionist demonstrations, see ch. 7.

[6] E. Cooper and M. Jahoda, 'The Evasion of Propaganda: How Prejudiced People Respond
to Anti-Prejudice Propaganda', *Journal of Psychology*, 23 (1947), 15–25.

effective, a propagandist must know the sentiments and opinions, the current tendencies and stereotypes, among the people he is trying to reach, and appeal to them in such a way as to win an individual over to his cause.[7] Therefore, most propaganda will reflect in some way the common opinions of the age. Yet what we have is a propagandist's view of those opinions, and the problem is to discern what is genuinely believed and what is propagandist fiction.[8] By setting the study of propaganda firmly in the context of London political culture, many of these problems can be overcome. We can see which prejudices and preconceptions the propagandist believed it worthwhile to focus on, whether he sought to invest these with a new meaning, and also assess what resonance such arguments were likely to have had for different groups. Since I am primarily concerned with how people become politicized, it is crucial to discover the way propaganda was interpreted. It is possible for a particular message to be misunderstood, or for a given audience to build on that message to reach conclusions beyond those which it explicitly contains. For example, I shall suggest that although rarely attacking the king, whig propaganda nevertheless created a context in which people could be encouraged to develop a critical opinion of Charles II. A sophisticated propagandist can use this fact to his advantage, helping to shape opinions which he would never dare advocate explicitly. I shall argue that using such an approach it is possible to detect a criticism of the anglican establishment within some propaganda forms which were never overtly hostile to the Church of England. This will be seen in particular with the pope-burning processions.

THE WHIG MASS PROPAGANDA CAMPAIGN

Low levels of literacy in pre-industrial societies have meant that mass propaganda in the early modern period has often been equated with visual and aural propaganda such as prints, plays, rituals and sermons.[9] To define mass propaganda in this way, excluding material which took a written form, would clearly be inappropriate for late seventeenth-century London. As was shown in chapter two, the adult male literacy rate in the capital at this time could have been as high as 70 per cent. Moreover, it is not always clear which propaganda types were dependent upon literacy. Many of the prints that I shall examine can only be fully understood by reading the mottos or speeches of those depicted, or the accompanying explanatory

---

[7] J. Ellul, *Propaganda: The Formation of Men's Attitudes*, trans. by K. Kellen and J. Lerner (New York, 1973), pp. 33–6.

[8] R. W. Scribner, *For the Sake of Simple Folk: Popular Propaganda for the German Reformation* (Cambridge, 1981), p.8.

[9] The best recent study of mass propaganda is Scribner, *Simple Folk*, where the author tries to reconstruct lower-class attitudes towards the Reformation in Germany through the use of wood-cut prints.

notes. It is a mistake to argue that written propaganda was invariably inaccessible to illiterates. Those who could not read could gather around one who could, and discover through an aural medium political views which were issued by the propagandists in the written medium.[10] This process is known as bridging.[11] Coffee-houses, in particular, were places where all sorts of people, even 'the rude Rabble', could go to read, or have read to them, political propaganda.[12] The laws regulating coffee-houses, which required owners of licensed houses to refuse to have political literature on their premises, seem to have been of little effect during the exclusion crisis.[13] In 1681 a contemporary complained that 'we have the Coffee-House Tables continually spread with the noisome Excrements of diseased and laxative Scribblers'.[14] In addition, it is important to realize that even for those who could read, literary propaganda would be mediated through oral communication. Tracts that had been read were often discussed in taverns and coffee-houses.[15]

If some written literature must be included in mass propaganda, clearly not all can come under this title. The price of a printed tract might provide a useful criterion of definition, on the assumption that the lower classes could not afford the lengthier and more expensive pamphlets. Yet even the shorter and cheaper prints, broadsides and newspapers might be too dear for poorer people, who nevertheless could still have access to such material. If literature was deposited in coffee-houses it did not have to be bought, whilst if a group of people wanted to purchase a certain item, they could always pool their resources and buy it between them.[16] One contemporary's complaint of how satires, which 'swarm in ev'ry Street', marched 'from Friend to Friend', shows how easily economic restrictions on circulation could be overcome.[17] The tory Edmund Bohun noted that 'you shall sometimes find a seditious libel to have passed through so many hands that it is at last scarce legible for dust and sweat'.[18]

Style seems the most important criterion for defining mass propaganda. Long, turgid and philosophically learned tracts were not easy to read aloud

[10] J. A. Downie, *Robert Harley and the Press: Propaganda and Public Opinion in the Age of Swift and Defoe* (Cambridge, 1979), p. 6.

[11] R. S. Schofield, 'The Measurement of Literacy in Pre-Industrial England', in J. Goody, ed., *Literacy in Traditional Societies* (Cambridge, 1968), pp. 312–13.

[12] BL, Add. MS 34,362, fol. 52, 'On the Coffee Houses'.

[13] CLRO, Journal 48, fols. 189–91.

[14] *Protestant Loyalty*, preface.

[15] Cf. J. Brewer, *Party Ideology and Popular Politics at the Accession of George III* (Cambridge, 1976), ch. 8.

[16] H. M. Atherton, *Political Prints in the Age of Hogarth: A Study of the Ideographic Representation of Politics* (Oxford, 1974), p. 61.

[17] *The Carman's Poem; Or, Advice to a Nest of Scribblers* [1680], in N. Thompson, ed., *A Collection of Eighty-Six Loyal Poems* (1685), pp. 192–3.

[18] E. Bohun, *The Third and Last Part of the Address to the Free-Men* (1683), epistle dedicatory.

for the benefit of illiterate people. Those who could read would probably not have the time to sit in a coffee-house for hours trying to decipher such a tract. The pithy and vitriolic statements found in newspapers, ballads, broadsides and the shorter pamphlets were more likely to have a mass appeal. Despite its vagueness, this consideration has the advantage of being accepted by contemporaries as important. In justifying the publication of his *Weekly Pacquet*, Henry Care wrote:

This good Design may possibly seem contemptible, by being Attempted in a Pamphlet course; but 'tis considered, though there be good Books enow abroad, yet every Mans Purse will not allow him to buy, nor his Time permit him to read, nor perhaps his Understanding reach to comprehend large and elaborate Treatises. This Method is therefore chosen, as most likely to fall into Vulgar hands.[19]

   In some respects it is misleading to talk of a whig propaganda campaign, if by that we assume coherence and careful party coordination. Jones has shown that the first whigs were far from being a united party, but constituted a rather heterogeneous coalition of different interests brought together by largely negative propositions and a desire to see exclusion succeed.[20] Haley has argued that the earl of Shaftesbury, for so long regarded as the leader of the whigs, should be seen simply as the head of a particular faction within the whig movement.[21] It has now been recognized that it is inappropriate to see the Green Ribbon Club, which met at the King's Head Tavern in Chancery Lane, as the central coordinating body of the whig movement.[22] Neither Shaftesbury nor the duke of Buckingham were members, Shaftesbury keeping his own clubs at the Swan, Fish Street, the angel Tavern, near the Old Exchange, the Queen's Arms and the Nag's Head,[23] and Buckingham holding a rival club at the Salutation Tavern, Lombard Street.[24] A total of 29 different whig clubs in the metropolis can be identified, and although many of these were rather improvised meetings of whig leaders who would have frequented a number of clubs, some of these societies seem to have represented different factional interests within the whig movement.[25]

   Some of the clubs seem to have been responsible for coordinating exclusionist propaganda, though the precise nature of their control is unclear. Lord Guilford perhaps exaggerated when he said that in 24 hours the Green

[19] H. Care, *The Weekly Pacquet of Advice from Rome* (5 vols., 1678–83), I, 2–3.
[20] Jones, *First Whigs*, pp. 9–19.
[21] Haley, *Shaftesbury*, pp. 349–53, 506–9, 523.
[22] Jones, 'Green Ribbon Club'. For the old view which greatly exaggerated the club's importance, see Sir G. R. Sitwell, *The First Whig* (Scarborough, 1894).
[23] *CSPD, 1679–80*, p. 296; *CSPD, 1682*, p. 237; *Hatt. Corr.*, I, 206.
[24] *CSPD, 1682*, p. 237.
[25] Allen, 'Political Clubs', p. 571; Smith, 'London and the Crown', p. 76; T. Sprat, *A True Account and Declaration of the Horrid Conspiracy* (1685), p. 39; J. Willcock, 'List Taken from the Official Narrative – Places which were Haunts for the Conspirators', *Notes and Queries*, 10th series, 11 (1909), 102.

Ribbon Club 'could entirely possess the City with what reports they pleased and in less than a week spread it over the entire country'.[26] Propagandists certainly frequented the clubs. Printer and bookseller Francis Smith was a member of the Salutation Club,[27] whilst poets Ayloffe and Shadwell, and pamphleteers Booth and Blount were Green Ribbon Club men.[28] It is impossible to say to what extent the clubs controlled the output of such authors. The Green Ribbon Club was responsible for organizing visual propaganda, in the form of pope-burning processions, at least for the years 1679–80.[29] But it did not hold a monopoly. The Sun Tavern Club, which met behind the Royal Exchange, was suspected of playing a role in organizing the procession of 1680.[30] Tory sources tell us the effigies of the popes were built by the carpenter Stephen College, who was not a member of the Green Ribbon Club. College was reputed to have built seven such popes during the exclusion crisis.[31] The playwright Elkannah Settle was allegedly hired by Shaftesbury to design the pageants, and neither he, nor his employer, were members.[32] Because so much of the written propaganda appeared anonymously, or under pseudonyms, it is impossible to say much about those who wrote in favour of the whig cause. More is known about the publishers of such material. The earl of Shaftesbury seems to have employed a small group of opposition stationers to produce and distribute whig tracts, among them Francis Smith. Yet much more propaganda was produced than the whig leaders could possibly have encouraged, and it seems plausible that much of the exclusionist literature came from writers and publishers who were working on their own initiative.[33]

A wide variety of propaganda types were used to advocate the exclusionist cause. One of the most direct ways of spreading whig arguments was by personal communication. One hostile writer complained that people were 'hired to ball in Coffee houses'.[34] Even whig MPs could occasionally be found in coffee-houses vindicating the position of parliament.[35] The reception was not always friendly. In late March 1681, newspaper publisher

---

[26] Jones, 'Green Ribbon Club', p. 19.
[27] Allen, 'Crown and Corporation', p. 177.
[28] Pepysian Library, Pepys Misc. VII, 465–91.
[29] Ibid., pp. 475, 484–5.
[30] *CSPD, 1680–1*, pp. 86–7.
[31] *A New Song on the Death of Colledge, the Protestant Joyner* [1681], in N. Thompson, ed., *A Choice Collection of One Hundred and Eighty Loyal Songs*, 3rd edition (1685), pp. 64–5.
[32] Furley, 'Pope-Burning Processions', p. 19; Williams, 'Pope-Burning Processions', pp. 106–7; Burke, 'Seventeenth-Century London', pp. 47–8.
[33] T. J. Crist, 'Francis Smith and the Opposition Press in England, 1660–1688', unpub. Cambridge PhD thesis (1977), pp. viii–ix.
[34] Bodl. Lib., MS Carte 104, fol. 18.
[35] *CSPD, 1680–1*, p. 107.

Langley Curtis was threatened in a coffee-house and forced to leave.[36] On Saturday, 14 May 1682, 'some honest Citizens [i.e. tories] being in a Coffee-house in Aldersgate street, vindicating the present Government, were interrupted by Mr Samuel Harris ... who affirm'd, the Government of this Nation lay wholly in the People'. Again, a brawl resulted.[37]

Another effective oral form of propaganda was preaching. Titus Oates was active giving sermons at this time.[38] Often a sermon could carry a very pointed political message. Tories, at least, believed the whigs were using this medium to teach radical theories of resistance.[39] One preacher used a sermon to attack the tory press, and reveal to his congregation its errors and lies.[40] Money was even provided by the French ambassador, Barillon, to finance two presbyterian ministers to preach against the Court.[41] Ballads may be regarded as a hybrid form of printed and oral propaganda. The whigs printed a large number of broadsides of 'new songs to an old tune'. The use of an old familiar tune meant that the words of the ballad might be more easily learned by anyone who read or heard it, and could then pass the message on. Occasionally new tunes were written specially for the ballad, and sheet music printed as well. Often these songs were performed publicly in the streets by ballad singers.[42]

In a deliberate appeal to the gambling and gaming side of London culture, a number of sets of playing cards depicting political scenes were produced, some of which survive in the Guildhall Library and the British Library.[43] How readily available such packs were during the exclusion crisis is difficult to say, but the fact that they were advertised in the press suggests that quite a number of each pack were produced. Some packs were quite expensive, at 1s per pack,[44] although cheaper editions sold at only 4d.[45]

[36] *Loyal Protestant Intelligence*, no. 7.
[37] Ibid., no. 23.
[38] T. Oates, *A Sermon Preached at St Michael's, Wood Street* (1679); LC, MS 18,124, VII, fol. 98; Verney, *Memoirs*, II, 329; *Protestant (Domestick) Intelligence*, nos. 59, 66, 67; Guildhall Library, MS 5026/1; *Loyal Protestant Intelligence*, nos. 38, 41.
[39] *Loyal Protestant Intelligence*, no. 141.
[40] Ibid., no. 59.
[41] George, *Political Caricature*, p. 55. During the exclusion crisis, Charles II was on bad terms with the French, only to be reconciled in 1681. For whig intrigues with the French at this time, see: Jones, *First Whigs*, pp. 147–51; Allen, 'Crown and Corporation', p. 178.
[42] LC, MS 18,124, VIII, fol. 192; *Loyal Protestant Intelligence*, no. 149; *CSPD, 1682*, p. 538.
[43] Guildhall Library, Playing Cards, nos. 236–88; Lady C. Schreiber, *Catalogue of the Collection of Playing Cards bequeathed to the Trustees of the British Museum* (1901); W. H. Willshire, *A Descriptive Catalogue of Playing and Other Cards in the British Museum* (1876). Some of these cards are reproduced in facsimile in Lady C. Schreiber, *Playing Cards of Various Ages and Countries* (3 vols., 1892–5), I.
[44] S. A. Hankey, 'Remarks upon a Series of Forty-Nine Historical Cards, with Engravings, Representing the Conspiracy of Titus Oates', *Archeological Journal*, 30 (1873), 187.
[45] *Impartial Protestant Mercury*, no. 62.

Plays were put on to carry the exclusionist message. The text of one – *The Coronation of Queen Elizabeth* – which was performed at Bartholomew and Southwark fairs in 1680, survives. Because of the expense of the theatre, fairs were the only places where ordinary people could see plays, and judging by the crowds that frequented the fairs, the whigs could reach a large number of people in this way.[46] Anyone who failed to see the play could always buy it in pamphlet form. The appeal to the lower orders was an obvious one, for in the above named play the heroes were a cook and a tinker, people of very low status.[47] A play called *Rome's Folly: Or, the Amorous Fryar*', dedicated to the earl of Shaftesbury and Lord Howard of Escrick, was put on at the house of a person of quality at the end of 1681.[48] William Bedloe wrote a play describing the Popish Plot, which he dedicated to the duke of Buckingham, but there is no evidence that it was ever performed publicly.[49]

The best-known forms of visual propaganda employed by the whigs were the pope-burning processions, which took place on Queen Elizabeth's accession day, 17 November. An effigy of the pope, seated in his chair of state, was carried through the City preceded by a long train of people dressed as catholic clergymen, in imitation of the papal coronation ceremony.[50] Whilst the leading figures were represented in effigy, all the rest of the entourage were played by male youths. In 1679 and 1680 the processions ended up at Temple Bar, the place of contact between the City and Westminster and a traditional site for demonstrations, where the effigies were burnt at a huge bonfire.[51] In 1681 the effigies were burnt at Smithfield, the place where many protestant martyrs had been burnt in Mary's reign. The pageantry served a triple function: a satire on the catholic faith; a narration of the Popish Plot, with an exposition of the sort of things one could expect if popery were ever to reign in England again; and a condemnation of all those who were hostile to the whigs as popishly affected. These themes will be examined below in the context of the whig message as a whole, although the details of the pageants can be learnt from the studies by Furley and Williams.[52]

Much of the catholic paraphernalia used in the processions was obtained

[46] Burke, 'Seventeenth-Century London', p. 40.
[47] *The Coronation of Queen Elizabeth, with the Restauration of the Protestant Religion; Or, The Downfall of the Pope* (1680).
[48] *Impartial Protestant Mercury*, no. 73.
[49] W. Bedloe, *The Excommunicated Prince; Or, The False Relique* (1679).
[50] P. Shaw, *American Patriots and the Rituals of Revolution* (Cambridge, Massachusetts, 1981), p. 206.
[51] L. W. Cowie, 'Temple Bar, London', *History Today*, 22 (1972), 402–9; De Krey, *Fractured Society*, pp. 60–1.
[52] Furley, 'Pope-Burning Processions'; Williams, 'Pope-Burning Processions'.

from the whig justice of the peace, Sir William Waller, who was active in prosecuting the Plot and searching out catholic relics and books.[53] A member of the Green Ribbon Club, he provided priests' vestments for the society's pope-burning procession of 1679.[54] On other occasions, Waller organized great bonfires to destroy the seized goods in ritualistic manner. On 3 November 1679 he discovered a huge quantity of popish goods in Lincoln's Inn Fields.[55] Two days later, on Gunpowder Treason Day, 'there was a Great Bonfire made in the Palace Yard at Westminster, and many of the Books, Garments, Crucifixes and others Popish Trinkets were there publickly burnt, with the Acclamations of the People'.[56] Such rituals were not necessarily reserved for festival days from the anti-catholic calendar. On 13 February that year, several popish relics were burnt in New Palace Yard by the common hangman.[57]

The processions were expensive to put on, the pope's effigy alone costing £100 in 1679, and the cost grew as the next two years witnessed ever more elaborate displays.[58] Such money was only well spent if as many people as possible saw the procession. Sometimes they were advertised in advance in the press, which would give detailed accounts of what one could expect to see.[59] The route of the processions was planned to take in most of the City, but if one still failed to see the procession, it was possible to read accounts of them in newspapers or in illustrated broadsides.[60]

The pope-burning processions reached vast numbers of people. According to one report, 200,000 witnessed the burning of the pope at Temple Bar on 17 November 1679.[61] To obtain a good view of the climax could be expensive, a place at a window or a balcony in Cheapside or Fleet Street

[53] *CSPD, 1679–80*, p. 83; Luttrell, I, 7; LC, MS 18,124, VI, fol. 171.

[54] Pepysian Library, Pepys Misc. VII, 484.

[55] *Domestick Intelligence*, no. 35.

[56] Ibid., no. 36.

[57] *CSPD, 1679–80*, p. 83.

[58] Luttrell, I, 29; Miller, *Popery and Politics*, pp. 185, 187.

[59] See, for example, *Domestick Intelligence ... Impartially Related*, no. 51.

[60] For the procession of 1679, see: *Domestick Intelligence*, nos. 39, 40; *London's Defiance to Rome* (1679); *The Solemn Mock Procession of the Pope, Cardinalls, Jesuits, Fryers, etc. ... November the 17, 1679* (1679). For 1680, see: *London's Drollery; Or, The Love and Kindness Between the Pope and the Devil* (1680), in *The Roxburghe Ballads*, ed. W. Chappell and S. W. Ebsworth (14 vols., 1869–95), IV, 221–4; *The Solemn Mock Procession of the Pope, Cardinals, Jesuits, Fryers, Nuns, etc. ... November the 17th 1680*, for I. Oliver (1680), engraving; ibid., for N. Ponder (1680), broadside; *The Solemn Mock Procession; Or, The Trial and Execution of the Pope and His Minister, on the 17 of Nov. at Temple Bar* (1680). For 1681, see: *True Protestant Mercury*, no. 91; *The Procession; Or, The Burning of the Pope in Effigy* (1681). See print 2.

[61] *Domestick Intelligence*, no. 40; *London's Defiance*. Others put the figure at 100,000 or 150,000: HMC, *7th Report*, p. 477; Verney, *Memoirs*, II, 330; Cowie, 'Temple Bar', p. 407.

2 The pope-burning procession of 1680

costing as much as a guinea in 1679, a room at Temple Bar costing £10.[62] Of course, many people might be intrigued to watch the pope-burning processions who would never be sympathetic to the whig cause. It has been pointed out that the processions are not very good evidence of popular support for whiggery.[63] But because of their entertainment value, and consequent ability to attract a large audience, they were an invaluable propaganda device. Such occasions had innumerable possibilities for assisting the politicization of the masses, beyond the simple publication of the whig message. People would discuss their shared experiences, exchange ideas about what they saw and talk about political affairs. Moreover, a 'crowd' had been created, and people would be aware of the possibilities of coordinated action in the future. It is also important to remember that the processions were

[62] Bodl. Lib., MS Carte 232, fol. 61: *HMC, 7th Report*, p. 477.
[63] Miller, *Popery and Politics*, pp. 183, 187; Allen, 'Trained Bands'; p. 300.

participatory. It was not just a question of the propagandist trying to impart his message to an audience – people actually dressed up as devils and catholic priests and acted out the pageants themselves. Even mere spectators could be participants in the songs that were sung.[64] In this sense the dichotomy between cause and effect was overcome, for people were being propagandized by expressing the propaganda themselves.[65]

Burke has suggested that the pope-burning processions were 'a kind of inverse lord mayor's show'; whereas the function of the latter was legitimation of civic authority, the former were designed to criticize those in power.[66] But because the two lord mayors from 1679–81 were whigs, the shows could be used for a legitimation of whig authority, and thus serve a propaganda purpose.[67] The shows took place on 29 October, when the new lord mayor went to Westminster to be sworn in, and then returned to the City where he was dined at the Guildhall. He was accompanied by the livery companies and other groups in a long procession, and his journey was broken up with several pageants, the function of which was to exhort the incoming mayor to perform his duties virtuously. Crowds gathered to witness these occasions, and those who failed to see them could read a printed version of the text, through which they could also learn about the songs and poems performed at the lord mayor's feast.[68]

Much of this chapter is concerned with what issued forth from the various whig presses. Many prints and woodcuts were produced, sometimes appearing separately, sometimes as illustrations to broadsides, books, or almanacs.[69] Some of the cartoons were drawn by the pope-maker, Stephen College.[70] Whig almanacs were produced by John Partridge.[71] There were also several whig newspapers. The first periodical was the *Weekly Pacquet of Advice from Rome* written by Henry Care and published by Langley Curtis, whose issues run from 3 December 1678 to 13 July 1683. Initially

[64] For the words of the song, see: *Domestick Intelligence*, no. 40; *London's Defiance*, p. 4.

[65] Cf. R. W. Scribner, 'Reformation, Carnival and the World Turned Upside-Down', *Social History*, 3 (1978), 322–4.

[66] Burke, 'Seventeenth-Century London', p. 47.

[67] For a brief description of the lord mayor's shows for Sir Robert Clayton in 1679 and Sir Patience Ward in 1680, see Fairholt, *Lord Mayors' Pageants*, I, 92–5.

[68] Burke, 'Seventeenth-Century London', pp. 44–5; Williams, 'Lord Mayors' Show'.

[69] The British Museum has the largest collection of such prints. A printed catalogue, describing each print in detail, exists. See F. G. Stephens, ed., *A Catalogue of Prints and Drawings in the British Museum* (1870), I.

[70] George, *English Political Caricature*, pp. 55–8; W. A. Speck, 'Political Propaganda in Augustan England', *TRHS*, 5th series, 22 (1972), 21; B. J. Rahn, 'A Ra-ree Show – A Rare Cartoon: Revolutionary Propaganda in the Treason Trial of Stephen College', in Korshin, ed., *Studies*, pp. 77–98.

[71] B. S. Capp, *Astrology and the Popular Press: English Almanacs, 1500–1800* (1979), p. 92.

it was concerned with developing a popular history of the beginnings of the Reformation on the continent, it did not print news or comment on current affairs for some time to come, and at first the periodical was licensed.[72] The first newspaper proper was the *Domestick Intelligence*, begun on 7 July 1679 and published by Benjamin Harris, which was continued as *The Protestant (Domestick) Intelligence* from 16 January 1680. Green Ribbon Club member Benjamin Claypoole was arrested in December 1679 for being the alleged author of this *Intelligence*.[73] Between April 1681 and May 1682 Richard Janeway published his *Impartial Protestant Mercury*, the first issue of which Care was indicted for writing,[74] whilst Langley Curtis published his *True Protestant Mercury* between December 1680 and October 1682. Quite a few other newspapers, with less continuous runs, were produced, including Francis Smith's *Protestant Intelligence*, and Benjamin Harris's *Weekly Discovery Strip'd Naked*.[75] Finally it should be added that there was a fair amount of political literature which circulated in manuscript form, usually because the views expressed were of such a nature as to be too risky for a publisher to print them.

It may be questioned if many people went out of their way to look at whig newspapers or broadsides, unless they already shared the points of view expressed in them. Attempts were made at overcoming this, and examples can be found of printed material being given away, or thrown into the coaches of passers-by.[76] Yet there was still no guarantee that it would be read by the recipient. Political statements were sometimes affixed to public buildings where many passers-by would be likely to see them. For example, on 21 October 1679, a day when the duke of York dined with the Artillery Company at Merchant-Tailors' Hall, an inscription was placed over the gate to the Hall condemning all those who accompanied the duke thither as 'Papists in Masquerade'.[77] Other obvious places to affix such notices were the houses of parliament, or the doors of the lodgings of public figures, and the fact that messages were sometimes reported as being written on walls in lead pencil suggests the existence of political graffiti.[78] It seems that even the most hostile or apathetic person would have had difficulty

[72] G. Kitchin, *Sir Roger L'Estrange: A Contribution to the History of the Press in the Seventeenth Century* (1913), pp. 232–3; J. G. Muddiman, *The King's Journalist, 1659–1689* (1923), p. 212.

[73] *London Gazette*, no. 1467; Pepysian Library, Pepys Misc. VII, 473, 489.

[74] PRO, KB 10/2, part 3.

[75] Full publishing details of these and also the tory newspapers are offered in the bibliography. See also R. S. Crane and F. B. Kaye, *A Census of British Newspapers and Periodicals, 1620–1820* (1927).

[76] *HMC, 7th Report*, p. 479.

[77] Bodl. Lib., MS Don b. 8, p. 597.

[78] Ibid., p. 644; BL, Add. MS 34,362, fol. 71; *A Lampoon on Scroggs Put on His Door* (1679), in *POAS*, II, 288; Bodl. Lib., MS Don b. 8, p. 183.

in avoiding exposure to whig arguments. Even the material that only reached people who were already sympathetic nevertheless had an important propaganda effect, serving to arouse latent prejudices, to make explicit existing assumptions, and to furnish people with arguments to use as ammunition against friends who did not share their political views.[79] Preaching to the converted, therefore, does serve a function, if it encourages them to go out and preach to the unconverted. Playing-cards, however, probably worked on a slightly different level. Perhaps only whig sympathizers bought whig playing-cards. But cards for games were often provided by the owner of the coffee-house or the tavern where the game was taking place. The people who were using the cards would not be the purchasers of the pack, and they might become exposed to ideas about which they had given little consideration in the past.

THE WHIG MESSAGE

The major aim of whig propaganda was to keep alive the anxieties aroused by the Popish Plot. There was certain circumstantial evidence which gave the Plot the semblance of truth. Middlesex justice of the peace, Sir Edmundbury Godfrey, who received depositions from Oates and others, was found dead in October 1678, presumed murdered by catholics. Edward Coleman, whom Oates named as a principal conspirator, was arrested and found to possess some highly incriminating papers concerning the enhancement of catholic interests.[80] The prosecution of the alleged leading conspirators, including the five English catholic lords, Arundel, Bellasis, Petre, Powis, and Stafford, the ensuing drive against catholics launched by the Court, and the raising of the trained bands to protect the City against conspirators, all helped to sustain fear of the Plot.[81] By 1679 the Popish Plot fever was beginning to lose some of its momentum, but the clumsy attempt by Madame Cellier to discredit the presbyterians in the Meal Tub Plot gave the whigs something extra to exploit. The execution of Stafford in January 1680 kept the excitement going still longer. The trial of Oliver Plunkett and the Irish conspirators was not to come until May 1681.

Godfrey's 'martyrdom' was inevitably exploited. Medals were produced commemorating the Middlesex JP, whilst playing cards often depicted how Godfrey was supposedly so cruelly murdered by catholics.[82] Daggers were

---

[79] It could have the important psychological effect of making people realize they were not alone in holding the beliefs that they did. Cf. D. Hoerder, *Crowd Action in Revolutionary Massachusetts, 1765–1780* (New York, 1977), p. 377; Scribner, *Simple Folk*, p. 248.

[80] Jones, *Country and Court*, pp. 201–2.

[81] Miller, *Popery and Politics*, pp. 158–69; Allen, 'Trained Bands', pp. 294–9.

[82] *BM Prints*, nos. 1057–63; Guildhall Library, Playing Cards 236.

even sold bearing Godfrey's name.[83] The pope-burning processions always started with a man ringing a bell and crying 'Remember Justice Godfrey.' The following description of how he was represented is taken from the 1679 procession. After the bellman

followed the dead Body of Sir Edmundberry Godfrey in the habit he usually wore, and Crevat wherewith he was murdered about his Neck, with spots of Blood on his Wrists and Breast, and White Gloves on his Hands, his Face Pale and Wan, riding upon a White Horse.

His murderers were positioned behind him, 'to keep him from falling', although they did this with their daggers.[84]

Two broad themes were emphasized in whig anti-catholic propaganda, namely the threat to the reformed religion and the political threat to the state. A typical development of the first can be seen in a print where the pope, satan, a monk, and a cardinal are shown vainly trying to blow out a lighted candle symbolizing the Reformation.[85] Much stress was put on the type of religion that would return to England should they succeed in extinguishing the light. The pope and his priests cared not for the people they were supposed to be serving, the whigs argued, but only for themselves. One print showed the pope wearing his usual tiara, against the three crowns of which were written 'Avarice', 'Lust', and 'Pride'.[86] The tiara, which was in fact the pope's crown, was also a symbol of that worldly corruption which the whigs despised in catholicism. The catholic church, it was argued, grew wealthy at the expense of the poor. In the pope-burning procession of 1680, the pope's officers and cardinals were represented as distributing pardons for money, crying 'For Money you may Heaven Buy:/But those that have no money got,/Hell is their Portion and their Lot.'[87]

The pope's moral failings also extended into his sex life. A play called the *Coronation of Queen Elizabeth* contained a scene in which the pope attempts to seduce a nun, and later the nun is seen to be pregnant.[88] Nuns were frequently depicted as whores or courtesans, as they were for example in the pope-burning processions.[89] One print showed two nuns seated on a basket which is filled with eggs, each holding an egg at the moment of

---

[83] Miller, *Popery and Politics*, p. 161.
[84] *Domestick Intelligence*, no. 39.
[85] *A True Account of the Rise and Growth of the Reformation; Or, The Progress of the Protestant Religion* (1680); *BM Prints*, no. 1096.
[86] *Rome's Hunting Match For Three Kingdoms: England, Scotland, and Ireland* [1680]. The same woodcut is used in *Rome's Hunting Match For Three Kingdoms; Or, The Papists Last Run for the Portestants Life and Estates too* [1680]. See *BM Prints*, nos. 1094, 1095.
[87] *Londons Drollery*, in *Roxburghe Ballads*, IV, 223; *BM Prints*, no. 1086.
[88] *Coronation of Queen Elizabeth*, pp. 12–13.
[89] See, for example, *Solemn Mock Procession of... 1680*, engraving and broadside; *BM Prints*, nos. 1084, 1085.

hatching, one of which 'brings foorth a Frier, and one a Nunne'.[90] The first issue of the first exclusionist newspaper contained a long account of how a catholic priest made a chamber-maid pregnant.[91]

It was the means whereby the counter-Reformation would be achieved that caused most alarm. One pack of playing cards contained 'an History of all the Popish Plots that have been in England' from Elizabeth's time to 1678, and a similar history was offered in an illustrated almanac of 1681.[92] Popery was seen as a political threat, both to the people and government of England. The threat to individuals was shown by recalling the experiences of Mary's reign and making references to contemporary experience overseas. Harris's tract, the *Protestant Tutor*, was illustrated with prints showing children being eaten, people hung by their feet, or being burnt or boiled alive.[93] In the play, the *Coronation of Queen Elizabeth*, Tim the Tinker recalled how, during Mary's reign, popish cardinals had burnt his neighbour.[94] The persecutions in France provided a reminder of the things that protestants could expect to experience at the hands of a catholic monarch, something which whig newspapers continually stressed. In December 1679, Benjamin Harris reported a rumour that a boy who had taken part in the pope-burning procession of 17 November had been enticed over to France and barbarously murdered by papists.[95] Emigrating to the New World would not necessarily help one escape such terrifying prospects. Richard Janeway recalled how catholics in Maryland were using Indians to murder protestants, whilst according to Harris and Smith, Boston, New England, had been the recent victim of catholic incendiarism.[96] *A Scheme of Popish Cruelties* contained a number of prints illustrative of its title: jesuits, monks and friars ravishing and abusing women; popish villains beating the brains out of tender infants and putting their mothers to the sword; and bloody papists cutting the throats of protestants or burning 'Martyrs for the True Religion'. It also contained references to the burning of London by catholics, and the invasion by catholic forces from overseas.[97]

---

[90] *A Nest of Nunnes Egges, Strangely Hatched, With a Description of a Worthy Feast for Joy of the Blood* [1680?]; *BM Prints*, no. 1101.

[91] *Domestick Intelligence*, no. 1.

[92] BL, Schreiber Cards, English 56; Schreiber, *Playing Cards*, plates 5–8; W. C. Ford, 'Benjamin Harris, Printer and Bookseller', *Proceedings of the Massachusetts Historical Society*, 57 (1923–4), 54–5; 'The Christian Four Year Almanac', advertised in *Impartial Protestant Mercury*, no. 62.

[93] *The Protestant Tutor* (1679); Ford, 'Harris', pp. 46–50.

[94] *Coronation of Queen Elizabeth*, p. 5.

[95] *Domestick Intelligence*, no. 44.

[96] *Impartial Protestant Mercury*, no. 34; *Domestick Intelligence*, no. 31; *Smith's Protestant Intelligence*, no. 12.

[97] *A Scheme of Popish Cruelties* (1681); Ford, 'Harris', pp. 57–8; Care, *Weekly Pacquet*, III, 160; Miller, *Popery and Politics*, p. 75.

Part of the plan of the Popish Plot, according to Oates, was to burn to the ground the staunchly protestant City of London. Such a claim was bound to touch a sensitive nerve, as the catholics had allegedly burnt the City as recently as 1666. Many prints recalled this 'fact' for those who needed reminding.[98] In 1681, whig lord mayor Sir Patience Ward had the following inscription put on the monument erected to mark the place where the fire began: 'This Pillar was sett up in Perpetuall Remembrance of that most Dreadfull Burning of this Protestant City, Begun and Carried on by the Treachery and Malice of the Papists.'[99] One print showed the pope with flames coming out of his mouth, with the scene of London burning in the background.[100] Playing cards sometimes showed jesuits offering money to people to burn houses.[101]

In exploiting the fears of a revived attempt to burn the City, the whigs were helped by an unusual number of fires in London during the exclusion crisis. In January 1679, the Temple caught fire, started supposedly at the instigation of papists.[102] In April of that year several maid servants were sent to prison on suspicion of firing their masters' houses, one of whom confessed she did it at the instigation of a popish priest.[103] In March 1680 a maid was executed for having fired a house in Southwark, allegedly as part of a popish conspiracy.[104] Whig agitators did their utmost to encourage the popular fear of catholic incendiaries. In March 1680, Robert West, a member of the Green Ribbon Club, was busy spreading rumours that Holborn was about to be burnt and that the streets would soon run with blood.[105] Fireworks, supposedly designed to start such conflagrations but fortunately discovered in time, were sometimes put on public display in coffee-houses.[106] The occasional convictions of arsonists gave the conspiracy theory that ring of truth which made the whig claims so convincing. For many, catholicism really did mean the threat of personal torture or burnt houses, and this partly explains why the cry in defence of 'Liberties and Properties' became so resonant at this time.

---

[98] See, for example, *The Catholick Gamesters; Or, A Dubble Matcht of Bowleing* (1680); *BM Prints*, no. 1077.

[99] CLRO, Journal 49, fol. 224; Rep. 86, fols. 151, 162. Today this inscription can be seen in the London Museum, Barbican.

[100] *Babel and Bethel; Or, The Pope in his Colours* (1679); *BM Prints*, no. 1076.

[101] Guildhall Library, Playing Cards 238, 7 diamonds.

[102] BL, Add. MS 17,018, fols. 143–5; Luttrell, I, 7–8. One Adlington was arrested for telling a friend about the fire 12 hours before it began. CLRO, Sessions File, February 1679, gaol calendar, committal of Adlington.

[103] Luttrell, I, 9; *HMC Ormond*, NS V, 69.

[104] *Protestant (Domestick) Intelligence*, nos. 61, 63, 75, 79.

[105] *CSPD*, 1679–80, p. 423. For West's membership of the Green Ribbon Club, see Pepysian Library, Pepys Misc. VII, 491.

[106] *Domestick Intelligence*, no. 27; *Protestant (Domestick) Intelligence*, nos. 102, 103.

The catholic threat was usually seen as being external to England. One pack of playing-cards produced at this time concentrated on recalling the attempted invasion by the Spanish Armada in 1588.[107] An illustrated ballad had references to an Irish army lying incognito, ready to join forces with one from Spain.[108] But the success of an invasion force would depend on having allies in England. An illustrated book contained one print showing jesuits and other conspirators going to England by boat. Another of its prints showed the English-based conspirators, the lords Arundel, Powis, Bellasis, Petre and Stafford, giving a jesuit purses of money as a contribution to the expenses of the Plot.[109] Langley Curtis even argued that one of the red-coats guarding the catholic priests in the Tower was a papist, although he had fled to avoid justice.[110] One writer believed that the army was infiltrated with people who were popishly affected, and was to be employed with the help of a French force in the work of reconverting England.[111] It was in this context that Danby was impeached. He was accused of having raised an army, ostensibly to make war against France, but in reality to introduce arbitrary government at home.[112] Whig propaganda repeated the charge that Danby was popishly affected. One print associated Danby with the firing of London in 1666 and with the murder of Godfrey.[113] The logical development of this tactic was to condemn all opponents of the whigs as 'Protestants in Masquerade' secretly working for the papists.[114] The implications of this are discussed below.

The Popish Plot, above all else, was a threat to the life of the king, and the whigs played on this to the utmost. They could therefore portray themselves as being loyal defenders of the Crown. *A Satire on Popery and Jesuitism* (1679) depicted the pope with his foot on the head of the king (who is prostrate on the ground) kicking off the royal crown.[115] The procession of 17 November 1680 also depicted the pope with his feet on a prostrate king.[116] One pack of playing cards showed a jesuit threatening 'if CR will

---

[107] BL, Willshire Cards, E185; Schreiber, *Playing Cards*, Plates 1–4.

[108] *A True Narrative of the Horrid Hellish Popish Plot*, first and second parts (1682); *BM Prints*, nos. 1092, 1093.

[109] Philopatris, *The Plot in a Dream; Or, The Discoverer in Masquerade* (1681).

[110] *True Protestant Mercury*, no. 6.

[111] P. Misopappas, *A Tory Plot; Or, the Discovery of a Design Carried on by Our Late Addressers and Abhorrers to Alter the Constitution of the Government, and to Betray the Protestant Religion* (1682), pp. 2–3.

[112] Miller, *Popery and Politics*, p. 172; C. Roberts, *The Growth of Responsible Government in Stuart England* (Cambridge, 1966), pp. 211–25.

[113] *Catholick Gamesters*; *BM Prints*, no. 1077.

[114] P. Misopappas, *The Tory Plot: The Second Part; Or, A Farther Discovery of a Design to Alter the Constitution of the Government, and to Betray the Protestant Religion* (1682), p. 8.

[115] *BM Prints*, no. 1075.

[116] *Solemn Mock Procession of . . . 1680*, engraving and broadside; *BM Prints*, nos. 1084, 1085.

not be RC he shall no longer be CR'.[117] The use of Queen Elizabeth as a symbol had royalist connotations. The pope-burning processions which marched to Temple Bar converged on four statues representing Elizabeth, James, Charles I and Charles II. A shield bearing the inscription 'Magna Charta et Religio Protestantium' was affixed to Queen Elizabeth's statue for the day of the procession.[118] Yet it was not so much Charles II in particular who was being defended, but protestant monarchy in general. A well-trodden theme in the anti-catholic tradition was that popery was incompatible with monarchical government. One illustrated ballad depicted the pope as 'This hawhty Prelat, who disdayneth Kings,/Nay Emperors with him, are petty things'.[119] The important thing to understand is that a standard was being set up to which Charles II would have to live himself. If not, he could be criticized within the context of a monarchical tradition.

Parliament was championed as the body that was to protect England against the popish onslaught. One print showed the pope crying to his confederate in evil, 'Wee Beseach thee, noe Parliament good Devill.'[120] This print was produced in November 1679, in the long gap between the first and second exclusion parliaments. Similar anxieties were voiced after the dissolution of the Oxford parliament. Now the popish party's chant was 'the Parliament's dissolved the Coast is Clear,/No other Obstacles we need to fear'.[121] The whig petitioning campaigns for a sitting of parliament, discussed in chapter seven, functioned as pro-parliament propaganda. 'Abhorrers of petitions and parliaments' were burnt in effigy in the pope-burning procession of 1680.[122] Criticism of the chief tory propagandist, Sir Roger L'Estrange, centred largely on his alleged anti-parliamentarian beliefs. In one pack of cards, the ten of clubs shows L'Estrange sitting at a desk writing a pamphlet. He looks over his right shoulder at an inset, which shows a council of men, and he murmurs 'who thought of a parliament'.[123] People were encouraged to see members of parliament as exercising a position of trust. Curtis's newspaper described them as 'our Representatives, in whose hands the Lives, Liberties and Properties of all English Subjects are intrusted'.[124] Before the elections to the Oxford parliament, the whigs com-

---

[117] Guildhall Library, Playing Cards 238, 3 hearts. The reference is taken from Oates's initial depositions. See *State Trials*, VI, fol. 1456, where it is reported that one Mr Jennison had said on 12 August 1678 'if the King did not become RC he should not be CR long'.
[118] *Domestick Intelligence*, no. 40; *Solemn Mock Procession of...1680*, broadside.
[119] *The Devills Tryumph over Romes Idoll* (1680); BM *Prints*, no. 1079.
[120] *A Tale of the Tubs; Or, Rome's Master Peice Defeated* (1679), in POAS, II, 300; BM *Prints*, no. 1071.
[121] *The Time-Servers; Or, A Touch of the Times* (1681); BM *Prints*, no. 1112.
[122] *Solemn Mock Procession of...1680*, engraving and broadside; BM *Prints*, nos. 1084, 1085.
[123] Guildhall Library, Playing Cards 238.
[124] *True Protestant Mercury*, no. 11.

posed a paper to all electors, which they deposited in coffee-houses and elsewhere. It read: 'Have your late Members of Parliament Betrayed your Trust, given away your Rights and Priviledges, stifled the Plot, or encouraged Popery? Then change them.'[125] Such advice was offered really only to people outside London, for in the City the MPs were whigs. In successive exclusion parliaments they therefore encouraged voters to choose the same men again, because they had fulfilled their trust.[126]

If we piece these arguments together, a distinctive whig ideology emerges, familiar to us from their more philosophical tracts, but clearly available in the popular medium. The Popish Plot was a threat to people's liberties and properties as guaranteed by Magna Carta, as well as a threat to protestant monarchy. Members of parliament were entrusted with the protection of these liberties and properties, and were accountable to the electorate in this respect. The king and council were not by themselves capable of protecting English liberties and properties; only parliament could do this, and successfully quash the plot, although by doing this they would also protect the king. It was not easy to spell this out in so many words in the type of propaganda I have been examining. Care came close in his *Weekly Pacquet* when he described a tory as an 'Abhorrer', an enemy to 'Magna Charta', 'a State Vultur, that gnaws out the Heart of Liberty and Property', and someone 'ready to sacrifice even his King'.[127]

This ideology, therefore, was not republican, nor was it necessarily radical. As I demonstrate in the next chapter, the tories showed themselves sensitive to the need to defend the king, Magna Carta, liberty and property, and parliament, although they were less keen on the idea of 'trust' or 'electoral accountability'. However, by taking the whig propaganda at face value, we fail to appreciate the radical implications it contained. People were being told about the evils of catholicism, but it soon became apparent that in order to be secure against the catholic threat fairly fundamental political changes might be necessary.

The obvious one was the need to alter the succession. Initially, the position of the catholic heir was ignored. Oates positively testified that the duke of York had not been involved in the Popish Plot.[128] The early prints did not mention him, and he did not feature in any of the pope-burning processions. But exclusion was first considered in November 1678, and a successful prosecution of the Plot by parliament more or less immediately implied the need to change the succession. By the spring of 1679, witnesses began

[125] *Observations on the Single Query Proposed Concerning the Choice of Parliament-Men for the City, Yesterday Diligantly Delivered to the Coffee-Houses and Elsewhere* (1681).
[126] *Smith's Protestant Intelligence*, no. 2.
[127] Care, *Weekly Pacquet*, III, 215–16.
[128] *State Trials*, VI, fols. 1435, 1438, 1457, 1470–1; *LJ*, XIII, 309. Cf. Haley, *Shaftesbury*, p. 460.

to accuse James of involvement in the Plot, and there was an attempt to indict the duke of York for recusancy in June 1680.[129] Attacks on him became more open. One print showed the pope talking about his 'presumptuous successor'.[130] The *Prospect of a Popish Successor*, published at the time of the Oxford parliament, provided the most blatant visual attack on York. Here he is represented as 'Mack', a double-headed figure, half-devil, half-papist, wearing a cross for a sword. He blows flames from a cruciform trumpet, in order to set fire to London, and he is also lighting a fire in which four protestant martyrs are tied to stakes. He is shown as an associate of the jesuits, the devil, and the tories.[131] Anonymous poems were often quite forthright in their attacks on the catholic heir. One styled him 'a plotting false Duke that delight[ed] in Blood'.[132] Some were just abusive: 'Tho' the Duke take Physic to make himself clean,/Yet he eats his owne Snivell which claps him again.'[133]

The whigs were not always clear about their preferred successor. Much interest has been focused upon the duke of Monmouth, the 'natural' son of the king, with the supposed proof of his legitimacy to be found in a 'Black Box' which contained his mother's marriage certificate.[134] But the whigs seldom directly advocated Monmouth's succession. The first exclusion bill said the succession should pass to the next in line after York, in other words, Mary, whilst the second bill left the question open.[135] Shaftesbury even contemplated the succession of the duke of Buckingham, arguing that he had a claim through the house of Plantagenet.[136]

However, looking for explicit references to Monmouth as an alternative successor misunderstands the way propaganda works. The whigs created an environment in which there was shown to be a need for an alternative heir, even if they did not name whom the heir should be. Monmouth was for many an obvious choice. A popular figure, he was always very keen to show himself as the 'protestant prince', going publicly to church in

---

[129] Miller, *Popery and Politics*, p. 174; *The Reasons for the Indictment of the Duke of York Presented to the Grand Jury of Middlesex* (1680); Haley, *Shaftesbury*, pp. 580–1.

[130] *The Contents (Hats for Caps) Contented* (1680); BM Prints, no. 1087. See print 3.

[131] *A Prospect of a Popish Successor, Display'd by Hell-Bred Cruelty* (1681); BM Prints, no. 1110. See print 4. Traditionally, two-headed figures were used to symbolize the spiritual and human aspects of the representative. See Shaw, *American Patriots*, pp. 219–20.

[132] BL, Add. MS 34,362, fol. 122, 'The Responses; Or, Letany for Letany, 1680'. Another MS copy gives it the title 'The Respondent', and dates it August 1680. BL, Sloane MS 655, fol. 1.

[133] BL, Add. MS 34,362, fol. 119, 'On the Duke of Y'.

[134] Haley, *Shaftesbury*, pp. 574–5; R. Clifton, *The Last Popular Rebellion: The Western Rising of 1685* (1984), pp. 81, 110, 121–4.

[135] Jones, *First Whigs*, pp. 69, 135–6.

[136] CLRO, Sessions File, November/December 1681, ind. of Shaftesbury (O + T); *Impartial Protestant Mercury*, no. 62; *Loyal Protestant Intelligence*, no. 82.

3 *The Contents* (1680)

London. The press was quick to report such activities.[137] The newspapers, in fact, followed all of Monmouth's activities with interest. Harris, for example, gave detailed accounts of the duke's whereabouts in the Low Countries during his exile in the autumn of 1679.[138] Monmouth went on a number of progresses through England to gain support, and whig leaders showed their favour towards him by welcoming him in style. Again, all this was reported in the press.[139] With rumours of Monmouth's legitimacy being rife anyway, people were being encouraged to see Monmouth as the obvious person who should succeed instead of York.

Harris, in particular, followed Monmouth's activities with interest.[140] He published the *Appeal from the Country to the City*, the only exclusionist tract specifically to advocate Monmouth's succession.[141] In other, less explicit ways, he helped to promote the duke's interests. In February 1681, when he republished *The Protestant Tutor*, a tract already mentioned, he dedicated it to Monmouth's son.[142] In his *Intelligence* he published a letter from inhabitants in Somerset concerning a girl who had been cured of the King's Evil by touching Monmouth.[143] If Monmouth could do this, then he must be the legitimate son of Charles II. This was how people who believed the report would react. In short, Harris was in effect saying that Monmouth should be king, but in a way which would safeguard him against prosecution.

Although the logic of the whig exploitation of the Popish Plot led them to claim they were protecting Charles II, their propaganda could carry an implicit criticism of the king. The problem with arguing by what I have termed negative inference is that the message being conveyed will in part be determined by how individuals or groups align themselves. The message is therefore outside the propagandist's control. Because the king was determined to protect the succession of his brother, he became guilty by association, even though many of the whigs might have sincerely wanted to absolve Charles II.

Blatant attacks on Charles II are to be found in anonymous pieces that often circulated in manuscript form. Whig parodies of the tory addresses that were presented in 1681 made clear what support for the policies of Charles II meant.[144] One mock address, from the inhabitants of the 'Corporation of Gotham', asserted 'that the truest liberty consists in an entire submission to the dictates of the Court. And that the onely way to secure

---

[137] *Protestant (Domestick) Intelligence*, no. 68.
[138] See, for example, *Domestick Intelligence*, no. 28.
[139] See, for example, *Protestant (Domestick) Intelligence*, no. 65.
[140] *Domestick Intelligence*, *passim*.
[141] [R. Ferguson], *Appeal from the Country to the City* (1679); Ford, 'Harris', p. 46.
[142] *Protestant (Domestick) Intelligence*, no. 94.
[143] Ibid., no. 86.
[144] For these addresses, see ch. 7.

the Protestant religion is to establish a Popish Successor, And that the best means to preserve the rights and libertyes of the people is the dissolving three parliaments togeather before they had brought any thing to perfection'. It ended by stating, with heavy sarcasm, that they were convinced that the king did not intend to extend his power beyond the rules of law and justice.[145] A similar mock address from those in debtors prisons in the London area thanked Charles for dissolving parliament, 'thereby having given us a blessed prospect of Seeing a General Gaole Delivery, of having opportunity of Plundering and cutting the throats of our Creditors, And of becomeing otherwise usefull Instruments to the Government'.[146]

Occasionally it is possible to find anti-monarchical propaganda coming from those closely associated with the whig leaders. Stephen College's 'Raree Show', an illustrated poem, was explicit in its attack on the king. The cartoon depicts a two-headed Charles II, half-protestant and half-papist, as a pedlar with a portable peep-show that is, the two houses of parliament, which he carries from city to city (London to Oxford) and displays for money (convenes only so that they might levy funds for him). The print shows men from the lower house resisting the king and the house of lords.[147] John Ayloffe, member of the Green Ribbon Club, was probably the author of a poem in 1681 which advocated a republican-style government with Monmouth as its head.[148]

SLANTING TOWARDS A NONCONFORMIST AUDIENCE

The tory publicist, Nathaniel Thompson, when justifying the launch of his *Loyal Protestant Intelligence* in March 1681, wrote that he would have been prepared to commend the whigs' 'endeavours against Popery (had they gone no further)' but, he added, 'in all their Libels, they seldom or never begin with the papists, but they are sure to end with the Church of England'.[149] This tory charge is certainly exaggerated. In 1679 Langley Curtis published an illustrated broadside which explicitly defended the Church of England. One print depicting the Popish Plot also showed the martyrdom of English bishops in the tradition of Foxe.[150] Nevertheless, it is clear that

---

[145] Bodl. Lib., MS Douce 357, fol. 91, 'The Humble Address of the Inhabitants of the Ancient Corporation of Gotham'. Gotham means a town of fools. See *OED*.

[146] Bodl. Lib., MS Douce 357, fol. 78.

[147] [S. College], *A Raree Show* (1681), repr. in *POAS*, II, 425–31; Rahn, 'A Ra-ree Show', pp. 77–98.

[148] J. Ayloffe, *Oceana and Brittania* [1681], in *POAS*, II, 393–405. The poem was published in 1689.

[149] *Loyal Protestant Intelligence*, no. 1. Cf. Sir R. L'Estrange, *The History of the Plot* (1679), preface; Sir R. L'Estrange, *A Further Discovery of the Plot: Dedicated to Dr. Titus Oates* (1680), p. 8. See ch. 6 for a discussion of this aspect of tory propaganda.

[150] *Babel and Bethel*; *BM Prints*, no. 1076.

the whig propaganda failed to meet the revelations of the Popish Plot head on. It more or less ignored the references in Oates's testimony to presbyterians or fifth monarchists being papists in disguise. In one pack of cards, the five of diamonds shows jesuits receiving commissions to stir the people to rebellion, a reference to the covenanters' rising in Scotland in 1679.[151] In another pack the knave of hearts shows the catholic priest Whitebread holding forth at a quakers' meeting.[152] Mostly the whigs showed themselves sympathetic towards dissent. Harris used the rising of 1679 to defend the dissenters, recounting how after the rebels in Scotland had been routed, the king nevertheless sent 'an indulgence thither, allowing them their Meeting Houses in the Cities and Towns'.[153] The clumsy attempt by Madame Cellier in the autumn of 1679 to lay blame for the Plot on the presbyterians, the famous Meal Tub Plot, in fact helped the whigs to exonerate the dissenters. When referring to this, their propaganda usually showed the victims of the sham plot as 'protestants', removing any suspicion that the interests of the dissenters might be different from those of the conformists, and associating them with those who were to suffer at the hands of the papists.[154] One illustrated broadside stated that the Meal Tub plotters' aim was 'to ruine all that were true Protestants, or honest Assertors of the Liberties and Property of the Subject'.[155] Thus whilst it cannot be said that they 'targeted' their propaganda at the nonconformists or against the Church of England, which clearly would have been a tactical mistake, it was certainly 'slanted' towards the dissenters.

Why this should have been the case becomes obvious when we consider who the whig propagandists were. Attitude towards dissent seems to have been an important criterion for membership of the Green Ribbon Club. All of the members for whom we have adequate information either actively supported or promoted the interests of dissenters, the vast majority being nonconformists themselves. Amongst the better-known members were the presbyterians Henry Booth and Pawlet St John, the independent Slingsby Bethell and four members of that famous west country nonconformist family, the Trenchards.[156] Buckingham's meeting at the Salutation Tavern, on the limited evidence of membership that survives, seems to have been a baptist

---

[151] Guildhall Library, Playing Cards 236; Schreiber, *Playing Cards*, plates 10–13; 'Picture Cards of the Popish Plot', *Gentleman's Magazine*, NS 32 (1849), 267.
[152] Guildhall Library, Playing Cards, 238.
[153] *Domestick Intelligence*, no. 1.
[154] See, for example, Guildhall Library, Playing Cards 236, 6 clubs; 'Picture Cards', p. 267.
[155] *The Popish Damnable Plot Against Our Religion and Liberties, Lively Delineated in Several of its Branches* (1680); BM Prints, no. 1088.
[156] This is based on my own prosopographical analysis of the members of the club, as listed in Pepysian Library, Pepys Misc. VII, 465–91. I hope to publish a more detailed account of my findings shortly.

club.[157] Shaftesbury, although he took the sacrament in accordance with the Test Act of 1673, was a consistent supporter of toleration for dissenters and a critic of episcopacy.[158] The man who made the revelations of the Popish Plot, Titus Oates, although a roman catholic convert and apostate, was the son of a leading baptist.[159]

Most of the whig newspaper publishers appear to have been nonconformists. The first newspaper proper to appear during the exclusion crisis, the *Domestick Intelligence*, was produced by a baptist, Benjamin Harris.[160] Other newspaper publishers were dissenters. Francis 'Elephant' Smith was also a baptist and a key figure in the whig machine.[161] During the exclusion crisis Smith worked with fellow baptists John Darby and George Larkin, as well as Harris.[162] Langley Curtis was probably a nonconformist, since in February 1682 he was charged with publishing seditious news saying that the Middlesex Grand Jury ought not to prosecute dissenters.[163] Henry Care was a dissenter, probably a presbyterian, who later became one of James II's nonconformist collaborators.[164] Richard Janeway disapproved of nonconformist persecution, and in November 1681 he inserted a piece in his *Mercury* to dissuade constables from executing warrants against conventicles.[165]

If we examine the pope-burning processions of 17 November, there is evidence of deliberate slanting towards a nonconformist audience. In 1679 the procession started in Moorfields, near Moorgate, proceeding to Bishopsgate, down Hounsditch to Aldgate and from thence through Leadenhall Street, Cornhill, and Cheapside to Temple Bar.[166] In 1680 the procession started at St George's Yard, Whitechapel, marched to Aldgate and then

---

[157] *CSPD*, 1682, pp. 356–8, 404–5, 494–5.

[158] GLRO, MR/RS/2, no. 217; Haley, *Shaftesbury*, pp. 28–9, 323–6, 740.

[159] Kenyon, *Popish Plot*, 46, 54. Whitley, 'Militant Baptists', p. 155, describes Titus Oates as a renegade baptist.

[160] Crist, 'Francis Smith', p. 116; J. G. Muddiman, 'Benjamin Harris, the First American Journalist', *Notes and Queries*, 163 (1932), 129–33.

[161] J. G. Muddiman, 'Francis Smith, "The Elder"', *Notes and Queries*, 163 (1932), 57–62; Crist, 'Francis Smith'. Smith was a baptist preacher in both London and Croydon, and took up a licence to preach under the 1672 declaration. See: *CSPD*, 1671–2, pp. 72–3, 94, 348, 356; W. T. Whitley, *The Baptists of London, 1612–1928* (1928), p. 114.

[162] Crist, 'Francis Smith', pp. x–xi.

[163] *CSPD*, 1682, p. 68; Kitchin, *L'Estrange*, p. 296.

[164] Guildhall Library, MS 9060, gives a Henry Care of St Sepulchre's as a dissenter in 1683–4. Care's indictment at King's Bench for publishing the *Weekly Pacquet* shows that he was from St Sepulchre's. See PRO, KB 10/1, part 4. See also: *DNB*, IX, 45–6; *An Epitaph on Harry Care* [ND], in *A Third Collection of the Newest and Most Ingenious Poems, Satyrs, Songs, etc. against Popery and Tyranny* (1689), pp. 7–8; Lacey, *Dissent*, p. 346, note 64; J. R. Jones, 'James II's Whig Collaborators', *HJ*, 3 (1960), 68.

[165] *Impartial Protestant Mercury*, no. 59.

[166] *Domestick Intelligence*, no. 39; *London's Defiance*, p. 2; BL, Add. MS 25,359, fol. 193.

took the same route as the previous year.[167] In 1681 it started in Katherine Wheel Alley, Whitechapel, took the above route to Temple Bar, but then went up Chancery Lane, down Holborn to Newgate and then to Smithfield, where the pope was burnt.[168] On all these occasions, the processions started with a detour around the northern and eastern outparishes, areas with heavy concentrations of nonconformists.[169] No other civic pageant ever took a similar route, so we might suppose the procession was intended to march through nonconformist areas. The switch to Smithfield was probably made for politico-religious reasons. Temple Bar was the border between the two high-church parishes of St Martin-in-the-Fields and St Dunstan-in-the-West. To demonstrate their hostility to the whig pope-burning of 1679, the apprentices of St Martin's decided they would burn an effigy of Jack Presbyter on 29 May 1680.[170] The parish officials of St Dunstan's do not seem to have been too sympathetic to the whig use of 17 November. The church-wardens' accounts record money paid to bell-ringers for duties performed on 17 November every year before exclusion, although no such entries occur in 1679 and 1680, and bell-ringing on that day was only resumed in 1681, after the procession had shifted its destination.[171] A tract describing the procession of 1681 said that it ended at Smithfield where a large fire was prepared 'by the Gentlemen of the Loyal Inns of Court'.[172] The implication is that the change was necessary because some of the Inns were no longer whig in sympathy, a reference to the desertion to the tory cause by the Templars, who had helped sponsor the pope-burning procession of 1679.[173] It was the adherence to high-church principles of hostility towards noncon-formists that motivated those Templars who now opposed the whigs; indeed, they decided to organize their own presbyter-burning procession for 17 November 1682.[174] The routes of the pope-burning processions are impor-tant, because they show the audience they were aimed at. There seems to have been an attempt to avoid high-church areas and focus on dissenting communities. As I argue below, what the rituals actually meant would be determined by who saw them.

Whig writers were often defensive about their association with dissent. For example, when Stephen College was indicted for treason, for his alleged part in a whig plot at the time of the Oxford parliament of March 1681, Henry Care denied the tory charge that College was a presbyterian, saying

[167] *Solemn Mock Procession of . . . 1680*, broadside.
[168] *True Protestant Mercury*, no. 91.
[169] Harris, 'Politics of the London Crowd', appendix one. See above, pp. 66–7.
[170] *Mercurius Civicus*, 24 March 1680. See below, pp. 166–8.
[171] Guildhall Library, MS 2968/5.
[172] *The Procession*, p. 3.
[173] *The Solemn Mock Procession . . . of 1679*; HMC, *7th Report*, p. 477.
[174] *Loyal Impartial Mercury*, no. 43; *Loyal Protestant Intelligence*, no. 232.

he was no frequenter of conventicles, but a member of the Church of England.[175] They sometimes sought to exonerate the Church of England from any guilt. Richard Janeway described a debauched evening in a parish church in September 1681, when a crowd of apprentices got drunk and set the bells ringing. But he declined to use this opportunity to attack anglicans, adding that the leaders had not received the sacrament and were therefore not members of the Church of England.[176] Presbyterian newspaper publishers frequently claimed that they were really members of the Church of England. Care complained of how people who accepted the 39 articles were condemned as fanatics.[177] He also argued that those whom the tories called dissenters shared the doctrines of the Church of England, administered the sacraments in their churches, and only dissented from 'certain Ceremonies and outward rites'.[178] According to Janeway, the Church of England was something 'for which every true Protestant has a profound deference and respect, though dissenting from some superfluous Ceremonies' so that people who 'so studiously make it their business to render dissenters odious and suspected ... are no real Sons of the Church of England'.[179]

More positive positions can be found. One tract argued that the tories spent their time condemning 'those who were most instrumental in the Kings Restauration', a clear reference to the presbyterians.[180] Henry Care described how in pre-Reformation times some people had had the vision to see further than Rome. These were the Lollards, 'they were the Puritans, the Fanaticks, the Whigs, the Brumminghams of those days'.[181]

The parliamentary whigs were committed to the repeal of the Act of 35 Elizabeth, a statute aimed originally at catholic recusants, but which Danby and the bishops had been using against protestant dissenters.[182] Whig writers argued that this was essential, because it would unite protestants in the face of the catholic threat.[183] When Shaftesbury was indicted in 1681 for conspiring to use force to obtain whig ends once parliamentary means had failed, the indictment recognized that this meant the repeal of the 35 Elizabeth as well as the exclusion of the duke of York.[184] This theme was

[175] Care, *Weekly Pacquet*, III, 511.
[176] *Impartial Protestant Mercury*, no. 47.
[177] Care, *Weekly Pacquet*, IV, 223.
[178] Ibid., III, 543–4.
[179] *True Protestant Mercury*, no. 17.
[180] Misopappas, *Tory Plot: Second Part*, p. 4.
[181] Care, *Weekly Pacquet*, IV, 97.
[182] H. Horwitz, 'Protestant Reconciliation in the Exclusion Crisis', *Journal of Ecclesiastical History*, 15 (1964), 201–17.
[183] *Smith's Protestant Intelligence*, no. 7; Misopappas, *Tory Plot*, pp. 25–7.
[184] CLRO, Sessions File, November/December 1681, ind. of Shaftesbury (O + T); *The Proceedings at the Sessions House in the Old Bayly... On the 24th of November* (1681), for J. Heathcote; ibid., for J. Mearne and J. Baker; *State Trials*, VIII, fol. 776; *True Protestant Mercury*, no. 93.

often present in whig propaganda. As one tract put it, 'Oh! let not Protestants devour one another, when their Popish Adversaries would devour all.'[185] One ballad asserted 'When the Subjects of England shall all be as one,/Then Popery out of this Nation will run.'[186] Often the argument was less explicit. Newspapers might advertise books advocating unity.[187] The main message in the two whig lord mayors' shows was the need for unity to face the popish challenge. This was particularly noticeable in the 1680 show for Sir Patience Ward. At the second pageant, 'Moderation' was shown speaking of 'wide divisions in the Land', stating that 'Divide them, and destroy them, is the Pope's/Maxim, and Ready road to all his Hopes'. The point was made most explicitly in a song performed at the dinner, and which was included in the printed text of the pageantry. Lamenting the fact that English protestants were fighting amongst themselves whilst enemies were hatching treason, it pleaded 'Let us not mingle our Faith with our Fancies,/And leave the Substance for Small Circumstances... Let true Protestants love one another.'[188]

One illustrated tract developed the argument that the catholics were trying to reverse the Reformation, and depicted the protestant reformers standing near to, or seated at, a table, on which was a lighted candle symbolizing the Reformation. In front of the table, the pope, satan, a monk and a cardinal are vainly trying to blow out the candle. The reformers depicted are Bulinger, Zanchi, Martyr, Zwingli, De Malorat, Bucer, Prague, Perkins, Wycliffe, Melancthon, Luther, Calvin, Beza, Tyndale and Hus.[189] This print, therefore, deliberately blurs the distinction between the more conservative religious tradition stemming from the lutheran reformers, and a more radical one associated with the Genevans Calvin and Beza. The implication here was that both anglicans and dissenters had an identity of interest in the face of the popish threat. Yet the whigs knew well that to anglican tories Calvin was 'a worse man than Ignatius Loyola'.[190] Because of this, a plea for unity could be divisive, alienating those who wanted to keep the Church of England free from calvinists.

There was a potential ambiguity in the visual symbolism employed by the whigs in their pope-burning processions. Bishops were depicted in all three pope-burning processions of November 17 between 1679–81, and

[185] *A Proposal of Union amongst Protestants* (1679), p. 2.
[186] *A New Ballad, Called, The Protestant Prophesie* [1680]; *BM Prints*, no. 1102.
[187] See, for example, *Domestick Intelligence*, no. 49.
[188] T. Jordon, *London's Glory; Or, the Lord Mayor's Show* (1680), pp. 9, 13. Cf. T. Jordan, *London in Luster, Projecting Many Bright Beams of Triumph at the Initiation and Instalment of... Sir Robert Clayton* (1679), p. 15.
[189] *True Account of the Rise and Growth*; *BM Prints*, no. 1096.
[190] Misopappas, *Tory Plot*, p. 29. For a tory attack on Calvin, see: *The Presbyterian Pater-Noster, Creed, and Ten Commandments* (1681); *A Congratulation on the Happy Discovery of the Hellish Fanatick Plot* (1682), in Thompson, ed., *Songs*, p. 62.

although they were meant to be catholic ones, some tracts did not describe them as such.[191] Other tracts described them as 'Popish bishops',[192] which could be ambiguous, since 'Popish' was a catch-all to describe those who supported catholic policies, although they might be protestant.[193] It is more important to understand how people interpreted the imagery. If we look at the 1679 procession, we find that there were four bishops 'in pontificalibus', wearing 'Purple with Surplices and Rich Imbroydered Copes, and Golden Mitres on their Heads'. The others were 'in Purple and Lawn Sleeves, with Golden Crosses on their Breast'. It might be assumed that the dress allows no doubt that they were supposed to be catholic bishops, especially in the context of a procession where all the other clergymen were catholic. But here were also symbols of anglicanism which were bitterly disliked by nonconformists. Edmund Hickeringill, former nonconformist although writing after he was in anglican orders, complained that he could not tell the difference between an anglican and a catholic bishop. In particular he complained of surplices, copes, rochets and hoods.[194] To nonconformists, crosses, surplices, lawn sleeves and mitres were examples of the relics of popery within the anglican church. When we remember that the procession marched through areas with heavy concentrations of nonconformists, then we see that an image of catholicism was being represented which reminded this particular audience of some of the things they hated most within the Church of England. This interpretation cannot be pushed too far. If it worked in this way at all, then it was on a subliminal level, and clearly different people would interpret the symbolism in different ways.

Overt attacks on the Church of England were rare, but whig propaganda did contain certain messages within it which could be interpreted as criticism of the anglican establishment, operating on various levels of subtlety. One polemicist styled himself Misopappas, which he acknowledged could signify either 'a hater of popes' or 'a hater of bishops', 'for a Pope and a Bishop are all one in Greek'.[195] The whig press often carried adverts for books which were critical of episcopacy. Summaries of the books were provided. Janeway advertised *The Bishops Courts Dissolved*, which argued that bishops did not have power to impose their wills on subjects.[196] He later advertised Hickeringill's *The Black Nonconformist*, summarizing the argument thus:

---

[191] *London's Defiance*, p. 3; *Solemn Mock Procession of . . . 1679*; *Domestick Intelligence*, no. 39.

[192] *London's Drollery*; *Solemn Mock Procession of . . . 1680*.

[193] Cf. L'Estrange, *History of the Plot*, preface; L'Estrange, *Further Discovery*, p. 8; Miller, *Popery and Politics*, p. 178.

[194] E. Hickeringill, *The Ceremony-Monger* (1689), pp. 15, 21.

[195] P. Misopappas, *The Charge of a Tory Plot Maintain'd, In a Dialogue Between the Observator, Heraclitus and an Inferior Clergy-man at the Towzer-Tavern* (1682), p. 29.

[196] *Impartial Protestant Mercury*, no. 20.

That Excommunication and Confirmation, the Two Great Episcopal Appurtenances, and Diocesan Bishops, are (as now in Use) of Human Make and Shape; And that not only some Lay-Men, but all the Keen-cringing Clergy, are NON-CON-FORMISTS. And, except they Repent, are liable to be Indicted and Presented by Grand-Juries.[197]

The condemnation of those who opposed the whigs as popish sympathizers could have an alienating effect, since many anti-exclusionists were widely regarded as staunch defenders of the Church of England. The tory propagandist, Sir Roger L'Estrange wrote that there was hardly anything

That has done us more Mischief then the Accusing this Lord, That Commoner; this Bishop, that Alderman, this Citizen, that Country-Gentleman; for Popishly Affected; when the whole world knows 'um to be Church-of-England Protestants.[198]

L'Estrange himself was attacked as a pretended member of the Church of England who was really promoting the cause of the papists.[199] Oates condemned him as a papist in orders.[200] He was burnt in effigy at the pope-burning processions of 1680 and 1681.[201] In *A Prospect of a Popish Successor*, L'Estrange is typically depicted as the dog Towzer, with a broom for his tail (a reference to his publisher Henry Brome), and with a cross and rosary on his head. He is fawning on a jesuit who is brandishing a dagger amidst his own cross and rosary.[202] In *Strange's Case, Strangly Altered*, Towzer is shown walking towards the pope, but with his head turned back towards the devil. Above him reads the inscription 'Your Case is Evill: twixt Pope and Devill'. But a manuscript addition to the British Library copy of this print, admittedly from a hostile hand, recalled how 'for the last 20 years' L'Estrange had been 'a zealous Voucher of the Church of England'.[203] Castigating all opponents of their cause as papists must have been counter-productive after a time, especially when a genuine popular tory position began to emerge as the crisis progressed.[204] For example, the leader of an intended tory apprentice demonstration in 1680 was attacked as working in collusion with papists even though it was widely publicized as a demonstration in defence of the established church.[205]

---

[197] Ibid., no. 75.

[198] Sir R. L'Estrange, *Citt and Bumpkin, the Second Part; Or, A Learned Discourse upon Swearing and Lying* (1680), p. 8.

[199] Miller, *Popery and Politics*, p. 177.

[200] *Strange's Case, Strangly Altered* (1680); *BM Prints*, no. 1083. Manuscript addition to the British Museum's copy of the print. See print 5.

[201] *Solemn Mock Procession; Or, the Trial*, p. 3; *The Procession*, pp. 2, 3; *Impartial Protestant Mercury*, no. 60; Williams, 'Pope-Burning Processions', pp. 109–10.

[202] *BM Prints*, no. 1110.

[203] *BM Prints*, no. 1083. See print 5.

[204] This is discussed in Ch. 7.

[205] Guildhall Library, Playing Cards 238, Ace and Knave of Spades; *A Protestant Prentices' Loyal Advice to all his Fellow Apprentices in and about London* (1680). The demonstration is discussed below, pp. 166–8.

4 *A Prospect of a Popish Successor* (1681)

5 *Strange's Case* (1680)

The emergence of an anglican anti-exclusionist position called for a re-adjustment of the whig propaganda to avoid being construed as an attack on anglicanism. Instead, the whigs tended to reinforce the divide that was already emerging. *The Contents* satirized those high-church clergy who opposed exclusion. In a print the pope is shown holding out a cardinal's hat to a crowd of clergymen.[206] The nickname for a church tory was a 'tantivy', and one engraving showed 'tory' and 'tantivy' galloping off towards the pope, who offers them protection.[207] Benjamin Harris asked whether 'that Maxim, No Bishop, no Pope, no Prelacy, no Popery was not more Infallible then no Bishop no King'.[208] Bishops were 'Protestants in Masquerade'. This was the subtitle to the knave of clubs in one pack showing three men sitting round a table: one has horns, hooved feet, claws for hands, and a tail; another is wearing a bishop's mitre. *A Prospect of a Popish Successor* showed a double-headed figure, half pope, half bishop, standing on the bible. One hand, supporting a crosier, holds a scroll offering a free pardon to all plots, and the other holds a crosier and is pushing out ministers from the Church. The figure mimics the typical tory propaganda cry 'out fanaticks in popery', his real intentions are shown by the Latin legend which proceeds from him: 'Confirmatio exit Reformatio'.[209] This print makes a typical nonconformist point that the still popish Church of England has put a stop to the Reformation.

The most blatant anticlerical statements can be found in anonymous verses. The illustrated ballad for which College lost his life was in part an attack on bishops.[210] The chorus of a crude verse which told of an act of buggery between a bishop and a lord near Whitehall ran:

> Help Deans and Chapters all
> The Tribe Episcopalian
> What Glorious Hopes
> You Have now to be Popes
> Since your Bishops turn Italian.[211]

A mock litany of 1680 asked, amongst other things, to be delivered 'From Church Tantive who rail at dissenters'.[212] Another poem ran 'Debaucht Circingle Clergy you're the Knaves/Whose Lives make Atheists and your Doctrines Slaves'.[213] Often the crown and church were condemned together. Another mock litany of 1681, which concentrated its attack on the anglican

---

206 *BM Prints*, no. 1087. See print 3.
207 *Time Servers*; *BM Prints*, no. 1112.
208 *The Weekly Discovery Strip'd Naked*, no. 2.
209 *BM Prints*, no. 1110. See print 4.
210 [College], *Raree Show*; Rahn, 'A Ra-ree Show'.
211 BL, Add. MS 34,362, fol. 19, 'The Man in the Moon; or, Bumm for a Bishop'.
212 Ibid., fol. 122, 'The Responses'.
213 Ibid., fol. 107, 'On the Prorogation to the 17 May, 1680'.

church, started by asking for deliverance 'From the Lawless Dominion of the Miter and Crowne/Whose Tyranny is so absolute growne'.[214] But anti-episcopalianism, even at this late stage, was not necessarily anti-monarchical. One poem, anxious about the day 'when James the 2d shall assume the Power', predicted that 'Strange Changes in ye Kingdom shall appeare,/All Sects and Hereticks must be pul'd down,/The Miter must advance above the Crowne.'[215]

CONCLUSION

This chapter has examined how the whigs sought to exploit the fears aroused by the revelations of the Popish Plot in order to win mass support for exclusion. I have argued that much of the whig propaganda was negative in nature, stressing the horrors that could be expected should the catholic plot succeed; the positive ideals, about which the propagandists were often silent, could be learnt by discovering what had to be done to avoid such horrors. At a minimum this meant a commitment to the parliamentary cause and exclusion, but had the potential for a far more radical extension, depending upon what political forces chose to position themselves against the whigs. At its most extreme, this was the possibility of a condemnation of the king or even monarchy in general, although this was something that was rarely done, except in the anonymous poems of the propaganda underworld. The whig propaganda campaign is usually assumed to have been successful because the whigs were able to exploit deep-seated anti-catholic prejudices held by the majority of the London populace. But it must be remembered that the anti-catholic tradition was an extremely ambiguous one, intimately bound up with the domestic religious tensions which had divided London political culture since the 1640s. We have seen how anglican royalists could use the rhetoric of no popery against the enemies of the monarchy and the Church of England, as too could the nonconformists in their critique of the established church. It is thus crucial to consider which aspects of the anti-catholic tradition the whigs chose to exploit. The printed versions of Oates's revelations incorporated aspects of the anti-nonconformist side to this tradition. The whigs ignored this, and not only defended the dissenters, but even attacked the Church of England. It was this whig bias towards dissent which was to give the tories room for manoeuvre in their counter-propaganda campaign.

---

[214] Bodl. Lib, MS Don b. 8, p. 696, 'The Antiphone to the Late Protestant Petition'. One source dates it 1681. See: BL, Add. MS 34,362, fol. 124, 'The Letany, 1681'; BL, Add. MS 27,405, fol. 45.
[215] BL, Add. MS 34,362, fol. 51.

6

The tory response

Charles was able to frustrate the attempts to enact an exclusion bill by skilful use of his prerogative powers for determining the calling, sitting and dissolution of parliaments. The parliamentary exclusion movement was effectively destroyed with the dissolution of the Oxford parliament in March 1681, since another parliament was not to be called for the rest of the reign. But driving the exclusionist movement 'out of doors' would not necessarily solve the crisis, especially since the whigs had tried to excite mass support for their cause. In the early 1660s the government had been seriously worried about the possible threat to the security of the state posed by a tiny minority of fifth monarchists. What potential havoc might the thousands who flocked to London's pope-burnings be able to cause, once they had been frustrated in their aims? To defeat exclusion safely and successfully, the government had to deal with the whig appeal to the people.

The main problem was the lack of an effective means of controlling the press after the lapse of the Licensing Act. It was possible to use the common law of seditious libel to deal with opposition publicists. A vigorous campaign conducted by Chief Justice Scroggs in the first half of 1680 led to successful indictments against Henry Care, Jane Curtis (the wife of Langley), Benjamin Harris and Francis Smith.[1] Yet once a tract had been produced, the damage had been done, and punishment after the deed could be counter-productive. When Harris appeared in the pillory on 17 February 1680 for publishing his *Appeal*, which advocated Monmouth's succession, he was treated very kindly by the assembled crowds, and one man was chased away because he dared to mention throwing eggs.[2] What thwarted the attempt to control the presses through the common law, however, was the fact that in the summer of 1680, two whigs, Slingsby Bethell and Henry Cornish, were elected sheriffs of London. The sheriffs were responsible for empanelling juries for London and Middlesex, and so they could ensure that only those sympathetic to the whigs were chosen to serve. The election of Thomas Pilkington and Samuel Shute in 1681 continued the whig domination of

[1] *State Trials*, VII, fols. 926–60, 1111–30; Crist, 'Francis Smith', pp. 107–41.
[2] Bodl. Lib., MS Carte 228, fol. 147; *CSPD, 1679–80*, p. 397.

the shrievalty. This domination made it impracticable for the government to try and prosecute stationers for seditious libel, since any indictments would be thrown out by packed juries.

The tories therefore decided to try and beat the whigs at their own game. A counter-propaganda campaign was launched, spearheaded by Sir Roger L'Estrange and Nathaniel Thompson, in an attempt, as Thompson put it, 'to undeceive the people' and 'reduce the deluded Multitude to their Just Allegiance'.[3] L'Estrange believed that since the press had 'made 'um Mad ... the Press must set 'um Right again ... there's no way in the World, but by Printing, to convey the Remedy to the Disease'.[4] But the task of persuading people to accept a catholic successor was a formidable one. The whigs' exploitation of the Popish Plot, appealing to deeply embedded anxieties over popery and arbitrary government, stimulated an intensity of emotion against which no propagandist could run counter. What the tory propagandists did was to appeal to the self-same anxieties, and try to re-direct them to their own advantage. The key to this was the identification of the whigs as nonconformists. They could then compare the activities of the whigs with those of the presbyterians in 1640–2, and emphasize the very arbitrary style of government that had emerged as a result in the 1640s and 1650s. It was the nonconformists, they argued, who had destroyed the Church of England and murdered the king in 1649, thereby achieving the aims which the papists had for so long unsuccessfully pursued. In this way they sought to turn the anti-catholic prejudice against the whigs.

However, the tory exploitation of fears of tyranny and popery, it will be argued, worked on a different level from that of the whigs. By claiming that the real threat to the Church of England came from the nonconformists, they exacerbated the tensions that the issue of dissent had already caused. By identifying the whigs as rabble-rousers who were promoting popular anarchy, their arguments took on a fiercely anti-populist tone. This is not to say that the tory position would have held little attraction for the lower classes. The religious arguments could have an extremely powerful resonance; indeed, popular hostility towards dissenters can be found earlier in the reign. But the tories appealed to different aspects of political culture than had the whigs, thus encouraging a polarization in political attitudes, and setting the context for divisions within 'the London crowd' over the issue of exclusion, which will be examined in chapter seven.

THE TORY COUNTER-ATTACK

Although the widespread initial belief in the Popish Plot made the tory task very daunting, time was to provide room for manoeuvre. As the persecution

---

[3] Thompson, ed., *Songs*, preface.
[4] L'Estrange, *Observator*, no. 1.

of the plotters became less important, and attention was focused on the problem of the duke of York's succession – exclusion was first broached as early as November 1678 – legitimism was to become an issue, the principle which was, in fact, to give definition to the tory party. The lack of success of the exclusion bill forced the whigs to promote extra-parliamentary activity in the form of petitioning and popular demonstrations, which enabled the tories to brand them as rabble-rousers. As whig tactics became more desperate, a number of supposed whig plots were uncovered. The Meal Tub Plot of December 1679 was revealed as a sham and so rebounded on the tories. But after the dissolution of the Oxford parliament in March 1681, the charge of whig plots became more credible, with a reputed plan to seize the king at Oxford, Shaftesbury's alleged 'Association' and the Rye House revelations of 1683.[5] The dynamics of the crisis, therefore, enabled the tories to label the whigs as a danger to the security of the state, and accuse them of using the threat of popular insurrection to undermine the monarchy. By late 1681, the tories were in a strong enough position to launch an attack on whig strongholds in the City and also on the nonconformists. An important prerequisite of this was regaining control of City government, with the installation of a tory mayor from 1681, and tory sheriffs from 1682. Tory propaganda grew in response to these developments during the exclusion crisis, and sought to manipulate them to a tory advantage.

The tory counter-attack was well conceived and carefully coordinated. In the papers of Francis North, lord chief justice of common pleas and a close adviser of the king, there is a list of guidelines 'for undeceiving the people about the late popish plott', which stresses the necessity of blaming England's troubles on republicans, presbyterians and sectarians, who had been disaffected ever since the restoration of monarchy and episcopacy.[6] Much of the propaganda was directed by Sir Roger L'Estrange, licenser of the press, and a seemingly indefatigable pamphleteer. There were a number of tory clubs. L'Estrange frequented Sam's Coffee-House in Ludgate Street, which was a tory meeting place in the early 1680s.[7] In the autumn of 1681 the duke of Ormond established a club at the Warder within Ludgate, a meeting place for both tory peers and citizens, which soon achieved a membership of some three hundred. The members were exhorted to use their influence in their respective wards to persuade people to vote for tory candidates in municipal elections, an example of propaganda by personal communication.[8] A group of Danby's supporters met at an unnamed tavern in

[5] For this basic narrative, see: Jones, *First Whigs*; Haley, *Shaftesbury*, chs. 21–30.
[6] BL, Add. MS 32,518, fols. 144–52.
[7] Care, *Weekly Pacquet*, IV, 167–8; *Loyal Protestant Intelligence*, no. 170; *The Procession*, p. 2.
[8] Earl of Ailesbury, *Memoirs*, ed. W. E. Buckley (2 vols., 1890), I, 64–5.

Fuller's Rents, and there were other tory clubs at the Sun Tavern in Aldersgate Street and the Queen's Head.[9]

The tories produced nothing to match the elaborate pope-burnings of 17 November. There were a number of presbyter-burning processions, although these were on a much smaller scale, and tended to be localized, community affairs. For this reason they are discussed in the next chapter under the activities of the tory crowd. Once the mayoralty was in tory hands, after October 1681, it was possible to use this civic ritual to make anti-exclusionist political points, although fear that doing so would provoke disorder probably explains why there were no pageants in 1682.[10] Neverthe-less, many of the other whig techniques were mimicked. Ballad singers could be found 'asserting the Rights of Monarchy, and proclaiming Loyalty in ev'ry street'.[11] Plays satirizing the whigs were put on, amongst them *City Politics* and *Venice Preserved*.[12] Anglican sermons often carried political messages. One whig pamphleteer referred to how 'our Pulpits began to eccho' with tory propaganda statements.[13] The same author believed that such activity was coordinated by the tory clubs, speaking of 'the scandalous Clubbs of our Coffee-house and Tavern-haunting Parsons'.[14] Playing cards and prints were used as visual forms of propaganda, whilst poems, pamph-lets, broadsides and the popular press carried written propaganda. Almanacs were produced by John Gadbury advocating an anti-exclusionist position.[15] L'Estrange had his own newspaper in the *Observator*, published first by Henry Brome, and then by Brome's wife Joanna. Thompson published the *True Domestick Intelligence* and the *Loyal Protestant Intelligence*. Benjamin Tooke produced another called *Heraclitus Ridens*, which seems to have been written by a club of tory writers headed by Edward Rawlins and the poet Thomas Flatman.[16]

TYRANNY AND POPERY

The crucial starting-point for the tories was the identification of the whigs as nonconformist subversives, who were a threat to the security of the

[9] Allen, 'Political Clubs', pp. 575–9; Care, *Weekly Pacquet*, IV, 168, 255; *Loyal Protestant Intelligence*, no. 2.

[10] [T. Jordan], *The Lord Mayor's Show; Being a Description of the Solemnity at the Inaugu-ration of . . . Sir William Pritchard* (1682); Fairholt, *Lord Mayors' Pageants*, I, 97–8.

[11] Thompson, ed., *Songs*, preface; *Loyal Protestant Intelligence*, no. 76; *CSPD, 1680–1*, p. 509.

[12] Morrice, I, 353; LC, MS 18,124, VIII, fols. 192, 283; Smith, 'London and the Crown', p. 137.

[13] Misopappas, *Tory Plot*, p. 5. Cf. Misopappas, *Tory Plot: Second Part*, p. 3.

[14] Misopappas, *Charge*, 'To the Reader'.

[15] Capp, *Astrology*, pp. 92–4.

[16] T. F. M. Newton, 'The Mask of Heraclitus: A Problem in Restoration Journalism', *Harvard Studies and Notes in Philology and Literature*, 16 (1934), pp. 145–60.

church and state. However, it was not the more extreme sects that were usually attacked. Occasionally, the label of anabaptist was employed to invite the stigma of association with the Munster rebels. Thus Thompson described Care's *Weekly Pacquet* as an 'Anabaptiscal Mercury', although Care was probably a presbyterian.[17] But, in general, the tories associated the whigs with the presbyterian cause. This was partly because the presbyterians were the largest and most powerful group of dissenters (numerically and politically), influential in support of exclusion,[18] and partly because the presbyterians were seen as having been responsible for the drift towards Civil War in 1641–2.[19] But it was also picking up on an element in Oates's narrative of the Popish Plot, which said that the jesuits, disguised as presbyterians, were to be sent to Scotland to stir the people to revolt, something given extra credence by the Covenanters' Rebellion of the late spring of 1679.[20] Several early tory pieces drew comparisons between a jesuit amd a Scottish presbyterian.[21]

Because they were nonconformists, the whigs were also republicans: they were 'Against the Church and State ... They Villify the Bishops,/And they cry the Stuarts down.'[22] According to the tories, the dissenters were against bishops, because 'this same Mitre does support the Crown'.[23] Conventicles were therefore seen as the sources of rebellion: 'They meet in private, and cry Persecution,/When Faction is their end, and State-confusion'.[24] Thompson argued that 'All Conventicles are Treasonable presumptively ... while men labour to withdraw the Love and Loyalty of the Subject from the Established Government of Church or State, thereby to weaken and discredit Both, there must lie hidden a Treasonable Purpose.'[25]

Typically the whigs were represented as trying to revive the 'good old cause'. This argument was so common that the whigs even satirized it in their propaganda.[26] The charge could be made in a variety of ways, the most blatant being through explicit parallels with the 1640s. For example, in March 1682, shortly after it had been revealed that Shaftesbury was

---

[17] *Loyal Protestant Intelligence*, no. 151.

[18] Lacey, *Dissent*, esp. chs. 6, 7.

[19] See, for example, *Presbyterian Paternoster*.

[20] *LJ*, XIII, 313, 326; Haley, *Shaftesbury*, pp. 534–7.

[21] *Simeon and Levi, Brethren and Iniquity. A Comparison Between a Papist and a Scotch Presbyter* [1679]; *Jockey's Downfall; A Poem on the Late Total Defeat Given to the Scottish Covenanters* (1679), in *Roxburghe Ballads*, IV, 541–2.

[22] *The Downfall of the Good Old Cause* [ND], in Thompson, ed., *Songs*, pp. 12–13.

[23] *The Dissenter Truly Described* (1681), in Thompson, ed., *Poems*, p. 168. Cf. *The Charter, A Comical Satyr* (1682), in ibid., p. 136; *The Ballad of the Cloak; Or, The Cloaks Knavery* [1679], in *Roxburghe Ballads*, IV, 605–7; *BM Prints*, no. 1109.

[24] [J. Phillips], *A Satire Against Hypocrites* (1680), p. 23.

[25] *Loyal Protestant Intelligence*, no. 123.

[26] See, for example, *Time Servers; BM Prints*, no. 1112. Here L'Estrange, characteristically depicted as the dog 'Towzer', is shown crying '41'.

forming an Association of protestants to provide against a popish successor, Thompson argued that the traitorous practices of the whigs were proven 'by a Parallel instrument with '41 the Association found in the E of S Closet'.[27] One of the pageants in the lord mayor's show of 1681 raised the spectre of 'Privy Conspiracies,/Seditious Cabals, where Spirits Consent/To Undermine all Peacefull Government', and advised Sir John Moore, the tory lord mayor elect, to 'Suppress Pamphlet-Contentions, for they are/The Serpentary Seed of Civil War'.[28]

Such techniques might have been less successful because of their very blatant nature. A political view was being starkly stated, and the choice was a clear one between accepting or rejecting it. Subtler techniques, pervading the consciousness at a more subliminal level, might have proved more persuasive. The tories dedicated one newspaper, the *Weekly Discovery of the Mystery of Iniquity*, entirely to recounting affairs in England in 1641, leaving the reader to draw his own conclusions as to whether present trends in politics suggested the likelihood of another civil war. The way such events were recounted usually left the reader little room for doubt. In February 1681, just before the last exclusion parliament met at Oxford, the paper pointed out that

there was nothing that contributed more effectually to the carrying on, supporting, contriving, and encouraging those wicked designs of the late Rebels, than their being convened at London, where they had so depraved the understanding of the common People, that ... they had a Tumult ready upon all occasions for holding up their Finger.

Charles I later admitted, the account continued, that had he 'called this parliament to any other place in England' he might have avoided trouble.[29] A subtler technique still was to set songs satirizing the whigs 'to an old tune of '41'.[30] One print showed an old man preaching from a tub, clearly intending to convey the antiquity of the whig's cause.[31]

In case the memory of imagination was lacking, the tory publicists produced reminders of just what horrors a commonwealth could bring. In this way they sought to invert the whig exploitation of fears of arbitrary government. Shaftesbury and his supporters, it was argued, 'would have no body Arbitrary but themselves'.[32] The same charge was repeated time and again:

[27] *Loyal Protestant Intelligence*, no. 123. Cf. Haley, *Shaftesbury*, p. 687.
[28] T. Jordan, *London's Joy; Or, The Lord Mayor's Show* (1681).
[29] *Weekly Discovery of the Mystery of Iniquity*, no. 3.
[30] *An Excellent New Hymne to the Mobile, Exhorting them to Loyalty the Clean Contrary Way* (1682), in *Roxburghe Ballads*, V, 60; *The Whig's Exaltation* (1682), Thompson, ed., *Songs*, pp. 6–8.
[31] [F. Quarles], *The Whig Rampant; Or, Exaltation* [1682]; *BM Prints*, no. 1100.
[32] *Heraclitus Ridens*, no. 11.

'Tho' the king mayn't, yet We [Whigs] may break the Laws.'[33] One tract, purporting to be a dialogue between a pope and a fanatic, made the same connection, the pope arguing that, since Cromwell, the cavaliers

have more reason to fear Arbitrary Government from you [fanatics], than from their Hereditary Kings, whose Interest it is to secure the Liberty and Property of their Loyal Subjects. 'Tis true, [replies the fanatic] the Saints have a right to an absolute Dominion ... and I grant that there shall be no Parliament in the Fifth Monarchy; but this Arbitrary Power must not be allowed to the Kings of the Earth.[34]

Tyranny was usually depicted as a dragon. One print showed the 'Commonwealth' as a dragon which had swallowed parliament, whilst its neck was covered with armed troops, alluding to how the head of the Commonwealth, Cromwell, derived his strength from military oppression.[35] The tyranny of the 1650s had been accompanied by anarchy. In a pack of playing-cards which satirized the interregnum, the ace of clubs is entitled 'a free state or toleration for all sort of villainy', and shows people looting houses and stealing goods. The other cards dwell on the tyranny of Cromwell and his army.[36] Tory propagandists also tried to manipulate the emotive symbol of Magna Carta, arguing that the whigs were seeking to destroy the liberties guaranteed by it.[37] The argument was made visually in a print by L'Estrange, where 'Magna Charta' is shown as having been rejected by a factious 'Committee' of nonconformists.[38]

What constituted tyranny, so far as the tories were concerned, was clearly different from the whig vision. Above all else, they feared the tyranny of popular government. The implications of the whig appeal to the masses to apply pressure for exclusion were spelt out. A tory parody of a whig petition printed in June 1681 asked the king, in the name of his 'dissenting Subjects', to

grant the Right of Calling and Dissolving Parliaments, Entring into Associations, Leagues and Covenants, The Power of the Militia: War and Peace: Life and Death:

---

[33] *The Deliquium; Or, The Grievance of the Nation Discovered in a Dream* (1681), in Thompson, ed., *Poems*, p. 13.

[34] *A Dialogue Between the Pope and a Phanatick, Concerning Affairs in England* (1680), p. 12.

[35] 'The Commonwealth Ruling with a Standing Army', frontispiece to [Sir T. May], *Arbitrary Government Display'd in the Tyrannick Usurpation of the Rump Parliament, and Oliver Cromwell* (1683); BM Prints, no. 1127. Cf. 'Carolus Everso Missus Succurer Seclo', frontispiece to E. Pettit, *Visions of Government, Wherein the Antimonarchical Principles and Practices of all Fanatical Commonwealths Men and Jesuitical Polititians are Discovered, Confuted, and Exposed* (1684); BM Prints, no. 1130. Here a print shows Charles II trampling on a three-headed dragon of Turk, Jesuit and Puritan.

[36] Guildhall Library, Playing Cards 239.

[37] *New Song on the Death of Colledge*, in Thompson, ed., *Songs*, p. 65.

[38] Sir R. L'Estrange, *The Committee; Or, Popery in Masquerade*; BM Prints, no. 1080. Cf. 'Britannia Mourning the Execution of Charles I', frontispiece to Nalson, *Impartial Collection*, I; BM Prints, no. 1122. See prints 6 and 7.

6 *The Committee* (1680)

the Authority of Enacting, Suspending and Repealing Laws, to be in your Leige People, the Commons of England.[39]

Tory propagandists explicitly defended the traditional hierarchy, and in that sense were self-consciously anti-populist. The whigs, they believed, wanted to '... teach the Nobles how to bow,/And keep their Gentry down/... The name of Lord shall be abhorr'd/For ev'ry Mans a Brother'.[40] It was not just lords, but lords and bishops that would fall.[41] The fear was lest the 'rabble' should rule church and state, as had happened in the 1640s and 1650s.[42] As one song expressed it, 'Each Cobler's Statesman grown, and the bold Rable/Convert each Ale-house-Board to Council-table'.[43] Men of property would suffer, as they had with the sequestrations of the 1640s; and this was exactly what the whigs wanted, for "Tis Rabble Property they

[39] L'Estrange, *Observator*, no. 27.
[40] *Whig's Exaltation*, in Thompson, ed., *Songs*, p. 6.
[41] Ibid., p. 8; *The Convert Scot and Apostate English* (1681), in Thompson, ed., *Poems*, p. 50.
[42] *The Mad-Men's Hospital; Or, A Present Remedy to Cure the Presbyterian Itch* (1681) in Thompson, ed., *Poems*, p. 57; *Advice to the City; Or, The Whigs Loyalty Explained* (1682).
[43] *The Solicitous Citizen; Or, Much Ado about Nothing* [ND], in Thompson, ed., *Poems*, p. 133.

own.'[44] Tories, therefore, prayed for deliverance from 'the Insolent Rabble'.[45] In short, the whigs were represented as offering the true threat to 'liberties and properties', inverting the whig claim that only exclusion could safeguard these.

Newspapers pursued similar themes, one asking whether 'they who are our Fellow-Subjects, and our Servants, and by Law are appointed Wages, ought to take it upon them, not only as if they were ours, but our Great Master's Master?'[46] So too did sermons:

The Liberties and Properties of the Subject, is an admirable pretence to deprive the Prince of his Liberties and Properties; and those who have any Liberty and Property, seldom gain any thing by this: for when they have secured Liberties and Properties against their Prince, it is a much harder task to secure themselves from their fellow-Subjects. Men who have no Property have some encouragement to Rebel and fight for Property; for it is possible they may get something in the scramble ... but methinks men of Honour and plentiful Fortune, should not be so zealous for transferring Properties, to enrich Beggars, and submit their necks to the Yoke and Government of their own Slaves; which our late experience has taught us to be the glorious effect of Rebelling for Liberty and Property.[47]

This anti-populist streak continued into the tory attack on the City government of London. After the tory Sir John Moore had become lord mayor in 1681 he was acclaimed as the man who would suppress the rabble – 'May Moore ne're cease to stand up for the Crown/'Gainst the Presumptuous Rabble of the Town.'[48] Sir William Pritchard was similarly celebrated when he became lord mayor the following year.[49] When the City lost its charter, tory propagandists had no qualms about showing their delight: 'As Sampson's Strength up in his Hair was ty'd,/Rebellions Strength was in the Charter hid.'[50] London deserved to lose its charter for its disloyalty: 'Oh London! Oh London! thou'dst better had none/Than thus with thy Charter to vie with the Throne.'[51]

It was not just the political radicalism of the nonconformists that was a threat, but their factiousness, something related to the fear of popular

[44] *Loyal Protestant Intelligence*, no. 145; *Convert Scot*, in Thompson, ed., *Poems*, p. 50.
[45] *A Litany from Geneva, in Answer to that from St. Omers* (1682). Cf. *The Cavaliers Litany* (1682); L'Estrange, *Observator*, no. 38.
[46] *Heraclitus Ridens*, no. 12.
[47] W. Sherlock, *Some Seasonable Reflections on the Discovery of the Late Plot, Being a Sermon Preacht on that Occasion* (1683), p. 2.
[48] *The Humble Wishes of a Loyal Subject* (1681), in Thompson, ed., *Poems*, p. 79. Cf. *A Congratulatory Poem to Sir John More Knight, Lord Mayor Elect of London* (1681) in ibid., pp. 189–91; *A New Song, on the Instalment of Sir John Moore, Lord Mayor of London* (1681), in Mackay, ed., *Songs*, pp. 103–8.
[49] *London's Joy and Triumph on the Instalment of Sir William Pritchard* (1682), in Mackay, ed., *Songs*, pp. 112–14.
[50] *The Charter*, in Thompson, ed., *Poems*, p. 134.
[51] *London's Lamentation for the Loss of their Charter* (1683) in Thompson, ed., *Songs*, p. 40.

anarchy. *Heraclitus Ridens* compared dissenters to 'a Dog made up of a matter of seven or eight-score Heads ... these Heads ... always snapping and snarling one at another'. Only when the bear – an anglican bishop – was to be baited, with 'every one hoping to have a share in his skin', did they 'all agree upon that point, and fall upon him tooth and nail'.[52] A print by L'Estrange, *The Committee*, developed this theme of factiousness in splendid detail. It shows nine persons sitting around a table: a muggletonian, raving; a ranter, ranting; a quaker, telling arguments on his fingers; an anabaptist, holding a dagger; a presbyterian, the chairman, holding an unwound scroll which reads, 'thanks to the Petitioners'; an independent arguing with the rest; a fifth monarchist; Naylor, preaching; and an adamite, naked. On the table are papers, inscribed 'Church and Crown Lands', 'Sequestrations', 'Remonstrances', 'Petitions', 'Court of Justice', and 'Humiliation'. At one side of the table is an 'Elders Mayd', wearing a book called 'The Protestutor', [i.e. Harris's *Protestant Tutor*] at her girdle, and shouting 'no service book'. Her dog, 'swash', is barking 'No bishops'. On the left side of the picture is a mob of men carrying a crown, mitre, and banners inscribed 'A Thorough Reformation', 'Liberty', 'Property', and 'Religion'. Before their feet are the sceptre, orb and bust of Charles I. They lead in chains the men who in the early 1640s had suffered for their support of Charles I, Gurney (the royalist lord mayor of London in 1641–2), Strafford, and Laud.[53] On the other side of the picture are reminders of what this alliance of mob and schismatics brought: sequestrated livings, excise, army accounts, ordinances, widows' tears and the blood of orphans. Amongst the things discarded by the 'Committee' are the symbols of anglicanism, including the common prayer. In the top right hand corner we see 'Little Isaack', that is, Alderman Pennington, who back on 11 December 1640 had presented the first 'root and branch' petition for the abolition of episcopacy.

This print by L'Estrange can be taken as a paradigm of the tory case against the whigs. They were nonconformists, factious, king killers, mob rousers, tyrants, and hostile to the Church of England. It also makes explicit comparisons with the politics of the 1640s. But L'Estrange went further, suggesting the whigs were working in alliance with the catholics. The print's subtitle is 'Popery in Masquerade', and in the top right hand corner, standing next to Isaac Pennington, is the pope, and the couple are encouraging the committee with the words 'courage mes enfants' and 'Wee'l be true to you.'[54]

---

[52] *Heraclitus Ridens*, no. 10.
[53] Gurney was the royalist lord mayor of London in 1641–2, who was impeached by parliament and sent to the Tower, where he died. *DNB*, XXIII, 364–5.
[54] L'Estrange, *Committee*; *BM Prints*, no. 1080. See print 6. For a general discussion of L'Estrange's use of anti-catholic arguments, see Miller, *Popery and Politics*, pp. 177–9.

In L'Estrange's print the pope speaks in French because the tories too recognized that the main catholic threat came from France. During his period of ascendancy, Danby had pursued an anti-French foreign policy, and during the parliamentary exclusion crisis Charles was on bad terms with Louis XIV, not being reconciled until 1681. In 1679 there had been several rumours of a French invasion. By fermenting domestic discord when there existed this external threat to national security, tories argued, the whigs and nonconformists were playing into the catholics' hands. *Heraclitus Ridens* said that dissenters were either papists in masquerade or French pensioners, 'for this is a Maxim, That the Discords of England are the great Interest of France and Rome'. Was 'the most prudent Method to secure the Nation against the formidable power of France . . . to embroyl us among ourselves?'[55] Would not divisions at home work in favour of the king of France?[56] It was therefore argued that the best way to diminish the pretensions of Rome and France was through a severe persecution of nonconformists. Discussing a directive from Whitehall of January 1682 ordering all local justices to enforce rigorously the penal laws against dissenters, Thompson's *Intelligence* suggested that

the Pope is going into a deep Consumption upon hearing of the Persecution of his dear friends the Fanaticks in England . . . he is more troubled for Them, then all the Persecution of the Papists; for that all his hopes consists in their dissentions, and endeavours to root out the Church of England as by Law established.[57]

The demand for toleration was another way the nonconformists might, if unwittingly, help promote the interests of catholics. Thompson believed 'if ever Popery comes in, it will be brought in under Jack Presbyter's Cloak', whilst others agreed 'Popery could never come into England, unless the Phanatiques let it in at the back door of Toleration.'[58] Previous plans for toleration, most notably the king's Declarations of Indulgence of 1662 and 1672, had indeed included catholics, and were bitterly opposed by the bishops and the anglican interest in parliament. Another indirect way the nonconformists could help to bring in popery was described by Mr Bohun in a sermon preached, significantly, on 5 November 1682. He feared that the dissenters might 'bring us againe into that corrupt religion, by provoking God to take away the light we have so long abused'.[59]

Tory propagandists went so far as to suggest that the protestant nonconformists were working in deliberate alliance with the pope. One pamphlet

---

[55] *Heraclitus Ridens*, nos. 2, 4.
[56] *Mad-Men's Hospital*, in Thompson, ed., *Poems*, p. 59.
[57] *Loyal Protestant Intelligence*, no. 104.
[58] *Loyal Protestant Intelligence*, no. 97; *Heraclitus Ridens*, no. 7. Cf. [J. Nalson], *Foxes and Fire-Brands; Or, A Specimen of the Danger and Harmony of Popery and Separation* (1680), preface.
[59] Evelyn, *Diary*, IV, 295.

showed the pope encouraging a fanatic to raise 'loud cries of Popery' as the best way to destroy the Church of England.[60] A similar point was made by a print which shows a double-headed man, one head wearing a jesuit's, the other a presbyterian's, cap, who is painting out the royal arms and substituting those of the commonwealth. He is exclaiming, 'we will Reform both Church and State'. The pope is shown removing the crown and saying, 'then rail at me at your old rate'.[61] The frontispiece to Nalson's *Impartial Collection* shows a two-headed figure, half puritan, half papist, at whose feet lie not only the symbols of anglicanism, but also the crown and the royal arms.[62] One manuscript poem warned Charles:

> Papist, and Presbyter boeth combine, ...
> To robb you of your Crowne, and to destroy
> With thee our Lives, Religion, Liberty.
> Rome, and Geneva boeth strive to pull downe
> The envy'd Mitre, and Imperial Crowne.[63]

In a sermon delivered in September 1683, in the aftermath of the Rye House revelations, William Sherlock examined the nonconformist demand for toleration. He argued that if it were to be granted for religious reasons alone, it should be extended to catholics as well, although dissenters did not advocate this:

I believe Popery to be a very corrupt Religion ... but yet I am so profest an enemy to Popery, that I abhor that Popish principle of persecuting men meerly for Religions sake, which can no more be justified in Protestants against Papists, than in Papists against Protestants.

But the need for persecution was political, to prevent seditious and treasonous activities which might threaten the security of the government.[64] Here the dissenters had shown themselves worse than the catholics. For the latter tried and failed to murder a monarch; the nonconformists actually succeeded. This argument was used to justify why the courts decided to act against the nonconformists in the 1680s. In December 1682 the grand jury of the hundred of Ossulston, which comprised urban Middlesex to the west of the City, made the following statement:

We present as Our Opinion That Popery, and Phanaticism, are equally dangerous to the Government by Law Established. The Papists, ever since the Reformation,

---

[60] *Dialogue Between the Pope and a Phanatick*, pp. 10, 12.
[61] 'The Visions of Thorough Reformation', frontispiece to E. Pettit, *Visions of the Reformation: Or, A Discovery of the Follies and Villanies that have been Practised in Popish and Fanatical Thorough Reformations, since the Reformation of the Church of England* (1683); *BM Prints*, no. 1126. See print 8.
[62] 'Britannia Mourning', frontispiece to Nalson, *Impartial Collection*, I; *BM Prints*, no. 1122. See print 7.
[63] Bodl. Lib., Don b.8, p. 595, 'Haile, Mighty Charles'.
[64] Sherlock, *Seasonable Reflections*, pp. 15–16.

'Visions of Thorough Reformation' (1683)

'Britannia Mourning the Execution of Charles I' (1682)

have Plotted and Continued many Designs against this Kingdome, but secretly, not by Appearance of open Force; but by God's Providence, and the Wisdome of the Government, they have been always disappointed. The Phanaticks made but one Attempt, and with a High Hand raised a Rebellion, Murdered the Best of Kings, many of the Loyal Nobility and Gentry, Tooke away their Estates, Laid aside the Monarchy, Destroyed the Church, and, for almost Twenty Yeares, excercised Arbitrary and Tyrannical Government against Law.[65]

The same charge was repeated time and again: 'the Papists they would Kill the King, but the Fanaticks did';[66] 'What is term'd Popery? To Depose a King. What's true Presbytery? To Act the Thing'.[67] Both presbyterians and jesuits shared 'the Self-same Treasonable mind'.[68]

The comparison between nonconformists and catholics could be stretched back to the Reformation. For the resistance theories of the radical calvinists, argued the tories, were derived from catholic political thought – the conciliarists, radical Thomists, jesuits – and from the pope's claim to be able to depose kings.[69] Issue no. 5 of *Heraclitus Ridens* carried an advertisement for a print of Pope Gregory the thirteenth, shaking hands with John Knox, with the inscription 'Agreed in the main, that Heretical Kings may be Excommunicated, Deposed and Murthered'. It also described another print, showing Mariana the jesuit and Buchanan the presbyterian as 'Concordia Discors'. In a sermon of 1683 on the anniversary of Charles I's execution, Edward Pelling cited a number of whig tracts which argued that 'the King's whole Power is derived from the People; that He is such a Trustee and Servant as may be called to Account', and the kings 'unfaithfull to their trust' might be deposed, and explained that 'Originally these Doctrines were taught by Mariana, by Bellarmine, by Azorius, and divers Jesuites more.'[70] The argument that the nonconformists had learnt their regicidal principles from the catholics was a theme common to lengthier and more philosophical tracts of the exclusion crisis, it simply being, as one pamphleteer reminds us, a popularization of Dr Stillingfleet's position.[71]

[65] GLRO, MJ/SBB/401, p. 42; *Presentment of the Grand Jury of . . . Ossulston; CSPD, 1682*, p. 534.
[66] *Downfall of the Good Old Cause*, in Thompson, ed., *Songs*, p. 13.
[67] *Interrogatories; Or, A Dialogue Between Whig and Tory* (1681), in Thompson, ed., *Poems*, p. 221.
[68] Sir J. Denham, *The True Presbyterian Without Disguise; Or, A Character of a Presbyterian's Ways and Actions* (1680), p. 2.
[69] Cf. Q. Skinner, *The Foundations of Modern Political Thought* (2 vols., Cambridge, 1978), II, Part 3; Q. Skinner, 'The Origins of the Calvinist Theory of Revolution', in Malament, ed., *After the Reformation*, pp. 309–30.
[70] E. Pelling, *A Sermon Preached on the Anniversary of that Most Execrable Murder of K. Charles the First, Royal Martyr* (1682/3), pp. 12–14.
[71] *The Way of Peace* (1680), p. 7. See also: E. Stillingfleet, *A Discourse Of the Idolatry Practised in the Church of Rome* (1671), pp. 343–50; J. N. Figgis, *The Divine Right of Kings* (Cambridge, 1914), pp. 185–9; Goldie, 'Locke', pp. 71–3.

THE ATTACK ON WHIG HEROES

It is possible to identify a number of individuals who, during the exclusion crisis, personified the struggle against catholicism. Not only had the whigs appealed to the popular cult surrounding Elizabeth, they had also sought to exploit the martyrdom of Godfrey, whilst those most active in pursuing the Plot, whether informers, such as Oates, or politicians, such as Shaftesbury, soon came to be seen as the nation's defenders against the popish threat. Tory propagandists saw the need to prevent the charisma surrounding such figures from working in a whig direction.

Manipulation of the popular legend surrounding Queen Elizabeth had proved extremely useful in aligning popular sentiment behind the whigs, and so regaining her for toryism could be of crucial significance. But once the whigs had been firmly identified with nonconformity, this might not be too difficult, for Good Queen Bess had been no lover of radical puritanism. *Heraclitus Ridens* asked if Elizabeth 'was not a Tory and Tantivy Queen, for making such humming Laws against Dissenting Protestants?'[72] A few issues earlier the same paper asked 'whether Q. Eliz. and the Parliament that made the Statute of 35. of Her Reign, were True Protestants, or whether they must not be roasted as Abhorrers the next seventeenth of November'.[73] Elsewhere the whigs were reminded that Queen Elizabeth thought unordained and unlicensed preaching a usurpation: 'was this Tyranny in Queen Elizabeth, or a wise and just Defence of the Protestant Religion'.[74] Attempts were also made to regain the martyr of the Plot, Sir Edmundbury Godfrey, for the tories. Being a justice of the peace, responsible for keeping order in Middlesex, he would surely have been alarmed at the rabble-rousing tactics of the whigs, fearful, as one poem put it, of 'our Disobedience to a Prince', and the possibility of another civil war.[75]

The duke of Monmouth was another figure the tories had to cope with. Some tracts did try to discredit him for his disloyalty as a son, and others for a republicanism which he had supposedly learnt from Algernon Sidney, although such arguments were most commonly adopted after Monmouth's alleged involvement in the Rye House Plot of 1683.[76] Before then, many

---

[72] *Heraclitus Ridens*, no. 10.
[73] Ibid., no. 3.
[74] [Nalson], *Foxes and Firebrands*, p. 11. Cf. *The Riddle of the Roundhead* (1681), in Thompson, ed., *Songs*, p. 16.
[75] *The Last Speech of Sir Edmundbury Godfrey's Ghost* [ND], in Thompson, ed., *Poems*, p. 322.
[76] *The Conspiracy; Or, The Discovery of the Fanatick Plot* (1683), in Thompson, ed., *Songs*, p. 4; Earl of Roscomman, *The Ghost of Tom Ross to His Pupil the Duke of Monmouth* (1680), in *POAS*, II, 249–52; *The King's Answer* (1680), in ibid., pp. 255–6; *Tom Ross's Ghost to his Pupil* (1683), in Thompson, ed., *Poems*, p. 24.

tory writers were more circumspect, appreciating the tremendous popular appeal of Monmouth, and realizing the advantage of trying to win him back. Monmouth's dilly-dallying between the whigs and the Court and, in particular, his several attempts to beg his father's mercy in the early 1680s, must have given the tories extra hope here. A two page tract was written in 1681 inviting Monmouth back to loyalty: 'So high you were Exalted, that nothing but a Crown could make you higher ... above all, you had the hearts of the People, and the Heart of Your Royal Father'. But now the devil had turned Monmouth, and Shaftesbury was 'pouring poison in the Ears of Poor Young Absalom'. The author asked Monmouth to forsake the devil, so that 'we shall see Monmouth as Great as ever ... At your Return, the Troops of the Ungodly Brethren shall be broken in Pieces, the Fury of the Giddy-headed Mobile shall be allayed, and the Enemies of the Crown laid Prostrate at the Feet of Majesty.'[77]

Tory propaganda tried to convince Monmouth's supporters that the whigs were not supporting his true interests. In February 1681 *Heraclitus Ridens* asked whether those

who now take the Insolent Liberty to make a Property of his Grace the D. of M. do not intend to serve him as they did Liberty and Property in the late Rebellious Reformation, which were the two first things which they cryed up, and the two first things which they pulled down.[78]

Another tract put these words into a fanatic's mouth, denying any genuine whig support for Monmouth:

No truly. We know the Natural Sons of Princes are begotten in an Arbitrary way, against the Proceedings of Law and Property, and therefore they are commonly born with an unhappy Inclination to unlimited Government; and it is not Empire, but Commonwealth that we are desiring.[79]

Other poems regretted how young Perkin, the 'dull mistaken fool', was being manipulated by the whigs who would discard him once they had achieved their ends.[80]

Those heroes the tories did not wish to reclaim, they sought to discredit. Of all the whig champions against popery, more was written about the earl of Shaftesbury than any other. He was represented as a turncoat, a traitor, a machiavellian politician, an agent of the devil and leader of the

---

[77] *A Seasonable Invitation for Monmouth to Return to Court* (1681), pp. 1–2.
[78] *Heraclitus Ridens*, no. 3.
[79] *Second Dialogue Between the Pope and a Phanatick, Concerning Affairs in England* (1681), p. 11.
[80] *Riddle of the Roundhead*, in Thompson, ed., *Songs*, p. 15; [Mrs J. Philips], *Advice to His Grace* [1681–2], in Thompson, ed., *Poems*, pp. 128–9. Cf. the discussion in Clifton, *Last Popular Rebellion*, pp. 133–4.

rabble.[81] Shaftesbury was accused of having invented the Popish Plot.[82] One poem put the following words into his mouth: 'On top of the Monument let my Head Stand,/Itself a Monument, where first began/The Flame that has endanger'd all the Land.'[83] He was 'that worm of Reformation/Who of Common Wealths has Laid Foundation'.[84] Not least of Shaftesbury's treachery, according to the tories, was his association with presbyterianism: 'I leave old Baxter my invenom'd Teeth,/To Bite and poison all the Bishops with.'[85] His physical disabilities, especially the tap inserted by Dr John Locke to drain fluid from his stomach ulcer, were mocked to make political points. One poem recalled how '... His Belly carries still a Tap,/Through which black Treason, all its dregs doth strain/At once, both Excrements of Guts and Brain'.[86] Another poem told how 'all his Imps drank Venom from his side:/His word was (then He out his Tap did pluck,)/Come my young Pugs of Treason, come and suck'.[87]

Most of those who were associated with promoting the exclusionist cause were vilified in the tory press. The Popish Plot informers, Oates, Bedloe and Tonge, were all condemned for their alleged perjury.[88] Often the attack was of a highly personal nature, tory propagandists engaging in a deliberate policy of character assassination. City MP Sir Thomas Player was charged with having had associations with the infamous London bawd, Mrs Cresswell.[89] Thompson described the author of the *Weekly Pacquet* as 'Monkey Care (so unlike Mankind, that an Indictment is preferred against his Wife at the Old-Baily for Bestiality, where he is to prove what species he is of)'.[90] Whig publishers Francis Smith and Benjamin Harris both came under attack for their alleged sexual immorality. Sometimes these government libels

---

[81] See, in particular, *Let Oliver Now Be Forgotten* [ND], in Thompson, ed., *Songs*, pp. 1–3; *The Recovery* [1682], in Thompson, ed., *Poems*, p. 33; *Tony's Soliloquies* [ND], in ibid., pp. 60–2; [J. Dean], *The Badger and the Fox-Trap; Or, A Satyr upon Satyrs* [1681], in ibid., pp. 62–78; *The Polititian's Downfall; Or, Potapski's Arrival in the Netherlands* (1684), in ibid., pp. 80–6.

[82] *Tony's Soliloquies*, in Thompson, ed., *Poems*, p. 62.

[83] *The Last Will and Testament of Anthony, King of Poland* (1682), in ibid., p. 197.

[84] *Treason Unmasqued; Or, Truth Brought to Light* (1681).

[85] *Last Will and Testament*, in Thompson, ed., *Poems*, p. 197. *Let Oliver*, in Thompson, ed., *Songs*, p. 1, sees Shaftesbury as the mouth of the presbyterians.

[86] *Sejanus; Or, The Popular Favorite now in his Solitude, and Sufferings* (1681), in Thompson, ed., *Poems*, pp. 16–17.

[87] *The Recovery*, ibid., p. 32.

[88] *A Dialogue Betwixt the Devil and the Ignoramus Salamanca Doctor* [1681], in Thompson, ed., *Poems*, pp. 120–3; *Titus Tell-Troth; Or, The Plot-Founder Confounded* (1682), in *Songs*, pp. 25–7; *The Compleat Swearing Master* (1682) in *POAS*, III, 3–8; [R. Duke], *Funeral Tears upon the Death of Captain William Bedloe* [1680], in Thompson, ed., *Poems*, pp. 42–4; *Poor Robin's Dream; Or, The Visions of Hell – Or, A Dialogue Between the Ghost of Bedloe and Tonge* (1681), in ibid., pp. 176–87.

[89] *London's Loyalty* (1679), in Thompson, ed., *Songs*, p. 80.

[90] *Loyal Protestant Intelligence*, no. 56.

carried a fraudulent whig imprint. For example, *The Leacherous Anabaptist* (1681), an attack on Smith, claimed to have been 'printed for B. Harris'.[91] Nonconformist ministers faced similar slurs. In September 1681, Thompson published an account of a certain dissenting minister who had picked up a prostitute in Moorfields, and recalled a report of two years earlier, that the same man 'had lain with two Wenches ten nights, at a Guinney a night; That he exercised one, whilst the other raised his Inclinations'.[92] In a sermon to the governors, boys, and maids of Bartholomew Hospital, an anglican preacher, 'forgetting Charity (the Usual Theme of those Sermons) Entertained the People with Invectives against Dissenters, and told them of a Presbyterian who had no less than fifty Bastards'.[93]

It was one thing for the tories to launch such an invective against the whigs; it was another to persuade people to believe it. The whigs were helped by the actuality of the Popish Plot. Whether there was any truth in Oates's revelations or not is irrelevant. It was how people reacted to it that counted. The tory charge that the whigs were really radical dissenters endangering the security of church and state required more substance to it than mere polemic to make it carry. Hence the need for the tories to provide evidence that a whig or nonconformist plot really existed.

The first attempt was the Meal Tub Plot. Leading London whig and member of the Green Ribbon Club, Sir Robert Peyton, was accused by Mr Gadbury and Mrs Cellier, the popish midwife, of saying that if the king were to die suddenly he would head 20,000 to resist York's title and establish a commonwealth.[94] Peyton was sent to the Tower in January 1680. Another member of the Green Ribbon Club, Colonel Mansell, had some forged papers related to a plot planted in his rooms.[95] The plot was laid at the hands of the Green Ribbon men and presbyterians in general, but it was soon revealed as a sham, and in the end was exploited more successfully by the whigs than the tories. Besides, Sir Robert Peyton had been expelled from the Green Ribbon Club the previous October for deserting to the Court.[96]

Throughout the exclusion crisis there were attempts to lay charges of seditious words against leading whigs. As early as October 1679 a man by the name of Ore swore that Titus Oates had declared 'it would never be well in England til the monarchy were elective'. No charge was brought, however, because another witness against Oates could not be found.[97] Lon-

---

[91] Crist, 'Francis Smith', pp. 188–9; Muddiman, *King's Journalist*, pp. 222–3.
[92] *Loyal Protestant Intelligence*, no. 52.
[93] *Impartial Protestant Mercury*, no. 48.
[94] *Hatt. Corr.*, I, 214; *True Domestick Intelligence*, no. 56.
[95] Luttrell, I, 23.
[96] Pepysian Library, Pepys Misc. VII, 475.
[97] *Hatt. Corr.*, I, 198.

don whig and member of the Green Ribbon Club Slingsby Bethell was accused in 1680 of having been of the view of 1649 that 'rather then the old king should have wanted an executioner, he would have done it himself'. Bethell brought a legal action against the man who made the accusation.[98] In 1681 baptist publisher Francis Smith was accused of saying he 'would never leave writing news till he had reduc'd this kingdome to a common wealth'.[99]

The year 1681 was notable for the charges laid against Stephen College, Sir John Rouse and the earl of Shaftesbury. All three were indicted for a supposed plot to seize the king when parliament met at Oxford, to force through the policy of exclusion and religious toleration, and to convert England into a republic. Shaftesbury was also accused of starting an 'Association' of protestants to protect themselves against the catholic threat. All three were originally tried at the Old Bailey, and their bills found *ignoramus*.[100] The fact that the London prosecutions were unsuccessful did not necessarily detract from their propaganda value. The whigs' ability to pack juries to secure favourable verdicts was well known. This was confirmed by College's retrial at Oxford, when he was found guilty. Likewise, Shaftesbury's release would not necessarily be regarded as proof of his innocence. It is often the case that an individual charged with some heinous crime finds it difficult to regain his public respect, even though he has cleared his name in a court of law. The fact that indictments were brought, the alleged offences widely publicized, and suspicion surrounded the way the verdicts were reached, could have been enough to discredit the whigs in many people's eyes. It was also alleged that College had said:

the People of England only made an idol of the Fool the Duke of Monmouth, on purpose to destroy the King and his Interest in England; for the True Protestants of England were all unanimously resolved, that the King, nor any of his Race, should ever rule over them.[101]

Again, the tories were trying to provide 'proof' that the whigs were not sincere in advocating Monmouth's position.

Whilst Shaftesbury was in the Tower, in the summer of 1681, some of his associates were reportedly plotting to release him and also to destroy the government of the Stuarts. An army of 25,000 men was to be mobilized against the king, and in London the 'rabble' was to be raised. Wilson, one of the chief suspects, was accused of planning to fire the City of London in several places, and to lay the blame on the papists.[102] The list of accusations

---

[98] Luttrell, I, 49, 187.
[99] Ibid., p. 75.
[100] CLRO, Sessions File, July 1681, ind. of College (O + T); ibid., October 1681, ind. of Rouse (O + T); ind. of Shaftesbury (O + T); Haley, *Shaftesbury*, ch. 25.
[101] *Loyal Protestant Intelligence*, no. 49.
[102] PRO, SP 29/417, no. 19; BL, Stowe MS 186, fols. 48–50.

against leading whigs can be extended. Green Ribbon clubber Lord Howard of Escrick was imprisoned in the Tower in 1681 for words against the king and duke of York.[103] In August 1681 Colonel Dering, whig MP for Kent at the Oxford parliament, was accused of words against the monarchy and against episcopacy.[104]

The revelations of the Rye House Plot in the summer of 1683, an alleged whig and nonconformist conspiracy against both Charles and James, seemed to provide final confirmation of the whig threat. Tory publicists naturally exploited this to the full. So too did the anglican clergy. September 9th was established as a day of thanksgiving for deliverance from the plot, and there were innumerable sermons preached that day inveighing against the regicidal principles of the dissenters. But the damage to the whigs had been done before Rye House; indeed, the exaggerated and often fabricated evidence about this conspiracy was only believed because it confirmed existing assumptions about whig rebelliousness emphasized by tory propaganda.[105]

THE TORY ALTERNATIVE

The tories had a very different image of the head of state to the whigs. For them the king was 'Gods Servant, not the Peoples Slave'.[106] One poem exclaimed 'How Great is Majesty, and how August?/How God-like'.[107] The house of commons, in attempting to decide the succession, tory propagandists argued, was attempting to usurp the powers of God.[108] Because the tories were critical of the parliamentary movement for exclusion, and because the house of commons wished to exclude York, it might be inferred that the tories were in favour of the forces working towards absolutism at this time. They could at times be fierce in their criticism of the house of commons. One verse said it was the aim of this house to make the king their slave.[109] Tories also argued that people's 'Possessions and Enjoyments' sprung solely from the good will of the monarch.[110] If we look at L'Estrange's print, the victims of the 'Committee' include not only the king, but also Laud and Strafford, the architects of Charles I's personal rule. But L'Estrange's imagery does not necessarily mean that the tories cherished a return to the regime of the 1630s. What is being presented is an indictment of

---

[103] *CSPD, 1680–1*, p. 556.
[104] PRO, SP 29/416, no. 92.
[105] Jones, *Country and Court*, p. 223.
[106] *The Parliament Dissolv'd at Oxford, March 28, 1681* (1681), in Thompson, ed., *Poems*, p. 29.
[107] *The Recovery*, in ibid., p. 35. Cf. *The Charter*, in ibid., p. 149.
[108] *Parliament Dissolv'd at Oxford*, in ibid., p. 29.
[109] BL, Add. MS 29,497, fol. 4.
[110] *An Heroick Poem on Her Highness the Lady Ann's Voyage into Scotland; With a Little Digression Upon the Times* (1681), in Thompson, ed., *Poems*, p. 266.

the type of government which followed on the execution of these three men.[111]

As already seen, the tories in fact portrayed themselves as defenders of the liberties guaranteed by Magna Carta. They were not anti-parliament. High anglicans had defended parliamentary power in print back in 1673, whilst the forerunners of the tory party in the 1670s, Danby's anglican interest, achieved their strength by working through a parliament which they dominated. The tory complaint was against parliaments controlled by the whigs, and what they wanted was not no parliaments at all, but a parliament in tory hands. In July 1679, shortly after the dissolution of the first exclusion parliament, the tory John Verney wrote to Sir Edmund Verney 'I hope the next will prove neither Popish or Phanatical, but the true medium betwixt both, an honest Church of England Parliament.'[112] In April 1681 the author of *Heraclitus Ridens* could still write 'I hope we shall have a Parliament yet will heal all, and take care to secure the foundations of the Government from the attempts both of Popish and Protestant Jesuits.'[113] Their ideal, it might be suggested, came again in 1685.

The tories, by definition, stood for the legitimate succession, but one must ask how their support for York was reconciled with their professed anti-catholicism. It could be argued that a defence of hereditary succession was running little risk, since James had no son, was not likely to outlive his brother by many years and the next heir was a protestant. Yet the next heir was married to a calvinist, equally as unpalatable to the tories as a catholic. The marriage of princess Anne to the protestant prince George of Denmark in 1683 gave some tories hope here. There was now the prospect of an eventual protestant succession deriving from the anglican Anne Stuart.[114]

To Nathaniel Thompson, at least, the prospect of a line of successors deriving from the catholic York aroused no fears at all. When it was confirmed that the duchess of York was with child in February 1682, he claimed this was 'to the great Joy and Happiness of all True English-men; and we hope it will prove a Son, who (if it please God he survive His Majesty) may many years hence succeed in the English Throne, and cut off all the vain hopes of Ambitious Pretenders'.[115]

Yet most people did not support York because they harboured catholic sympathies. Many thought he would not promote catholicism. One tract claimed that he might desert Rome's cause, and if he became king, he 'would

---

[111] L'Estrange, *The Committee; BM Prints*, no. 1080. See print 6.
[112] *HMC, 7th Report*, p. 473.
[113] *Heraclitus Ridens*, no. 13.
[114] *A New Song on the Arrival of Prince George and his Intermarriage with the Lady Anne* (1683), in Thompson, ed., *Songs*, pp. 23–4.
[115] *Loyal Protestant Intelligence*, no. 113.

never have render'd his short Reign uneasie, by removing the boundaries of an establish'd Religion and Government, but would have thought himself oblig'd, in Generosity, to have been Defender of that Faith, and of that People, who had never given him the least disquiet'.[116] A sequel to this tract was later to claim that the duke of York was so fond of his brother, that if Charles were assassinated by catholics, he would turn protestant and massacre all papists in England.[117] Looking at the several songs and poems in defence of York in the collected editions by Thompson, one sees that the question of James's catholicism was usually ignored by tory propagandists. Instead, they stressed the fact that York was legitimate, unlike Monmouth, and that he had a right to the crown which could not be denied him.[118] It was ironic, tory publicists argued, with all the whigs' talk about laws and rights, that they 'would make a Law against the Law' and deny 'Great York ... his Right'.[119]

The tories tried to win further support for York by appealing to xenophobic and patriotic sentiments. After all, York was a 'great Hero of loud Fames First Rate', there being no braver man than 'our Great Duke of York'.[120] He had 'oft for haughty England fought', showing himself to be a successful naval commander, in particular in the wars against the Dutch.[121] Such arguments were a counter to the whig attempts to exploit the military achievements of the duke of Monmouth.

Because the tories set themselves up as the champions of order and the traditional hierarchy, and of the propertied against the propertyless, it might be thought that their arguments must have held little attraction for the lower classes. Whilst the anti-populist streak in tory propaganda might be valuable in works aimed at the elite, was it not disfunctional in the sphere of mass propaganda? In fact, the tories were aware of the need to try and dissuade the poor or economically depressed classes from joining with the whigs. This they did by showing how little the whigs had to offer the lower

---

[116] *Second Dialogue Between a Pope and Phanatick*, pp. 10, 13.

[117] *A Third Dialogue Between the Pope and a Phanatick Concerning Affairs in England* (1684), pp. 8–9.

[118] *Old Jemmy* (1681), in Thompson, ed., *Songs*, p. 20; *London's Joy and Loyalty on His Royal Highness the Duke of York's Return from Scotland* (1682), in ibid., pp. 82–3.

[119] *The Whig's Down-fall*, in ibid., p. 10.

[120] *The Charter*, in Thompson, ed., *Poems*, p. 150; *Convert Scot*, in ibid., p. 53.

[121] *A Congratulatory Poem upon the Happy Arrival of His Royal Highness James Duke of York, at London, April 8th, 1682* (1682), in ibid., p. 251. See also: *A Panegyrick to His Royal Highness, Upon His Majesties Late Declaration* (1680); *To His Royal Highness, the Duke* [1679]; *To His Royal Highness the Duke, Upon His Arrival* [1679]; *To His Royal Highness the Duke of York, Upon His Return to the Care and Management of the Navy of England* [1684]; *A Welcome to His Royal Highness into the City, April the 20th, 1682* (1682); *A Farewell to His Royal Highness, James Duke of York, on His Voyage to Scotland, October 20, 1680* (1680); *The Duke's Welcom from Scotland to London* [ND]. All these poems can be found in Thompson, ed., *Poems*, pp. 243–65.

classes, who had fared very badly under the commonwealth.[122] As I mentioned in chapter three, there was an anglican vision of a 'natural' hierarchy which alone could work for everyone's interests. One tract denied that the tories were enemies to the common good of the people. Although it admitted that 'they are persuaded that the chief business of the People, is to mind their own vocations, obey their Superiors, pay their Tithes and their Taxes chearfully, and if occasion be, fight for the Glory and Honour of their Prince and the Church ...' it argued that only in this way would peace, plenty and happiness be brought to the people, whilst republicanism would bring confusion, ruin and slavery.[123] The tory press was, of course, quick to praise the London apprentices who demonstrated in support of the succession,[124] but even here the emphasis was on the submission of the lower orders. They were 'Brave Loyal Youths' because they 'Joyn'd Zeal to God with Duty to the King'.[125]

This leads me to the most obvious positive element in the tory propaganda, which incorporated everything else, the commitment to anglicanism. The tories argued that if the whigs were to be successful, the established Church of England would be undermined. In short, they raised the cry later to be associated with Dr Sacheverell, namely 'the danger the Church ... [was] in from Fanaticks'.[126] Judging from L'Estrange's vision of what whig success would bring, they clearly sought no middle ground, but were uncompromising in support of a fairly high anglicanism. In *The Committee*, L'Estrange defended not just religion in general terms (the committee is shown to have discarded the bible), but also the common prayer, the surplice, the canons, the apochrypha and the cross in baptism. These were the areas of dispute which had prevented the anglican church from becoming a broader establishment that comprehended the more moderate nonconformists. Laud was certainly championed. By linking the moderate nonconformists with the radical fanatics, and allowing the only alternative to be a fairly high anglicanism, this print presented a stark polarization to the view.[127]

THE PROPAGANDA WAR

Fierce competition between whigs and tories developed as they sought to win the people over to their rival ideologies. We find whig and tory hawkers working in the same neighbourhood trying to out-shout each other in the

---

[122] This is discussed in full in ch. 8.
[123] *Protestant Loyalty*, p. 7.
[124] For these demonstrations, see ch. 7.
[125] *An Answer to the Whiggish Poem on the Loyal Apprentices Feast* (1682).
[126] Misopappas, *Tory Plot*, p. 5.
[127] See print 6.

streets to ensure the appropriate type of literature was bought.[128] The struggle between the whig and tory propagandists grew so intense, that it became
the occasion of collective violence itself, leading literally to a propaganda
war. On 31 December 1679 the whig writer Henry Care was attacked at
his house by a crowd of 8 or 9 people. One called him 'dog and rogue',
broke his windows, and tried to enter the house, although the intruder
was frightened away when someone cried murder.[129] A threatening letter
was sent to whig publisher Richard Janeway in March 1682.[130] The author
of a tory play was cudgelled in St Martin-in-the-Fields whilst the performance
was going on.[131] Of the tories, Nathaniel Thompson seems to have suffered
most, and he frequently reported having been assaulted or threatened.[132]

The law courts also became a battle-ground for control over the circulation
of propaganda. Whig control of the shrievalty and hence also of the composition of London juries encouraged them to use the common law of seditious
libel against tory publicists. In October 1681 indictments were presented
at the Guildhall against Joanna Brome, Benjamin Tooke and Nathaniel
Thompson for publishing *The Observator, Heraclitus Ridens*, and *A Dialogue Betwixt the Devil and the Ignoramus Doctor* respectively. All three
had their cases removed to King's Bench by writs of *a certiorari*, where
they knew they would receive more favourable hearings.[133] Thompson in
particular became the target for whig legal recriminations. In June 1682
a jury found him guilty of publishing a tract where it was suggested that
Sir Edmundbury Godfrey had killed himself, and he was fined £100 and
ordered to stand in the pillory.[134] The government tried to control the whig
output by putting pressure on the Stationers' Company to enforce its own
by-laws regulating the publishing trade. In June 1681, by royal mandate,
six loyal stationers were added to the Court of Assistants to ensure tory
domination of this company. A complete purge of whig influence was
achieved in April 1684 with the *quo warranto* proceedings. But it was the
tories' regaining control of the shrievalty in the summer of 1682 which
really enabled the government to clamp down on the press. In December
1682 thirteen indictments were presented at the Guildhall to the new tory
jury for seditious libel or for printing without authority. All were returned
billa vera.[135] In this way, the publication of most whig newspapers was

---

128 *Protestant (Domestick) Intelligence*, no. 96.
129 *Domestick Intelligence*, no. 53.
130 *Impartial Protestant Mercury*, no. 99.
131 Morrice, I, 353.
132 *Loyal Protestant Intelligence*, nos. 79, 130, 133, 178.
133 CLRO, Sessions File, October 1681, inds.; PRO, KB 10/2, part 2.
134 *London Gazette*, no. 1729; *Loyal London Mercury*, no. 3; J. B. Williams, 'Nathaniel
     Thompson and the "Popish Plot"', *The Month*, 138 (1921), 31–7.
135 CLRO, Sessions File, December 1682.

stopped, and also some of the lesser tory ones. Although it was impossible to totally silence the press, by the end of the reign only small and weak voices remained.[136]

CONCLUSION

In this chapter I have argued that once the whigs were identified as nonconformists and republicans, it became possible for the tories to use some of the whig arguments against their authors. Whiggery is often supposed to have had such a strong base in the London area because it exploited fears of popery and tyranny and anxieties over the security of liberties and properties. Yet these same fears and anxieties could equally well lead to a tory position. The tory appeal, however, came from a different perspective, namely an anglican and anti-nonconformist one. To assess the impact the rival propaganda campaigns had on streets politics, it is necessary to turn to a consideration of crowd activity in London during the exclusion period.

[136] Crist, 'Francis Smith', ch. 6.

≪ 7 ≫

Crowd politics and exclusion

It has become a historiographical commonplace that the majority of the London population were whig in sympathy during the exclusion crisis.[1] The assumption is that given the prevalence of deep-seated anti-catholic prejudices, it was only natural for the mass of the people to support the whigs in their attempts to secure a protestant succession. Although Arthur Smith, in his unpublished thesis, acknowledged that demonstrations in support of the duke of York did occur, he dismissed these as a reflection of elite manipulation, rather than a genuine expression of the opinion of the people.[2] In this chapter I propose to challenge this orthodoxy. A detailed examination of seditious words, petitioning, and crowd unrest reveals that a basic split between whig and tory positions existed in the years after the Popish Plot scare.

This split reflected a fundamental divide in London political culture, generated by tensions which, as we have seen, were primarily of a religious character, centring around the issue of dissent. It is true that most Londoners had an intense hatred of everything associated with popery. But this shared hatred did not serve as a unifying force, smoothing over the tensions within English protestantism, since both anglicans and nonconformists used the rhetoric of anti-catholicism to justify their opposition to each other. Whig propaganda during the exclusion crisis, it has been shown, contained within it a distinct bias towards dissent. Tory polemicists were able to exploit this, arguing that the real popish threat came from the whigs and nonconformists. When we look at collective agitation during the exclusion period, we find that supporters of both the whigs and the tories were motivated by a desire to preserve the protestant monarchy against the popish threat. For most whigs this meant shifting the succession in favour of the duke of Monmouth. Although it would be wrong to suggest that all who supported the whigs were nonconformists, it is nevertheless clear that dissenters played

---

[1] J. Miller, *The Glorious Revolution* (1983), p. 2; Allen, 'Crown and Corporation', p. 203; Stevenson, *Popular Disturbances*, p. 53; J. Stevenson, ed., *London in the Age of Reform* (Oxford, 1977), p. xvi.

[2] Smith, 'London and the Crown', pp. 97, 150.

a prominent part in the agitation against the duke of York's succession. The tories' supporters, in contrast, defended the hereditary succession and defined themselves primarily in terms of anglican hostility towards nonconformists. Yet the tory position, also, was of an anti-catholic nature, since for tories any perceived threat to the monarchy and the Church of England was equated with popery.

Collective agitation during the exclusion period fulfilled two basic functions. I shall start by looking at crowds which were simply manifestations of public opinion, rituals designed to reveal to the rulers the wishes of the people. By exhibiting their anti-catholicism, hostility to the duke of York and support for the duke of Monmouth, whig groups sought to demonstrate to the government that the people wanted a change in the succession. No direct pressure was applied, and the tactic only stood a chance of success if the whigs truly did speak for the mass of the people. Tory rituals emerged in response in order to show that, on the contrary, large numbers of people remained loyal to the succession and were more worried by the whig and nonconformist challenge. I shall then examine the attempts to use collective agitation in a more coercive way, to influence government policy directly. In the period 1681–2 we find both whig and tory groups stating their preparedness to take action themselves, if necessary, in defence of their cause. In one aspect, this involved trying to suppress the crowd rituals of one's opponents. For the whigs, it also meant attempting to frustrate the tory attack on leading whigs and nonconformists after the Oxford parliament.

HOSTILITY TOWARDS THE DUKE OF YORK'S SUCCESSION

The whig exploitation of the Popish Plot produced a new intensity in street politics in the capital, as people sought to give expression to their anxieties about the catholic menace and their opposition to the duke of York's succession. The huge crowds that gathered to celebrate the burning of the pope on 17 November are usually singled out by historians as evidence of the anti-catholic fever which gripped the London populace at this time. There continued to be pageants on 5 November, although these tended to be smaller and more localized affairs, without the elaborate procession around London.[3]

Predictably, there are many examples of hostility towards the duke of York. The catholic heir could anticipate a rough reception whenever he made a public appearance in London. When, in January 1679, York came to try and deal with a fire that had broken out at the Temple, he had to

---

[3] *Domestick Intelligence*, no. 36; LC, MS 18,124, VI, fol. 292; HMC, *7th Report*, p. 477; *Hatt. Corr.*, I, 201; BL, Add. MS 25,361, fol. 46; HMC, *10th Report*, IV, 174.

leave for fear of the crowds which called him a popish dog.[4] He was similarly
jeered by hostile crowds in October that year, at the time of the Artillery
Company's feast.[5] Sedition cases reveal the types of reason why York was
so hated. A Shadwell mariner said 'the Duke of York is a Papist and this
is his Plott.'[6] Nonconformist Robert Humes from Stepney was charged with
saying in February 1683 'Popery is coming into this Kingdome, and if the
Duke of Yorke should succeede his brother, hee would be a worse popish
tyrant than ever Queene Mary was.'[7] In April 1685, just before James's
coronation, Elizabeth Bedbury, the wife of a shoemaker from Bishopsgate
without, supposedly believed that a great massacre of protestants would
follow within two or three days of the coronation.[8] These were the conclusions which anyone who had swallowed the whig propaganda was bound
to reach.

Although the whig leaders were ambiguous as to their preferred alternative
to York, most of their supporters at the grass-roots level seem to have wanted
the succession to pass to James, duke of Monmouth. His popularity is easily
explicable. The eldest illegitimate son of Charles II, and a favourite of the
king, there had been rumours from as early as 1662 that he was to be
made legitimate.[9] Monmouth was relatively young (he reached the age of
thirty in April 1679), attractive, and had already achieved success as a military commander. His talents were appropriately rewarded by his father.
In 1668, when still only 19, Monmouth had been made Captain of the
Life-Guards, and in 1678 he was created Captain-General of all the troops
and land forces in the country.[10] Monmouth was also conspicuous in his
protestantism. After the Test Act of 1673, partly aimed at the duke of York,
he made his qualification by taking the sacrament in St Martin-in-the-Fields,
Westminster.[11] During the exclusion crisis, he usually followed a return
to London with a visit to church, something commented upon in the whig
press.[12] In short, Monmouth was seen as the dashing, young, heroic and
protestant prince.[13]

---

[4] BL, Add. MS 25,358, fol. 139.
[5] Wood, *Life*, II, 466–7.
[6] GLRO, MJ/SR/1636, recs. 37 (to prosecute), 316; Jeaff., IV, 224.
[7] GLRO, MJ/SR/1633, rec. 220; ind. 3 (O + T); Jeaff., IV, 201. Robert Humes was indicted
     for recusancy in October 1683. See GLRO, MJ/SR/1636, ind. 79. Cf. *CSPD, 1682*, p.
     246, case of Caper.
[8] CLRO, Sessions File, January 1686, rec. 64, ind. of Bedbury.
[9] Pepys, *Diary*, III, 238; Clifton, *Last Popular Rebellion*, pp. 86–8.
[10] B. Bevan, *James, Duke of Monmouth* (1973), pp. 43, 73–4; C. Chenevix Trench, *The
     Western Rising: An Account of the Rebellion of James Scott, Duke of Monmouth* (1969),
     p. 66; Clifton, *Last Popular Rebellion*, pp. 93–4.
[11] GLRO, MR/RS/1/2, no. 218; Bevan, *Monmouth*, p. 73.
[12] *Protestant (Domestick) Intelligence*, no. 68; *True Protestant Mercury*, no. 19.
[13] For Monmouth in general, see Clifton, *Last Popular Rebellion*. A summary of why Mon-
     mouth was popular can be found on p. 124.

The majority of the exclusionist crowds were also Monmouth crowds. The festivities of 5 and 17 November were obvious occasions for championing the cause of 'the protestant duke'. For example, at the pope-burning of 17 November 1681 the crowd assembled at the large bonfire in Smithfield drank the healths of the king and the duke of Monmouth 'conjunctively'.[14] But most public expressions of support for Monmouth were more spontaneous, responding to immediate political developments rather than conforming to a particular calendar. The first example of public support for Monmouth can be found in November 1678. On the 9th, when exclusion was being discussed for the first time, Charles promised parliament he would assent to 'such reasonable bills as should be presented, to make them safe in the reign of any successor, so as they tend not to impeach the right of succession, nor the descent of the crown in the true line'. The news leaked out, but became distorted, 'some reporting it to be a resolution declared of choosing a Protestant successor, and in other places that the Duke of Monmouth was to succeed the King'. Bonfires burned in celebration throughout London, healths being drunk to the king, the earl of Shaftesbury and the duke of Monmouth.[15]

From this time onwards, Monmouth seemed to be able to attract large crowds of cheering supporters whenever he made a public appearance in the capital. When Monmouth dined with leading whigs at the Crown Tavern in Fleet Street in January 1681, hundreds of well-wishers came to the tavern, and cheered him as he left.[16] On 27 February 1681, the day after he had returned from a visit to Chichester, Monmouth went to church in St Martin-in-the-Fields, 'and the people expressed their joy to see him, Crying out, God Bless the Protestant Duke'.[17] In the heightened political atmosphere of 1682 it was virtually the case that Monmouth could not leave his residence in the Strand without attracting a crowd to cheer him on his way.[18]

Sometimes official ceremonies were perverted into a celebration of Monmouth. On 17 September 1679 the Court returned to Whitehall from Windsor, the king having just recovered from a severe bout of fever. The lord mayor gave an order that the churchwardens should arrange for the bells to be rung and organize bonfires for the evening, to express the City's joy at the king's recovery.[19] Although there was much genuine rejoicing at the king's return, at some bonfires people used the opportunity to drink the

---

[14] *HMC, 10th Report*, IV, 174; Furley, 'Pope-Burning Processions', p. 22.
[15] *HMC, Ormond*, NS IV, 470; LC, MS 18,124, VI, fol. 138; Jones, *First Whigs*, p. 26; Clifton, *Last Popular Rebellion*, pp. 109–10.
[16] *Protestant (Domestick) Intelligence*, no. 87.
[17] *True Protestant Mercury*, no. 19.
[18] Smith, 'London and the Crown', p. 117.
[19] CLRO, Journal 49, fol. 61; LC, MS 18,124, VI, fol. 272; *Domestick Intelligence*, no. 22.

duke of Monmouth's health, who was then under royal displeasure, having recently been ordered into exile by Charles II. It is probable that no affront was meant to the king, it having been rumoured that 'his Majesty had changed his mind, and the Duke of Monmouth was to stay in England'. The tory, John Verney, recalled how he was stopped at one bonfire and asked 'to drink the King's and the Duke's health', and at another 'asked for money to do it; but because I would not give them any, they cried out a Papist, a Papist'.[20]

Shortly afterwards Monmouth went to Holland, in accordance with his father's orders, but on the night of Thursday 27 November he surreptitiously slipped back into London. The news of his arrival was spread by the night watch, and before daybreak bonfires had been made in several places. The main celebrations took place on the following day. In many places the church bells were rung, and at St Alphage, London Wall, the churchwardens even contributed 1s 6d from the parish coffers towards the cost of a bonfire. At St Giles-in-the-Fields several flambeaus or torches were placed on top of the steeple. The guards at Whitehall lit fires to welcome back their commander. On the evening of the 28th, according to Charles Hatton, 'ther wase more bonnefires... then ever was since those for the restoration of his Majesty', a testimony to the amount of support which Monmouth enjoyed at this time. Hatton counted more than sixty along the Strand alone, between Temple Bar and Charing Cross. In addition to the efforts of the guards and the churchwardens, the people, or 'the rabble' as our sources describe them, developed their own techniques for sponsoring bonfires. Coaches were stopped, and their passengers made to cry out 'God Bless the Duke of Monmouth.' Some were forced out of their coaches before giving this salute, and several were 'offer'd kennel water', and told 'they must drinke the Duke's health in yt, or pay for better liquor'. Even the lord chancellor had his coach stopped, and was asked for money to drink Monmouth's health. When he 'spoke roughly' to the crowd, 'they answered him in the like language', so he gave them a shilling, which, they said, 'though 'twas so little, they'd have it out in ale'. Charles II was furious at Monmouth's uninvited return, and shortly afterwards Monmouth was stripped of most of his offices, command of the guards passing to Christopher, duke of Albemarle.[21]

The above examples illustrate how artificial it often is to try and distinguish between demonstrations that were organized and prompted from above, and those which were spontaneous and initiated from below. There are

[20] HMC, *7th Report*, p. 475; *Hatt. Corr.*, I, 195.
[21] *Domestick Intelligence*, no. 43; Guildhall Library, MS 1432/5; *Hatt. Corr.*, I, 203; HMC, *7th Report*, p. 478; LC, MS 18,124, VI, fol. 302; *CSPD, 1679–80*, p. 295; Evelyn, *Diary*, IV, 189; Jones, *First Whigs*, p. 114; Clifton, *Last Popular Rebellion*, pp. 115–16.

also ambiguities concerning the extent to which the activities of the whig crowds should properly be described as conservative or radical. On the one hand we find that support for Monmouth and Charles II was commonly linked, and most people probably saw Monmouth simply as an alternative, protestant successor, rather than someone who would initiate radical constitutional change. Sedition cases suggest that many saw Monmouth as the rightful 'heir to the Crown'.[22] In August 1682 ironmonger William Baker of Little Queen Street was charged with saying 'The Duke of Monmouth is as lawfully begotten as I am... and the Duke of York will never be King; we are all bound by our oaths to fight against Popery.'[23]

On the other hand, forcing the rich to dismount from their coaches and drink kennel water exhibited a lack of deference that would have been terrifying to most conservatives. Hostility expressed towards upper-class supporters of the catholic succession might easily assume overtones of class resentment. On 4 September 1682, according to Nathaniel Thompson, a 'Holding-forth Brother', returning home drunk that night, staggered into the path of a coach which only narrowly missed him. He therefore struck the horses and the coachman, crying out 'Tory, Arbitrary Power'. This prompted a crowd to gather, who proceeded to break the windows of the coach, and we are told that a cobbler shouted to the passenger, a 'Lady of Honour', that he was as good or better a man than her husband.[24] The story should be treated with suspicion, since our source, Nathaniel Thompson, was keen to suggest that the whig crowds were an ill-disciplined and levelling rabble. Even if this type of thing did happen, it is difficult to know whether the grievances were genuinely social or primarily political. Not only Monmouth, but other upper-class whigs, such as the earl of Shaftesbury, were customarily accorded all due deference by their supporters, whereas lower-class tories, as will be seen below, were equally likely to receive rough handling by whig crowds.

Sedition cases reveal a more critical attitude towards the monarchy, as might be expected. Yet even these suggest that initially criticism was more likely to be levelled against the king's ministers, rather than the king himself. In February 1681 Thomas Monckfield, a weaver from Petticoat Lane, was indicted for saying 'No Men but Rogues served the King.'[25] As the crisis progressed, and especially after the dissolution of the Oxford parliament – by which time it was clear that Charles himself was determined to protect the succession – the king increasingly became the target for seditious speeches. In August 1681 one John Baynes of Westminster was accused

[22] PRO, Assi 35, 126/6, ind. 34; GLRO, WJ/SR/1670, gaol calendar, committal of Ley.
[23] *CSPD, 1682*, p. 334.
[24] *Loyal Protestant Intelligence*, no. 204.
[25] CLRO, Sessions File, February 1681, rec. 33, ind.

of saying: 'That the King is a great Favourite of the Papists, that he perjured himself otherwise he would not have dissolved his Parliament at Oxford, and that he was sworne both in France and Spaine to maintaine the Papists religion here in England.'[26] In April of that year tailor John Groves, of St Martin-in-the-Fields, supposedly said 'the King was as great a Papist as the Duke of York, and I wonder the Parliament doth not chop off his head'.[27]

A certain egalitarian element can be detected in some of the crude statements which tainted the rulers with the sins of the common folk. Today many such opinions seem quite tame, but set against the traditional image of a king, the god-like nature of majesty, they probably had more powerful overtones.[28] Thomas Moore, a weaver from St Leonard's Shoreditch, apparently exclaimed that the king was a bastard. His 'proof' was that 'his mother was a Common Whore and lay with her fidlers, begott him, and that was the cause of his loveing musick soe well'.[29] Cutler Samuel Wright from New Street supposedly believed that 'the late old King was a Cuckold and that his Queen was a whore and that his children were all Jermins'.[30] Ann Fenney believed that she was as good a woman as Queen Catherine.[31] When James II became king, Maria Jefford thought he was only fit to kiss her arse,[32] framework-knitter Isaac Belchcraft believed himself 'as good a man as the King',[33] and Solomon Heath thought he himself should wear the crown of England.[34]

Extreme caution is needed when using the evidence of seditious words, since informations were often brought by paid spies, who knew how to exploit the sensibilities of the government. Thus in 1682 Constant Oates reported that a fifth monarchist, George Kettle, who was a victualler in Southwark, had said 'The King and all the Court Party had best look to themselves, For the people would not always bear with them', adding that the nonconformists and old Oliverian boys were arming against the king.[35] In September 1683, shortly after the revelations of the Rye House Plot, John Robinson, a mariner from Shadwell, was bound over for saying 'I

---

[26] GLRO, MJ/SBB/389, p. 59; GLRO, WJ/SR/1602, gaol calendar, committal of Baynes.

[27] GLRO, MJ/SR/1596, recs. 17 (to prosecute), 95, ign. ind.; Jeaff., IV, 153.

[28] This is what Scribner has termed desacralization – reducing someone from an elevated status to the mundane. See Scribner, 'Reformation', p. 324. The concept is adapted from M. M. Bakhtin, *Rabelais and His World*, trans. by H. Iswolsky (Cambridge, Massachusetts, 1968), p. 19.

[29] GLRO, MJ/SR/1633, ign. ind.; Jeaff., IV, 217–18.

[30] CLRO, Sessions File, October 1681, rec. 8, ind. of Wright.

[31] GLRO, MJ/SR/1591, rec. 40.

[32] CLRO, Sessions File, December 1685, ind. of Jefford.

[33] GLRO, MJ/SR/1678, rec. 181; Jeaff., IV, 298, who gives the name as 'Botchcraft'.

[34] CLRO, Sessions File, December 1681, rec. 26 (GD, to prosecute).

[35] BL, Stowe MS 186, fol. 45; PRO, SP 29/420, no. 6.

care not a fart for the King of England himselfe; my father was a soldier
to Oliver and fought against the King, and I would do the like if there
were occasion.'[36] Yet I can find no evidence that successful indictments
were brought against either of these two. And although sedition cases very
often reveal republican sentiments, crowds never made anti-monarchical
gestures. It will be seen below how whig groups always claimed that they
were acting out of loyalty to Charles II and the protestant monarchy.

To argue that most of the whigs' supporters were monarchists and not
republicans, however, is perhaps to miss the point, since the whigs clearly
had a different vision of monarchy from the tories. Because up until March
1681 all hope was placed in the possibility of passing a bill to exclude
York from the succession, the whig position became intimately involved
with a defence of parliament. Hence the choice of representatives was crucial.
On 7 October 1679, after the freemen of the City had returned four exclusionists to the coming parliament, there were bonfires in several parts to
celebrate the particular selection.[37] Hence also the frustration felt when
Charles II tried to stall the exclusionists by prematurely proroguing or dissolving parliament. The prorogation of 30 December 1678 supposedly
prompted John Tregoose, a salesman from Blackfriars, to say to a company
of drinking companions that 'if I had fiftie or three score thousand Men...
I would question him, or them, that prorogued them'.[38] Sedition cases suggest
that some people were aware of the constitutional implications of a shift
in the succession. Deborah Hawkins, of St Andrew's Holborn, supposedly
said in March 1685, shortly after York's accession, 'Hee is noe King but
an Elective King', and went on to express her support for Monmouth.[39]

The whig support for monarchy also contained within it a criticism of
the intolerant religious policies of the anglican establishment. At the pope-
burning procession of 17 November 1680 the crowd shouted 'No Popery,
God bless the King, Protestant Religion, The Church, and Dissenting Protestants, both whom God Unite'.[40] In November 1682 Thomas Ludlam from
St Giles-in-the-Fields argued that the Church of England, in alliance with
the papists, had been responsible for the execution of Charles I, 'and that
the Presbyterians had noe hand in itt, and that the Presbyterians were the
King's [Charles II's] only Friends, and that he was crowned a Presbyterian'.[41]
More will be said about the whig support for parliament and association

---

[36] GLRO, MJ/SR/1636, recs. 37 (to prosecute), 316; Jeaff., IV, 224.
[37] *Domestick Intelligence*, no. 28; Allen, 'Crown and Corporation', p. 106.
[38] CLRO, Sessions File, January 1679, rec. 3, ind. of Tregoose; CLRO, Sessions Papers,
January 1679, information of Brooke. For the prorogation, see: Haley, *Shaftesbury*, p.
494; Jones, *Country and Court*, p. 204.
[39] GLRO, MJ/SR/1682, ind. 2 (O + T); Jeaff., IV, 285.
[40] *Solemn Mock Procession of ... 1680*, broadside.
[41] GLRO, MJ/SR/1619, recs. 10 (to prosecute), 65, ind. 19; Jeaff., IV, 187.

with the cause of dissent a little later. However, it is impossible to explore fully the contours of the whig position unless it is realized that as the crisis progressed whig crowds came to define themselves increasingly in terms of opposition to an emerging tory presence in the streets. It is thus first necessary to consider the nature of the support in London for the duke of York's succession.

THE EMERGENCE OF AN ANTI-EXCLUSIONIST POSITION

Initially most people believed in the Popish Plot, and the wave of anti-catholic hysteria which swept the country in late 1678 and early 1679 probably reflected a genuine consensus. But it was difficult to maintain this level of excitement for long, and with time the Plot tended to die a natural death, although the fears aroused by it lasted longest in London.[42] In the spring of 1680 L'Estrange wrote that 'the Nation is nothing near so hott upon the business now, as they were Ten or Twelve months agoe: and they grow still cooler and cooler, methinks, every day'.[43] The moderates among the upper classes became more concerned with the whig exploitation of the Plot, causing them to rally behind the crown in defence of the succession. But it would be wrong to assume that the tories just won back the elite, since this process of redefinition was going on at all levels of London society. It is true that the liverymen remained predominantly whig, as evidenced by their repeated choice of four whig MPs for the City for the three exclusion parliaments and their preference for whig sheriffs. Yet this is largely explicable in terms of the power structures of the livery companies, which were controlled by the courts of assistants, self-perpetuating oligarchies which for most companies were dominated by whigs. Moreover, the tory minority amongst the liverymen was a high one at some 40 per cent, and the tories seem to have had as much support amongst the lesser companies as they had in the twelve great companies.[44]

A better sense of the mood of the City is achieved by looking at the much wider municipal electorate, the 15,000 or so freemen who voted in the common council elections. The freemen certainly seem to have been changing their allegiances. The whigs held a narrow majority on the common council at the beginning of the exclusion crisis; they lost this at the elections of December 1680, although if we exclude the non-elected aldermen, who were predominantly tory, the whigs won the election by five seats. In December 1681 there was a further reaction, the tories now clearly dominant among the electorate, and their majority increased still further the following year, although this time it was in large part due to the fact that care was

---

[42] Miller, *Popery and Politics*, pp. 154, 161.
[43] L'Estrange, *Citt and Bumpkin, The Second Part*, p. 5.
[44] Smith, 'London and the Crown', pp. 38, 218, 341–2, 344–5.

taken to prevent nonconformists from voting. The evidence shows that the tories were winning votes from the poorer freemen as well as the more prosperous.[45] A study of London's citizen's militia, the trained bands, also reflects the rise and decline of the general belief in the Popish Plot. By 1681–2 they were acting as keenly against the whig crowds as they had earlier against the papists. The bands were controlled by the tory-dominated lieutenancy, who could ensure the tory credentials of the officer corps. Yet there is little evidence of disaffection amongst the rank and file, the political complexion of whom it was less easy to manipulate.[46]

We can also detect growing support for the tory position at the level of street politics. A number of sedition cases were brought before the London courts during the exclusion crisis which reflect views hostile towards the exclusionists. Some of these involved catholics indicted for seditious words which tended to 'prove' the reality of the Popish Plot. Other cases reveal attempts by catholics to defend themselves against what they considered a sham plot, one man stating that all persons convicted in the Plot 'were by false and mendacious oaths'.[47] Yet a number of the anti-whig speeches do not seem to have been pro-catholic. In April 1679 one James Douglas supposedly said 'that the Duke of Monmouth was illegitimate, And he hoped no bastard would reign here'.[48] In January 1681 one Matthew Michael said 'the duke of Monmouth was a bastard and his mother a whore'. Michael also cursed the parliament for being rogues, and in the same month one Edward Rawlins spoke out against the exclusionist house of commons.[49] One Joseph Pagett, discussing a vote of the house of commons which declared the duke of York to be a papist and that his hope of coming to the throne gave the Popish plotters great hopes, dismissed it as 'a damned lye'.[50] Sometimes seditious words were uttered in an explicitly anglican context. In December 1680, one Michael Benstead, of St Giles-in-the-Fields, was accused of saying 'the lord Stafford was cheated out of his life, and that ere long, noe bishopps should weare lawne sleeves, nor the King's armes stand in

---

[45] Allen, 'Crown and Corporation', pp. 197–9; Smith, 'London and the Crown', pp. 24, 129, 211–12, 218–19, and appendix tables 4, 5.

[46] Allen, 'Trained Bands', pp. 288, 302; Smith, 'London and the Crown', p. 228.

[47] CLRO, Sessions File, January 1681, ind. of Mazott; *London Sessions Records, 1605–1685*, ed. Dom H. Bowler (1943), pp. 315–16; *True Protestant Mercury*, no. 18.

[48] CLRO, Sessions File, April 1679, rec. 27 (GD); *London Sessions Records*, pp. 234–5. It should be remembered that this Catholic Record Society publication includes 'all the records which have any bearing on the history of the Plot, even such as do not immediately concern catholics', including the charges levelled against those who were 'so rash as to question the reality of the Plot'. See ibid., pp. liv, lix. Unless explicitly stated, there is no reason to assume an author of seditious words who appears in this source was a catholic.

[49] CLRO, Sessions File, January 1681, recs. 21, 26.

[50] Ibid., ind. of Pagett.

any churches'.[51] The sedition cases of Edward Sing, Peter Lamporte and John Winde expressed the opinion that Sir Edmundbury Godfrey had been murdered by presbyterians.[52]

Individual expressions of hostility to exclusion were not enough, since the whigs had laid claim to speak for the whole of London through their exploitation of crowd rituals. Tory supporters therefore saw it necessary to organize their own public rituals, to show that the whigs did not monopolize people's sympathies. A planned demonstration for 29 May 1680 serves as a paradigm for the popular tory position. In the spring a group of apprentices from the Strand area, St Martin-in-the-Fields, Westminster, began meeting in a house in Chancery Lane to organize a demonstration for the king's birthday as a deliberate counter to the first exclusionist pope-burning of the previous November. They clearly identified the whigs as republicans and nonconformists, since they proposed to burn effigies of the Rump and Oliver Cromwell, and afterwards pull down all conventicles and bawdy houses in London and Westminster. One of those involved later confessed that they 'had agreed among themselves to burne the Rump as the phanaticks had done the Pope'. The apprentices organized themselves in militaristic fashion. Thomas Alford, a 22-year-old bell-founder's apprentice, was to be their captain, whilst a cobbler's apprentice was to be lieutenant and an oilman's apprentice was to be ensign.

The apprentices accepted the reality of the Popish Plot, but also seem to have believed Mrs Cellier's allegations of the previous autumn that there was a presbyterian plot against the monarchy. At one meeting, Captain Tom delivered this speech to a group of his followers:

Gentlemen and Brethren, there hath been of late 2 Horrid Plots; the one by the Papists, and the other by the Presbyterians: that of the Papists is pretty well over, but the Presbyterians is not; We are young men and therefore the strength of the Nation, and on whom the Presbyterians much depend, but to show them to the contrary, we will once again burn the Rump and stand so for our King and his Government, and Protestant Religion, as it is now established by Law; and we'l drink the Kings Good Health to the confusion of both Papists and Presbyterians.

The demonstration never took place. On Sunday 21 March 1680, whig JP Sir William Waller received an anonymous letter informing him of the design, and on the following day a number of those involved were arrested on a charge of high treason, for conspiring to levy war against the king.[53]

---

[51] GLRO, MJ/SBB/380, p. 52.
[52] CLRO, Sessions File, February 1681, rec. 25 (GD); August 1681, rec. 10 (GD), ind. of Lamporte; September 1682, rec. 18, ind. of Winde; *London Sessions Records*, pp. 320, 337–9, 356–7.
[53] *Mercurius Civicus*, 24 March 1680; LC, MS 18,124, VII, fols. 34, 35; *CSPD, 1679–80*, p. 422; Luttrell, I, 38; *Protestant (Domestick) Intelligence*, no. 76.

Appropriate preventative measures were taken. The Privy Council issued an order prohibiting bonfires and fireworks on 29 May, the lord mayor sent instructions to all masters to make sure that their apprentices did not get involved in any such conspiracies and tumults, and the apprentices from the Strand area that were of age were required to take oaths of allegiance.[54] It is therefore difficult to assess how much support this type of action would have won. Under examination it was revealed that the apprentices had listed their supporters in two rolls, but our sources demonstrate just how inaccurate contemporary reporting of numbers could be. According to one account the apprentices confessed that 7–8,000 were listed; another says the enquiry revealed that 4–5,000 were involved; whilst a third states that Alford confessed to having listed only 'several hundreds'. By the time the Venetian ambassador heard of the episode, the number who were going to burn the Rump had risen to 30–40,000, clearly a wild exaggeration.[55] When the apprentices were in prison they were visited by one John Climps, who assured them that 'if they were not released by the Councel that Night, 5 or 6 thousand prentices would come out of the City and set them free'. However, no such rising happened, even though the apprentices were not to be released on bail until mid-April, and Climps, for his pains, was committed to the Gatehouse.[56]

Critics believed that the apprentices had been 'animated and encouraged by some persons to this rising'. It was reported that under examination Alford admitted that he had told his associates that 'he could command 3 or 400 pounds... and that the Guards [now under the command of the duke of Albemarle] would join with them', and that the earl of Ossory 'would assist them and encourage them in it'. Our source describes this as a ridiculous allegation, 'yet is made great use of by some persons who would maliciously lay an aspersion on his lordship'.[57] The whig press won greatest mileage from arguing that the design had been coordinated by the papists, and according to Benjamin Harris a 'Romish Priest' was committed to Newgate as being one of the 'principall promoters'.[58] Tory propagandist Nathaniel Thompson was arrested for involvement in the design, the ground for suspicion being that he had printed an account of a similar intrigue in his *True Domestick Intelligence* some six or seven weeks before the design

---

[54] PRO, PC 2/68, p. 473; *Protestant (Domestick) Intelligence*, nos. 78, 81; CLRO, Journal 49, fols. 119, 125; *London Gazette*, no. 1502.

[55] *Mercurius Civicus*, 24 March 1680; *CSPD, 1679–80*, pp. 422, 423; BL, Add. MS 25,360, fol. 13.

[56] GLRO, WJ/SR/1576, gaol calendar; *Protestant (Domestick) Intelligence*, no. 76; *A Narrative of the Proceedings of the Sessions House, 21st April, 1680* (1680), p. 4.

[57] HMC, *Ormond*, NS V, 296.

[58] *Protestant (Domestick) Intelligence*, no. 79; *A Protestant Prentice's Loyal Advice to all his Fellow-Apprentices in and about London* (1680).

became publicly known.[59] Whether Thompson was leader of the apprentices or not, the symbolism they were to adopt did parallel the arguments used by Thompson in his propaganda.

Although we cannot be certain whether or not there was outside leadership, it is hard to believe that the apprentices were merely being 'put upon', and that their only concern was with the 'delights of bonfires and ales'.[60] Although the treason charge in this case was eventually dropped, only 12 years previously some apprentices had been hanged, drawn and quartered for combining an attack on brothels with a political demonstration, and the apprentices of 1680 must have been aware that this was a risky way of having a good time. The apprentices' position is certainly intelligible, given the latent antagonism towards nonconformists which anti-exclusionist propagandists like Thompson had sought to exploit. Moreover, the points which the apprentices had intended to make were repeated on a number of occasions in tory rituals which did take place.

The typical tactic for tory crowds was to organize bonfires at which loyal healths were drunk, effigies of leading whigs and/or Jack Presbyter burnt, along with associated symbols such as a mock bill of exclusion or solemn league and covenant. Royal birthdays were obvious occasions for such demonstrations. For example, on 29 May 1682 there were anti-whig and anti-presbyterian rituals in a number of places. At a bonfire in Whitefriars Shaftesbury's 'Association' was first read and then committed to the flames 'by vote of the vast multitude'. Healths were drunk to the king, queen, and duke of York. The societies of the Middle and Inner Temples held bonfires at their gates where they burnt the covenant and the Association. In Covent Garden, near one Mr Erwin's house, the effigy of Oates was burnt in a tub, along with the Association, solemn league and covenant and 'A New Scheme of a Plot'.[61] The queen's birthday also provided a focus for loyalist crowds, and falling as it did on 15 November, it served as an immediate counter to the whig rituals of that month. On 15 November 1681, Mr Rutland at the Angel, Cheapside, the queen's laceman, apparently according to his annual custom, had a bonfire made at his own door and expense, and gave 12d in beer to those who kindled it. A crowd gathered and drank healths to the king and queen, and 'the rabble', we are told, did their normal trick of laying 'contributions on coaches'. The demonstration was not explicitly anti-exclusionist, but for loyalist crowds to celebrate the birthday of a catholic queen was of dubious wisdom. Some

[59] GLRO, WJ/SR/1576, gaol calendar; *Protestant (Domestick) Intelligence*, nos. 76, 77; L. Rostenberg, 'Nathaniel Thompson, Catholic Printer and Publisher of the Restoration', *Transactions of the Bibliographical Society*, 3rd series, 10 (1955), 196–7.
[60] *London Gazette*, no. 1497; HMC, *Ormond*, NS V, 296.
[61] *Loyal Protestant Intelligence*, no. 162; LC, MS 18,124, VIII, fol. 63.

apprentices, hearing a report that the promoters were drinking the health of the pope, proceeded to put out the bonfire and then break the windows of Rutland's house.[62]

As seen, tory propagandists had not only sought to disassociate themselves from the catholic cause, but had even defined their position in anti-catholic terms. It was therefore natural for tory crowds to poach the anti-catholic calendar. November 5th, 1681, witnessed the first actual presbyter-burning procession, organized by the scholars of the Society of St Peter's College, Westminster. They 'dresst up Jack Presbyter in his proper Habit' and set him on a tub. In his right hand was placed a mock whig tract, *Vox Patriae*, and in his left a scroll marked 'solemn league and convenant'. On his cloak was pinned a piece of parchment which read 'Ignoramus'. After a short procession from the Bowling Alley to the Dean's Yard, they burnt him.[63] There were also whig pope-burning processions on this day. In 1682 preparations were even made to use Elizabeth's coronation day to tory advantage, perhaps reflecting the success of tory propaganda in reclaiming the queen from association with the whigs. The young gentlemen of the Temples made an elaborate effigy of Oliver Cromwell which they intended to burn.[64] Another paper reported a plan to burn 'Jack Presbyter in his Formallitys' alongside the pope on that day.[65] The plans were frustrated by a royal order of 10 November forbidding bonfires on the 17th, because there had been trouble involving whig crowds on the previous Gunpowder Treason day.[66]

Although I have already commented on the rough reception that might await the duke of York whenever he made a public appearance in London, especially during the early months of the exclusion crisis, from 1680 such appearances began to serve as a trigger for anti-exclusionist demonstrations. On 24 February 1680 the duke and duchess of York returned to Whitehall after some months of exile in Scotland. They arrived by river, and an official welcome was given by the firing of guns from the ships and from the Tower. The king told people who had intended to make bonfires that night that

---

[62] *Loyal Protestant Intelligence*, no. 78; *Impartial Protestant Mercury*, no. 60; *CSPD, 1680–1*, pp. 571–1; HMC, *10th Report*, IV, 173; Luttrell, I, 144.

[63] *Loyal Protestant Intelligence*, no. 74; *A Dialogue upon the Burning of the Pope and a Presbyter in Effigy at Westminster* (1681); LC, MS 18,124, VII, fol. 264; Luttrell, I, 142; HMC, *10th Report*, IV, 174; Furley, 'Pope-Burning Processions', p. 22. A manuscript addition to a British Library copy of the *Solemn Mock Procession of... 1679* says that the effigy was supposed to represent the presbyterian divine, Vincent Alsop. See *BM Prints*, no. 1072.

[64] *Loyal Protestant Intelligence*, no. 232.

[65] *Loyal Impartial Mercury*, no. 43; *Loyal London Mercury; Or, Currant Intelligencer*, no. 24.

[66] PRO, PC 2/69, p. 566; *London Gazette*, no. 1772; *Loyal Protestant Intelligence*, no. 233; *Loyal Impartial Mercury*, no. 45; Luttrell, I, 237. The Gunpowder Treason day disturbances are discussed below, pp. 186–7.

he did 'not think it convenient', and ordered the lord mayor to forbid any celebrations in the City. Nevertheless there were numerous bonfires and other 'demonstrations of joy' in Westminster.[67] At the beginning of February there had been rumours that, at his return, York would 'goe to Church, take the Test and be restored to his Charges', and so this perhaps explains the enthusiasm with which he was greeted.[68] On 8 March Charles and James went to dine with the lord mayor, and on their journey to the City they were attended with a great many of the nobility, with numerous 'Lights and Flambeaus being placed in the Balconies to lighten the streets they passed'. Crowds of ordinary people were at the mayor's house to welcome them. When the royal brothers left at about 1 a.m., bells were rung, 'a great many bonfires were made', and they were followed 'by a great multitude of people who by their loud acclamations of God Bless the King, God Bless the Duke, awakened the Inhabitants every where they passed'.[69]

In October York was sent back into exile. He was eventually allowed to return in the spring of 1682, landing at Yarmouth on 10 March and stopping first at Newmarket before going on to London.[70] From this date we see a number of elaborate anti-exclusionist demonstrations whenever York appeared in London. There were numerous demonstrations on 8 April 1682, when Charles brought his brother back to London from Newmarket. One Captain Simons built a bonfire at the Dog-Wonder Tavern within Ludgate. Ropes were tied from St Martin's, Ludgate, to St Paul's, upon which squibs and crackers burnt to amuse the people. A loyalist song was chanted by some youths. The same men brought an effigy of Jack Presbyter from Little Britain, and burnt him along with the Rump, the Association, and the bill of exclusion, amidst great acclamations from the spectators. At Will's Coffee-House in Covent Garden a pole was erected over a bundle of faggots, and on it placed the Rump, covenant, Association, and green ribbons, which were burnt together. At the Dog Tavern, Drury Lane, Shaftesbury was burnt in effigy. On a pole was fixed the figure 'of a little meager fac'd wither'd old Conjurer, with a Tap and Spiggot in his side. In his right hand was writ THE ASSOCIATION; In the left, TREASON; on his Breast, ANARCHY, in large capitals'. In the Hay Market an effigy of a whig was burnt. At the Globe Tavern in Cornhill a great fire was made, and Jack Presbyter brought out, leaning over a board nailed to a tub – that is, the Meal Tub – and holding in his right hand the solemn league and covenant, and in his left hand the Association. Between both was the inscription 'The Pope is an Ass to ME'. He was cast into the fire to the

---

[67] Bodl. Lib., MS Carte 39, fol. 111; *Protestant (Domestick) Intelligence*, no. 68; HMC, *Ormond*, NS, IV, 580; LC, MS 18,124, VII, fol. 23; Haley, *Shaftesbury*, pp. 565–6.
[68] Bodl. Lib., MS Carte 39, fol. 107.
[69] LC, MS 18,124, VII, fol. 28; *London Gazette*, no. 1493.
[70] Haley, *Shaftesbury*, pp. 591, 692.

shouts of 'No whig, no whig'. Whig newspapers, such as Janeway's *Mercury* and Care's *Weekly Pacquet*, 'were design'd to accompany him, but by a mistake it is reserved till another opportunity'.[71]

On 20 April 1682, crowds gathered to cheer the duke of York when he attended the Artillery Company's feast. In the evening there were further demonstrations. In particular, the Dog-Wonder Tavern in Ludgate was again the focus of tory groups. Crowds shouted 'God Bless the King and his Royal Highness; No Bill of Exclusion; No Associators', and tried to force passers-by to do the same.[72] There were also bonfires on 27 May, when York made another entry into Whitehall, the tory press claiming that he was 'received with more glad than sorrowful countenances'.[73]

Most whig accounts dismiss the tory demonstrations as unauthentic expressions of public opinion, carefully coordinated from above and poorly supported on the ground. One whig alleged that the bonfires in his street on 8 April were 'so thin, that there might be reckoned a whole halfe myle betwixt them'.[74] Commenting upon the greetings York received from crowds on 20 April, Richard Janeway wrote that 'the Noise was not extraordinary', and 'several of the Guards were often pleased to put the Boys and Mobile in mind of their Duty, to Shout and Hallow'.[75] Not all whig accounts were so dismissive, however, and Langley Curtis conceded that York was greeted with 'great Acclamations' from 'numerous spectators'.[76] It is true that official encouragement was often given to pro-York demonstrations. On 8 March 1682 the king wrote to the lord mayor from Newmarket telling him of his intention to bring his brother back to London, and asking him to lay on an appropriate reception. To that end an order was to be given for the trained bands to be in arms, 'to keep the people from tumulting', and encouragement was to be given to the 'loyall apprentices in London' to 'make a body for his receptione'.[77] Some of the bonfires of April and May 1682 seem to have been sponsored by the duke of York's servants and captains of the guards.[78] But encouragement from above could only have been effective if there was fertile ground upon which to work. People were more likely to be provoked into hostility by organized demonstrations in

---

[71] LC, MS 18,124, VIII, fol. 40; Bodl. Lib., MS Carte 216, fol. 29; *Loyal Protestant Intelligence*, no. 140; *Impartial Protestant Mercury*, no. 101; L'Estrange, *Observator*, no. 122; *London Mercury*, no. 2; *London Gazette*, no. 1710; HMC, *7th Report*, p. 479.

[72] *Loyal Protestant Intelligence*, no. 145.

[73] LC, MS 18,124, VIII, fol. 63; *True Protestant Mercury*, no. 147; *Heraclitus Ridens*, no. 70.

[74] LC, MS 18,124, VIII, fol. 40.

[75] *Impartial Protestant Mercury*, no. 104. Cf. Haley, *Shaftesbury*, p. 694; Smith, 'London and the Crown', p. 150.

[76] *True Protestant Mercury*, no. 135.

[77] LC, MS 18,124, VIII, fol. 27.

[78] *Impartial Protestant Mercury*, nos. 104, 105; *True Protestant Mercury*, no. 147; LC, MS 18,124, VIII, fol. 40.

favour of a cause for which they held little sympathy. Indeed, this is precisely what happened in London. Increasingly we see rival whig and tory groups defining themselves in terms of mutual hostility towards each other, as they each strove to achieve dominance of the streets.

RIVALRY BETWEEN WHIG AND TORY GROUPS

The type of crowd activity so far considered has been that of a public expression of opinion, rituals designed simply to show how people felt, and not backed up by any coercive threat. Such public expressions were intended to influence policy indirectly, on the assumption that if the people's will was made known, the government might be persuaded to take some account of it. Such crowds could only lay claim to moral authority, and they could only do this if it was clear that they reflected a true consensus. One of the prime functions of the tory demonstrations was to disinvest the whig crowds of any moral authority. Another problem with these mere demonstrations of opinion was that they were a rather weak form of pressure, which could easily be ignored by the government.[79] Yet we also witness during the exclusion crisis collective agitation, from both whig and tory groups, which was deliberately coordinated in order to influence governmental policy. We see this with regard to the use of petitions and addresses, and also to the direct action taken by crowds in order to enforce or frustrate the enforcement of a particular measure.

Faced with a predominantly whig house of commons, Charles II dissolved his first exclusionist parliament in July 1679. But fresh elections in August and September did not produce a more sympathetic body, so Charles prevented this parliament from sitting for almost a year by a series of prorogations. The king's attempt to frustrate the sitting provoked mass petitioning, coordinated by the whig organization, but extending down to the lowest orders. In late 1679 forms were being printed and distributed throughout the country where agents went from parish to parish collecting signatures. A nonconformist brewer called Manly was one of those employed by a club of whig lords which met at the Swan Tavern, Fish Street, to collect signatories in the City of London. Another whig agent in the capital was the baptist, Samuel Harris, whilst Titus Oates was busy helping organize the petition in Southwark. A number of London taverns were provided with tables, petition forms and pen and ink for the purpose. A mammoth petition from the inhabitants of London, Westminster and Southwark was presented to the king on 13 January 1680 by Sir Gilbert Gerard and other whig leaders. It formed a roll three hundred feet long, and allegedly contained 50–60,000 signatures.[80]

---

[79] Cf. Miller, *Popery and Politics*, p. 184.
[80] *Hatt. Corr.*, I, 206, 215; Luttrell, I, 31; LC, MS 18,124, VI, fols. 313, 315; LC, MS

In a campaign that was obviously so well organized from above, we might be sceptical about using the petition as evidence of public opinion. Signatures could easily be forged or fraudulently obtained. The government, on the other hand, seems to have been genuinely concerned about the petitioning movement, and took action to try and discourage subscriptions.[81] Yet if it is fair to suggest that the whigs were just attempting to mobilize what was in reality genuine mass support for their cause, they certainly could not claim to speak for the whole of the metropolis. To match this unofficial petition, the whigs wanted an official petition presented by the City government, but on 20 January the common council voted by a small majority not to proceed with such a petition.[82] The following April the justices and grand jury of the Westminster Quarter Sessions, claiming to speak on behalf of the inhabitants of that City, publicly disowned the petition of 13 January and expressed their support for the king, his heirs, and lawful successors. A similar abhorrence was presented in May by the Middlesex justices.[83] These were official organs, and so it is difficult to know if they reflect popular opinion. But they had to come through this channel, as one of Charles II's complaints about the whig petitions was that they did not come from an official body, but merely from 'a company of loose and disaffected people'.[84]

When signatures were being collected in the Strand in December 1679, a group of three forcibly seized the whig petition and threw it into the flames, believing they were acting, as they said later, 'as Loyal and Dutiful Subjects to His Majesty'.[85] In January 1680 another petition form was seized by a captain in the guards, although this time the promoters rescued it and the captain was arrested by a constable.[86] In December a project to form a 'Loyal Protestants' Association' got underway. Signatures were collected of those who abhorred whig petitions, something which the promoters believed was their 'Duty to Church and State'.[87] In the middle of January

18,124, VII, fols. 1, 6; *Domestick Intelligence*, no. 51; *True Domestick Intelligence*, no. 83; *London Gazette*, no. 1477; Jones, *First Whigs*, p. 117; *CSPD, 1679–80*, p. 296; Haley, *Shaftesbury*, pp. 559, 561, 563.

[81] CLRO, Journal 49, fol. 85; *London Gazette*, nos. 1467, 1468; Haley, *Shaftesbury*, p. 562.

[82] CLRO, Journal 49, fol. 90; LC, MS 18,124, VII, fol. 9; Jones, *First Whigs*, p. 119.

[83] *London Gazette*, nos. 1504, 1509; *True Domestick Intelligence*, no. 83.

[84] *London Gazette*, no. 1480; N. Landau, *The Justices of the Peace, 1679–1760* (Los Angeles, 1984), pp. 49–51.

[85] PRO, KB 10/1, part 4, ind. of Whitfield *et al.*; I.C, MS 18,124, VII, fol. 17; *London Gazette*, nos. 1477, 1485; *True Domestick Intelligence*, no. 56. The three were William Laud, John Smallbone (Woodmonger), and Thomas Whitfield – all of St Martin-in-the-Fields. Smallbone was to serve as churchwarden of St Martin-in-the-Fields between 1682–4. See Victoria County Library, F2004, fols. 339–54; ibid., F39, F40.

[86] *Domestick Intelligence*, no. 53.

[87] Ibid., no. 50.

a bonfire was going to be made in Cheapside 'by the prevailing party against petitions'. The lord mayor forbade it, as the whigs opposed it and a disturbance was feared.[88] The king's known preference for official addresses probably explains why no abhorrence was ever presented at this time.

The prorogation of the second exclusionist parliament on 10 January 1681, followed by its dissolution and the king's decision to hold the next one at Oxford, produced another bout of petitioning from the whigs.[89] After the dissolution of the Oxford parliament in March 1681, petitioning reached new heights, but now the tories seized the initiative. Loyal addresses flooded in from all over the country thanking Charles for the way he had handled the tumultuous parliaments and for his promise to preserve the government as established in church and state. By 1682, the petitions concentrated on expressing an 'abhorrence' of the supposed Association found in the earl of Shaftesbury's closet. Nearly everyone of significance in the London area now petitioned the Crown to such an effect – the lieutenancy of the City, the lawyers of the Temple, the Middlesex bench, the Southwark grand jury.[90]

So too did the tory apprentices. At the end of June 1681 a group of apprentices from the City presented an address to the king at Hampton Court, with 18,000 hands to it. One of the young men who presented it supposedly told the king 'we hope your Majesty will continue the succession... in the right line, that they would all fight for it, if need were, and that there were not above 4,000 Dissenters of their quality in all the City'.[91]

Two months later, some 5,000 apprentices from Westminster presented a similar address to the king. After disowning the politics of 'some young men in Forty One... prevailed upon by a company of religious Pretenders', they went on to thank the king for his

Promises to maintain the true Protestant Religion by Law established, by which we have been taught, that to Fear God and Honour the King is the chief Character of a true Christian... We therefore... do resolve as one man (Providence having placed us about your Royal Palace) to be ready day and night with our Lives and Fortunes, to assist your Majesty, in Defence of your Royal Person, Prerogative, and the Church of England, against all Opposers whatsoever.[92]

It seems that neighbourhood vigilante groups were being formed to guard the king, as one tract put it, 'from his Enemies under what names so ever

[88] CLRO, Rep. 85, fol. 58; *CSPD, 1679–80*, p. 376.
[89] Jones, *First Whigs*, p. 162.
[90] CLRO, Lieutenancy Court Minute Book, 1676–84, fol. 87; *Petition of the Lieutenancy to the King* (1682); *London Gazette*, nos. 1716, 1717, 1727; Haley, *Shaftesbury*, pp. 640, 687.
[91] *HMC, Ormond*, NS VI, 91.
[92] *London Gazette*, no. 1647; *Loyal Protestant Intelligence*, no. 51.

distinguished'. The aim of the apprentices was to acquaint the king of numerous loyal youths

whose Hearty Affections to His Person and Government, and their Loyal Union among themselves, would make them not afraid when by him Commanded, To Confront the most Resolute and Formidable Rebel: and whose Number would render them (if occasion should be) no inconsiderable Guard to his Royal Person.[93]

The whig apprentices of the City were quick to respond to this tory initiative. In June they published a recantation of the loyal address of the City youths in Janeway's *Mercury*.[94] By 9 August a whig petition had been drawn up, arguing that the only effectual means 'for the security of His Majesty and the Nation' was the sitting of a parliament.[95] The petition of the City whig apprentices was presented to the whig lord mayor, Sir Patience Ward, on 2 September. This day was chosen since it was 'the Day appointed by Act of Parliament to be Yearly observed in Commemoration of the Burning that Famous Protestant City by Papists, Jesuits, and Tories, Anno 1666'. It purported to be from over 20,000 'of the Loyal Protestant Apprentices of London'. They represented themselves as defenders of the protestant religion who were prepared to sacrifice their lives for the king. They disowned the late address of the tory apprentices, 'boasting themselves the only Royal Young Men of this City', claiming that the tory address had less than 3,000 subscribers. The tory address was 'of a tendency dishonourable to Parliaments ... the Bulwark (under his Sacred Majesty) of English Liberties'. They replied explicitly to the tory call to be ready to rise in defence:

we shall never be behind any of our Fellow-Apprentices in Demonstrations of Loyalty to his Sacred Majesty, even to the last drop of our Blood, whenever His Service shall require it, against Traitors or Rebels whatsoever ... as we do ... abhor Popery, and all its Bloody Traiterous Practices; so we do utterly disapprove and dislike any such Proceedings from Private Persons as tend to reproach Parliaments.

It went on to express unanimous support for the mayor and common council in the petitions to the king for a parliament. The youth who presented the address to the mayor supposedly assured him that it was not promoted by dissenters, but only by 'True Sons of the Church of England', although it would have been a tactical error to have admitted anything different.[96]

---

[93] *Vox Juvenilis; Or, The Loyal Apprentices Vindication* (1681), pp. 2, 4.
[94] *Impartial Protestant Mercury*, no. 18.
[95] *CSPD, 1680–1*, p. 394; *Loyal Protestant Intelligence*, no. 46; *Impartial Protestant Mercury*, no. 33.
[96] *The Address of above 20,000 of the Loyal Protestant Apprentices of London, Humbly Presented to the Right Honourable Lord Mayor, September 2nd, 1681* (1681); *Just and Modest Vindication of the Many Thousand Loyal Apprentices that Presented an Humble Address to the Lord Mayor of London* (1681); PRO, SP 29/416, nos. 136, 137, 138; *Impartial Protestant Mercury*, nos. 33, 39.

There were more addresses in the following year. On 14 April 1682 an abhorrence of Shaftesbury's intended Association from a large number of tory apprentices was delivered by 'a worthy Gentlemen of the City'.[97] According to Janeway, 'divers other young men of the City, altogether as Loial and Zealously Affected towards His Majesties happy Government and the Established Church', were not in sympathy with this last address.[98] In early June the whig youths drafted an alternative address to the king, although it seems never to have been presented. Complaining that 'your Majesties most Loyale and Obedient subjects have been abused and scandalized as being phanatically affected and given to tumults by the enemyes of your Royall person and Government and the publick peace of the kingdome', they asserted that they were the only 'true Loyalists and Zealous Protestants'. They therefore declared

that we will Lay our Lives at your Majesties feet in defence of your sacred persone and Authority and the Protestant Religion against all opposers whatsoever... we reckon ourselves concerned as Englishmen and Loyall Subjects, and even under the Character of the Loyall young freemen and Apprentices of this your Citty of London, with our Bloods and utmost hazard of our Lives to assert this and all Protestant Monarchy, in detestatione of all the foull and villainous plotts of the Papists to the Contrarie, who have so often attempted the dethroneing of your Majestie and setting up an Arbitrary and Bloody Monarchy in this Kingdome.[99]

On 13 July the tory young freemen and apprentices of the City presented another address to the king, signed by 12,000 hands, vindicating their position in abhorrence of Shaftesbury's Association, and denying that they were 'Popishly and Tumultously inclined'. Nevertheless, they repeated their declaration that 'we will lay our Lives at your Majesties Feet in defence of your Sacred Person and Authority, the Rights of Your Lawful Successors, and the True Protestant Religion as it is Established by Law, against all opposers of the same'.[100]

Whig and tory polemicists alike complained that the other side only obtained signatures through intimidation and that only poor labourers and youths, the types who could be most easily bribed, supported their opponent's cause.[101] The question of the relative social composition of the two groups is a complex one, which is considered in depth in chapter eight. It certainly seems that the activities of the youths on both sides were well coordinated, and given strong encouragement from above. The whigs alleged

[97] *Domestick Intelligence ... Impartially Related*, no. 94.
[98] *Impartial Protestant Mercury*, no. 115.
[99] LC, MS 18,124, VIII, fol. 64.
[100] *London Gazette*, no. 1738; *Loyal Protestant Intelligence*, no. 181.
[101] *A Vindication of the Loyal London Apprentices* (1681), p. 2; *Vox Juvenilis*, pp. 2–3; *A Friendly Dialogue Between Two London Apprentices* (1681), p. 3; *Impartial Protestant Mercury*, no. 15.

that the tory addresses were organized by a club that met every night at the Crown Tavern in Ivy Lane.[102] On 4 August 1681 a select number of the tory apprentices, as a reward for their efforts, were treated to a sumptuous feast at Sadlers' Hall. The king provided a brace of the fattest bucks from Hyde Park for the occasion.[103] A year later the king donated three brace of bucks for a feast for the loyal young men held at Merchant Tailors' Hall on 9 August. The dukes of Ormonde and Albemarle and the earls of Halifax and Sunderland, along with several other 'great persones of quallity', were present at the feast, and the apprentices had 'the Kings Kettle drumes and Trumpets and most of the Kings and dukes Musick attending them all the while they were at dinner'.[104]

Predictably the whigs suggested that the tory youths acted more from a 'Love to Venison then Loyalty', but it should not be assumed that support was simply being bought.[105] It is perhaps better to think of a dialectical process, with the activities of the propagandists helping to prompt an initiative from below, which in turn is further encouraged by elite rewards. This is clearly the case for the whig apprentices, where we have more evidence of how they were organized. John Dunton later wrote that it was he and his companion Joshua Evans who made the first moves to organize the whig petitions in opposition to the tory ones in 1681. Dunton was then an apprentice to the bookseller Thomas Parkhurst, although at 22 years of age he was virtually at the end of his service. In a short time they had formed a society of 300 apprentices, with a chairman and a treasurer.[106] One Mr Stillingfleet, who counted himself among 'the Apprentices of London', was the man responsible for coordinating whig apprentice demonstrations.[107] In May 1682 Stillingfleet presided over a meeting of 30 apprentices, at which he gave a long speech warning of the dangers of popery and tyranny:

His Majestie being too Credelous entertained and harkened to the faneing words of Papists and tymeserving Rogues... By the Councill and Advice of such; all who Protest for Protestantisme and the banishment of Papists were banished the Court, Reputed as Seditious Persones and Enemyes to King and Government; The Parliament was likewise dissolved and dissipat... Then was our best Protestants accused and Imprisoned for high Treason, and Papists brought to swear against them.

---

[102] *Friendly Dialogue*, p. 2.
[103] *Loyal Protestant Intelligence*, nos. 43, 44; *Impartial Protestant Mercury*, no. 30; LC, MS 18,124, VII, fol. 220.
[104] *Domestick Intelligence ... Impartially Related*, no. 126; *Loyal London Mercury; Or, Moderate Intelligencer*, nos. 17, 18; LC, MS 18,124, VIII, fol. 220.
[105] LC, MS 18,124, VIII, fol. 64.
[106] J. Dunton, *Life and Errors* (1705), p. 50; B. S. Capp, 'English Youth Groups and the Pinder of Wakefield' in Slack, ed., *Rebellion*, p. 214.
[107] LC, MS 18,124, VIII, fol. 47; Smith, 'London and the Crown', pp. 106–7.

Stillingfleet ended the speech by exhorting them to be unanimous

for the secureing of our selves against Popery and Tyranii... as we are born free Subjects and bred Protestants, so Let us endeavour to defend our Rights and Libertyes and Religion, for when it is gon our Lives goe Likewise.[108]

Yet if these initiatives came from the whig apprentices themselves, they were certainly given full encouragement from above. Like the tories, the whig elite wanted to reward their apprentice supporters with a lavish feast, which they proposed to hold at Haberdashers' Hall on 21 April 1682, although the king forbade it.[109] Instead, the apprentices put on a pope-burning display the following day for a number of whig lords. The pope's effigy

was by above 600 apprentices carried through the Streets to my Lord Colchester's lodgings, where the Pope was magnificently burnt, ther being many thousand of spectators Looking on, who all and every one of them expressed their Loyalty and Good will to the Protestant Religione by calling alwayes no Pope, no Papist, God Bless the King and the Duke of Monmouth.

Afterwards Stillingfleet and 40 other youths were presented to Monmouth, Stillingfleet saying 'Long Live your grace, and forever let the Protestant Religion flourish, and you remaine its protector.' The lords expressed their pleasure at overseeing the pope's tragedy, and by special order from the duke of Monmouth, Colchester invited 23 of the youths to a dinner, where Monmouth gave Stillingfleet a large ring.[110] On 1 May 1682, Sir John Lawrence, who had been the foreman on Shaftesbury's ignoramus jury, gave another 'treat', and after dinner Sir John made 'a great Bonfire round which they Drunk the Kings health'. This meeting, however, was broken up by the lord mayor.[111] John Dunton recalled that his group were 'regal'd... very plentifully' after they had delivered their petition to Sir Patience Ward in September 1681.[112]

A striking feature about these whig apprentice groups is their close association with dissent. Dunton's group used to meet in the house of Mr Russell, a nonconformist minister in Ironmonger Lane. Dunton was probably a presbyterian himself, and in August 1682 he married Elizabeth Annesley, the daughter of the famous presbyterian minister. Dunton later described the whig petitions as coming from 'the Dissenting Party'.[113] We learn about

[108] LC, MS 18,124, VIII, fol. 57.
[109] *Domestick Intelligence ... Impartially Related*, no. 96; *London Mercury*, no. 5; *The Loyal Feast, Designed to be Kept in Haberdasher's Hall, on Friday, 21st April, 1682* (1682); *CSPD, 1682*, p. 173; Maitland, *London*, I, 473.
[110] LC, MS 18,124, VIII, fols. 46–7.
[111] Ibid., fol. 51.
[112] Dunton, *Life and Errors*, p. 50.
[113] Ibid., pp. 50, 96; T. G. Crippen, 'The Tombs in Bunhill Fields', *TCHS*, 4 (1909–10), 361. For Russell's nonconformist conventicle in Ironmonger Lane, see CLRO, Sessions File, July 1684, rec. 67.

Stillingfleet's activities from a newsletter which was regularly written throughout 1682 by one of his apprentice associates. From the internal evidence of the newsletters, there is no doubt that this youth was a non-conformist.[114]

The threat made by the whig and tory apprentices to take direct action themselves in defence of their cause was not an idle one. Both sides sought to suppress the crowd rituals of their opponents. Most of the tory demonstrations examined above were disrupted by whig apprentices. On 8 April 1682 about 300 of Stillingfleet's associates armed with long canes set out to extinguish all the bonfires lit to mark the duke of York's return from exile. They marched from Aldersgate to Charing Cross, shouting 'a Monmouth, a Monmouth, no York, no York', trying to put out all the fires they met with. There was a scuffle with the crowd at the bonfire outside Captain Simons's house in Ludgate, the Monmouth men getting the better of things. Further trouble broke out at the Queen's Head Tavern, near Temple Bar, where the youths encountered a group toasting the king's, queen's and duke of York's healths. Nathaniel Thompson was one of them, and he came out of the tavern brandishing a sword, but he was thumped by a young whig apprentice named Killingworth, dropped his weapon, and rushed back inside. The whig apprentices threw stones at the windows, the tories threw chairs and stools out of the windows at the crowd. Undismayed, the whig youths made 'a handsome Bonfire' from this material, calling out always 'no Papist, no Papist'. This group then went off to disperse the tory demonstration in Covent Garden. However, Stillingfleet sent orders to the youths to return by 11 o'clock, and to 'bring forth our show'; which accordingly they did, burning an effigy of the pope in Charing Cross, within sight of St James's and Whitehall.[115]

We see the same pattern on 20 April, and on 27 and 29 May that year, with whig crowds trying to suppress the tory demonstrations and replace them with their own. On 29 May, for example, the whig crowds burnt effigies of the pope and Sir Roger L'Estrange at Temple Bar, just outside the Green Ribbon Club, because the Templars were holding anti-whig demonstrations at the gates of their societies nearby. Scuffles broke out between rival groups shouting 'a Monmouth, a Monmouth' or 'a York, a York'. The Templars, we are told, routed the whigs, throwing down their tubs of ale, so they then only had kennel water with which to toast Monmouth. The Templars broke the windows of the King's Head Tavern,

---

[114] LC, MS 18,124, VII, fols. 297–311; ibid., VIII, fols. 1–132; ibid., IX, fols. 326–31; Smith, 'London and the Crown', p. 17, footnote 11.
[115] LC, MS 18,124, VIII, fol. 40; *Impartial Protestant Mercury*, no. 101; *Loyal Protestant Intelligence*, no. 140; L'Estrange, *Observator*, no. 122.

captured one of the leaders of the whig crowd, and took him captive to the pump, where they forced him to do penance on his knees.[116]

The tories likewise sought to suppress the activities of whig groups. Thus on 5 November 1681, in addition to holding their presbyter-burning procession, the tories sought to disrupt the whig pope-burnings. One whig procession was set upon as it was passing along Aldersgate Street, a group of tories having hid in Charterhouse Yard waiting to ambush it, and the effigies of the pope and the devil were seized. A similar thing happened in Crutched Friars, on the eastern limits of the City, and also in King Street, in Bloomsbury.[117]

There seems to have been no attempt to disrupt the whig procession of 17 November, probably because on this day there tended to be just the one massive pageant and not the smaller and more localized affairs of the 5th which were undoubtedly easier to break up. However, in the new year some students of the Inner Temple decided to hit at the organizational centre on the Queen Elizabeth's day pope-burnings, the Green Ribbon Club. They attacked the King's Head Tavern late on the night of 13 January, broke the windows and pulled down the sign. The watch came to disperse the crowds, but some watermen, armed with halberds, came to assist the Templars, and in the ensuing riot one of the watermen was seriously injured.[118]

THE WHIGS ON THE DEFENSIVE

After the dissolution of the Oxford parliament, the whigs were put increasingly on the defensive. The government became less concerned with catholic recusants and alleged Popish Plotters, and turned its attention on the whigs and nonconformists. From this time on we see the deliberate attempt to use crowd pressure to frustrate this tory counter-attack. We can see this with regard to the trial of the earl of Shaftesbury, which took place at the Old Bailey on 24 November. After the depositions were given in, the court adjourned to dinner, and all the king's evidences departed for the Fountain Tavern. As they went, a crowd followed them, crying out 'Bogtrotters' and 'Perjured Rogues' and 'There go the Rogues... that swear against the Earl.' At the door of the tavern the witnesses were met by Titus Oates, who said he would fill the tavern with porters before the perjured rogues should have any place here. Oates had apparently been plying his followers with wine. When the witnesses returned to court they were met, so one

---

[116] LC, MS 18,124, VIII, fol. 63; *Loyal Protestant Intelligence*, no. 162; *Impartial Protestant Mercury*, no. 105; *True Protestant Mercury*, no. 147.

[117] *True Protestant Mercury*, nos. 88, 89; *Impartial Protestant Mercury*, no. 57; *Loyal Protestant Intelligence*, no. 75.

[118] Luttrell, I, 158; *Impartial Protestant Mercury*, no. 77.

of them later claimed, by 'thousands of people with long poles, half-pikes and halberts in their hands hindering our passage, calling us rogues and rascals and offering to strike at home'. The intimidation was not without effect. One of the prime witnesses, Stephen Dugdale, fearful that they would 'have our braines knocked out before we can give our Evidence', slipped away from the Fountain and did not appear in court.[119] When the bill was found *ignoramus*, there were attempts to assault the witnesses against the earl. The news of the verdict was allegedly brought outside the court by Oates, who ran through the streets shouting 'An Ignoramus'. The whig sheriff, Shute, who came out of the court room pretending to discharge the crowds, according to one report waved his hat and exclaimed 'Shout boys, shout'. The court ordered the sheriffs to see the witnesses safely out of the City, 'to avoid the Complements of the Croud'. They were seen beyond Temple Bar, but were still pursued by some of Shaftesbury's more enthusiastic supporters, and had to seek sanctuary in the Savoy.[120]

The evening of the 24th witnessed numerous celebratory bonfires in the City. Nathaniel Thompson wrote that there were more bonfires 'than ever yet was seen on the 29th of May', though by this he was trying to suggest that the whigs were more loyal to Shaftesbury than to Charles II. In Aldersgate Street alone there were eight or ten bonfires upon this 'Feast of St Ignoramus'. All coaches that passed the bonfires were stopped, and passengers made to give money to drink the healths of Shaftesbury and the 'worthy jury men'. A crowd stopped the coach of one Mr Hamilton, who was returning that night from a dance in the City, but when he refused to give any money his coachmen and footmen were 'lustily mauled'. Some of the officers of the Tower, making their way to the Tower gate, found that there was a stop put on all coaches in Tower Street. The officers got out of their coaches, but refused to give any money, and after receiving some rather rough handling, they managed to make a run for it, with the crowd 'at our heels, hallowing like mad'.

Although we should expect tory reports to exaggerate the aggressiveness of the whig crowds, it is difficult to believe Langley Curtis when he wrote in his whig *Mercury* that there was no tumult nor 'Damage done to any Person, but that everyone went peaceably home'. Some of the whig groups seem to have been looking for trouble. At about 11 p.m. a group of around 40, led by John Harrington (Shaftesbury's kinsman) and a Wiltshire MP, came down St Paul's Churchyard with their swords drawn, crying 'No Popish

---

119 PRO, SP 29/418, no. 186; *CSPD, 1682*, pp. 162–3; *Currant Intelligence*, no. 62; *Impartial Protestant Mercury*, no. 62; *Heraclitus Ridens*, no. 48; Haley, *Shaftesbury*, p. 676.

120 *Impartial Protestant Mercury*, no. 63; *True Protestant Mercury*, no. 93; *CSPD, 1680–1*, p. 583; *Loyal Protestant Intelligence*, no. 84; Ailesbury, *Memoirs*, p. 63; LC, MS 18,124, VII, fols. 272, 311.

Successor, No York, A Monmouth, A Buckingham'. Buckingham was cheered because one of the charges against Shaftesbury was his supposed desire to settle the succession in Buckingham's favour. Miles Prance, one of the original evidences against the Popish Plot, took a group into a coffee-house and set upon some tories. When Captain Griffith, an officer in the lieutenancy and a common council man, came to disperse the crowd that had made a bonfire in Warwick Lane, he was cudgelled by a group shouting 'A Tory, A Tory', and he received a fractured skull. Although, according to the captain's later testimony, the crowd's aim was murder, shouting 'kill him, kill him', it is questionable how far the violence was indiscriminate. One of his assailants apparently said 'Oh, that he had but drawn his sword', implying that they could not have justified seriously hurting him unless he had first threatened their lives. The crowd continued to bait the captain. At about midnight they made a fresh bonfire just outside his precinct, 'where they wished he would come again'. Griffith did not, perhaps because he was too badly injured, perhaps for fear of the legal risk involved in acting outside his own precinct.[121]

The government also began to turn its attention against the noncon-formists, whom it believed provided the corps of whig support. Although most of the attempts to persecute dissent in the years 1681–2 were frustrated by packed whig juries, a number of conventicles were disturbed either by informers or by local peace-keeping agents. Often we find whig youths com-ing to the rescue of the conventiclers. In May 1682 Dr Parker's conventicle in Southwark was disturbed by a company of footguards, but as Parker was being carried away 'the Apprentices rose to his rescue ... beat off the soldjars' and 'made them run for it'. The night was spent celebrating the victory in the streets. When this news reached the ears of the apprentices in the City, they 'Likewise gathered togither and went rambling through the streets, Comitting severall insolences as they past, breaking windows, etc.' The lord mayor called on Mr Stillingfleet to persuade the apprentices to disperse, which he eventually did, although not until after 'they had fallen on two bawdy houses in Butcher Row'.[122]

There are a number of accounts of attacks on informers in 1682. On 25 June one informer, with the help of the city marshal and some soldiers from the trained bands, was escorting twenty conventiclers to a JP's house, when he was assaulted by a 'rude multitude' who rescued his prisoners. They then fell upon the informer, 'kick'd him, thrust him up and down,

[121] PRO, SP 29/417, no. 115; BL, Add. MS 25,363, fol. 125; *Loyal Protestant Intelligence*, nos. 82, 84; *Heraclitus Ridens*, no. 64; HMC, *Ormond*, NS VI, 237; HMC, *12th Report*, V, 61; *True Protestant Mercury*, no. 63; Haley, *Shaftesbury*, p. 681.
[122] LC, MS 18,124, VIII, fol. 56.

and with nasty Dirt, defac'd Him, and his Cloathes'.[123] Occasionally such attacks occurred with the encouragement of sympathetic local constables. For example, in August 1682 Charles Dadley, the constable of Fleet Street, was approached by a man with a warrant to disturb a conventicle in Goldsmith's Court. Dadley therefore decided to raise the hue and cry, but he shouted 'Informer, Informer', and this encouraged a group of about 200 to assemble, who chased the informer away.[124] As well as attempting to frustrate the execution of the laws against the conventicles, whig groups also sought to enforce the laws against catholic worship. That same month the countess of Sussoins was 'most dreadfully abused... in one of the Duke of Yorks Coaches by a number of Boyes that fell upon there Coach as she was going to Somerset House to publick masse'. They broke all the windows, and forced the coachman to turn back.[125]

To effectively defeat the exclusionists, the Court realized it was necessary to destroy the whig influence in the government of the City of London. The whigs were far from dominating the Corporation. The tories outnumbered the whigs on the court of aldermen by 14 to 9 (with 3 whose allegiances are uncertain), and they controlled the lieutenancy. From December 1680 they even had a narrow majority on the common council, although until after the elections of December 1682 the whigs could gain the ascendancy here if they won the support of the uncommitted councillors. But it was the whig control of certain key areas which gave them so much power. Their control of the courts of assistants which ran the livery companies gave them the dominant voice in common hall, where the liverymen elected the sheriffs and proposed two nominees for lord mayor, from which the court of aldermen chose one. It was the whig hold on the mayoralty (1679–81), the shrievalty (1680–2) and their activism in the common council which made the exclusionists so influential within the Corporation.[126]

Most of the whig petitions of the exclusion period were directed to the common council. Because the deliberations of this body became so crucial, exclusionist crowds would often flock to the Guildhall to learn what was being decided. On 13 January 1681 the common council voted to address the lord mayor to ask him to put pressure on the king for the sitting of parliament. A man by the name of Coxcomb, coming into the Guildhall, expressed his disapproval of the vote,

but being over-heard by some zealous Lovers of the City and its Representatives, was severely rebuked for that his unbecoming Character, and the croud falling upon him, did so trace his fat sides from one part of the Hall to another, calling him

---

[123] *Conventicle Courant*, no. 1; *Loyal London Mercury; Or, Moderate Intelligencer*, no. 5.
[124] *Conventicle Courant*, no. 5.
[125] LC, MS 18,124, VIII, fol. 98; Smith, 'London and the Crown', p. 50.
[126] Smith, 'London and the Crown', ch. 2.

Rascall, Papist, and Abhorrer of Parliaments... till at last by giving good words, and promising to answer it before a Magistrate, he gravely sneaked off, with 100 Boys at his heels.[127]

Theoretically the whig activity in the common council should have been of little concern to the tories, since they dominated the court of aldermen which had the power of veto over decisions taken by the commons. But the aldermanic veto had been successfully challenged in the 1640s, was the subject of some controversy in the mid 1670s and now again came under attack. In May 1681 the common council successfully withstood an attempt by the court of aldermen to veto their petition to the king calling for a new parliament, and the whig lord mayor, Sir Patience Ward, was able to override aldermanic protests. It was not until May 1683 that the aldermen successfully reclaimed their negative voice.[128]

As well as destroying the independence of the common council, the tories also needed to obtain a sympathetic lord mayor. Although common hall voted for two nominees, from which the aldermen chose one, it was customary for the alderman next in seniority to be 'elected'. In 1681 it was Sir John Moore's turn. Moore had once been a dissenter himself, and it was thought that he had conformed to the church only to qualify for office. He thus enjoyed the support of many dissenters, and won many natural votes in the election of September. Although some whigs suspected Moore's reliability, especially once it became clear that he was being strongly supported by the Court, they were unable to muster enough votes around their rival candidates of Sir John Shorter and Sir Thomas Gold. Moore was not really a party man, but was 'flexible and faint-hearted', and more amenable to government pressure than his predecessors had been.[129] At times the whigs were able to exploit Moore's timidity. In January 1682 the two previous whig lord mayors, Sir Patience Ward and Sir Robert Clayton, managed to persuade Moore to deliver a petition to the king subscribed by several thousand citizens in defence of the conventicles, and to urge the need for unity to face the catholic threat. A bemused Charles II could only ask 'My Lord Mayor, how longe since you turned Presbyterian?'[130] During 1682, however, it became increasingly clear that Moore was an agent of the Court, especially after his role in the shrieval elections of the summer. Whig disillu-

---

[127] *Protestant (Domestick) Intelligence*, no. 89.
[128] CLRO, Rep. 80, fols. 17, 130, 143, 152, 269; Rep. 82, fols. 28–33; Rep. 86, fol. 128; Smith, 'London and the Crown', pp. 34, 36–7; Pearl, *London*, pp. 146–59, 280–1; Elliot, 'Elections', p. 152; BL, Add. MS 33,051, fols. 206–11; *CSPD, 1680–1*, p. 632.
[129] *True Protestant Mercury*, no. 77; *Impartial Protestant Mercury*, no. 47; Burnet, II, 335; *CSPD, 1680–1*, p. 473; Lacey, *Dissent*, p. 151; Jones, *First Whigs*, p. 201; Haley, *Shaftesbury*, p. 668. Moore had been a member of Cockayne's congregational church. B. C. Cockett, 'George Cockayn', *TCHS*, 12 (1933–6), 230.
[130] LC, MS 18,124, VIII, fol. 3.

sionment with Moore is well captured by the following words, allegedly spoken by Stephen College's sister in July. She said 'she would take my Lord Sh's Monkey, and put a Jack-Chain about him; and setting a Mastiff-Dog, with a Kennel-raker carrying a Lath before him, send him to Guild-hall, and he would make as good a Judge as the Lord Mayor'.[131] Shortly before the end of his term in office Moore, returning home in his coach from Whitehall, was pursued by a number of youths who 'called into the coach to him, Torrie, Papist, etc. and giveing him much scoffing Language'. Unfortunately for Moore, the man he had arrested for encouraging this tumult was able to produce alibis in court, and he sued Moore for £200 for wrongful imprisonment.[132]

The whigs were determined not to repeat their mistake the following year, especially since the person 'next the chair' was the vehement tory, Sir William Pritchard. The only way to avoid Pritchard being chosen was to ensure that the two nominees put forward by common hall were both whigs. Although there were two tory nominees, most of the tory liverymen were persuaded to vote for Pritchard; yet despite this, the whigs successfully divided their votes between their two candidates, Henry Cornish and Sir Thomas Gold, and Pritchard was forced into third place. However, after a scrutiny of the poll, a significant number of whig votes were struck out as being those of quakers, excommunicants, and dissenters, and Pritchard was declared mayor.[133] Certain of the City companies refused to accompany Pritchard on lord mayor's day when he went to Westminster to be sworn in. Some of the tickets sent out by the Mercers' Company for their members 'to attend that day were made with unusuall and unfitting expressions in contempt of the lord mayor and court of aldermen'.[134]

Perhaps the most important power base for the whigs in the City was their control of the shrievalty, because the sheriffs determined the selection of juries and could thus affect the extent to which whigs and nonconformists were persecuted in the courts. Although theoretically the lord mayor chose one sheriff, this right had been successfully challenged in the past, and in 1680 common hall elected both sheriffs, the whigs Slingsby Bethell and Henry Cornish. In 1681 the whig lord mayor, Sir Patience Ward, nominated Sir Thomas Pilkington to be sheriff, though Pilkington refused to serve without obtaining the votes of common hall, and so effectively both he and the other sheriff Samuel Shute could claim to have been elected. In 1682

---

[131] CLRO, Sessions Papers, July 1682, information of Goodwin; *Loyal Protestant Intelligence*, nos. 184, 185.

[132] LC, MS 18,124, VIII, fol. 130.

[133] Luttrell, I, 231–2; *CSPD, 1682*, pp. 475–6; Smith, 'London and the Crown', p. 200; Haley, *Shaftesbury*, p. 704; Jones, *First Whigs*, pp. 205–6.

[134] CLRO, Rep. 88, fols. 13–14; *Loyal London Mercury; Or, The Currant Intelligencer*, no. 17.

Sir John Moore sought to re-establish the mayor's right of selecting one sheriff, and expressed his preference for the tory Dudley North. When Moore tried to insist to common hall in July that they could only elect one sheriff, he was shouted down and then jostled out of the court, whilst the out-going whig sheriffs held a poll for two places. The election was violent and farcical. The whigs claimed their candidates Papillon and Dubois had won, but the tory candidate Ralph Box was declared elected. Box then decided to fine rather than accept such a contentious office, and so fresh elections were held in September. The whigs, believing that Papillon and Dubois had already been properly elected, refused to participate in the poll, and Sir Peter Rich was elected by a show of a mere 500 hands.[135]

The whig youths were aware that dominance of the shrievalty by the tories would enable them to take successful legal action against the whigs. One Jerome Batty 'composed and dispersed a circular to his brethren the apprentices, that they had to league themselves at this juncture', and he exhorted them to

contribute some sums according to the exigency of the enterprise and to appoint among them some treasurers to receive such moneys to be distributed hereafter according to the order they should receive and particularly whenever any of them should be imprisoned or assailed by the law in defending their cause.[136]

The crowd agitation of the exclusion crisis reached its climax in November 1682. This year the 5th fell on a Sunday, and so Gunpowder Treason day was celebrated on the Monday, there being many bonfires throughout the City. The festivities had been planned in advance. A group of about 40 youths met first at the White Hart alehouse in Butchers Hall Lane for a dinner that had been appointed three weeks previously, before going to their bonfires. Exactly what type of activity had been planned is uncertain, since events took a dramatic turn when a group appeared chanting 'a York, a York', and proceeded to extinguish several of the fires. This provoked the whig apprentices, who 'gathered together in a Body... sowndly beat off these persones that were putting out their fires', and 'proceeded to go through the Streets calling No York, a Monmouth, a Monmouth; No Pritchard, a Gold, a Gold, No North and Rich, a Papillion and Dubois'. The violence escalated as whig youths proceeded to attack not just the symbols of toryism, but also the property of known tories. Distasteful pub signs were destroyed. In Cheapside a group fell on the Cardinal's Head and the Duke of York's Head, although interestingly they decided to leave the sign of the King's Head. At the Stocks Market a group led by one John Langham burned the sign of the Mitre. The quaker Edward Billing was another

---

[135] Smith, 'London and the Crown', pp. 178, 186–99; Jones, *First Whigs*, pp. 203–5; Haley, *Shaftesbury*, pp. 657, 697, 699–703.

[136] *CSPD*, *1682*, pp. 327–8.

involved in this, crying out as he looked on 'the Mitre burns bravely'. Mr Chamberlain, the king's poulterer, had his windows smashed by an angry crowd shouting 'This is a Tory Rogue, He Serves the King and Duke.' Some of the youths threatened to pull down the house of Captain Simons at the Dog-Wonder Tavern within Ludgate, where there had been pro-York demonstrations the previous spring. A great part of Nathaniel Thompson's house was pulled down, and a crowd besieged L'Estrange's house in Holborn, removing wooden items such as chairs, stools and beds, out of which they made a great bonfire. They stopped people and asked for money to buy drink, so that they could toast 'the destructione of Towzer and the Pope'. Lord Mayor Pritchard, his predecessor Sir John Moore, and the two tory sheriffs North and Rich had the windows of their houses smashed by stone-throwing crowds.

Local constables and the watch were unable to suppress the riots. A constable managed to seize one of the rioters at Mr Chamberlain's house, but he was soon rescued by his fellow apprentices. The trained bands were therefore called out, but they fared little better. When the captain of the yellow regiment told one group to disperse in the lord mayor's name, the cry came 'who was my lord mayor'. He replied Sir William Pritchard, 'at the naming of which one knocked him down, and then a great hallow past amongst them of No Pritchard, a Gold, a Gold'. One of the crowd placed a hat on a stick, and shouted 'stand to it, fall on, fall on', and then the crowd charged the trained bands and forced them to retire. It was several hours before the crowds were eventually dispersed, but even so few arrests were possible, and by 8 o'clock the next morning only a handful had been seized.[137]

This proved to be the last exclusionist demonstration. On 10 November Whitehall issued an order against bonfires and fireworks on days of public celebration, an order which was enforced with extraordinary efficiency for the rest of Charles II's reign.[138] But the government faced the immediate problem of bringing the arrested rioters to justice, and the use of the traditional punishment of a spell in the pillory revealed the limitations of leaving the execution of the sentence to the crowd. On 9 December six of the ringleaders stood in the pillory: three in Gracechurch Street, two in Cheapside and one at the Royal Exchange. Crowds gathered at all these places, and threatened everyone who spoke against the convicted, saying 'they would be for a Monmouth and would burn the Pope for all this'. The three in Gracechurch Street had a bottle of 'sack' sent to them by a surgeon called

---

[137] LC, MS 18,124, IX, fol. 331; PRO, SP 29/421, no. 67; *Loyal Protestant Intelligence*, no. 231; *Domestick Intelligence... Impartially Related*, no. 155; HMC, *12th Report*, VII, 190; CLRO, Sessions File, December 1682.
[138] PRO, PC 2/69, p. 566; *London Gazette*, no. 1772.

Bateman, who was a baptist. They drank a health to the king, the duke of Monmouth and the earl of Shaftesbury. Meanwhile, Bateman had drinks with some friends, looking on from the balcony of John Price, upholsterer, who was preacher at the conventicle Bateman frequented in Paul's Alley. Others gave them money. The one who stood at the Royal Exchange had oranges given him, whilst those in Cheapside received wine and money.[139]

CONCLUSION

I have argued for the existence of a fundamental divide along whig/tory lines at the level of the London crowd during the exclusion crisis. There are no strong reasons for assuming that support for the whig position must have been more genuine than that for the tories. Although some of the tory crowds were given strong encouragement from above, this is also true for a number of the whig crowds. On the other hand, sometimes we find the elite responding to initiatives which came from below. It is also necessary to distinguish whether elite organization of demonstrations merely created a vehicle for the expression of public opinions, or whether they actually manufactured an artificial statement of those opinions. From the context so far established in this book, it seems that the divide which emerged between whig and tory crowds corresponded to fundamental tensions within the political culture of Londoners, tensions which centred on the issue of dissent and rival interpretations of the anti-catholic tradition. Yet so far my analysis has concentrated on the ideological aspects of the political conflict, and it might be objected that material factors were more significant in explaining why people took to the streets in Charles II's reign. It is to an examination of the role played by economic considerations that I turn next.

---

[139] *CSPD, 1682*, p. 572–3; *HMC, 7th Report*, pp. 406, 480–1. For the religious denominations of Bateman and Price, see CLRO, Conventicle Box 2.1. They were general baptists.

8

The economics of crowd politics

It might seem that a purely ideological explanation of crowd unrest is inappropriate. Most contemporaries believed that the masses were swayed more by material considerations than by political principles. For example, Sir Arthur Hesilrige in 1659 expressed his view that the people cared not what government they lived under, so long as they could plough and go to market.[1] Agitators, it was believed, could easily obtain mass support for their cause whenever 'the vulgar' were 'pricked by exactions of money'.[2] Economic recession invariably instilled fear of popular unrest amongst the upper classes. Thus, one contemporary feared tumults in London in response to the Conventicle Act of 1664, which would occur not for political or religious reasons, but because trade was 'greatly restrained' since the Act had been passed, meaning that the 'poor will raise tumults for want of bread'.[3] In the 1680s, the government was anxious lest the whigs might be able to exploit the material grievances of the poor, and especially of the weavers in Spitalfields, to raise a popular insurrection against the Stuarts.[4]

Historians have usually warned against positing too simple a relationship between material conditions and collective political or religious unrest. Geoffrey Holmes saw no connection between economic distress and involvement in the Sacheverell riots of 1710, and emphasized the causal role of high-church ideology.[5] George Rudé, in his work on the 1760s, argued that whilst it might seem likely that workers suffering from unemployment or low wages would more easily be swayed by the slogan 'Wilkes and Liberty', the available evidence does not give much support to the view.[6] In her work on crowd disorder in sixteenth-century France, Natalie Zemon Davis has shown how religious beliefs could cut across simple class loyalties.[7] The recent studies

[1] T. Burton, *Diary*, ed. J. T. Rutt (4 vols., 1828), III, 257.
[2] *CSPD, 1661–2*, p. 412.
[3] PRO, SP 29/99, no. 9.
[4] *CSPD, July–Sept. 1683*, pp. 71–2; *CSPD, 1683–4*, p. 261; Smith, 'London and the Crown', pp. 100–1.
[5] Holmes, *Trial*, pp. 177–8.
[6] Rudé, *Wilkes and Liberty*, p. 104.
[7] N. Z. Davis, 'The Rites of Violence: Religious Riot in Sixteenth-Century France', *PP*, 59 (1973), 78–81; N. Z. Davis, 'A Rejoiner', *PP*, 67 (1975), 133. But see her interview in *Radical History*, 24 (1980), 115–39.

by Keith Lindley and Buchanan Sharp, on the fenland and west country riots of the first half of the seventeenth century, have shown that economic hardship did not encourage people in these areas to adopt a radical political ideology during the Civil War.[8] It has also been demonstrated that even when disturbances were explicitly over bread-and-butter issues, as in the case of food riots, these cannot simply be explained in terms of crude economic stimuli. Food riots typically occurred only when there was a perceived abuse in the control of the market during times of grain shortage. It was the perception of a legitimate grievance, an ideological response, rather than starvation, that provoked disorder. At other times, dearth would merely provoke death.[9]

Having said this, there does seem to be a strong case for suggesting that economic factors were a prime cause of crowd disaffection in Charles II's reign. As seen in chapter three, grievances over the decline of trade and the high incidence of regressive taxation figured prominently in the agitation against the republican government in 1659–60. Not only did the Restoration regime fail to remove that most hated of taxes, the excise, but it also introduced another bitterly resented imposition in the form of the hearth tax. Although in general commerce flourished in the period after 1660, most of the benefits were experienced by the larger merchants. For many smaller producers, this was a time of continued decline in prosperity, with high levels of under- or unemployment. Severe problems in the weaving trade were to provoke widespread rioting in 1675. In the early 1680s there were a series of bad winters, with the Thames freezing over on a number of occasions. Many who earned their living from the river experienced much hardship, and of course most Londoners faced a dramatic increase in their fuel bills. J. R. Jones has suggested that when there was 'dislocation to trade ... a shortage of employment and high prices for food and fuel' it was fairly easy for political agitators to mobilize mass support for their cause.[10] Arthur Smith, when considering the whig agitation of the exclusion period, concluded that 'economically' the time was 'ripe for unrest'. The London poor, he asserts, 'were ready to swell any mob as a release for their frustrations. The political issue of the moment did not matter.'[11]

If the interpretation that the London populace was divided on the issue

[8] Lindley, *Fenland Riots*; Sharp, *In Contempt*. But cf. the recent critique of Lindley by C. Holmes, 'Drainers and Fenmen: the Problem of Popular Political Consciousness in the Seventeenth Century', in Fletcher and Stevenson, eds., *Order and Disorder*, pp. 166–95.

[9] Thompson, 'Moral Economy'; J. Walter, 'Grain Riots and Popular Attitudes to the Law: Maldon and the Crisis of 1629', in J. Brewer and J. Styles, eds., *An Ungovernable People: The English and their Law in the Seventeenth and Eighteenth Centuries* (1980), pp. 47–84; J. Walter and K. Wrightson, 'Dearth and the Social Order in Early Modern England', in Slack, ed., *Rebellion*, pp. 108–28.

[10] Jones, *Revolution of 1688*, p. 306.

[11] Smith, 'London and the Crown', pp. 97–101.

of exclusion in the late 1670s and early 1680s is to be sustained, the argument that economic recession, bad winters and tax grievances were driving people into the whig camp needs to be confronted. Two interrelated questions need to be considered. First, what were the political implications of disputes which seem to have been primarily economic in causation, and secondly, to what extent were the political allegiances of the London masses determined by economic factors? I shall start by looking at the weavers' riot of 1675. Although the weavers were not motivated by an ideology of political opposition to the Stuart regime, the riots were nevertheless reflective of a deep-seated hostility towards French immigrant workers, and this economic xenophobia, it will be argued, helped shape political attitudes during the exclusion crisis. Other economic grievances will then be considered, in particular the distress caused by regressive taxation and also by the hard winters of the early 1680s. The tories certainly feared that economic hardship was driving people into a radical political position, but they responded to this possibility on both an ideological and a material level. By developing arguments to show that the lower classes would be worse off should the whigs have their way, and also by a careful distribution of relief to the poorest groups at the (economically and politically) most sensitive times, they were able to prevent many of those hardest hit by economic misfortune from being easy prey to radical agitators. But it will also be shown that, on both these levels, the tory response demonstrated a marked hostility towards nonconformists, and in this way helped reinforce religious tensions and divisions that already existed.[12]

THE WEAVERS' DISPUTES

The most severely depressed group of London workers were the weavers. As with many of the traditional artisanal occupations, structural changes in the organization of the weaving trade had led to an increasing polarization between the merchant dealers and the producers of cloth. The wealthier master was ceasing to practise his craft, and was becoming a specialized merchant, trader, or shopkeeper. On the other hand, the small master's direct dealings with his customers became steadily fewer, and he sank back into dependence upon the merchant for whom he now worked. A class of permanent journeymen had also come into existence, men who had neither the capital nor the opportunity to set up an independent business of their

---

[12] It should be noted that there were no 'food riots' in London in this period. It is not my intention to re-examine this question here. Useful discussions can be found in: W. J. Shelton, *English Hunger and Industrial Disorders: A Study of Social Conflict During the First Decade of George III's Reign* (1973), pp. 155–6; Rudé, *Hanoverian London*, pp. 202–4; Pearl, 'Social Policy', pp. 119–20; Lindley, 'Riot Prevention', pp. 116–17; Stevenson, *Popular Disturbances*, pp. 99–100.

own. Work was irregular and unemployment frequent, and the small masters and journeymen experienced not only a humiliating loss of status but also a decline into real poverty.[13] In Charles II's reign, the continued decay of the trade meant that the weavers had come to be despised. A tract written in 1682, at the height of the political tension of the end of the reign, mapped out the weavers' plight and, perhaps with hints of class antagonism, lay most blame on the wealthy shopkeepers:

> Poor Weavers, they constrained are to live
> Meanly, and sometimes ready to want Bread,
> While the other are both richly cloath'd and fed,
> And in their shops, (like Lords) most stately are,
> With the profit they get by the Weavers' Ware;
> And the poor Weaver, by his cruelty,
> Forc'd to spin out his life in poverty;
> Which brings a scandal on our Trade, while he
> That is the cause, doth flourish gallantly.[14]

The plight of the small producers was made even more acute by the threat of mechanization. Engine-looms for the production of silk ribbons had been in use earlier in the century, but they grew more common after the Restoration.[15] By enabling goods to be produced much more cheaply, the machines posed a threat to the livelihood of 'the poor men who with their wives worked with the ordinary looms'.[16] Large-scale rioting against the use of engine-looms occurred in August 1675. The complaint of the weavers, as one contemporary observer tells us, was that 'one man with an engine loome can doe more worke in one day than 10 men with loomes without engines', with the result that weavers were becoming so desperate for employment and thus food that 'they had rather venter hanging than starving'.[17] One of the rioters explained why he joined in the destruction of the looms in an examination taken after his arrest:

the Noise that was made concerning these Engine-Loomes, how that they would destroy their trade, That where as hee might get his Master 10s per week, if these were continued hee could not get 7s weekly, And being near out his Time, the consideration thereof, with the other disadvantage, Did stir him up to what hee did.[18]

[13] H. N. Brailsford, *The Levellers and the English Revolution*, ed. C. Hill (1976), pp. 102–4; Dunn, 'Weavers' Riot', pp. 13–14.

[14] R.C., *The Triumphant Weaver; Or, The Art of Weaving Discussed and Handled* (1682), p. 36.

[15] A. Plummer, *The London Weavers' Company, 1600–1970* (1972), p. 165.

[16] *CSPVen, 1673–5*, p. 447.

[17] *Hatt. Corr.*, I, 120. See also: *HMC, 10th Report*, p. 80; *HMC, 12th Report*, VII, 124. Another account put the ratio at 20 to 1. See *HMC, 7th Report*, pp. 465, 466.

[18] PRO, Assi 35, 116/9, examination of Guest.

Trouble started on the night of Sunday 8 August around Moorfields, and over the next four days spread to Spitalfields, Stepney, Whitechapel, Cloth Fair and Blackfriars on the outskirts of the City, and also beyond that to Stratford le Bow, Westminster, and Southwark (and surrounding urban Surrey).[19] One report claimed that during the days of rioting there were 'reckoned to be above 30,000' tumultuous weavers in the City of London alone, although this is surely an exaggeration.[20] 2,000 were supposed to have assembled together at Stratford le Bow to destroy looms there.[21] But the indictments for the City, Middlesex and Surrey suggest that the rioters mainly launched their attacks in groups of 40, 60 or 100.[22] We learn from the indictments that at least 85 engine-looms belonging to 24 different owners were destroyed, the damage to property being estimated to be in excess of £780, though these figures in reality were probably somewhat higher.[23]

Most of the rioters were male weavers. However, it is significant that a number of weavers' wives were involved in the disturbances, and of the 201 suspects who eventually appeared in court, 11 were females. This is in contrast to the more specifically political riots of the reign, for which there is no evidence of female participation.[24] This female participation in part probably reflects the important role that women played in textile production in the early modern period. It may also be that women were particularly likely to be involved in economic disputes, perhaps feeling that their role as managers of the household economy gave them a special licence to take direct action when the livelihood of their family was at stake. The prominence of women in food riots in the early modern period is a well-documented phenomenon.[25] In addition, 15 males who were not weavers were suspected of involvement in the disturbances, although it is impossible to tell whether these were genuine 'allies' of the weavers, anxious to assist

---

[19] CLRO, Sessions File, September 1675; CLRO, Sessions Papers, September 1675; GLRO, MJ/SR/1491, 1492; GLRO, MJ/GSR/1493; GLRO, WJ/SR/1494; PRO, Assi 35, 116/9; PC 2/64, fols. 490–7; PRO, SP 44/43, pp. 46–9; SP 29/372, nos. 189–90; *CSPD, 1675–6*, pp. 253–9; Jeaff., IV, 60–5; Dunn, 'Weavers' Riot'.

[20] *HMC, 7th Report*, p. 465.

[21] PRO, SP 44/43, p. 48.

[22] PRO, Assi 35, 116/9, inds. 1–5, 7, 8; GLRO, MJ/GSR/1493, inds. 1–12; CLRO, Sessions File, September 1675, inds. (O + T); Jeaff., IV, 60–5.

[23] The precise loss for some of the victims is not identified in the sources. The value of only 80 looms can be learnt from the indictments, totalling £783 10s.

[24] This is not to suggest that women were uninterested in the political controversies of the reign. 37 women (out of a total of 323 for whom sex is known) were accused of speaking anti-Stuart or pro-whig seditious words during Charles II's reign, and a further 4 (out of 48) uttered anti-exclusionist speeches. Harris, 'Politics of the London Crowd', p. 301.

[25] Walter, 'Grain Riots', pp. 62–3; Thompson, 'Moral Economy', p. 116.

in the suppression of the looms, or whether they were innocent observers who were wrongly arrested.[26]

There does at least seem to have been quite widespread sympathy for the actions of the weavers. Local constables and the London and Tower militias were unwilling to suppress the riots.[27] One informant stated that in Newington Butts the trained bands, instead of suppressing the weavers, seemed to side with the rioters, some of whom were escaping arrest with the soldiers' connivance.[28] In Shoreditch William Tindall, ensign of one troop of trained bands, was ordered to safeguard one rioter, but instead of taking him before a JP, decided to set him free.[29] Even the Lieutenant of the Tower, Sir John Robinson, refused to send his forces against the rioters. Indeed, four weavers from Southwark were sent to meet with Sir John to seek his advice and help, and he apparently told them: 'Every man of you go away to your Own houses. And I will seek to get some thing done for your own good, According to my Power.'[30] The royal guards under the command of the duke of Monmouth eventually had to be called in to restore order.[31] When some of the rioters appeared in the pillory in October, the Venetian ambassador noted that none of the usual atrocities were committed on this occasion, 'but there was rather a sentiment of universal sympathy'.[32]

The weavers took action, of course, in order to try and protect their economic livelihood. The precise trigger, which explains why a long-standing grievance erupted into unrest at that exact moment, may have been the dearth of 1674–5. Wheat prices rose to nearly 70s per quarter.[33] A depression in the Essex weaving trade led also to disturbances in Colchester in the summer of 1675.[34] But it would be wrong to say that disorder was a response to crude economic stimuli. The affair provides a classic example of collective bargaining by riot, unrest being an extension of the bargaining process after the failure of more peaceful methods.[35] In a broad sense, the weavers' protest was both political and ideological in nature. The weavers made complaints about the engine-loom to all the appropriate political authorities, local and

---

[26] Dunn, 'Weavers' Riot', p. 21. The 15 were: butcher, cordwainer, goldsmith, innkeeper, leatherseller, porter, silversmith (2), tailor, tallowchandler, tobacco-pipe maker, victualler (2), vintner (2).

[27] Dunn, 'Weavers' Riot', pp. 18–21. However, Dunn has missed some material relating to this which can be found in PRO, Assi 35, 116/9.

[28] PRO, Assi 35, 116/9, information of Vaughan.

[29] GLRO, MJ/GSR/1493, ind. 3; Jeaff., IV, 64.

[30] PRO, Assi 35, 116/9, examination of Guest. For the government's attempts to deal with the recalcitrance of Sir John and others, see: PRO, PC 2/64, pp. 490–7; CSPD, 1675–6, pp. 258–9.

[31] PRO, PC 2/64, p. 490.

[32] CSPVen, 1673–5, p. 466.

[33] Maitland, London, I, 460.

[34] PRO, PC 2/65, p. 17.

[35] Hobsbawm, 'Machine Breakers', pp. 58–62.

central, before resorting to riot, and it was clear that they recognized that there could only be a political solution to the problem. Riot, when it happened, was constrained by self-imposed norms determining what action was regarded as legitimate, revealing an ideological control on the violence.

The peaceful presentation of grievances concerning engine-looms had had a long, if frustrated, history. As far back as James I's reign there had been complaints about their use.[36] In 1638 Charles I presented a solution by including in his letters patent granted to the Weavers' Company an express prohibition of the use of engine-looms.[37] Little is heard of the affair during the Civil War and Commonwealth period, but by late 1666 and early 1667 we find informations being presented to the court of the Weavers' Company against people who kept engine-looms.[38] In December 1667 the Yeomanry of the Company presented a paper to the court of the names of engine-loom owners, and a committee was set up to endeavour the suppression of such machines.[39] The next step was to take the case to the court of aldermen and the common council of London, which was done in February 1668. The aim was to get the City authorities to procure an act of parliament for suppressing the engine-loom.[40] A bill was eventually discussed in parliament, but after a second reading on 18 January 1671, and the injection into the debate of a counter petition submitted by engine-loom owners on 16 February, nothing more was heard of it.[41]

The legal situation with regard to the use of the engine-looms was thus far from clear. The last explicit decision on this matter had been the royal prohibition of 1638, and prohibition seems to have been the official line adopted by the Weavers' Company and the court of aldermen in the 1660s. The weavers therefore had good reason to believe that the use of engine-looms was illegal, although they were being frustrated in their efforts to secure the suppression of these machines. They therefore decided to take action themselves. The rioting of 1675 appears to have been a well coordinated attempt by the weavers to enforce what they perceived to be the law when the authorities had failed in their responsibilities. The riot was certainly planned in advance. The lord mayor knew of the intended action a day beforehand, and ordered a double watch as a precaution.[42] Informations given in Southwark, admittedly in the aftermath of the riot, claimed that a good week before unrest erupted, weavers in and around the urban area could be heard discussing 'a greate rising ... to pull downe the engine

[36] *CSPD, 1611–18*, p. 397; *CSPD, 1619–23*, p. 271.
[37] *CSPD, 1637–8*, p. 454; Plummer, *Weavers' Company*, pp. 280–1.
[38] Guildhall Library, MS 4655/4, fols. 5, 9, 51.
[39] Ibid., fol. 93.
[40] CLRO, Rep. 73, fol. 67; CLRO, Journal 46, fol. 211.
[41] CLRO, Rep. 76, fol. 46; *CJ*, IX, 190, 202–3; Dunn, 'Weavers' Riot', p. 15.
[42] CLRO, Journal 48, fol. 168.

loomes'.[43] On the weekend before the riot, claimed one informant, the wife of a weaver from Newington Butts was heard to say 'if the weomen (sic) would rise to pull downe the engine loomes shee would ... healpe and assist them'.[44] A pamphlet called *In Honour of the Weavers* was produced at the time of the rioting, which perhaps served as a manifesto, although unfortunately the tract has not survived.[45]

The aims of the riot were clearly limited to the destruction of machines.[46] The weavers were under strict instructions to 'Meddle only with the Looms.'[47] They went to the houses of those known to own engine-looms, first asked – but if necessary forced – them to deliver up their looms, which they then removed and burnt in a ritualistic fashion outside the owner's door.[48] The rioters seem to have had specific victims in mind. Thomas Bibby was the one who had suffered most from the riot in Southwark, and it was he who was the first owner to be named in person to the Weavers' Company back in November 1666.[49] Another victim was Edward Berstowe, who was actually an assistant of the Weavers' Company at this time.[50] But there seems to have been no general pillaging or theft, and no violent assaults on individuals. This contrasts with those who were determined to defend their property, as two of the rioters lost their lives.[51]

The weavers continued to hope for a political settlement even after violence had erupted. Shortly after the royal guards had managed to quieten the unrest, the weavers were expressing their intention 'to wait for the meeting of parliament in order to make their appeal to it'.[52] Meanwhile the Weavers' Company was forced to take action. Money was given to some of the weavers in Newgate, and further investigations concerning the looms were launched.[53] The Company presented a petition to the house of commons on 13 November 1675, linking an attack on the engine-loom with complaints against foreign importation.[54] In December that year a further petition against the machines was made to the privy council.[55] Such petitions came

[43] PRO, Assi 35, 116/9, informations of Pratt and Tilsley.
[44] Ibid., information of Ratcliffe.
[45] CLRO, Sessions File, September 1675, rec. 3.
[46] *HMC, 12th Report*, VII, 124.
[47] PRO, Assi 35, 116/9, examination of Guest.
[48] *HMC, 12th Report*, VII, 124; PRO Assi 35, 116/9, information of James Bradshaw.
[49] Guildhall Library, MS 4655/4, fol. 5.
[50] Ibid., MS 4655/6, fol. 72. Berstowe's membership of the Weavers' Company Court went back at least to 1661. See ibid., MS 4655/3–5, *passim*.
[51] William Hewes and William Evans lost their lives. See PRO, Assi 35, 116/9, ind. 6, note of acquittal for murder, and information touching death of William Evans.
[52] *CSPVen, 1673–5*, p. 449.
[53] Guildhall Library, MS 4648/1, renter bailiff's accounts from August 1675 to April 1676, *passim*.
[54] Ibid., MS 4655/8, fols. 66, 67; *CJ*, IX, 375.
[55] *CSPD, 1675–6*, p. 434; Guildhall Library, MS 4655/8, fol. 72.

to nothing, and Richard Dunn has argued that this was due to the Weavers' Company's half-hearted commitment to the suppression of engine-looms, becoming more concerned with the threat of foreign importation.[56]

The central government initially feared that the riot might have been political in a narrower sense, and that it had dangerous radical overtones. A proclamation was issued in the king's name threatening the rioters with prosecution for treason.[57] The Venetian ambassador believed this was done 'not so much because of the rioting of these poor folk as from the danger of its providing an opportunity for other unquiet spirits and malcontents to come together and that these wretched, unarmed and half desperate people might be supplied with money and arms by those ill affected to the court'.[58] Some of the weavers marched wearing green aprons, a colour traditionally associated with the levellers, and perhaps symbolizing certain political sympathies.[59] Indeed, in the 1640s the weavers, and especially the silk-weavers of Spitalfields, had won support from Lilburne and the levellers.[60] Radical sectarians were feared to have been agitating the rioters. John Mason, a weaver and a fifth monarchist, was charged with being involved in the riot and encouraging the weavers with seditious words.[61]

Yet despite these initial anxieties the government soon became convinced that the insurrection was 'unpollitically designed'.[62] The king himself came to believe the ground was 'no other than what is pretended'.[63] Secretary of State, Sir Joseph Williamson, said the riot was 'without any design or foundation more than the interest these common weavers have to suppress ... the use of this engine'.[64] And it was decided not to proceed against the rioters for high treason, as had been the case with the bawdy house riots of 1668, when wider political implications were strongly suspected.[65] Much of the evidence which gave the government initial cause for concern did not stand closer scrutiny. The fifth monarchist Mason, it turned out, was a victim and not an instigator of the riots, having one engine-loom destroyed.[66] A quaker from Newington Butts was another victim of the

---

[56] Dunn, 'Weavers' Riot', pp. 22–3.
[57] PRO, PC 2/64, p. 490; Charles II, *A Proclamation for the Suppression of Riots* (1675).
[58] *CSPVen, 1673–5*, p. 448.
[59] CLRO, Journal 48, fol. 168; Dunn, 'Weavers' Riot', p. 17; C. Hill, *Reformation to Industrial Revolution* (Harmondsworth, 1969), p. 143.
[60] Brailsford, *Levellers*, pp. 104, 289, 297.
[61] *CSPD, 1675–6*, pp. 258, 259.
[62] BL, Add. MS 25,124, fol. 43.
[63] Ibid., fol. 39.
[64] *CSPD, 1675–6*, p. 255.
[65] *State Trials*, VI, fols. 893–5.
[66] GLRO, MJ/SR/1491, gaol calendar, committals of Herberd and Conway, rec. 5 (O + T, to prosecute).

riot.[67] It was such radical separatists who were most commonly regarded as 'unquiet spirits' and 'those ill-affected to the court'.

The significance of green aprons used for colours can be questioned. Some people claimed they had been falsely arrested because they had been wearing their normal work clothes, namely green aprons.[68] In Surrey some of the rioters wore blue feathers,[69] a colour later associated with the duke of Monmouth, who on this occasion played the key role in suppressing the riots.[70] Some of the rioters even wore red ribbons,[71] a practice associated with support for the duke of York during the exclusion crisis.[72] It cannot be convincingly argued that the colours were chosen in order to show affinity with a particular political cause. A more likely explanation is that different colours depicted the different regiments into which rioters customarily grouped themselves during the course of a riot.[73]

There seems little evidence, then, to suggest that the weavers were motivated by an ideology of political opposition to the Stuart regime, or that the riots were instigated by radical subversives. But looking for such a direct link between economic unrest and political opposition is perhaps a misguided approach. It is better to consider the way in which the weavers' disputes helped shape certain aspects of London political culture, and thus influence the way people might perceive the political crisis at the end of the reign. For example, propagandists during the exclusion period sought to exploit the chauvinism and xenophobia of the London populace, the catholic threat typically being represented as an external one, posed by hostile foreign powers, and in particular by France. The reason why such arguments were so powerful was because many London artisans, and particularly the weavers, did perceive that their own difficulties were created largely by foreigners, and especially by the French. In other words, economic xenophobia reinforced anti-French and anti-catholic sentiments, and helps explain the intensity of emotion aroused after the revelations of the Popish Plot.

The engine-loom which the weavers had wanted to suppress had always been associated with foreigners. Invented in Gdansk in the early 1580s, it was banned in that city, but was taken up by the Dutch at Leiden in 1604, and when it found its way into England became known as the Dutch loom.[74] Silk textile production, concentrated as it was in the eastern outparishes of London, was exposed more than any other part of the textile

[67] *HMC, 7th Report*, p. 465.
[68] CLRO, Sessions Papers, September 1675, examination of Staherne.
[69] PRO, Assi 35, 116/9, examination of Guest.
[70] Allen, 'Clubs', p. 569.
[71] CLRO, Journal 48, fol. 168.
[72] Allen, 'Clubs', p. 569.
[73] See above, p. 25.
[74] Plummer, *Weavers' Company*, p. 163.

industry to foreign competition. It had grown up largely under the influence of Dutch and French weavers in the sixteenth century, who had come to England to escape the persecutions of the continent. By 1583 there were 5,141 aliens in the City, Southwark and Westminster. A return of aliens in 1618 showed that the majority were silkweavers.[75] By the autumn of 1612 the Weavers' Company was complaining that foreign silkweavers practising in and around London were eating 'the bread out of our people's mouths', and that 'our own people are grown into the most extreme wants, and know not what to do in winter-time when work will fail and be more scant'.[76]

As the seventeenth century progressed the threat from aliens and from mechanization came to be regarded as more interrelated, and to understand this we need to be aware of the peculiar position of alien weavers in England, which could make the use of machines seem more attractive than manpower. Hobsbawm and Rudé have argued that action against machines is only necessary if they are seen as a threat to livelihood, and are likely to be particularly resented at times of un- or underemployment. Yet at such times there is a reservoir of cheap labour, which could make the need for labour-saving devices unnecessary. Any savings that machines brought would be likely to be offset by a rise in the poor rates.[77] Un- and underemployment were prevalent under the domestic system. Even when times were relatively prosperous, weavers were rarely fully occupied the whole year round, as the above-cited complaint of the Company in 1612 shows. In addition to this, the economic thought of the period seems to have been unsympathetic to labour-saving devices.[78]

Alien weavers were admitted by the London Company, but at lower grades. No foreigners could be freemen, but they could achieve one of three positions: that of foreign master, allowed to take apprentices; foreign weaver, allowed to work independently, but not to set up as householders; and journeymen, not permitted to work independently.[79] To the middle group, in particular, the use of machines might seem especially attractive. This sets the context for a 1616 petition from the Weavers' Company, which urged that alien weavers

should entertain English apprentices and servants to learn these trades, the neglect thereof giveth them advantage to keep their misteries to themselves, which hath made them bold of late to devise engines for working of tape, lace, ribbon and

[75] Ibid., p. 144.
[76] HMC, *Salisbury*, XXII, 5–6.
[77] E. J. Hobsbawm and G. Rudé, *Captain Swing* (1969), p. 359.
[78] T. E. Gregory, 'The Economics of Employment in England, 1660–1713', *Economica*, 1 (1921), 48.
[79] Plummer, *Weavers' Company*, pp. 16–17.

such, wherein one man doth more among them than seven English men can do, so that their cheap sale of those commodities beggareth all our English artificers of that trade and enricheth them.[80]

In 1621 the protest was made against 'that devilish invention of looms brought in by strangers ... [which] are the destruction of many poor',[81] whilst in the reign of Charles I the Weavers' Company sought to obtain control over aliens who had invented machines, and who refused to employ English journeymen or apprentices.[82] The engine was also associated with the production of silk goods of inferior quality,[83] a problem aggravated by the importation of cheap goods. On 29 March 1671, in a petition to the house of lords, the weavers asserted that they had 'attained great skill in the making of all sort of ... [silk] stuffs ... and could, if encouraged, supply the nation cheaply. They are, however, impoverished by the importation of foreign goods, chiefly French', which they wanted to have stopped. The weavers argued that the 'English do maintain the French Kings poor at work (whilst the Natives here are ready to starve and perish through want of work)'. However, a counter-petition by the merchants of London in favour of free trade meant that nothing was done.[84] The merchants explicitly linked the case against foreign prohibition with a defence of the engine-loom in a pamphlet written that year.[85]

By 1671, it seems, the threat from unfair foreign competition (domestic and overseas), from the engine-loom and from alien artisans, was coming to be seen as part and parcel of the same problem. Importantly, it was increasingly the French who came to be most resented, even though until Charles II's reign the majority of alien silkweavers in London were Dutch. It is normally argued that the bulk of the influx of French artisans did not come until the 1680s, with the 'dragonnades' and then the revocation of the Edict of Nantes in 1685 forcing huguenots to flee in the face of persecution.[86] Yet earlier French immigration seems to have been on a sufficient scale to cause severe anxieties. As early as November 1660 some MPs had expressed their concern over the 'multitude of French now in town, who eat the bread out of the mouths of natives, there being as they say no less than 35,000 silk weavers come hither since '57'.[87] Although the

---

[80] Cited in E. Lipson, *The Economic History of England*, III (1931), 52–3.

[81] *CSPD, 1619–23*, p. 271.

[82] *CSPD, Addenda, 1625–49*, pp. 313–14.

[83] The Weavers' Company petition of February 1668 makes this point. See CLRO, Rep. 73, fol. 67.

[84] HLRO, Main Papers, H. L., 29 March – 1 April 1671; *HMC, 9th Report*, II, 14.

[85] *Reasons Humbly Offered Against a Bill for Regulating and Encouraging the Art of Weaving* (1671).

[86] R. Gwynn, 'The Arrival of Huguenot Refugees in England, 1680–1705', *Proceedings of the Huguenot Society*, 21 (1969), 366–73.

[87] *HMC, 5th Report*, p. 195.

precise figure might be an exaggeration, the minutes of the Weavers' Company show that they were accepting huguenot refugees from as early as 1668.[88]

Tension between native weavers and French immigrants first became explicit in 1669, when certain of the yeomanry of the Weavers' Company preferred indictments against four members of the French congregation in London for flouting the laws regulating the work of aliens.[89] The French and Dutch churches petitioned the king, complaining about such molestation, and demanding the release of the four. The Weavers' Company replied by pointing out that too many aliens were coming over to England, even though there was no 'want of Workmen (there being now Severall hundreds that cannot gett Imployment and are ready to Starve and Perish)', and that the aliens had more workmen 'then they will or can imploy'. They suggested that the aliens were worried because the natives were surpassing their skill in the production of silk goods, and were 'willing to prejudice themselves by inviting over more', at a time when trade was dead and when they could not sell all they produced anyway, 'in the hopes that Natives will be much more prejudiced and discouraged'. The petition concluded by expressing the hope that 'little Incouragement shall be given to others to come over, for certainly Charity ought to begin at home' and that foreigners should not be allowed 'to eat the bread out of the Natives Mouths and Incouraged whilst they looke on are ready to Starve and perish through want'.[90]

The weavers' riot was believed to have been 'occasioned ... by the dangerous discontent that the silk weavers and others have taken up against the French inhabitants in the city and suburbs, robbing them as they conceive of their trade and livelihood'.[91] The French were apparently the first to be attacked.[92] According to one contemporary, the reason why many local officers refused to act against the rioters was because they 'sought to see the French inventions (as they called them) burnt'.[93] The weavers were not alone in their hostility towards foreign artisans. The petition of the French and Dutch churches to Charles II of 1669 mentioned that 'other Companyes of Artificers in London', besides the weavers, had been molesting them.[94] In the petition to the house of lords of 1671 against imported silk stuffs, already mentioned, several other London mercers joined with the weavers in their expressions against the French.[95] Shortly after the riot of August

[88] Guildhall Library, MS 4655/5, fol. 24.
[89] Bodl. Lib., MS Rawlinson A 478, fol. 97.
[90] BL, Harleian MS 2262, fols. 8–11.
[91] *HMC, 6th Report*, p. 372. See also: *HMC, 7th Report*, p. 492; *CSPD, 1675–6*, p. 253.
[92] *Hatt. Corr.*, I, 120.
[93] *HMC, 7th Report*, p. 466.
[94] BL, Harleian MS 2262, fol. 8.
[95] HLRO, Main Papers, H.L., 29 March 1671; *HMC, 9th Report*, II, 14.

1675 it was noted that the English hatters had 'made a move against the French ones, as well as some other artisans in order to drive away from London all the workmen who are not natives or subjects of these realms'. Rumour had it that 'they were going to massacre all the French, who have introduced various manufactures and who work for less than the English'.[96]

The problems affecting the weavers were part of a wider crisis of foreign competition facing many domestic artisans. This was certainly true of the hatters, or feltmakers. An act of common council of 3 and 4 Philip and Mary had forbidden citizens to employ foreigners, but a special clause had excluded the feltmakers from the provisions of this act. In February 1662 the feltmakers petitioned the common council for the repeal of this clause, complaining that they had become impoverished as a result of their masters' taking on cheap foreign labour. Some, they alleged, had even been forced into other employment, such as working as porters. The masters and wardens of the Feltmakers' Company petitioned against the repeal, stating that the journeymen would not work 'but for unreasonable wages'. A repeal, they said, would be prejudicial to the government of the Company, since many freemen would move into Southwark where they could employ foreigners. In May 1663 the common council decided to support the journeymen and repeal the clause in the act, but their threatened action in 1675 suggests that this did not succeed in solving their problems.[97]

Another group facing similar difficulties were the carpenters. In November 1674 they petitioned the court of aldermen complaining 'that diverse Masters of the said trade under pretence of wanting Freemen have and doe imploy Forreynors to the impoverishment of the petitioners and their familyes'. They asked that they might be allowed to congregate at the back of the Royal Exchange in Threadneedle Street each morning between 5 and 7 'to the end it might appeare that there are Journeymen sufficient of that trade free of this Citty'. The masters and wardens of the Carpenters' Company stated that they would be happy with this arrangement, and so the court of aldermen conceded the demand.[98] In October 1675, the fishmongers complained to this court 'of great Numbers of persons forreigners unlicensed that take upon them to ingrosse great quantityes of fish and sell the same in the streets, being not shopkeepers', which was in violation of an act of common council of 6 March 1661. The aldermen ordered an enquiry, although there is no record of any final decision being reached in this matter.[99]

The first group to contemplate taking direct action against foreign artisans

[96] *CSPVen*, 1673–5, p. 449.
[97] CLRO, Journal 45, fols. 159, 311.
[98] CLRO, Rep. 80, fols. 29, 40–1.
[99] Ibid., fol. 283.

were the tailors. In 1670, a group of journeymen tailors met to draw up their grievances in writing, in order to encourage other artisans to resist the French threat. Their paper read:

To all Gentlemen Apprentices and Journeymen Inhabitants of London and Suburbs. This is to acquaint you that by foureigne Nations wee are impoverished by them tradinge within our Nation, espetially by the French ... we will not suffer it noe longer, for by your assistance, we are resolved to meet in Morefields betwixt eight and nine of the Clocke in the afternoone on Mayday next. Therefore faile NOT, for wee your Brethren Apprentices and Journimen will not faile you, for wee will not have them raigne in our kingdome. So God save the King and all the Royall Family. Procure what armes you can for we are resolved to doe it.[100]

The plans were leaked to the government and so came to nothing, but the tailors' paper does reveal the intensity of anti-French feeling in the capital.

Following the failure of this insurrection, more peaceful methods were tried. At the end of July 1675 the journeymen tailors petitioned the court of aldermen to ask the city chamberlain to take action against the employment of foreigners. In September the master tailors responded with a counter-petition stating that it would be prejudicial to them if they were not allowed to take on foreigners, but the court resolved that they could only do so if they were granted a special licence by the city chamberlain.[101] In October 1681 the masters complained to the common council about the inconvenience this arrangement was causing them. The English journeymen, they said, 'supposeing themselves only can be imployed, are grown so unruly and undutiful to the Masters, that they cannot be Indured'. Moreover, there were too few English journeymen for their needs, but having to apply for licences to take on foreigners, 'when their work requires Expedition is very troublesome and Dilatory'. They reminded the common council that if they did 'remove tho' but two doores out of the Libertyes of this Citty they might Enjoy the same without any trouble or molestation'. The common council conceded that the masters should be free to take on foreigners, provided that journeymen who were free of the City were employed first.[102] In June 1686 the masters complained again to the court of aldermen that they were being molested 'for setting on Worke journimen of their trade not free of this citty', even though they took on journeymen freemen first. The journeymen freemen responded by stating that several master tailors were 'preferring foreigners before them contrary to the lawes of this city', causing them great hardships.[103]

This history of competition from immigrant workers created an intense

---

[100] PRO, SP 29/274, nos. 205, 206.
[101] CLRO, Rep. 80, fols. 258, 274, 299.
[102] CLRO, Journal 49, fols. 254, 277–8.
[103] CLRO, Rep. 91, fols. 110, 116, 141–2.

hatred of foreigners, and especially of the French, amongst many English artisanal groups. The situation became particularly tense in the 1680s, when French immigration reached its peak, and it even seemed likely that violent protest would erupt once more.[104] In August 1683 there were rumours that the Spitalfields weavers were engaged in a secret conspiracy against the French. They intended to petition the king against the French weavers, but supposedly claimed that 'if they can get a sufficient number together, they will rise and knock them on the head'.[105] A year later there were further reports that weavers in Moorfields and Spitalfields were preparing 'to rise and brake all the Loomes of the weavers that underworke them'.[106]

This anti-French sentiment informed people's political outlook during the exclusion crisis. At first this might seem odd, since it was the catholic threat from France that was the issue at this time, whilst the immigrants were French calvinists fleeing from catholic persecution. In 1681 Charles II made a public appeal on behalf of the huguenot refugees, a move which was supported by whig and tory leaders alike.[107] However, not only were English journeymen and apprentices less hospitably inclined towards the huguenots, but they interpreted what they perceived to be a further French threat to their livelihood in terms of their existing preconceptions and assumptions. Thus it was widely rumoured that the French protestants were really papist spies sent by Louis XIV to assist him in preparation for an invasion.[108] The group of whig apprentices led by Mr Stillingfleet certainly shared these anxieties. In May 1682 these apprentices seem to have contemplated 'pull-[ing] downe the Post house where the French said Protestants are', as our whig apprentice source puts it. The mayor took anticipatory action to prevent any disorder, so instead Stillingfleet held a meeting of his followers where he inveighed against the popish threat. Amongst other things, he complained that 'French Papists' were 'brought in and allowed the benefit of Free denizen to the great prejudice of his Majesties free born subjects'.[109]

OTHER ECONOMIC GRIEVANCES AND THEIR POLITICAL
IMPLICATIONS

Before I consider in more detail whether it was those groups hardest hit by immigrant competition which were most likely to support the whigs

---

[104] Smith, 'London and the Crown', pp. 58–9.
[105] *CSPD, July–Sept., 1683*, pp. 267, 325, 330.
[106] LC, MS 18,124, IX, fol. 100.
[107] M. A. Goldie, 'The Huguenot Experience and the Problem of Toleration in England' (forthcoming).
[108] LC, MS 18,124, VIII, fol. 10; *London Gazette*, no. 1661; Smith, 'London and the Crown', p. 59.
[109] LC, MS 18,124, VIII, fol. 57. Other aspects of this speech are discussed above, pp. 177–8.

after 1678, it is necessary to look at some of the other material grievances of the lower orders during Charles II's reign. Prime amongst these was the issue of regressive taxation. I have already commented on the influence of anti-excise sentiment in shaping attitudes at the time of the Restoration. After 1660, the excise continued to be a regular form of indirect taxation, and the number of goods which had to pay it began to grow.[110] Marvell believed that excise was now 'a monster worse than e're before', used to support a land army and the extravagance of the Court.[111] In addition, there was now the hearth tax, introduced in 1662, being a yearly tax of two shillings on all domestic hearths, payable in half-yearly instalments except by the very poorest people. It was repealed shortly after the Glorious Revolution by an act of 1 William and Mary, c. 10 for the following reasons: 'it is in itselfe not onely a great Oppression to the Poorer sort, but a Badge of Slavery upon the whole People, Exposeing every mans House to be Entred into and Searched at pleasure by persons unknown to him'.[112]

The hearth tax was hated right from its introduction. In 1662 Pepys wrote that there was 'much clamour against the Chimney Money', people saying 'they will not pay it without force'.[113] A Southwark critic said it was 'heavier than any other tax, falling mostly on such as through inability never contributed to former taxes'.[114] In June 1662, one Henry Parnby supposedly said 'if the King upholds the Act for Chimnies he would not own him to be King'.[115] In May 1664 one Henry Phillips was charged with uttering seditious words which suggest how some people might have reacted to the new tax: 'the King that now is did take the same waies that his father did to be ill beloved, and that the Chimnie-monie would prove a worse burden then formerly the Ship-monie was'.[116]

Other taxes which hit the lower classes were also resented. In August 1679 Richard Selwin, a victualler from St Katherine's by the Tower, was bound over for assaulting a collector of the poll tax and saying 'they were the Heads of Hell that first Caused that Tax'.[117] Resentment ran highest when those who could afford to pay seemed to be escaping taxes, or when taxes collected were not being used for their appropriate ends. In September 1686, one Henry Curle supposedly uttered these scandalous words: 'My Arse upon the Justices, for they do not pay their taxes.'[118] In November

[110] Beloff, *Public Order*, p. 93; Kennedy, *English Taxation*, ch. 4.
[111] Marvell, *Last Instructions*, in *POAS*, I, 106.
[112] *Statutes of the Realm*, VI, 61–2.
[113] Pepys, *Diary*, III, 127.
[114] *CSPD, 1665–6*, p. 179.
[115] GLRO, MJ/SBB/198, p. 41.
[116] GLRO, MJ/SR/1287, unnumb. rec.; Jeaff., III, 338–9.
[117] GLRO, MJ/SR/1566, rec. 220.
[118] GLRO, MJ/SR/1696, ind. 6.

1666 Humphrey Dewell, a cooper from All-Hallows, Barking, levelled the charge that 'Sir Richard Ford hath wronged the poore and will not pay them their due. And I will send the poore to his doore. And they shall not stirre thence till they be paid itt.'[119]

Having said this, collective action against the imposition of taxes was uncommon. Excise disputes normally happened when the duties were being levied at the markets. For example, on 28 July 1677, in Leadenhall market, a group of about fifteen butchers assembled against the farmers of the rights and duties of meat, attempting to impede them in their business.[120] Crowd unrest against hearth tax collectors was also very rare. In August 1666 one William Barret was accused of assaulting the officers of Hackney collecting the hearth money, and for inciting the people against the payment of that duty.[121] Collective passive resistance could occur. The 1664 hearth tax returns for Finsbury division show that in the White Cross Street liberty of St Giles-without-Cripplegate, Middlesex division, 42 people (out of a total of 254 whose hearths were chargeable) were entered as refusing to give account.[122] This was greatly in excess of the normal number of non-payers, and the fact that the people were grouped together in one neighbourhood, often living next door to each other, suggests some coordinated design. But it is only possible to draw these implications from this evidence because it stands out for its uniqueness.

Much more common were individual assaults on hearth tax collectors.[123] One detailed account of such an assault survives. In May 1682 the collector of the tax for Clerkenwell came to the house of Ralph Kingston, and found eight hearths, although previously Kingston had only been paying for seven. The collector, one Grascombe, asked for two years' arrears for the new hearth, which Kingston refused to pay. The collector therefore tried to distrain a tankard, which led to the assault by Kingston in order to regain his property.[124]

If the problems caused by the depression in the weaving trade and taxation of the lower orders were not severe enough, there were additional difficulties facing Charles II's government in the early 1680s. At the politically most sensitive time of the reign – when Charles defeated exclusion by refusing to summon parliament, when there was an attack on whig strongholds in the City of London and in other corporations throughout England and when a severe policy of religious persecution was vigorously pursued – there were

[119] CLRO, Sessions File, December 1666, ind. of Dewell.
[120] Ibid., September 1677, ind. of Holland *et al.*
[121] *CSPD*, 1666–7, p. 48.
[122] GLRO, MR/TH/1, fols. 3–5.
[123] For example, see: CLRO, Sessions File, October 1682, rec. 1; ibid., May/June 1682, ind.; GLRO, MJ/SR/1504, rec. 52; GLRO, MJ/SR/1604, rec. 182.
[124] GLRO, Acc 591/9.

a series of bad winters which caused much hardship. In January 1681 there was 'a great frost, so that the Thames in some places was frozen'.[125] But it was the winter of 1683–4 which witnessed the really big freeze, leading to the famous frost fairs on the Thames.[126] According to Luttrell, the freeze was responsible for 'raiseing the price of all commodities', with the result that 'all provisions were at an excessive rate, and fireing very dear', causing much anxiety about the plight of the poor in and around the capital.[127] One poem noted that the great frost was '... hard and grievous to the poor,/who many hungry bellies did endure'.[128] Those whose livelihood depended on river traffic, and especially the watermen, were also adversely hit. The Thames again froze over in January 1685, although this time only in the area around Chelsea.[129]

It is possible to understand, then, how the time might have been 'ripe for unrest' in the early 1680s. There was certainly a large pool of economically depressed artisans and labourers whose grievances political agitators sought to exploit. This can be seen by looking at the intrigues of those few radical whigs who seem to have contemplated the idea of a popular rebellion after the defeat in the shrieval elections of 1682. Until his flight to Holland in December 1682, Shaftesbury was heavily involved in these intrigues, and it was rumoured that he had '10,000 brisk boys' ready to do his business. One group of workers he seems to have been particularly cultivating were the seamen and watermen.[130] In the summer of 1683 came the revelations of the Rye House Plot, a supposed plan to murder the king and the duke of York on their return from Newmarket. It was also alleged that some whigs had planned to coordinate a nationwide rebellion, centred on London. Richard Goodenough, member of the Green Ribbon Club, had apparently employed a crape-weaver to manage the weavers in Spitalfields on that account. Some of the conspirators seem to have expected 5,000 weavers to join the rising.[131] The duke of Ormonde believed that many of 'the meaner sort that were in the conspiracy' were 'broken or indigent tradesmen'.[132] One of the manifestoes drawn up by the plotters at this time promised, amongst other things, the abolition of the hearth tax.[133]

---

[125] Luttrell, I, 62.
[126] R. A. Beddard, 'The London Frost Fair, 1683–4', *Guildhall Miscellany*, IV, no. 2 (April, 1972), 63–87.
[127] Luttrell, I, 294, 296.
[128] *A True Description of Blanket Fair upon the River Thames* (1684) in E. F. Rimbault, ed., *Old Ballads Illustrating the Great Frost of 1683–4 and the Fair on the River Thames* (1844), p. 9.
[129] Luttrell, I, 324.
[130] Ailesbury, *Memoirs*, I, 66.
[131] *CSPD, July–Sept. 1683*, pp. 5, 71–2; Smith, 'London and the Crown', p. 101.
[132] *HMC, 36 Ormond*, NS VII, 65.
[133] *CSPD, July–Sept. 1683*, p. 56.

The problem with the Rye House intrigues is that it is difficult to distinguish fact from fiction. All that can be said for certain is that plotters, informers and the government believed it credible that economically impoverished groups might be easily persuaded to join in a rebellion. There is no evidence to suggest that such groups ever did contemplate such a rebellion. On the other hand there is a lot of evidence which leads us to cast doubts on the assumption that material hardship must have automatically been driving people into the hands of the whigs.

Although I argued in chapter six that tory propaganda was in many respects anti-populist in tone, the tories were nevertheless sensitive to the need of trying to cultivate the poorer classes. Tory propaganda of the exclusion crisis continually argued that the lower orders would gain nothing from supporting the whigs. The commonwealth period, they asserted, had offered the lower classes less than they wanted; the levellers and radical religious sects had had no luck under Cromwell, whilst expenses of government and foreign policy had led to the introduction of taxes which hit the lower classes. One tory print showed a puritan, recognizable by his cloak, preaching from a tub. The accompanying poem warned: 'To blind People's Eyes, This Cloak was so wise,/It took off Ship-money but set up Excise.'[134] Another depicted the 'fruits of the Commonwealth' as including taxes, excise, and monthly assessments.[135] Similar points were made by L'Estrange's print, *The Committee*, which recalls how nonconformist rule had meant the excise and army accounts, as well as sequestrated livings.[136]

Any pretended concern for the poorer classes by the whigs, the tories argued, was a trick. As one satire put it, 'Religion is the surest Cloak,/To hide our Treachery;/The Rabble we'll confine to th' yoak/Pretending to set Free.'[137] *The Observator* asked what care the whigs took

for the Good of the Subject; and for the securing of the well-affected Porters, and Watermen, in their Liberties and Estates? ... I cannot call to mind that ever I saw my Lord Whirligig, Sr. Popular Typsie, or Thomas Troublesome Esquire, carrying Sacks at Queen Hithe, or Tugging at a Western Barge, to Ease any of these Free-born Commoners, of their Bodily Labours or Burdens ... [In the late Commonwealth] they shar'd all the Offices of Dignity, Power, and Profit, among themselves, and left the Deluded Multitude to shift it in Raggs, betwixt Hell and their Consciences, without so much as an Obolus to Pay the Ferry-man.[138]

In this context an illustrated broadside of 1680 by Thomas Lanfière is of especial interest. Discussing the current bad times, he asked when things

---

[134] *Ballad of the Cloak*, in *Roxburghe Ballads*, IV, 606; *BM Prints*, no. 1109.
[135] 'The Commonwealth Ruling with a Standing Army', frontispiece to [May], *Arbitrary Government; BM Prints*, no. 1127.
[136] *The Committee; BM Prints*, no. 1080.
[137] *The Whigs Down-fall* [ND], in Thompson, ed., *Songs*, p. 11.
[138] L'Estrange, *Observator*, no. 38.

would be right again, and suggested a number of answers:

> When great rates and taxes are took away ...
> When as all the rich men so liberal will grow
> That to the poor part of their means they bestow ...
> When trading is quick as it formerly was ...
> When Roundheads and Quakers their Religion remove,
> To turn Cavaliers, and Church government love.[139]

It was even possible to offer ideological explanations of material hardship apparently caused solely by natural phenomena, such as the weather. This tactic was used a lot immediately after the Restoration. A fast was held in January 1662 'to avert Gods heavy judgment on this Land, there having fallen so greate raine without any frost or seasonable cold'. A sermon preached in St Margaret's, Westminster, to members of parliament, blamed 'the neglect of exacting justice on' the old king's murderers as the main cause of the unwelcome weather. The preacher went on to praise parliament for restoring the bishops, whilst that afternoon in the same church another argued 'how our living contrary to that holiness and righteousnesse ... was the occasion of all our publique calamities'. The fast did the trick, as there was 'an immediate change of wind and season'.[140] Similar ideological interpretations were put forward to account for the lean years of 1683–4. The freezing over of the Thames was represented as a punishment from god for whig sins: 'Was ever a vengeance so wonderful shown,/That a river so great should be turn'd to a town?'[141] Tory propagandists advised the watermen where they should apportion the blame for the loss of their livelihood: "Tis some Lapland acquaintance of conjurer Oates,/That has ty'd up your hands and imprisoned your boats.'[142]

Such ideological explanations were clearly not regarded as enough by themselves, and so more concrete steps were taken to alleviate the plight of the poor. Valerie Pearl has stressed London's relatively sophisticated system of poor relief as important in helping to preserve political stability.[143] The king responded to the harsh winters of the 1680s by asking the bishop of London to organize the collection of a benevolence for the benefit of the poor.[144] Particular attention was paid to the plight of the watermen. A petition of the watermen inhabitants of Stepney for relief in January 1684 was met with a gift of £100.[145] On 1 February 1684 the king ordered

---

[139] T. Lanfière, *The Citty Prophesier; Or, The Country Fortuneteller* [1680].
[140] Evelyn, *Diary*, III, 311.
[141] *The Whigs' Hard Heart for the Cause of the Hard Frost* (1684), in Rimbault, ed., *Old Ballads*, p. 18.
[142] *Blanket-Fair; Or, The History of Temple Street* (1684), in ibid., p. 10. Cf. *Freezland-Fair; Or The Icy Bear-Garden* (1684), in ibid., pp. 12–15.
[143] Pearl, 'Social Policy'.
[144] *CSPD, 1680–1*, pp. 129–30; *CSPD, 1683–4*, p. 199; Luttrell, I, 296.
[145] PRO, PC 2/70, p. 106.

another collection for 'the poor Watermen, Seamen, and other indigent Housekeepers in and about the Cities of London and Westminster, and the Parishes within the Bills of Mortality'.[146] Relief sent to the weavers seems to have helped keep them quiet. A government spy heard of reports that the weavers, because of their economic plight, were intending 'to go to the king, but he had been gracious and sent them money to relieve them, so they were satisfied'.[147]

But the way relief operated could sometimes reinforce the anglican/non-conformist divide. Both conventicle acts contained provisions that fines levied on nonconformists should go to 'the reliefe of the Poore of the Parish where such offender did last inhabite'.[148] In 1682 the Middlesex justices gave strict orders that fines taken from recusants or conventiclers should be distributed for the relief of the poor, 'which are very numerous in this County'.[149] A petition made to the Middlesex sessions by the churchwarden of Stepney, which complained that the fines were being inequitably distributed amongst the Tower Hamlets, and that his area was not receiving its fair due, suggests the policy was being enforced to some degree.[150] In December 1682 there was a dispute between the parishes of St Dunstan-in-the-West and St Bride as to which could claim the fines levied on the presbyterian Richard Baxter for the use of the poor. Eventually the poor of St Dunstan's were awarded the whole sum, which totalled £57 5s. 6d.[151] During the persecution of the 1680s, it was a tactic of arrested conventiclers to claim that they had met in an unoccupied house whose owner was unknown, so that no-one could be prosecuted for allowing the meeting to take place. To overcome this, the courts ordered that if the owner of the house did not come forward, the churchwardens were 'to place some of their poor Inhabitants therein for their abode and reliefe'.[152] It could be that at the time of fiercest persecution, which coincided with the severe winter of 1683–4, poor anglicans were benefiting at the expense of dissenters. The problems for poor nonconformists, on the other hand, increased. In 1681 the Middlesex justices issued an order stating that 'poore people who frequent Conventicles and doe not come to their parish Church and receive the Sacrament there (except in case of Sickness and Necessity ...) should not be given parish money for their relief', on the grounds that 'such persons who never come to parish Church ought not to be reckoned of the parish'.[153]

---

[146] Ibid., p. 110.
[147] *CSPD, 1683–4*, p. 269.
[148] *Statutes of the Realm*, V, 517, 649.
[149] GLRO, MJ/SBB/394, p. 35; ibid., 401, p. 43; *The Presentments of the Grand-Juries for the County of Middlesex* (1682).
[150] GLRO, MJ/SBB/424, p. 40.
[151] Ibid., 401, p. 46.
[152] Ibid., 422, p. 50.
[153] Ibid., 391, p. 44.

It would take a detailed study of poor law administration to discover the real extent to which the nonconformists were actually excluded from the parochial system of relief.[154] But there is one incident which suggests that nonconformists were being excluded. At the end of July 1684, during the height of the tory reaction, a number of constables from the Tower Hamlets area were imprisoned for their refusal to assist in suppressing conventicles. When in court the constables had warned the justices that they should 'look to the poor'. The following day there was a large demonstration of poor dissenters outside the door of the minister of Stepney, and they 'threatened they would come, a great multitude of them, on Sunday to the Church, to demand relief there'.[155] The implication is that they had either not been willing or been able to claim parish poor relief hitherto. We know that nonconformists had their own schemes to help their poor at this time. The White's Alley Baptist Church, which had many poor members in the northern and eastern suburbs, operated its own system of poor relief in the 1680s.[156] In the late 1670s the Six Weeks Meeting of London Quakers began a flax-spinning scheme to employ poor Friends, which continued to provide employment until the end of the century.[157] Anglicans, too, had their own forms of private charity. In 1681, a 'Society of Young Men of St Martin-in-the-Fields' was formed, condition of membership being regular attendance at the parish church and the receiving of the holy sacrament. Its main aim seems to have been to make monthly collections for the benefit of the poor, the money received to be given to the minister of St Martin's to distribute 'as he thinks fit'.[158]

There are thus no strong *a priori* reasons for assuming that the tories could not have enjoyed support amongst London's less prosperous classes. What is needed is some means of testing the relative socio-economic contours of whig and tory support. Unfortunately this is extremely difficult to do. An obvious approach would be to follow the technique pioneered by George Rudé of using the sessions records to put faces to the crowd. The problem is that most of the crowd activity of the exclusion period never led to any

---

[154] Although there is a thesis on poor relief in London at this time, it does not investigate this issue. See S. M. Macfarlane, 'Studies in Poverty and Poor Relief in London at the End of the Seventeenth Century', unpub. Oxford DPhil thesis (1982).

[155] GLRO, MJ/SBB/417, pp. 62–3; *The Proceedings of His Majesties Justices of the Peace, at the Sessions of Oyer and Terminer* (1684).

[156] Guildhall Library, MS 592, fol. 11.

[157] I. Grubb, *Quakerism and Industry Before 1800* (1930), pp. 136–7; A. Raistrick, *Quakers in Science and Industry: Being an Account of the Quaker Contribution to Science and Industry during the Seventeenth and Eighteenth Centuries* (1950), p. 84; Braithwaite, *Second Period*, pp. 570–1; A. R. Fry, *John Bellers, 1654–1725: Quaker, Economist, and Social Reformer* (1933), pp. 6–7; S. Macfarlane, 'Social Policy and the Poor in the Later Seventeenth Century', in Beier and Finlay, eds., *Making of the Metropolis*, p. 259.

[158] BL, Add. MS 38,693, fol. 137.

arrests. The crowds, therefore, retain their anonymity. Only for the proposed Rump burning of 1680 and the Monmouth disturbances of November 1682 do we have any information on those accused of involvement, and even here, taking both disturbances together, we know the names and occupations of a mere twelve alleged participants. This limited material can be supplemented by looking at the evidence of seditious words, but a major problem arises concerning the question of why certain individuals came to court. Prosecutions could be vexatious, they might be initiated by informers who were seeking to make money by exploiting government sensibilities, or charges might be brought in a deliberate attempt to discredit one's political opponents. It is by no means clear, then, that those accused of speaking pro-whig seditious words provide a reasonable cross-section of grass roots support for exclusion.[159]

Descriptive sources can shed light on the relative social composition of rival crowds, but they need to be treated with great caution, since many contemporary accounts were designed to serve a propaganda function. Polemicists on both sides liked to claim that only the better sort supported their own cause, whilst the 'vulgar' supported their opponents. Whig publicist Richard Janeway claimed that the tory apprentices who subscribed to the loyal address to the king in June 1681 were 'Ruffians and Beggarly Vermine', and that the better sort of apprentices, who were vehemently whig, refused to sign it.[160] Nathaniel Thompson was quick to deny that any disrespectful elements were supporting the tories: 'those that carried the Address were of the most eminent Rank, (viz) 4 Merchants, 2 Mercers, 2 Drapers, and a Goldsmith'.[161] A whig tract argued that many of the subscribers to this address were not even apprentices, but rather 'Journeymen, Carmen, Porters, Tapsters … [and] many others of a far more inferior degree'. These were the types who were easier to bribe.[162] The tract immediately prompted a tory denial, claiming that the whigs were the experts in bribery, and asserting that one of their petitions earlier that year had been subscribed to by 'Porters and broom-men'.[163] The 'fat buck youths' address' of 1682, according to a whig newsletter writer, had been subscribed to by 'porters, watermen and chimney sweepers'. When they were treated to their feast of venison at Merchant Tailor's Hall, some of them, our source

---

[159] A detailed consideration of the methodological problems together with a full analysis of riots and seditious words can be found in Harris, 'Politics of the London Crowd', appendix two.
[160] *Impartial Protestant Mercury*, no. 15.
[161] *Loyal Protestant Intelligence*, no. 35. Cf. L'Estrange, *Observator*, no. 30, for similar counter-accusations.
[162] *Friendly Dialogue*, p. 3.
[163] *Vox Juvenilis*.

continues, turned up so shabbily dressed that they had to be turned away.[164] A tory newsletter writer believed that the pro-Monmouth crowd which rioted on 6 November 1682 was comprised of 'hundreds of Butchers men and other mean fellowes'.[165]

What little can be learnt from the sessions records does not suggest that the whigs were more likely to enjoy a lower class constituency than the tories. We know the occupations of only 6 of the tory youths implicated in the design to burn the Rump on 29 May 1680, but they were all in occupations of low social status. Thus we have the apprentices of a bell-founder, a cobbler, a cutler, an oilman, a salesman and an embroiderer.[166] Of the 6 charged with involvement in the Monmouth disturbances of November 1682, only the two plumbers were people in unprestigious trades, whilst the others comprised a pharmacist, a grocer and two vintners.[167] From the evidence of seditious words we find that about 55 per cent of those accused of uttering pro-whig seditious speeches in the period 1678–85 (49 out of a total of 87 for whom occupation is known) can be described as petty shopkeepers, artisans and labourers in low-status trades. Yet an analysis of those who appeared in court to prosecute these speeches suggests that those who were hostile to the expression of such views came from the same type of social background. Thus some 60 per cent of prosecutors (30 out of 49 for whom occupation is known) can also be described as petty shopkeepers, artisans and labourers in low-status trades.[168] The evidence is thin, but it does suggest that there was no simple economic distinction between the two parties' supporters amongst the London masses. This view is further reinforced by the research of other historians on different aspects of London politics at this time. For example, David Allen has shown that the trained bands, which comprised many people of menial status, remained loyal to the government. His conclusion is that 'when the urban rabble flocked to London's pope-burning processions during the Exclusion Crisis they were kept in check by militiamen who were often of their own class'.[169] In his examination of the political affiliations of London's livery-men, Arthur Smith found no significant difference in economic status between those who supported whig or tory candidates at common council elections.[170]

Were there, then, perhaps particular occupations which were more prone

---

[164] LC, MS 18,124, VIII, fols. 83, 98.
[165] LC, MS 18,124, VIII, fol. 257.
[166] GLRO, WJ/SR/1576; *Mercurius Civicus*, 24 March 1680; *Protestant (Domestick) Intelligence*, no. 80.
[167] CLRO, Sessions File, December 1682.
[168] Harris, 'Politics of the London Crowd', p. 308.
[169] Allen, 'Trained Bands', p. 302.
[170] Smith, 'London and the Crown', pp. 128–9.

to either a whig or tory position? Smith has argued that tory support in the streets was strongest amongst the students of the Inns of Court, a high-status group, and also with the Thames watermen, a low-status group.[171] For example, on 13 January 1682 it was a group of young gentlemen from the Temple, aided by some watermen, who attacked the home of the Green Ribbon Club.[172] The extent to which these groups were unanimously or consistently tory, however, can be questioned. It was the young Templars who planned the anti-whig demonstration for 17 November 1682,[173] yet three years earlier the Templars had been responsible for financing a whig pope-burning procession.[174] In June 1682 the gentlemen of the Inner Temple, Middle Temple, Gray's Inn and Lincoln's Inn all presented loyal addresses in abhorrence of Shaftesbury's Association.[175] But even the tory Nathaniel Thompson acknowledged that the men of Lincoln's Inn could not agree as to whether to present the address or not.[176] In August 1681, 2,000 Thames watermen presented a loyal address.[177] Yet back in January the Thames watermen had petitioned the king against removing the parliament to Oxford, and although this was apparently for fear that their livelihood would be ruined if parliament did not sit at Westminster,[178] tory sources interpreted this petition as evidence of support for the whig cause.[179] There are good reasons to believe that the watermen might have been divided at this time. Whilst some of them were 'privileged' to wear the king's livery, others wore the crests of noblemen, and many were dependent for their livelihood on the influx of people to London during the sittings of parliament.[180] Such economic dependency, coupled with the various webs of patronage tying them to a politically divided elite, suggests that the adoption of a united front would have been unlikely. On the other hand, we might suggest that it was the careful attention paid to the needs of the watermen by the government during the harsh winters of the early 1680s that helped regain their loyalty. We can see a redefinition of allegiance amongst other groups. In June 1682 the seamen presented an abhorrence of Shaftesbury's Association.[181] Yet in May 1681 the seamen of the Tower Hamlets (where, in

---

[171] Ibid., p. 151.
[172] Luttrell, I, 158.
[173] *Loyal Protestant Intelligence*, no. 232; *Loyal London Mercury*, no. 24.
[174] *HMC 7th Report, Appendix*, p. 477; *Solemn Mock Procession . . . of 1679*.
[175] *London Gazette*, no. 1727; *Loyal Protestant Intelligence*, no. 165.
[176] *Loyal Protestant Intelligence*, no 160. Passions ran so high between whigs and tories, that two students of Lincoln's Inn fought a duel to defend the honour of their parties in December 1681. Huntington Library, MS HA9614. I am grateful to Mark Goldie for this reference.
[177] *London Gazette*, no. 1642.
[178] *True Protestant Mercury*, no. 10.
[179] *Heraclitus Ridens*, no. 2.
[180] Humpherus, *Company of Watermen*, I, 5–6, 242.
[181] *London Gazette*, no. 1728.

fact, most of the seamen were concentrated) had been 'most forward in promoting' a whig petition for the sitting of parliament.[182] The evidence is not incompatible with a view that Londoners, at all status levels, were split at the exclusion period, and also that the tories were winning support from people who had previously supported the whigs.

It does seem, however, that particular groups were likely to be distinctively whig in their outlook. Taking the evidence of seditious speeches over the reign as a whole, we find that four occupational groups were most prone to the expression of either anti-Stuart or pro-exclusionist sentiment. These were the trades of carpenter, shoemaker, tailor and weaver. These were of course among the most numerous trades in the London area. Yet it is significant that these trades do not appear amongst those accused of anti-whig activity.[183] It has been generally observed that these were the notoriously radical crafts, and that this was in part due to the sedentary and reflective nature of their work and their higher than average literacy.[184] But this is surely more accurately a recipe for political activism rather than radicalism. We still need to ask why these groups rejected the views expressed in tory propaganda which they might have had time to sit, read and think about. In this respect it is perhaps significant that the four most common occupations that suffered persecution for nonconformity were those of tailor, shoemaker, weaver and carpenter. Moreover, as seen earlier in this chapter, the carpenters, tailors and weavers were particularly vociferous in their complaints against the threat posed by immigrant, and especially French, workers in the 1670s and 1680s. In short it seems that it was those occupations where economic xenophobia was reinforced by nonconformist convictions which were likely to be prominent in support of the whigs.

CONCLUSION

The relationship between economic hardship and political disaffection is clearly an extremely complex one. What does seem clear from the analysis offered in this chapter is that a simple reductionist account is inappropriate, and that one must stress the important mediating role played by ideological factors. The weavers' riot of 1675 was no simple 'rebellion of the belly', but formed part of a complex process of bargaining and negotiation, and the weavers' actions were informed by an acute sense of grievance and injustice. The weavers, as with a number of other depressed artisanal groups

---

[182] *Impartial Protestant Mercury*, no. 11.
[183] Harris, 'Politics of the London Crowd', pp. 299–300.
[184] Reay, 'Early Quaker Activity', p. 231; Burke, *Popular Culture*, pp. 36–9; Clifton, *Last Popular Rebellion*, pp. 257–61; E. J. Hobsbawm and J. W. Scott, 'Political Shoemakers', *PP*, 89 (1980), 86–114.

in London, believed that many of their difficulties could be blamed on unfair competition from immigrant workers, and especially the French. It was this economic xenophobia, this anti-French ideology, rather than purely economic suffering, I have argued, that helped forge these domestic artisans' political consciousness, and fed in to support for the whigs during the exclusion crisis.

Ideological factors must also be taken into account when considering the politicizing effect of other material grievances, such as regressive taxation or the problems caused by bad weather. Those who suffered from the excise and high prices of fuel in the early 1680s may have had cause to side with the whigs; it is also possible that they could have internalized their grievances in such a way so as to blame the whigs for their sufferings. Tory polemicists certainly saw the value of offering their explanation of economic hardship in their propaganda. The tories also saw the value in backing up such arguments with the injection of money to relieve those hardest hit by the economic crisis. Yet it does seem that the discriminatory way in which relief operated might have reinforced the religious tensions that existed in London at this time. In short, though it might be fair to suggest that economic factors probably did play some part in politicizing the masses in Charles II's reign, it is wrong to assume that they must have forced the lower orders into the opposition camp. Indeed, from the little that can be known about the rank and file support for the two parties, it seems clear that the tories, as much as the whigs, were able to command a following amongst the lower classes.

9

A divided society

When I initially started research for this book, my prime intention was to study the politics of the London crowd in the reign of Charles II. However, one of my major conclusions has been that *the* London crowd did not exist at this time. By setting crowd activity in the context of London political culture as a whole, and examining the interaction of the constitutional, religious and economic grievances which underlay collective unrest, I have documented the existence of fundamental political divisions amongst the London masses. Religious tensions, although not the only cause of strife, were at the root of much of the discord. The apparent unanimity in favour of the return of monarchy in 1660 disappears when we consider the very different expectations of the Restoration held by anglicans, presbyterians and separatists. The failure to achieve a satisfactory religious settlement in 1662, and the centrality of the issue of dissent in politics for the rest of the reign, are crucial to understanding the genesis of the party divide, and the rivalry between whig and tory crowds apparent during the exclusion controversy.

In discussing crowd politics in the reign of Charles II I have deliberately eschewed using the word 'popular'. To some this may seem pedantic, since in many respects it is fair to suggest that this has been a study of 'popular politics'. I have concentrated on those below the level of the elite, looking not at political institutions such as parliament or the common council, but at the theatre of the street, which imposed no formal franchisal limitations on the right to participate. The political attitudes under examination were often expressed in a peculiarly popular idiom. In this respect we may note how the medium of the brothel riot was often used to make political points: in 1668, for example, by those who wanted 'liberty of conscience' and 'reformation and reducement'; again in May 1682, by whig apprentices protesting against the suppression of nonconformist meetings; and also in the spring of 1680, when the tory apprentices had planned to combine their burning of the Rump with an attack on all conventicles and bawdy houses in London.[1]

[1] Harris, 'Bawdy House Riots'; LC, MS 18,124, VIII, fol. 56; *Mercurius Civicus*, 24 March 1680.

On the other hand, there seems to have been nothing distinctly 'popular' about the political opinions of the London masses. They were heavily caught up in the partisan divide of the end of the reign, their political identity being determined by attitudes towards the succession and the issue of dissent. The masses themselves were divided, and political alliances tended to be vertical rather than horizontal. A close interaction of elite encouragement and popular activity can be found in many types of collective agitation in the streets, whether of a whig or tory kind. In fact, it seems inappropriate to discuss London political culture in terms of a simple popular/elite dichotomy. My examination of exclusionist propaganda, for example, has demonstrated the extent to which the issues of 'high politics' were debated in the public arena, permeating all levels of London society. Moreover, the distinction between high and low politics – if by that we mean a distinction between the political and the sub-political nation, or between the rulers and the ruled – itself seems of questionable value for seventeenth-century London. A consideration of the mechanisms of government in the capital reveals that a much larger number of people were involved, to some degree, in the processes of 'ruling' than is usually recognized. This can be seen in particular in the area of law-enforcement. Those responsible for policing crowds, or suppressing conventicles, say, were often drawn from the same levels of society as those who took part in demonstrations or protested against the enforcement of the penal laws. London was a politically divided society, but the divide was neither a popular/elite one, nor a simple socio-economic one.

It would be invaluable if some insight could be shed into the relative numerical strength of support for the whigs and tories amongst the London populace. Although there might have been a 'popular tory position', is it not nevertheless fair to suggest that the whigs were the more 'popular' party, or at least that the whig presence in the streets was the more significant? Unfortunately, it is difficult to see how such an assessment can be made. Contemporary estimates of the numbers of people who participated in riots or demonstrations, or who subscribed to petitions, are seldom trustworthy, whilst partisans on both sides liked to suggest that only a minority supported their opponents' cause. The picture is further complicated by the fact that relative support for the two sides did not remain stable, since it seems to have been the case that the tories gained ground at the expense of the whigs as time progressed.

Even if it were possible to assess whether the tory or whig position was more 'popular' in London as a whole, the conclusion reached might not in itself be particularly revealing. London was a sprawling metropolitan conurbation, and it would be necessary to discover whether specific areas were more inclined to support exclusion, say, than others. However, this is a question we can begin to answer, using the evidence provided by descriptive sources in conjunction with what can be gleaned from the sessions records about the geography of protest.

The general impression is that whig support amongst the London populace was most extensive within the City proper, whilst the tories were strongest in the Westminster area and in the western extra-mural ward of Farringdon without.[2] The duke of York's arrival at Whitehall on 24 February 1680 caused 'many bonfires in this end of town', wrote one observer, but there were none 'up in London' of which he knew.[3] The absence of Yorkist demonstrations in the City is explicable because the king ordered the lord mayor to forbid bonfires in the area under his jurisdiction, for fear that they would provoke disturbances, although this in itself is testimony to the fact that the City was thought to be more hostile to York than Westminster.[4] The tory apprentices who proposed to burn the Rump on 29 May 1680 came predominantly from around the Strand area.[5] From the sessions records we can only identify the places of habitation of two accused of involvement in this planned demonstration, and a further four who stood as sureties, but all of these six came from Westminster parishes.[6] The first actual tory presbyter-burning procession, that of 5 November 1681, took place in Westminster.[7] Tory demonstrations on 8 April 1682 were concentrated in the ward of Farringdon without – Little Britain, Ludgate and Fleet Street – as well as in the Westminster area – Covent Garden and Drury Lane.[8] A Yorkist demonstration of 27 May 1682 was in Westminster, and tory celebrations of Charles's birthday two days later were in Whitefriars and Covent Garden.[9]

At first glance an analysis of whig demonstrations seems to confirm this picture. The Florentine ambassador, discussing the popular celebrations when Shaftesbury's bill was found *ignoramus* in November 1681, noticed the 'infidelity' of the City of London, but remarked that such demonstrations were to be found in 'no part of Westminster'.[10] The pope-burning processions of 17 November marched both through the City and around its perimeters, but did not venture west of Temple Bar.[11] The pro-Monmouth disturbances

[2] Cf. Smith, 'London and the Crown', p. 152.
[3] Bodl. Lib., MS Carte 39, fol. 111.
[4] *HMC, Ormond*, NS IV, 580.
[5] *Mercurius Civicus*, 24 March 1680.
[6] GLRO, WJ/SR/1576. It was fairly common for those who put up sureties to come from the same neighbourhood as the accused. See Boulton, 'Southwark', pp. 295–303.
[7] *True Protestant Mercury*, nos. 88, 89; *Impartial Protestant Mercury*, no. 57; *Loyal Protestant Intelligence*, no. 75.
[8] LC, MS 18,124, VIII, fol. 40; *Impartial Protestant Mercury*, no. 101; *Loyal Protestant Intelligence*, no. 140.
[9] *True Protestant Mercury*, no. 147; *Loyal Protestant Intelligence*, no. 162.
[10] BL, Add. MS 25,363, fol. 125.
[11] *Domestick Intelligence*, no. 39; *London's Defiance*, p. 2; *Solemn Mock Procession of . . . 1680*, broadside; *True Protestant Mercury*, no. 91.

of 6 November 1682 started in Cheapside, in the heart of the City.[12] Of the 16 accused and sureties for whom we know place of habitation, all 16 came from the area under the lord mayor's jurisdiction.[13] Such a geographical divide would make sense of the fact that the whig position of the exclusion period was intimately tied up with a defence of the privileges of the Corporation, whilst those who supported the tories seemed less concerned about the implications for the City of the defeat of exclusion.

Although the general impression of an east/west divide contains some merit, it is too simple. It will be remembered that tory apprentices in the City presented an address to the king in June 1681, which they claimed was signed by some 18,000 hands, although the whigs argued that the figure was only 3,000.[14] There were tory demonstrations in Cheapside on 15 November 1681, and also in Cornhill, on 8 April 1682, both these locations being in the heart of the City.[15] On 5 November 1679, the whigs held pope-burning processions in Westminster, although the later use of this date for presbyter-burning processions in this area might reflect a change of opinion amongst people living here.[16] Yet on 5 November 1681, there was another whig procession in Westminster, marching down the Strand and then up to King Street, Bloomsbury, before it was attacked by a group of tories. On that day, too, tories attacked whig groups both in Aldersgate Street, on the west of the City, and also in Crutched Friars, in the east.[17]

This last example can perhaps be dismissed as evidence of tory groups seeking out whig processions in areas where tories were not strong. But that leads to another difficulty involved with giving a frequency breakdown for the geographical incidence of riot, namely, the question of whether an incident shows an area where support for that cause was strong, or whether it shows an area that was attacked because of its sympathy to a hostile cause. The location of the unrest on 24 November 1681, after Shaftesbury's release, was in part determined by where people hostile to exclusion lived. The victims of the whigs came not only from the Ludgate area to the west of the City, but also from Cornhill in the centre and from the Tower area in the east.[18] On 6 November 1682, tories in Cornhill and in Gracechurch Street were attacked by whigs.[19]

An analysis of sedition cases warns against stressing a simple east/west

[12] PRO, SP 29/421, no. 67; LC, MS 18,124, IX, fol. 331; *Loyal Protestant Intelligence*, no. 231.

[13] CLRO, Sessions File, December 1682.

[14] HMC, *Ormond*, NS VI, 91; *The Address of Above 20,000*.

[15] *Impartial Protestant Mercury*, no. 60; *Loyal Protestant Intelligence*, no. 140.

[16] *Domestick Intelligence*, no. 36.

[17] *Impartial Protestant Mercury*, no. 57; *True Protestant Mercury*, nos. 88, 89.

[18] *CSPD, 1680–1*, pp. 588–9.

[19] PRO, SP 29/421, no. 67.

divide. For the period 1678–85, out of a total of 79 accused of uttering pro-whig seditious speeches for whom we know place of habitation 21 came from Westminster, and only 13 from the City. Of course, we have to ask why such cases came to court, and it is true that often with regard to seditious words prosecutions were initiated by local inhabitants unsympathetic to the views being expressed. It might be suggested that these figures show that anti-Stuart statements were more likely to receive a hostile reception in Westminster than in the City, but the answer is not that straightforward. If we look at those who prosecuted whig sedition between 1678–85, out of 74 for whom place of abode is known, 23 came from within the City walls, and 19 from Westminster.[20]

Even less can be known about the political sympathies of those in the urban Middlesex parishes of London's east end or south of the river in Southwark, since they did not experience any major crowd disturbances or demonstrations during the exclusion period. Both areas, of course, provided many of the participants in the bawdy house riots of 1668 and the weavers' riots of 1675.[21] Both areas housed a sizeable nonconformist population.[22] An order of sessions of September 1684 described the inhabitants of the Tower Hamlets area as 'generally very factious'.[23] During 1682 Shaftesbury was allegedly seeking to obtain recruits for a possible insurrection from amongst the population of Wapping.[24] In the period 1678–85, 13 sedition cases (out of a total of 79 for whom habitation is known) involved accused from east Middlesex, that is the same number as came from the City of London. Yet against this must be set the fact that 15 (out of 74) prosecutors of whig sedition also came from this area.[25] The promoters of a tory address of August 1681 certainly believed there were plenty of 'loyal' signatures to be collected in London's east end. When someone did speak out against such an address circulating in the parish of Trinity Minories, the promoters sought to indict him for seditious words.[26] In Southwark, too, the tories enjoyed a certain amount of popularity. The tories won the 1681 Southwark election by an extension of the franchise to include the poorer people of the borough.[27] In August 1681, the Thames watermen presented a loyal address, and Southwark, of course, housed large numbers

---

[20] Harris, 'Politics of the London Crowd', p. 306.
[21] Jeaff., IV, 8–12, 60–5; PRO, Assi 35, 116/9; PRO, PC 2/64, p. 491; *CSPD, 1667–8*, p. 306; *CSPD, 1675–6*, p. 255.
[22] For the 1680s I have identified 86 nonconformist meeting-places in London's east end, and 78 in the Southwark area, compared to 97 in the City proper, 106 in the extra-mural parishes and 37 in Westminster. Harris, 'Politics of the London Crowd', p. 278.
[23] GLRO, MJ/SBB/417, p. 56; *The Proceedings of His Majesties Justices*.
[24] Ailesbury, *Memoirs*, I, 66; Ferguson, *The Plotter*, p. 72; Haley, *Shaftesbury*, p. 712.
[25] Harris, 'Politics of the London Crowd', p. 306.
[26] GLRO, MJ/SR/1654, ign. ind.
[27] *Smith's Protestant Intelligence*, no. 6. Cf. Johnson, *Southwark*, p. 281.

of watermen.[28] By January 1683, a grand jury comprising 'the numerous party of Honest Trading men' of Southwark were appealing to the lord mayor to be more vigorous in suppressing conventicles.[29]

Rather than seeing London as divided into zones which were either predominantly whig or tory in sympathy, it might be more appropriate to suggest that partisan political attitudes were more likely to find expression in communities which were bitterly divided amongst themselves. As already mentioned, most of the tory demonstrations took place either in the Farringdon without or Westminster areas. Although dissent was not as strong here as in other parts of London, there was nevertheless a noticeable nonconformist presence in Westminster and in Farringdon without, where a total of 66 different meeting-places can be identified during the first half of the 1680s.[30] The parish of St Martin-in-the-Fields, Westminster, in particular, seems to have been a trouble spot. The anti-presbyterian apprentices who proposed to burn the Rump in 1680 came from this area. Yet 13 nonconformist meeting-places can be identified here during the time of the tory reaction. Moreover, St Martin's provided more people accused of speaking anti-Stuart or pro-whig seditious words than any other parish in the London area, with a total of eight for the period 1678–85 and 25 taking the reign as a whole.[31] St Giles-without-Cripplegate was another bitterly divided community. To judge from the records of persecution, St Giles possessed one of the heaviest concentrations of nonconformists in the whole of the London area.[32] Yet here in August 1660 a petition from some of the parishioners successfully resulted in the removal of the presbyterian minister who then held the living, Dr Annesley, in favour of a man appointed under Charles I.[33] During the height of the tory reaction the wardmote of Cripplegate without was busy persecuting nonconformist meetings, even though the government had not specifically been encouraging the wardmotes to do this.[34] If Valerie Pearl's view of the wardmote as an arena for the expression of public opinion is still valid for the later seventeenth century, this might be indicative of pressure from below for persecution.[35] The latitudinarian minister Dr Edward Fowler, who was rector of St Giles in the early 1680s, was certainly very concerned about the extreme high-church and aggressively

---

[28] *London Gazette*, no. 1642. For the occupational structure of Southwark, see Boulton, 'Southwark', ch. 2.

[29] PRO, SP 29/422, no. 22; *Presentments of the Grand-Jury for the Town and Borough of Southwark* (1683). For the party politics of the Southwark Sessions, see Johnson, *Southwark*, pp. 254–5.

[30] Harris, 'Politics of the London Crowd', p. 278.

[31] Ibid., pp. 293, 306.

[32] See above, pp. 66–7.

[33] PRO, SP 29/12, no. 114.

[34] CLRO, Ward Presentments 1683, Cripplegate without.

[35] Pearl, 'Change and Stability', p. 16.

anti-nonconformist views of some of his parishioners. He often criticized them for their lack of charity towards their dissenting brethren. His parishioners, however, took their revenge on Fowler by prosecuting him in the Court of Arches for whiggish practices, and as a result Fowler was suspended in December 1685.[36]

Nathaniel Thompson's claim that the effect of the tory propaganda effort was to 'reduce the deluded Multitude to their just Allegiance' by 1685 is clearly an exaggeration.[37] Rather, the early 1680s witnessed a sharp polarization in London political culture. But Thompson's statement does contain an element of truth, in the sense that by the time of James's accession in February 1685 crowd unrest in London had ceased to be a major problem for the government. Admittedly, there was a rebellion in the west country that summer led by the duke of Monmouth, but there were no disturbances in the capital, and indeed the streets of London had been free from any disturbances since the Gunpowder Treason day riots of 1682.

In accounting for this sudden disappearance of crowd activity, emphasis has normally been placed on the forces of repression. Careful policing by the trained bands, controlled by the tory dominated lieutenancy, meant that it was possible to effectively enforce the royal proclamation of 10 November 1682 against public demonstrations. The tory control of the shrievalty from the summer of 1682 enabled the government to launch a successful campaign against London whigs and nonconformists through the courts. The *quo warranto* proceedings against the City charter in 1683 finally removed any vestiges of the whig power base within the Corporation which had served as a focus for popular agitation. By 1685 the first whig party had been virtually destroyed. The earl of Shaftesbury had fled to Holland at the end of 1682 where he died in exile early the following year. The revelations of the Rye House Plot in the summer of 1683 led to the execution of the whig radicals Algernon Sydney and Lord Russell, whilst many others were forced to flee to the continent to save their necks. The ravages of the persecution left the nonconformists dispirited, the majority had retreated into a position of political quietism, and a number of nonconformist pastors were either in prison or had emigrated to Holland or the New World.[38]

But the government's response to the mass exclusionist movement was much more sophisticated than this analysis would seem to imply. It would

---

[36] E. Fowler, *The Great Wickedness, and Mischievous Effects of Slandering* (1685), preface.

[37] Thompson, ed., *Songs*, preface.

[38] Jones, *First Whigs*, pp. 206–10; Smith, 'London and the Crown', parts 4, 5; Allen, 'Trained Bands'; Marshall, 'Protestant Dissent', pp. 135–8, 173; J. Levin, *The Charter Controversy in the City of London* (1969).

be wrong to suggest that the tories thought public opinion counted for little, that they could ride roughshod over the wishes of the people. As we have seen, much energy was invested in trying to disarm the whigs of their support amongst the London populace. In part, this was done by paying close attention to the needs of London's economically depressed groups, whom the government feared might be an easy target for political agitators if nothing were done to relieve their material hardships. In the main it was achieved by a careful cultivation of public opinion through their anti-exclusionist propaganda campaign. By setting themselves up as the true defenders of the protestant interest, namely 'the Church of England as by law established', the tories sought to turn the anglicans, who formed the majority of London's population, against the whigs and nonconformists. When the government embarked on its policy of repression, the mood in the capital had already begun to swing against the exclusionists.

Was public opinion worth cultivating simply because of the moral legitimacy it lent to the government's policies, or did it count for more than this? This is a difficult question to answer, but certainly merits further investigation. Given the widespread participation of ordinary Londoners in the processes of law-enforcement, the ability of the government not only to keep the streets of London quiet in the years 1683–5, but also to launch an extensive legal campaign against nonconformists is certainly extremely impressive. London's citizen militia, the trained bands, had typically shown themselves reluctant to suppress crowd disturbances or other illegal activities, if they knew those activities retained a large amount of support amongst the local community. The weavers' riot of 1675 is a case in point where, as we have seen, the army had to be called in to restore order. Yet never once was recourse had to the army in the period from the exclusion crisis to the end of the reign, since the trained bands remained loyal. Of course, care was taken to ensure the tory credentials of the officer corps, but it was far from easy to control the actions of the rank and file. It may be that the trained bands would not have policed the streets so effectively against the whig crowds but for the evidence of tory demonstrations, which revealed that the exclusionists did not hold a monopoly of people's sympathies. As a result, those who chose to act against the whigs need not fear that they were acting against a popular consensus, but could do so in the full knowledge that there were many in London who would welcome the suppression of the whigs.

The enforcement of the nonconformist persecution is another area which would repay closer study. For this, the authorities relied extensively on the traditional local agents of police, the trained bands again, the constables and other local officers, and also on informations brought before them by members of the public. There were, of course, complaints made about the remissness of local officers in enforcing the laws against nonconformists.[39] Yet given the dependence upon unpaid, part-time and local agents to enforce the penal laws, the extent of the persecution is truly remarkable. Nearly 4,000 different nonconformists (and many of these more than once) appeared before London courts charged with attendance at a conventicle between 1682–6, and about 400 different meeting-houses were successfully disturbed in the same period.[40] Nonconformist writers frequently complained that constables and other local officers were 'acting too officiously against their honest Neighbours upon the Conventicle Act'.[41] A study of the conventicle certificates reveals that those who were willing to inform against nonconformists were much more numerous than is usually recognized.[42] A number of the more moderate anglican clergymen in London remarked on the violent anti-nonconformist reaction at the parish level during the tory reaction, and even had to exhort their parishioners to be a little more generous towards their dissenting neighbours. Edward Fowler's experience in his parish of St Giles-without-Cripplegate has just been discussed. Benjamin Hoffman, who ministered at St George, Bottolph Lane, believed it was just to put the penal laws into operation, but was shocked to find that those that 'do it, rejoyce in their Brothers' sufferings'.[43] It seems likely that the anti-nonconformist enthusiasm which the tory propagandists had sought to stir up probably facilitated the enforcement of the persecution.

The alleged attempts by some radical whigs to encourage a popular rising after the parliamentary defeat of exclusion might seem to indicate a widespread alienation from the Stuarts during the years of the tory reaction. At the trial of Stephen College in 1681 witnesses swore that College had claimed that 30,000 men were ready to rise in London at the time of the Oxford parliament.[44] Shaftesbury allegedly had '10,000 brisk boys' ready to do his business in 1682.[45] The truth behind the supposed plot of 1683 to murder the king and duke of York at a rye house in Hertfordshire on their return from Newmarket is impossible to ascertain. Yet some plans do seem to have been laid for a coordinated insurrection in London, Cheshire, the West Country, and other parts at this time.[46] And, of course, some of the radical whigs did lead a rebellion in the west country in 1685, headed

[39] *The Presentment of the Grand Jury for the City of London* (1683); LC, MS 18,124, IX, fol. 10.

[40] See above, p. 67.

[41] T. Ellwood, *A Caution to Constables and Other Inferiour Officers Concerned in the Execution of the Conventicle Act* (1683), p. 1.

[42] CLRO, Conventicle Boxes 2.1–2.6; GLRO, MR/RC/3–10.

[43] B. Hoffman, *Some Considerations of the Present Use* (1683), p. 22.

[44] *HMC, 36 Ormond*, NS VI, 95.

[45] LC, MS 18,124, VIII, fol. 354; BL, Harleian MS 6845, fol. 268; Grey, *Secret History*, pp. 38–9; Ailesbury, *Memoirs*, I, 66; Smith, 'London and the Crown', p. 245.

[46] Salmon, 'Sydney', pp. 698–705.

by the duke of Monmouth, and the rebels clearly hoped that London would rise at the same time.[47]

What needs remarking is not so much the fact that radical whigs contemplated trying to raise London at this time, but that London, despite the economic difficulties, despite the legal recriminations, despite the attack on the whig power-base in the City and despite the efforts of political agitators, remained absolutely quiet in the period 1683–5. In the immediate post-exclusion climate, there was, I believe, very little chance that radical whigs would be able to launch a popular rebellion based on London. Not only had efficient policing and vigorous persecution left the whigs and nonconformists dispirited, but it was also far from certain whether they still enjoyed the support of the London populace as a whole. The Rye House plotters certainly had doubts as to whether they could carry the people of London with them. Monmouth expressed his exasperation to Robert Ferguson, the plotter, in early 1683 when he said that he had often heard of Shaftesbury's 10,000 brisk boys, but he did not know where to find them.[48] In March 1685 Monmouth wanted Wildman to raise London on his behalf, but Wildman declined to do so, believing it was impossible at that time.[49]

As is well-known, James II only started to run into difficulties when he upset the tory anglican interest in England. The same is also true with regard to crowd unrest in the capital. Trouble broke out in the streets of London again in 1686, by which time James's intentions of promoting the interests of catholics, with the concomitant threat to anglican hegemony, had become all too apparent. There were crowd attacks on catholic chapels in the spring and summer, and in November the pope-burnings began again. But now the trained bands and the constables, who in the previous years had shown themselves such reliable agents of law-enforcement, declined to take action to preserve the peace.[50] What is significant is that it was the anglican clergymen who were now trying to excite public anxiety about James's policies, preaching openly against catholicism in the sermons. The nonconformist ministers, on the other hand, remained silent, and were bitterly condemned by the high churchmen for refusing to join in their condemnation of popery.[51] In short, the Stuarts lost control of the streets of London again, not because of their harsh recriminations against whigs and dissenters, nor because of the problems caused by the harsh winters, the effects of both of which were most severe in the years 1681–5, but only when James began to alienate

---

[47] The best studies of the Monmouth rebellion are P. Earle, *Monmouth's Rebels: The Road to Sedgemoor* (1977); Clifton, *Last Popular Rising*.

[48] Grey, *Secret History*, p. 38.

[49] *HMC, 12th Report*, VI, 395–6; Clifton, *Last Popular Rebellion*, p. 154.

[50] Luttrell, I, 375; Morrice, I, 530–1; CLRO, Shelf 552, MS Box 3, no. 5; *The Ellis Correspondence, 1686–88*, ed. G. A. Ellis (2 vols., 1829), I, 118, 180–1.

[51] Marshall, 'Protestant Dissent', pp. 366–88.

the very support that the tories had striven so hard to cultivate during the years of the exclusion crisis.

James II's reign is a complex period from the point of view of crowd politics, which would merit a detailed study in its own right. The questions raised here are only intended as pointers for future research. In the light of my findings, a re-evaluation of the anti-catholic agitation of 1688 is clearly necessary.[52] It is no longer safe to regard this simply as a continuation of the anti-catholic agitation of the exclusion crisis. For too long the prevalence of the theme of 'no popery' in crowd activity in the decade from the Popish Plot to the Glorious Revolution has led historians to assume that the London populace was overwhelmingly whig in sympathy at this time. Historians working on the period after 1689, however, have been impressed by the strength of popular toryism under the last two Stuarts and the early Hanoverians.[53] This high-church, anti-nonconformist position was nothing new after the Revolution. It was a powerful force in London political culture during the exclusion crisis, and the roots of it can be traced back at least to 1660, and perhaps even earlier. For too long also students of high politics have dismissed crowd agitation as a rather ephemeral affair, insignificant so far as the 'real' political struggles were concerned. This view might be misguided. The loss of the support of the London masses could seriously jeopardize the stability of a regime: as it did in 1641–2; as it did also in 1659–60; and as it did once again in 1688. That Charles II did not face a comparable crisis in 1681–5 was, of course, due to a complex array of factors, not the least of which was the king's ability to retain the support of the powerful at the upper levels of society. Yet given the nature of government in seventeenth-century London, Charles's ability to police the streets and enforce the laws so effectively might have been due, at least in part, to the fact that he continued to enjoy a significant amount of support amongst the London populace.

[52] Sachse, 'The Mob and the Revolution'.
[53] Holmes, 'Sacheverell Riots'; Rogers, 'Popular Protest'; De Krey, *Fractured Society*; Colley,

BIBLIOGRAPHY

MANUSCRIPT SOURCES

BODLEIAN LIBRARY

Carte	30	Miscellaneous Papers
	39	Ormonde Papers, 1679–82
	73	Montague Papers, 1656–61
	104	Miscellaneous Papers
	213	Ormonde Papers, 1650–60
	214	Ormonde Papers, 1660–3
	216	Ormonde Papers, 1679–84
	228	Wharton and Huntingdon Papers
	232	Miscellaneous Irish Letters and Papers, 1567–1695
Clarendon	60–72	Clarendon Papers, 1659–60
Don	b. 8	Poems, Satires, etc.
Douce	357	Poems and Songs
Firth	c. 15	A Choice Collection of Poems, Lampoons, and Satires
Rawlinson A	478	fol. 97 Proposals made by the French Congregational Church in London to the Weavers' Company, 1669
	Poet 173	State Lampoons, temp. Cromwell to Anne
Tanner	47	Collection of Letters and Papers, 1663–4
	125	Diocese of Canterbury Papers, 17th Century

BRITISH LIBRARY
Additional

10,116–17	T. Rugge, 'Mercurius Politicus Redivivus; Or, A Collection of the Most Materiall Occurances and Transactions in Publick Affaires, Since Anno Domini 1659'
15,057	fols. 44–5 Letter of 1676 Relating to the Firing of London in 1666
17,018	fols. 143–5 Report on the Fire in Fetter Lane, 1679
25,124	Extraordinary Correspondence of Henry Coventry, Secretary of State, vol. III, 1672–80
25,358–63	Correspondence of the Florentine Minister in London, vols. I–VI, 1675–83
27,407	Political Poems, 17th and 18th Centuries
29,497	Political Poems
32,518	Guilford Papers

	33,051	fols. 206–11 Inquiry into the Common Council's Claim to a Negative Voice, 1676
	34,362	Poems
	38,693	fol. 137 The Articles for the Society of Young Men in St Martin-in-the-Fields, 1681
	38,856	Hodgkin Papers, vol. XI
Harleian	2262	fols. 6–12 Disputes of the Weavers' Company over the Admission of Aliens, 1669–70
	6194	Satirical Poems
	6845	fols. 251–96 Papers Relating to the Duke of Monmouth's Landing in the West
	7317	Political and Other Poems
	7319	A Collection of Choice Poems
Sloane	655	Poetry
	970	fols. 35–6 Examinations and Informations about the Firing of London, 1666
Stowe	185	fols. 171–6 'Present State of the Nonconformists, 1672'
	186	fols. 39–50 Papers Concerning Shaftesbury's Trial

CORPORATION OF LONDON RECORD OFFICE

Sessions Files, 1661–87
Sessions Minute Books, vols. 3–58, 1662–87
Sessions Papers, Charles II's reign (only a few)
Southwark Sessions Files, 1667–87
Southwark Box 17, Sessions Papers 1654, 1667–1784
Conventicle Boxes 1, 2
Common Council Journals, vols. 41x, 45–50, years 1649–61, 1661–86
Lieutenancy Court Minute Books, 1676–88
Repertories of the Court of Aldermen, vols. 67–91, years 1659–86
Repertories Index, vols. 5, 6, years 1649–72, 1672–92
Shelf 552, MS Box 3
Waiting Books, vols. 13, 14, years 1681–4
Ward Presentments, 1681–1683

GREATER LONDON RECORD OFFICE

MJ/SR/1204–1697	Sessions of the Peace and Oyer and Terminer Rolls, Middlesex, 1659–86
MJ/GSR	Middlesex Gaol Delivery Rolls, numbered as part of above series
WJ/SR	Westminster Sessions of the Peace Rolls, numbered as part of above series
MJ/SBB/188–442	Sessions of the Peace and Oyer and Terminer Books, Middlesex, 1660–86
WJ/SBB	Sessions of the Peace and Oyer and Terminer Books, Westminster, numbered as part of above series
MJ/SBP/5–7	Process Registers of Indictments, Middlesex, 1660–87
WJ/SBP/1	Process Register of Indictments, Westminster, 1660–79
MJ/SP	Sessions Papers, 1666–8 (only a few)

Calendar of Sessions Books, vols. 3–7, years 1656–86

Calendar of Sessions Papers, 1617–1709
Acc 591/9   Description of an Assault on a Hearth Tax Collector, 1 June
                   1682
Acc 591/12   Information on Westbury Street Conventicle, 1684
MR/RC/1–10   Certificate of Convictions for Holding Conventicles, 1664–87
MR/RS/1/1–2   Sacrament Oaths, 1673
MR/TH/1   Hearth Tax Returns, Finsbury Division, 1664

GUILDHALL LIBRARY
MS 592   Minutes of White's Alley Baptist Church, 1681–1708
MS 4648/1   Weavers' Company, Renter Bailiffs Accounts, 1666–82
MS 4655/3–8   Weavers' Court Minute Books, 1661–83
MS 9060   Archdeaconry of London, Assignation Book in Respect of Pro-
                   ceedings taken against Dissenters, 1680s
MS 9583/2–5   Episcopal Visitations, 1664, 1669, 1677, 1680
Churchwarden's Accounts:
MS 1432/5   St Alphage, London Wall, 1631–77
MS 2968/5   St Dunstan-in-the-West, 1665–81
MS 5026/1   All Hallows, Honey Lane, 1618–1743

HOUSE OF LORDS RECORD OFFICE
Main Papers, H.L., years 1660–85

LIBRARY OF CONGRESS
MSS 18,124   vols. I–IX

PEPYSIAN LIBRARY, MAGDALENE COLLEGE, CAMBRIDGE
Pepys Miscellanies, VII pp. 465–91 Transcript of the Minutes of the Green Ribbon
   Club

PUBLIC RECORD OFFICE
Surrey Assize Files:
Assi 35 101/2   3 September 1660
         102/6   22 July 1661
         103/6   22 February 1662
         104/7   4 March 1663
         104/8   8 August 1663
         105/7   22 February 1664
         105/8   25 July 1664
         106/7   22 February 1665
         106/8   28 June 1665
         107/5   19 March 1666
         107/6   23 July 1666
         108/6   4 March 1667
         109/4   24 February 1668
         109/9   29 June 1668
         111/4   28 February 1670
         111/5   4 July 1670
         112/11   31 July 1671
         113/1   Lent 1672

113/7	23 July 1672
114/6	7 July 1673
115/6	30 March 1674
115/7	20 July 1674
116/6	8 March 1675
116/7	10 June 1675
116/8	19 July 1675
116/9	2 September 1675
117/7	6 March 1676
117/8	4 July 1676
118/7	6 March 1677
118/8	Summer 1677
121/5	19 July 1680
122/5	7 March 1681
122/6	20 July 1681
123/5	23 March 1682
123/6	3 August 1682
124/6	26 July 1683
125/5	17 July 1684
126/6	19 March 1685
126/7	June and July 1685
126/8	10 September 1685

King's Bench:

KB 10/1–3	Indictments, 1675–83
KB 15/1	Amercements and Recognizances Forfeited
KB 33/5/5	Informations Concerning Sedition, Libel and Slander, Charles II – Anne
PC 2/54–70	Privy Council Registers, Reign of Charles II
SP 18	State Papers Domestic, Interregnum
SP 29	State Papers Domestic, Reign of Charles II

SURREY RECORD OFFICE
Surrey Quarter Sessions Files, 1666–86

VICTORIA COUNTY LIBRARY, WESTMINSTER
F 39, F 40	St Martin-in-the-Fields, Churchwardens Accounts, 1682–4
F2004	St Martin-in-the-Fields, Vestry Minutes, 1666–83

DR WILLIAMS'S LIBRARY
Morrice, Roger	Entring Books, 3 vols.

PRINTED PRIMARY SOURCES

NEWSPAPERS

Care, H., *The Weekly Pacquet of Advice from Rome*, 5 vols. (1678–83), pub. L. Curtis

The Currant Intelligence; Or, An Impartial Account of Transactions both Forraign and Domestick, pub. J. Smith, nos. 1–70, 14 February–24 December 1681

Domestick Intelligence; Or, News both from City and Country, pub. B. Harris, nos. 1–55, 9 July 1679–13 January 1681 (continued as *Protestant (Domestick) Intelligence*)

The Domestick Intelligence; Or, News both from City and Country Impartially Related, pub. T. Benskins, nos. 64–155, 29 December 1681–16 November 1682

Heraclitus Ridens, At a Dialogue Between Jest and Earnest, pub. B. Tooke, nos. 1–82, 1 February 1681–22 August 1682

[Hilton, J.], *The Conventicle Courant*, nos. 1–30, 24 July 1682–14 February 1683

The Impartial Protestant Mercury; Or, Occurrences Foreign and Domestick, pub. R. Janeway, nos. 1–115, 27 April 1681–30 May 1682

The Kingdome's Intelligencer of the Affairs now in Agitation, pub. H. Muddiman, for the years 1660–3

L'Estrange, Sir R., *The Observator: In Question and Answer*, pub. H. and J. Brome, nos. 1–469, 13 April 1681–7 January 1684 (subtitles vary)

The London Gazette, for the years 1660–85, pub. by authority

The London Mercury, pub. T. Vile, R. Baldwin, nos. 1–6, 6 April–17 October 1682

The Loyal Impartial Mercury; Or, News Both Foreign and Domestick, pub. E. Brooks, nos. 1–46, 9 June–17 November 1682

The Loyal London Mercury; Or, The Currant Intelligencer, pub. G. Croom, nos. 1–25, 23 August–15 November 1682

The Loyal London Mercury; Or, The Moderate Intelligencer, pub. G. Croom, nos. 1–20, 14 June–19 August 1682

The Loyal Protestant, and True Domestic Intelligence; Or, News both from City and Country, pub. N. Thompson, nos. 1–247, 9 March 1681–20 March 1683

Mercurius Civicus; Or, A True Account of Affairs both Foreign and Domestick, nos. 1–14, 4 March–6 May 1680

Mercurius Politicus, for the years 1659–1660

Mercurius Publicus, for the years 1660–1

The Protestant (Domestick) Intelligence; Or, News from Both City and Country, pub. B. Harris, nos. 56–114, 16 January 1680–15 April 1681

Smith's Protestant Intelligence; Domestick and Foreign, pub. F. Smith, nos. 1–22, 1 February–14 April 1681

The True Domestick Intelligence; Or, News both from City and Country, pub. N. Thompson, June 1679–May 1680

The True Protestant (Domestick) Intelligence; Or, News From Both City and Country, pub. B. Harris (?), nos. 1–7, 1 April–14 May 1680 (published during a suspension of the *Protestant (Domestick) Intelligence*)

The True Protestant Mercury; Or, Occurrences Foreign and Domestick, pub. L. Curtis, nos. 1–188, 28 December 1680–25 October 1682

The Weekly Discoverer Strip'd Naked; Or, Jest and Earnest Expos'd to Publick View in his Proper Colours, pub. B. Harris, nos. 1–5, 16 February–16 March 1681

The Weekly Discovery of the Mystery of Iniquity; In the Rise, Growth, Methods, and Ends of the Late Unnatural Rebellion in England, Anno 1641, pub. B. Tooke, nos. 1–30, 5 February–27 August 1681

PLAYING CARDS
British Library, Schreiber Cards, English 56, 'All the Popish Plots, 1588–1678'
British Library, Willshire Cards, E 185, 'The Spanish Armada', c. 1680
British Library, Willshire Cards, E 189, 'The Rye House Plot'
Guildhall Library, Playing Cards 236, 'The Pretended "Popish Plot" of 1678'

Guildhall Library, Playing Cards 237, 'The Pretended "Popish Plot" of 1678' (imperfect pack of 49)

Guildhall Library, Playing Cards 238, 'The Meal Tub Plot of Thomas Dangerfield and Madame Cellier'

Guildhall Library, Playing Cards 239, 'A Pack of Cavalier Playing Cards temp. Charles II, Forming a Complete Political Satire of the Commonwealth'

Schreiber, Lady C., *Playing Cards of Various Ages and Countries*, 3 vols. (1892–5)

BOOKS, PAMPHLETS, BROADSIDES, ETC.

The Address of above 20,000 of the Loyal Protestant Apprentices of London, Humbly Presented to the Right Honourable Lord Mayor, September 2nd, 1681 (1681)

Adis, H., *A Fanaticks Alarm, Given to the Mayor in his Quarters* (1661)

Advice to the City; Or, The Whigs Loyalty Examined (1682)

Advice to His Grace [1681–21], repr. in Thompson, ed., *Poems*, pp. 128–9

Ailesbury, Earl of, *Memoirs*, ed. W. E. Buckley, 2 vols. (1890)

Albemarle, Duke of, *Observations upon Military and Political Affairs* (1671)

An Answer to the Whiggish Poem on the Loyal Apprentices Feast (1682)

The Arraignment of the Anabaptists Good Old Cause (1660)

[Ayloffe, J.], *A Dialogue Between the Two Horses* [1676], repr. in *Poems on Affairs of State*, I, 274–83

[Ayloffe, J.], *Oceana and Britannia* [1681, first published 1689], repr. in *Poems on Affairs of State*, II, 393–405

Babel and Bethel; Or, The Pope in His Colours (1679)

The Ballad of the Cloak; Or, The Cloaks Knavery (1679), in *Roxburghe Ballads*, IV, 605–7

A Ballad in Praise of London Prentices and What They Did at the Cockpit Play-House, in Drury Lane (1617), repr. in Mackay, ed., *Songs*, pp. 94–7

Baxter, R., *A Key For Catholicks to Satisfie All Whether the Cause of the Roman or Reformed Churches be of God* (1659)

Bedloe, W., *The Excommunicated Prince; Or, The False Relique* (1679)

Behold a Cry; Or, A True Relation of the Inhuman and Violent Outrages of Divers Soldiers, Constables, and Others (1662)

Besse, J., *A Collection of the Sufferings of the People called Quakers*, 2 vols. (1753)

Blanket-Fair; Or, The History of Temple Street (1684), repr. in Rimbault, ed., *Old Ballads*, pp. 9–11

Bohun, E., *The Third and Last Part of the Address to the Free-Men* (1683)

Burnet, G., *The Life and Death of Sir Matthew Hale, Kt.* (1682)

The Burning of the Whore of Babylon, as it was Acted, with Great Applause, in the Poultrey (1673)

Burton, T., *Diary*, ed. J. T. Rutt, 4 vols. (1828)

By the Committee of Safety ... A Proclamation Prohibiting the Contrivance or Subscription of any Petitions or Papers for the Promoting of Designs Dangerous to the Common-Wealth (1659)

[C., R.], *The Triumphant Weaver; Or, The Art of Weaving Discuss'd and Handled* (1682)

Calamy Revised. Being a Revision of Edmund Calamy's Account of the Ministers and Others Ejected and Silenced, 1660–2, by A. G. Matthews (Oxford, 1934)

Calendar of the Clarendon State Papers Preserved in the Bodleian Library, ed. F. J. Routledge, 5 vols. (Oxford, 1872–1932)

Calendar of State Papers Domestic, for the years 1659–86

Calendar of State Papers Venetian, for the years 1659–75

Calendar of the Middlesex Sessions Records, NS I, 1612–14, ed. W. Le Hardy (1935)

The Carman's Poem; Or, Advice to a Nest of Scribblers [1680], repr. in Thompson, ed., *Poems*, pp. 191–5

Carte, T., *A Collection of Original Letters and Papers Concerning the Affairs of England from the Year 1641 to 1660* (1739)

The Catholick Gamesters; Or, A Dubble Matcht of Bowleing (1680)

The Cavaliers' Litany (1682)

The Character of a Coffee House (1673)

The Character of an Informer (1675)

Charles II, *A Proclamation for the Suppression of Riots* (1675)

The Charter. A Comical Satyr (1682), repr. in Thompson, ed., *Poems*, pp. 134–55

A City Ballad [1659–60], repr. in *Collection of Loyal Songs ... Against the Rump*, II, 80–8

Clapinson, M., ed., *Bishop Fell and Nonconformity: Visitation Documents from the Oxford Diocese, 1682–3* (Oxford, 1980)

Clarendon, Earl of, *Life. In Which is Included, A Continuation of His History of the Great Rebellion*, 2 vols. (Oxford, 1857)

Clarendon, Earl of, *The History of the Rebellion and Civil Wars in England*, ed. W. D. Macray, 6 vols. (Oxford, 1888)

A Collection of Loyal Songs Written Against the Rump Parliament, Between the Years 1639 and 1661, 2 vols. (1731)

[College, S.], *A Raree Show* (1681), repr. in *Poems on Affairs of State*, II, 425–31

The Compleat Swearing Master (1683), repr. in *Poems on Affairs of State*, III, 3–8

A Congratulation on the Happy Discovery of the Hellish Fanatick Plot (1682) repr. in Thompson, ed., *Songs*, pp. 62–4

A Congratulatory Poem to Sir John More Knight, Lord Mayor Elect of London (1681), repr. in Thompson, ed., *Poems*, pp. 189–91

A Congratulatory Poem upon the Happy Arrival of His Royal Highness, James, Duke of York, at London, April 8th, 1682 (1682), repr. in Thompson, ed., *Poems*, pp. 249–54

The Conspiracy; Or, The Discovery of the Fanatick Plot (1683), repr. in Thompson, ed., *Songs*, pp. 3–5

The Contents (Hats for Caps) Contented (1680)

The Convert Scot, and Apostate English (1681), repr. in Thompson, ed., *Poems*, pp. 45–54

The Coronation of Queen Elizabeth, with the Restauration of the Protestant Religion; Or, the Downfall of the Pope (1680)

The Country-Mans Complaint and Advice to the King (1681), repr. in Thompson, ed., *Poems*, pp. 95–6

[Cowley, A.], *A Satyre. The Puritan and the Papist* (Oxford, 1643)

[Dean, J.], *The Badger in the Fox-Trap; Or, A Satyr upon Satyrs* [1681], repr. in Thompson, ed., *Poems*, pp. 62–78

A Declaration of all the Watermen in and about the City of London between Gravesend and Staines; Or, A Hue and Cry after Col. Whitton and his Decoys (1660)

A Declaration from the Harmless and Innocent People ... Called Quakers (1661)

A Declaration of Many Thousand Well-Affected Persons, Inhabitants in and about the Cities of London and Westminster (1660)

Delaune, T., *A Plea for the Non-Conformists* (1684)

The Deliquium; Or, The Grievance of the Nation Discovered in a Dream [1681], repr. in Thompson, ed., *Poems*, pp. 7–14

Denham, Sir J., *The True Presbyterian Without Disguise; Or, A Character of a Presbyterians Ways and Actions* (1680)

The Devils Tryumph over Romes Idoll (1680)

A Dialogue Betwixt the Devil and the Ignoramus Salamanca Doctor [1679], repr. in Thompson, ed., *Poems*, pp. 120–3

A Dialogue betwixt an Excise-Man and Death (1659)

A Dialogue Between the Pope and a Phanatick, Concerning Affairs in England (1680)

A Dialogue Betwixt Tom and Dick, the Former a Country Man, the Other a Citizen (1660), repr. in Mackay, ed., *Songs*, pp. 88–94

A Dialogue upon the Burning of the Pope and Presbyter in Effigy at Westminster (1681)

Dictated Thoughts upon the Presbyterians Late Petition for Compleat and Universal Power (1646)

Dictionary of National Biography

The Discovery of the Popish Plot, Being the Several Examinations of Titus Oates, D.D., Before the High Court of Parliamant (1679)

Disney, J., *A Second Essay upon the Execution of the Laws against Immorality and Prophaneness* (1710)

The Dissenters Address, To His Majesty (1683)

The Dissenter Truly Described (1681), repr. in Thompson, ed., *Poems*, pp. 166–9

A Door of Hope; Or, A Call and Declaration, (1661)

The Downfall of the Good Old Cause [ND], repr. in Thompson, ed., *Songs*, pp. 12–14

[Duke, R.], *Funeral Tears upon the Death of Captain William Bedloe* [1680], repr. in Thompson, ed., *Poems*, pp. 42–4

The Duke's Welcom from Scotland to London [ND], repr. in Thompson, ed., *Poems*, pp. 264–5

Dunton, J., *Life and Errors* (1705)

The Ellis Correspondence, 1686–1688, ed. G. A. Ellis, 2 vols. (1829)

Ellwood, T., *A Caution to Constables and Other Inferior Officers Concerned in the Execution of the Conventicle Act* (1683)

Ellwood, T., *History of His Life,* ed. S. G. Graveson (1906)

The Engagement and Remonstrance of the City of London, Subscribed by 23,500 Hands (1659)

The Englishman; Or, A Letter from a Universal Friend ... With Some Observations Upon the Late Act against Conventicles (1670)

An Epitaph on Harry Care [ND], repr. in *Third Collection ... Against Popery*, pp. 7–8

Estwicke, N., *A Dialogue Betwixt a Conformist and a Nonconformist, Concerning the Lawfulness of Private Meetings* (1668)

Evelyn, J., *A Character of England, as it was Later Presented in a Letter, to a Noble Man of France. With Reflections upon Gallus Castratus* (1659)

An Excellent New Hymne to the Mobile, Exhorting them to Loyalty the Clean Contrary Way (1682), in *Roxburghe Ballads*, V, 60

A Farewell to His Royal Highness, James Duke of York, On His Voyage to Scotland, October 20, 1680 (1680), repr. in Thompson, ed., *Poems*, pp. 263–4

[Ferguson, R.], *Appeal from the Country to the City* (1679)

[Ferguson, R.], *An Historical Account of the Heroick Life and Magnanimous Actions of the Most Illustrious Protestant Prince, James, Duke of Monmouth* (1683)

Ferguson, R., 'Manuscript Concerning the Rye House Plot', in J. Ferguson, *Robert Ferguson – The Plotter; Or, The Secret of the Rye House Conspiracy and the Story of a Strange Career* (Edinburgh, 1887), pp. 409–37

The Final Protest, and Sense of the Cittie (1659)

For General Monk's Entertainment at Cloth-Worker's Hall (1660), repr. in *Collection of Loyal Songs ... Against the Rump*, I, 263–4

Fowler, E., *The Great Wickedness and Mischievous Effects of Slandering* (1685)

Freezland-Fair; Or, The Icy Bear-Garden (1684), in Rimbault, ed., *Old Ballads*, pp. 12–15

Freshfield, E., ed., *The Vestry Minute Book of St. Bartholomew Exchange* (1890)

A Friendly Dialogue Between Two London Apprentices (1681)

The Gracious Answer of the Most Illustrious Lady of Pleasure, the Countess of Castlem ... To the Poor-Whoores Petition (1668)

The Grand Cheat, Cry'd Up Under-Hand by Many in the Factious and Giddy Part of the Army (1659)

Grey, Ford Lord of Wark, *The Secret History of the Rye House Plot and Monmouth's Rebellion* (1685)

Guide to the Middlesex Sessions Records, 1549–1889 (1965)

Hale, Sir M., *Historia Placitorum Coronae: the History of the Pleas of the Crown*, facsimile of the 1736 edition, with an introduction by P. R. Glazebrook, 2 vols. (1971)

Hansard, T. C., *The Parliamentary History of England* (1808)

Harrington, J., *The Commonwealth of Oceana* (1656), repr. in J. G. A. Pocock, ed., *The Political Works of James Harrington* (Cambridge, 1977), pp. 155–359

An Heroick Poem on Her Highness the Lady Ann's Voyage into Scotland: With a Little Digression upon the Times (1681), repr. in Thompson, ed., *Poems*, pp. 266–9

Hickeringill, E., *The Ceremony-Monger* (1689)

Historical Manuscripts Commission, 5th Report

Historical Manuscripts Commission, 6th Report

Historical Manuscripts Commission, 7th Report

Historical Manuscripts Commission, 9th Report, II

Historical Manuscripts Commission, 10th Report, IV

Historical Manuscripts Commission, 11th Report, VII

Historical Manuscripts Commission, 12th Report, VII

Historical Manuscripts Commission, Leyborne-Popham

Historical Manuscripts Commission, Ormond, NS IV–VII

Historical Manuscripts Commission, Salisbury, XXII

The History of the Life and Death of Hugh Peters, that Arch-Traytor, from his Cradell to the Gallowes (1661)

Hoffman, B., *Some Considerations of the Present Use* (1683)

The Honest Cryer of London (1660)

The Honour of London Apprentices (1647)

Hugh Peters' Last Will and Testament (1660)

The Humble Apology of Some Commonly Called Anabaptists ... With their Protestation against the Late Wicked and Most Horrid Treasonable Insurrection and Rebellion Acted in the City of London (1661)

The Humble and Grateful Acknowledgment of Many Ministers of the Gospel in and about the City of London (1660)

The Humble Wishes of a Loyal Subject (1681), repr. in Thompson, ed., *Poems*, pp. 78–80

Interrogatories; Or, A Dialogue Between Whig and Tory (1681), repr. in Thompson, ed., *Poems*, pp. 221–2

J[essey], H., *The Lord's Loud Call to England* (1660)

Jockey's Downfall; A Poem on the Late Total Defeat Given to the Scottish Covenanters (1679), repr. in *Roxburghe Ballads*, IV, 541–2

Jones, D., *The Secret History of White-Hall From the Restoration of Charles II Down to the Abdication of the Late K. James* (1697)

Jonson, B., *Bartholomew Fair*, ed. D. Duncan (Edinburgh, 1972)

Jordan, T., *London in Luster, Projecting Many Bright Beams of Triumph at the Initiation and Instalment of . . . Sir Robert Clayton* (1679)

Jordan, T., *London's Glory; Or, The Lord Mayor's Show* (1680)

Jordan, T., *London's Joy; Or, The Lord Mayor's Show* (1681)

[Jordan, T.], *The Lord Mayor's Show; Begin a Description of the Solemnity at the Inauguration of . . . Sir William Pritchard* (1682)

Journals of the House of Commons

Journals of the House of Lords

Just and Modest Vindication of the Many Thousand Loyal Apprentices that Presented an Humble Address to the Lord Mayor of London (1681)

Kidder, R., *Life*, ed. A. E. Robinson (1924)

The King's Answer (1680), repr. in *Poems on Affairs of State*, II, 255–6

The Lamentation of the Safe Committee (1660), repr. in *Collection of Loyal Songs . . . Against the Rump*, II, 166–7

A Lampoon on Scroggs Put on His Door (1679), repr. in *Poems on Affairs of State*, II, 288–9

Lanfière, T., *The Citty Prophesier; Or, The Country Fortuneteller* [1680]

The Last Speech of Sir Edmundbury Godfrey's Ghost [ND], repr. in Thompson, ed., *Poems*, pp. 322–4

The Last and Truest Discovery of the Popish Plot, by Rumsey, West, and Other Great Patriots of their Countrey (1683)

The Last Will and Testament of Anthony, King of Poland (1682), repr. in Thompson, ed., *Poems*, pp. 196–8

Lawrence, W., *Marriage by the Moral Law of God*, 2 vols. (1680–1)

L'Estrange, Sir R., *The History of the Plot* (1679)

[L'Estrange, Sir R.], *Citt and Bumpkin, The Second Part; Or, A Learned Discourse upon Swearing and Lying* (1680)

[L'Estrange, Sir R.], *The Committee; Or, Popery in Masquerade* (1680)

L'Estrange, Sir R., *A Further Discovery of the Plot: Dedicated to Dr. Titus Oates* (1680)

Let Oliver Now Be Forgotten [ND], repr. in Thompson, ed., *Songs*, pp. 1–3

A Letter from a Person of Quality to his Friend in the Country (1675)

A List of Conventicles or Unlawful Meetings Within the City of London and Bills of Mortality (1683)

A Litany from Geneva, in Answer to that from St. Omers (1682)

[Lockyer, N.], *Some Seasonable and Serious Queries upon the Late Act Against Conventicles* (1670)

London Sessions Records, 1605–85, ed. Dom H. Bowler (1943)

London's Defiance to Rome (1679)

London's Drollery; Or, The Love and Kindness Between the Pope and the Devil (1680), repr. in *Roxburghe Ballads*, IV, 221–4

Londons Glory; Or, The Riot and Ruine of the Fifth Monarchy Men, and their Adherents (1661)

London's Joy and Loyalty, On His Royal Highness the Duke of York's Return from Scotland (1682), repr. in Thompson, ed., *Songs*, pp. 82–3

London's Joy and Triumph on the Instalment of Sir William Pritchard (1682), repr. in Mackay, ed., *Songs*, pp. 112–14

London's Lamentation for the Loss of Their Charter (1683), in Thompson, ed., *Songs*, pp. 40–2

London's Loyalty (1679), repr. in Thompson, ed., *Songs*, pp. 79–80

The Loyal Feast, Designed to be Kept in Haberdasher's Hall, on Friday, 21st April, 1682 (1682)

Mackay, C., ed., *A Collection of Songs and Ballads Relative to the London Prentices and Trades* (1841)

The Mad-Men's Hospital; Or, A Present Remedy to Cure the Presbyterian Itch (1681), repr. in Thompson, ed., *Poems*, pp. 57–60

Marriot, T., *Rebellion Unmasked, A Sermon Preached at Poplar . . . Upon the Occasion of the Late Rebellious Insurrection in London* (1661)

Marvell, A., *The Last Instructions to a Painter* (1667), repr. in *Poems on Affairs of State*, I, 97–139

Marvell, A., *The History of Insipids* (1674), repr. in *Poems on Affairs of State*, I, 243–51

Marvell, A., *An Account of the Growth of Popery and Arbitrary Government in England* (1677)

Marvell, A., *Poems and Letters*, ed. H. M. Margoliouth, 2 vols. (Oxford, 1971)

[May, Sir T.], *Arbitrary Government Display'd: In The Tyrannick Usurpation of the Rump Parliamant, and Oliver Cromwell* (1683)

Misopappas, P., *The Charge of a Tory Plot Maintain'd, in a Dialogue between the Observator, Heraclitus and an Inferiour Clergy-man at the Towzer-Tavern* (1682)

Misopappas, P., *A Tory Plot; Or, The Discovery of A Design Carried on by Our Late Addressers and Abhorrers to Alter the Constitution of the Government, and to Betray the Protestant Religion* (1682)

Misopappas, P., *The Tory Plot: The Second Part; Or, A Farther Discovery of A Design to Alter the Constitution of the Government, and to Betray the Protestant Religion* (1682)

Misson, H., *Memoirs and Observations in his Travels over England*, trans. by Mr Ozell (1719)

[Nalson, J.], *Foxes and Fire-Brands; Or, A Specimen of the Danger and Harmony of Popery and Separation* (1680)

Nalson, J., *An Impartial Collection of the Great Affairs of State*, 2 vols. (1682–3)

A Narrative of the Proceedings at the Sessions House, 21st April, 1680 (1680)

A Narrative of the Sufferings of Thomas Delaune (1684)

A Nest of Nunnes Egges, Strangely Hatched, with the Description of a Worthy Feast for Joy of the Blood [1680?]

A New Ballad, Called, The Protestants Prophesie [1680]

A New Song on the Arrival of Prince George, and His Intermarriage with the Lady Anne (1683) repr. in Thompson, ed., *Songs*, pp. 23–4

A New Song on the Death of Colledge, The Protestant Joyner [1681], repr. in Thompson, ed., *Songs*, pp. 64–6

A New Song, On the Instalment of Sir John Moore, Lord Mayor of London (1681), in Mackay, ed., *Songs*, pp. 103–8

A New Year's Gift for the Rump (Oxford, 1660), in *Collection of Loyal Songs ... Against the Rump*, II, 41–4

North, R., *Examen; Or, An Enquiry into the Credit and Veracity of a Pretended Complete History* (1740)

Oates, T., *A Sermon Preached at St. Michael's, Wood Street* (1679)

Observations on the Single Query Proposed Concerning the Choice of Parliament-Men For the City, Yesterday Diligently Delivered to Coffee-Houses and Elsewhere (1681)

Ogilby, J., *The Relation of His Majesties Entertainment Passing through the City of London to His Coronation* (1661)

Old Jemmy (1681), repr. in Thompson, ed., *Songs*, pp. 20–2

Oxford English Dictionary

A Panegyrick to His Royal Highness, Upon His Majesties Late Declaration (1680), repr. in Thompson, ed., *Poems*, pp. 243–7

The Parliament Dissolv'd at Oxford, March 28, 1681 (1681), repr. in Thompson, ed., *Poems*, pp. 29–31

Pelling, E., *A Sermon Preached on the Anniversary of that Most Excerable Murder of K. Charles the First, Royal Martyr* (1682/3)

Petition of the Lieutenancy to the King (1682)

Pettit, E., *Visions of Government, Wherein the Antimonarchical Principles and Practices of all Fanatical Commonwealths Men and Jesuitical Polititians are Discovered, Confuted, and Exposed* (1684)

Pettit, E., *Visions of the Reformation; Or, A Discovery of the Follies and Villanies that have been Practised, in Popish and Fanatical Thorough Reformations, Since the Reformation of the Church of England* (1683)

Phillips, H. D., *Catalogue of the Collection of Playing Cards of Various Ages and Countries* (1903)

[Phillips, J.], *A Satyr against Hypocrites* (1680)

Philopatris, *The Plot in a Dream; Or, The Discoverer in Masquerade* (1681)

Poems on Affairs of State, ed. G. de F. Lord, *et al.*, 7 vols. (Yale, 1963–75)

The Polititian's Downfall; Or, Potapski's Arrival at the Netherlands (1684), repr. in Thompson, ed., *Poems*, pp. 80–6

Poor Robin's Dream; Or, The Visions of Hell – Or A Dialogue Between the Ghost of Bedloe and Tonge (1681), in Thompson, ed., *Poems*, pp. 176–87

The Poor-Whores Petition. To the Most Splendid, Illustrious, Serene and Eminent Lady of Pleasure, The Countess of Castlemayne (1668)

The Pope Burnt to Ashes (1676)

The Popish Damnable Plot Against Our Religion and Liberties, Lively Delineated in Several of its Branches (1680)

Portrait of Hugh Peters (1660)

The Presbyterian Pater-Noster, Creed, and Ten-Commandments (1681)

The Presentment of the Grand Jury for the City of London (1683)

The Presentment of the Grand-Jury of the Hundred of Ossulston, for the County of Middlesex (1682)

The Presentments of the Grand-Juries for the County of Middlesex (1682)

Presentments of the Grand-Jury for the Town and Borough of Southwark (1683)

The Proceedings of His Majesties Justices of the Peace, at the Sessions of Oyer and Terminer (1684)

The Proceedings at the Sessions House in the Old-Bayly ... On the 24th of ... November, for J. Heathcote (1681)

The Proceedings at the Sessions House in the Old-Bayly ... On the 24th of ... November, for S. Mearne and J. Baker (1681)

The Procession; Or, The Burning of the Pope in Effigy (1681)

A Proposal of Union amongst Protestants (1679)

A Prospect of a Popish Successor, Displayed by Hell-Bred Cruelty (1681)

Protestant Loyalty Fairly Drawn (1681)

A Protestant Prentice's Loyal Advice to all his Fellow-Apprentices in and about London (1680)

The Protestant Tutor (1679)

[Quarles, F.] *The Whig Rampant; Or, Exaltation* [1682], repr. in *Roxburghe Ballads*, IV, 264–6

The Reasons for the Indictment of the Duke of York Presented to the Grand Jury of Middlesex (1680)

Reasons Humbly Offered Against a Bill for Regulating and Encouraging the Art of Weaving (1671)

The Recovery [1682], repr. in Thompson, ed., *Poems*, pp. 31–4

The Remonstrance of the Apprentices in and about London (1659)

A Renunciation and Declaration of the Ministers of Congregational Churches (1661)

A Reply to Dictated Thoughts, by a More Proper Emblem (1646)

The Resolve of the Citie (1659)

The Riddle of the Roundhead (1681), repr. in Thompson, ed., *Songs*, pp. 14–17

Rimbault, E. F., *Old Ballads Illustrating the Great Frost of 1683–4 and the Fair on the River Thames* (1844)

Rome's Hunting-Matcht for Three Kingdoms: England, Scotland, and Ireland (1680)

Rome's Hunting Matcht for Three Kingdoms; Or, The Papists Last Run for the Protestants Life and Estates Too, Because This Plot has e'en Beggar'd Them (1680)

Roscommon, Earl of *The Ghost of Tom Ross to His Pupil the Duke of Monmouth* (1680), repr. in *Poems on Affairs of State*, II, 249–52

The Roxburghe Ballads, ed. W. Chappell and S. W. Ebsworth, 14 vols. (1869–95)

The Royale Virgine; Or, The Declaration of Several Maydens in and about the once Honourable City of London (1660)

Rugge, T., *Diurnal*, ed. W. L. Sachse (1961)

The Rump Carbonado'd [1659–60], repr. in *Collection of Loyal Songs ... Against the Rump*, II, 119–28

The Rump Serv'd in with a Grand Sallet (1660), repr. in *Collection of Loyal Songs ... Against the Rump*, II, 175–83

The Rump Ululant; Or, Penitence per Force (1660), repr. in *Collection of Loyal Songs ... Against the Rump*, II, 244–8

Sadler, A., *The Loyall Mourner, Shewing the Murdering of King Charles the First, Fore-shewing the Restoring of King Charles the Second* (1660)

A Satire on Popery and Jesuitism (1679)

A Scheme of Popish Cruelties (1681)

Schreiber, Lady C., *Catalogue of the Collection of Playing Cards Bequeathed to the Trustees of the British Museum* (1901)

A Seasonable Invitation for Monmouth to Return to Court (1681)

A Second Dialogue Between the Pope and a Phanatick, Concerning Affairs in England (1681)

Sejanus; Or, The Popular Favorite now in his Solitude, and Sufferings (1681), repr. in Thompson, ed., *Poems*, pp. 15–20

[Shepherd, S.], *The Times Displayed in Six Sestyads: The First a Presbyter, an Independent, etc.* (1646)

Sherlock, W., *Some Seasonable Reflections on the Discovery of the Late Plot, Being a Sermon Preacht on that Occasion* (1683)

Simeon and Levi, Brethren and Iniquity. A Comparison Between a Papist and a Scotch Presbyter [1679]

The Solemn Mock Procession of the Pope, Cardinalls, Jesuits, Fryers, etc. ... November the 17th, 1679 (1679)

The Solemn Mock Procession of the Pope, Cardinals, Jesuits, Fryers, Nuns, etc. ... November the 17th, 1680, for I. Oliver (1680), (engraving)

The Solemn Mock Procession of the Pope, Cardinalls, Jesuits, Fryers, Nuns, etc. ... November the 17th, 1680, for N. Ponder (1680), (broadside)

The Solemn Mock Procession; Or, The Trial and Execution of the Pope and His Minister, on the 17. of Nov. at Temple Bar (1680)

The Solicitous Citizen; Or, Much Ado about Nothing [ND], repr. in Thompson, ed., *Poems*, pp. 130–3

Sprat, T., *A True Account and Declaration of the Horrid Conspiracy* (1685)

Standish, J., *A Sermon Preached at the Assizes at Hertford, 9 March 1682/3* (1683)

State Trials, ed. T. B. Howell, 33 vols. (1809–26)

Statutes of the Realm, V (1963)

Stillingfleet, E., *A Discourse Concerning the Idolatory Practised in the Church of Rome* (1681)

The Story of Ill May Day, in the Time of King Henry the Eighth [ND], repr. in Mackay, ed., *Songs*, pp. 11–22

Strange's Case, Strangly Altered (1680)

Strype, J., ed., *John Stow's Survey of the Cites of London and Westminster*, 2 vols. (1720)

Surrey Quarter Sessions Records, 1659–66, ed. H. Jenkinson and D. L. Powell, 3 vols. (1934–8)

A Tale of the Tubs; Or, Rome's Master Peice Defeated (1679), repr. in *Poems on Affairs of State*, II, 298–304

Tatham, J., *London's Glory, Repeated by Time, Truth and Fame* (1660)

[Taylor, J.], *Religions Enemies, with a Brief and Ingenious Relation, as by Anabaptists, Brownists, Papists, Familists, Atheists, and Foolists, Sawcily Presuming to Tosse Religion in a Blanquet* [1641]

A Third Collection of the Newest and Most Ingenious Poems, Satyrs, Songs, etc., Against Popery and Tyranny (1689)

A Third Dialogue Between the Pope and a Phanatick, Concerning Affairs in England (1684)

Thompson, N., ed., *A Collection of Eighty-Six Loyal Poems* (1685)

Thompson, N., ed., *A Collection of One Hundred and Eighty Loyal Songs* (1685)

Thorndike, H., *Theological Works*, 6 vols. (Oxford, 1844–56)

The Time-Servers; Or, A Touch of the Times (1681)

Titus Tell-Troth; Or, The Plot-Founder Confounded (1682), repr. in Thompson, ed., *Songs*, pp. 25–7

To His Excellency the Lord General Monck. The Unanimous Representation of the Apprentices and Young Men Inhabiting in the City of London (1660)

To His Royal Highness the Duke [1679], repr. in Thompson, ed., *Poems*, pp. 247–9

To His Royal Highness, the Duke, Upon His Arrival [1679], repr. in Thompson, ed., *Poems*, pp. 255–8

To His Royal Highness the Duke of York, Upon His Return to the Care and Management of the Navy of England [1684], repr. in Thompson, ed., *Poems*, pp. 259–61

To Our Worthy and Grave Senators ... the Lord Mayor, etc. ... The Further Humble Petition and Remonstrance of the Freemen and Prentices of the City of London (1659)

To the General Council of Officers. The Representation of Divers Citizens of London, and Others Well-Affected to the Peace and Tranquility of the Commonwealth (1659)

To the Right Honorable, the High Court of Parliament ... The Illegal and Immodest Petition of Praise-God Barebone, Anabaptist and Leatherseller of London (1660)

To the Right Honourable, the Lord Mayor ... The Humble Petition and Address of the Sea-men and Water-men, in and about ... London (1659)

To the Right Honourable, the Lord Mayor ... The Humble Petition of Divers Well-Affected Householders and Freemen (1660)

To the Right Honourable ... the Lord Mayor ... The Most Humble Petition and Address of Divers Young Men, on Behalf of Themselves and the Apprentices, in and about this Honourable City (1659)

To the Supreme Authority, the Parliament of the Commonwealth. The Humble Address and Congratulation of Many Thousands of Watermen belonging to the River Thames (1660)

Tom Ross's Ghost to His Pupil (1683), repr. in Thompson, ed., *Poems*, p. 24

Tony's Soliloquies [ND], repr. in Thompson, ed., *Poems*, pp. 60–2

Treason Unmasqued; Or, Truth Brought to Light (1681)

A True Account of the Rise and Growth of the Reformation; Or, The Progress of the Protestant Religion (1680)

A True Description of Blanket Fair upon the River Thames, in Rimbault, ed., *Old Ballads*, pp. 5–9

A True Narrative of the Horrid Hellish Popish Plot ... The First Part (1682)

A True Narrative of the Horrid Hellish Popish Plot ... The Second Part (1682)

A True Narrative of the Horrid Plot and Conspiracy of the Popish Party against the Life of His Sacred Majesty, the Government, and the Protestant Religion (1679), repr. in *State Trials*, VI, fols. 1429–72

Turner, G. Lyon, ed., *Original Records of Early Nonconformity under Persecution and Indulgence*, 3 vols. (1911–14)

Verney Family, *Memoirs*, ed. M. M. Verney, 4 vols. (1892–9)

A Vindication of the Loyal London Apprentices (1681)

Vindiciae Libertatis Evangelii; Or, A Justification of our Present Indulgence, and the Acceptance of Licenses. By Way of Reply to ... Queries upon the Declaration (1672)

Vox Juvenilis; or, The Loyal Apprentices Vindication (1681)

Ward, Rev. J., *Diary, 1648–1679*, ed. C. Severn (1839)

The Way of Peace (1680)

A Welcome to His Royal Highness into the City, April the 20th, 1682 (1682), repr. in Thompson, ed., *Poems*, pp. 261–2

The Whig's Down-fall [ND], repr. in Thompson, ed., *Songs*, pp. 10–12

The Whig's Exaltation [1682], repr. in Thompson, ed., *Songs*, pp. 6–8

The Whigs' Hard Heart for the Cause of the Hard Frost (1684), repr. in Rimbault, ed., *Old Ballads*, pp. 15–18

The Whores Petition to the London Prentices (1668)

Willshire, W. H., *A Descriptive Catalogue of Playing and Other Cards in the British Museum* (1876)

Wood, A., *Life and Times, 1632–1695. Collected from his Diaries, etc.*, ed. A. Clark, 5 vols. (Oxford, 1891–1900)

A Word of Advice to the Two New Sheriffs of London (1682)

SECONDARY SOURCES

Abbott, W. C., 'English Conspiracy and Dissent, 1660–74', *American Historical Journal*, 14 (1908–9), 503–28, 696–722

Abernathy, G. R., *The English Presbyterians and the Stuart Restoration, 1648–1663* (Philadelphia, 1965)

Allen, D. F., 'The Political Role of the London Trained Bands in the Exclusion Crisis, 1678–1681', *English Historical Review*, 87 (1972), 287–303

Allen, D. F., 'Political Clubs in Restoration London', *Historical Journal*, 19 (1976), 561–80

Allen, T., *The History and Antiquities of London, Westminster, Southwark, and Parts Adjacent*, 4 vols. (1927–9)

Allport, F. H., 'Towards a Science of Public Opinion', *Public Opinion Quarterly*, 1 (1937), 7–23

Ashley, M., *John Wildman, Plotter and Postmaster: A Study of the English Republican Movement in the Seventeenth Century* (1947)

Ashton, R., 'Popular Entertainment and Social Control in Later Elizabethan and Early Stuart London', *London Journal*, 9 (1983), 3–19

Atherton, H. M., *Political Prints in the Age of Hogarth: A Study of the Ideographic Representation of Politics* (Oxford, 1974)

Aylmer, G. E., ed., *The Interregnum: The Quest for Settlement, 1646–1660* (1974)

Bakhtin, M. M., *Rabelais and His World*, trans. by H. Iswolsky (Cambridge, Massachusetts, 1968)

Bate, F., *The Declaration of Indulgence, 1672: A Study in the Rise of Organised Dissent* (1980)

Beddard, R. A., 'The London Frost Fair, 1683–4', *Guildhall Miscellany*, IV, no. 2 (April, 1972), 63–87

Beddard, R. A., 'Vincent Alsop and the Emancipation of Restoration Dissent', *Journal of Ecclesiastical History*, 24 (1973), 161–84

Bedford, J., *London's Burning* (1966)

Behrens, B., 'The Whig Theory of the Constitution in the Reign of Charles II', *Cambridge Historical Journal*, 7 (1941), 42–71

Beier, A. L. and R. Finlay, eds., *The Making of the Metropolis: London, 1500–1700* (1986)

Beloff, M., *Public Order and Popular Disturbances, 1660–1714* (1938)

Besant, W., *London in the Time of the Stuarts, 1603–1714* (1903)

Bevan, B., *James, Duke of Monmouth* (1973)

Bolam, C. G. and J. Goring, 'The Cataclysm', in C. G. Bolam *et al.*, eds., *The English Presbyterians: From Elizabethan Puritanism to Modern Unitarianism* (1968), pp. 73–92

Bosher, R. S., *The Making of the Restoration Settlement, 1649–1662* (1957)

Boulton, J. P., 'The Limits of Formal Religion: The Administration of Holy Communion in late Elizabethan and early Stuart London', *London Journal*, 10 (1984), 135–54

Boulton, J. P., *Neighbourhood and Society: A London Suburb in the Seventeenth Century* (Cambridge, 1987)

Brailsford, H. N., *The Levellers and the English Revolution*, ed. C. Hill (1976)

Braithwaite, W. C., *The Second Period of Quakerism* (Cambridge, 1961)

Brett-James, N. G., *The Growth of Stuart London* (1935)

Brewer, J., *Party Ideology and Popular Politics at the Accession of George III* (Cambridge, 1976)

Brewer, J. and J. Styles, eds., *An Ungovernable People: The English and their Law in the Seventeenth and Eighteenth Centuries* (1980)

Brigden, S., 'Youth and the English Reformation', *Past and Present*, 95 (1982), 37–67

Burke, P., 'Popular Culture in Seventeenth-Century London', in Reay, ed., *Popular Culture*, pp. 31–58

Burke, P., *Popular Culture in Early Modern Europe* (1978)

Burke, P., 'Popular Culture between History and Ethnology', *Ethnologia Europaea*, 14 (1984), 5–13

Burrage, C., 'The Fifth Monarchist Insurrections', *English Historical Review*, 25 (1910), 722–47

Capp, B. S., *The Fifth Monarchy Men: A Study of Seventeenth-Century English Millenarianism* (1972)

Capp, B. S., *Astrology and the Popular Press: English Almanacs, 1500–1800* (1979)

Capp, B. S., 'English Youth Groups and the Pinder of Wakefield', in Slack, ed., *Rebellion*, pp. 212–18

Chenevix Trench, C., *The Western Rising: An Account of the Rebellion of James Scott, Duke of Monmouth* (1969)

Christianson, P. K., *Babylon and Reformers: English Apocalyptic Visions from the Reformation to the Eve of the Civil War* (Toronto, 1978)

Clark, P. and P. Slack, *English Towns in Transition, 1500–1700* (1976)

Clark, R., 'Why was the Re-Establishment of the Church of England in 1662 Possible? Derbyshire – A Provincial Perspective', *Midland History*, 8 (1983), 86–105

Clifton, R., 'Fear of Popery', in Russell, ed., *Origins*, pp. 144–67

Clifton, R., *The Last Popular Rebellion: The Western Rising of 1685* (1984)

Clifton, R., 'The Popular Fear of Catholics during the English Revolution', in Slack, ed., *Rebellion*, pp. 129–61

Cockett, B. C., 'George Cockayn', *Transactions of the Congregational Historical Society*, 12 (1933–6), 225–35

Colley, L., 'Eighteenth-Century English Radicalism before Wilkes', *Transactions of the Royal Historical Society*, 5th Series, 31 (1981), 1–19

Cooper, E. and M. Jahoda, 'The Evasion of Propaganda: How Prejudiced People Respond to Anti-Prejudice Propaganda', *Journal of Psychology*, 23 (1947), 15–25

Corrigan, P., *Schooling the Smash Street Kids* (1979)

Cowie, L. W., 'Temple Bar, London', *History Today*, 22 (1972), 402–9

Cragg, G. R., *Puritanism in the Period of the Great Persecution* (Cambridge, 1957)

Cragg, G. R., 'The Collapse of Militant Puritanism', in G. V. Bennett and J. D. Walsh, eds., *Essays in Modern English Church History in Memory of Norman Sykes* (1966), pp. 76–103

Crane, R. S. and F. B. Kaye, *A Census of British Newspapers and Periodicals, 1620–1820* (1927)

Cressy, D., *Literacy and the Social Order: Reading and Writing in Tudor and Stuart England* (Cambridge, 1980)

Crippen, T. G., 'The Tombs in Bunhill Fields', *Transactions of the Congregational Historical Society*, 4 (1909–10), 347–63

Cross, C., 'The Church in England, 1646–1660', in Aylmer, ed., *Interregnum*, pp. 99–120

Cross, C., *Church and People, 1450–1660: The Triumph of the Laity in the English Church* (1976)

Davies, G., *The Restoration of Charles II, 1658–60* (San Marino, 1955)

Davis, N. Z., 'The Reasons of Misrule: Youth Groups and Charivaris in Sixteenth-Century France', *Past and Present*, 50 (1971), 41–75

Davis, N. Z., 'The Rites of Violence: Religious Riot in Sixteenth-Century France', *Past and Present*, 59 (1973), 51–91

Davis, N. Z., 'A Rejoinder', *Past and Present*, 67 (1975), 131–5

Davis, N. Z., 'An Interview', *Radical History Review*, 24 (1980), 115–39

De Krey, G. S., 'Political Radicalism in London after the Glorious Revolution', *Journal of Modern History*, 55 (1983), 585–617

De Krey, G. S., *A Fractured Society: The Politics of London in the First Age of Party 1688–1715* (Oxford, 1985)

Dickinson, H. T., 'The Poor Palatines and the Parties', *English Historical Review*, 82 (1967), 464–85

Downie, J. A., *Robert Harley and the Press: Propaganda and Public Opinion in the Age of Swift and Defoe* (Cambridge, 1979)

Dunn, R. M., 'The London Weavers' Riot of 1675', *Guildhall Studies in London History*, I, no. 1 (October, 1973), 13–23

Durkheim, E., *The Elementary Forms of Religious Life*, trans. by J. W. Swain (1915)

Earle, P., *Monmouth's Rebels: The Road to Sedgemoor* (1977)

Eisenstadt, S. N., 'Archetypal Patterns of Youth', in E. H. Erikson, ed., *Youth: Change and Challenge* (New York, 1963), pp. 24–42

Elliot, D. C., 'Elections to the Common Council, December 21st, 1659', *Guildhall Studies in London History*, IV, no. 4 (April, 1981), 151–201

Ellul, J., *Propaganda: The Formation of Men's Attitudes*, trans. by K. Kellen and J. Lerner (New York, 1973)

Fairholt, F. W., *Lord Mayors' Pageants: Being Collections Towards a History of those Annual Celebrations*, 2 vols. (1843–4)

Feiling, K. G., *A History of the Tory Party, 1640–1714* (Oxford, 1924)

Ferguson, J., *Robert Ferguson – the Plotter; Or, The Secret History of the Rye House Conspiracy and the Story of a Strange Career* (Edinburgh, 1887)

Figgis, J., *The Divine Right of Kings* (Cambridge, 1914)

Finlay, R., *Population and Metropolis: The Demography of London, 1580–1650* (Cambridge, 1981)

Finlay, R. and B. Shearer, 'Population Growth and Suburban Expansion', in Beier and Finlay, eds., *Making of the Metropolis*, pp. 37–59

Firth, C. H., 'The Early Life of Pepys', *Macmillan's Magazine*, 69 (November, 1893), 32–6

Firth, C. H., 'London during the Civil War', *History*, 11 (1926–7), 25–36

Fitts, J. L., 'Newcastle's Mob', *Albion*, 5 (1973), 41–9

Fletcher, A. J., *Tudor Rebellions* (1968)

Fletcher, A. J., *A County Community in Peace and War: Sussex, 1600–1660* (1975)

Fletcher, A. J., *The Outbreak of the English Civil War* (1981)

Fletcher, A. J. and J. Stevenson, eds., *Order and Disorder in Early Modern England* (Cambridge, 1985)

Forbes, T. R., 'Weaver and Cordwainer: Occupations in St. Giles without Cripplegate, London, in 1654–93 and 1729–43', *Guildhall Studies in London History*, IV, no. 3 (October, 1980), 119–32

Ford, W. C., 'Benjamin Harris, Printer and Bookseller', *Proceedings of the Massachusetts Historical Society*, 57 (1923–4), 34–68

Foster, F. F., *The Politics of Stability* (1977)

Foster, Sir W., 'Venner's Rebellion', *London Topographical Record*, 18 (1942), 27–33

Fraser, P., *The Intelligence of the Secretaries of State and their Monopoly of Licensed News, 1660–1688* (Cambridge, 1956)

Freud, S., *Group Psychology and the Analysis of the Ego* (1922)

Fry, A. R., *John Bellers, 1654–1725: Quaker, Economist, and Social Reformer* (1933)

Furley, O. W., 'The Whig Exclusionists: Pamphlet Literature in the Exclusion Campaign', *Cambridge Historical Journal*, 13 (1957), 19–36

Furley, O. W., 'The Pope-Burning Processions of the Late Seventeenth Century', *History*, 44 (1959), 16–23

Gennep, A. Van, *The Rites of Passage*, trans. by M. B. Vizedom and G. L. Caffee (1960)

Gentles, I., 'The Struggle for London in the Second Civil War', *Historical Journal*, 26 (1983), 277–305

George, M. D., *London Life in the Eighteenth Century* (1925)

George, M. D., *English Political Caricature to 1792: A Study of Opinion and Propaganda* (Oxford, 1959)

Gilmour, M., *The Great Lady. A Biography of Barbara Villiers, Mistress of Charles II* (1944)

Glass, D. V. and D. E. C. Eversley, eds., *Population in History: Essays in Historical Demography* (1965), pp. 159–220

Glass, D. V., *London Inhabitants within the Walls, 1695* (1966)

Glass, D. V., 'Socio-Economic Status and Occupations in the City of London at the End of the Seventeenth Century', in A. E. J. Hollaender and W. Kellaway, eds., *Studies in London History Presented to Philip Edmund Jones* (1969), pp. 373–89

Goldie, M. A., 'John Locke and Anglican Royalism', *Political Studies*, 31 (1983), 61–85

Goldie, M. A., 'The Huguenot Experience and the Problem of Toleration in England' (forthcoming)

Green, I. M., *The Re-Establishment of the Church of England, 1660–1663* (Oxford, 1978)

Gregory, T. E., 'The Economics of Employment in England, 1660–1713', *Economica*, 1 (1921), 37–51

Grigg, D., *Population Growth and Agrarian Change: An Historical Perspective* (Cambridge, 1981)

Grubb, I., *Quakerism and Industry Before 1800* (1930)

Gwynn, R., 'The Arrival of Huguenot Refugees in England, 1680–1705', *Proceedings of the Huguenot Society*, 21 (1969), 366–73

Gwynn, R., 'The Distribution of Huguenot Refugees in England, II: London and its Environs', *Proceedings of the Huguenot Society*, 22 (1976), 509–68

Haley, K. H. D., *The First Earl of Shaftesbury* (Oxford, 1968)

Haley, K. H. D., '"No Popery" in the Reign of Charles II', in J. S. Bromley and E. H. Kossman, eds., *Britain and the Netherlands*, V (The Hague, 1975), 102–19

Halfpenny, E., '"The Citie's Loyalty Display'd": A Literary and Documentary Causerie of Charles II's Coronation "Entertainment"', *Guildhall Miscellany*, I, no. 10 (September, 1959), 19–35

Hammerton, E. and D. Cannadine, 'Conflict and Consensus on a Ceremonial Occasion: The Diamond Jubilee in Cambridge in 1897', *Historical Journal*, 24 (1981), 111–46

Hankey, S. A., 'Remarks Upon A Series of Forty-Nine Historical Cards, with Engravings, Representing the Conspiracy of Titus Oates', *Archeological Journal*, 30 (1873), 185–9

Harris, T. J. G., 'The Bawdy House Riots of 1668', *Historical Journal*, 29 (1986), 537–56

Hart, W. H., 'Further Remarks on some of the Ancient Inns of Southwark', *Surrey Archeological Collections*, 3 (1865), 193–207

Herlan, R. W., 'Social Articulation and the Configuration of Parochial Poverty in London on the Eve of the Restoration', *Guildhall Studies in London History*, II, no. 2 (April, 1976), 43–53

Herrup, C., 'New Shoes and Mutton Pies: Investigative Responses to Theft in Seventeenth-Century East Sussex', *Historical Journal*, 27 (1984), 811–30

Hibbard, C., *Charles I and the Popish Plot* (1983)

Hill, C., *Reformation to Industrial Revolution* (Harmondsworth, 1969)

Hill, C., *The World Turned Upside Down: Radical Ideas during the English Revolution* (Harmondsworth, 1975)

Hill, C., *Milton and the English Revolution* (1977)

Hill, C., 'From Lollards to Levellers', in C. Cornforth, ed., *Rebels and their Causes: Essays in Honour of A. L. Morton* (1978), pp. 49–67

Hill, C., *Some Intellectual Consequences of the English Revolution* (1980)

Hill, C., 'Robinson Crusoe', *History Workshop*, 10 (1980), 6–24

Hill, C., *The Experience of Defeat: Milton and Some Contemporaries* (1984)

Hill, C., 'Censorship and English Literature', in his *Collected Essays*, I (Brighton, 1985), pp. 32–71

Hirst, D., *The Representative of the People? Voters and Voting in England under the Early Stuarts* (Cambridge, 1975)

Hobsbawm, E. J., 'The Machine-Breakers', *Past and Present*, I (1952), 57–70

Hobsbawm, E. J., *Primitive Rebels: Studies in Archaic Forms of Social Movement in the Nineteenth and Twentieth Centuries* (Manchester, 1959)

Hobsbawm, E. J. and G. Rudé, *Captain Swing* (1969)

Hobsbawm, E. J. and J. W. Scott, 'Political Shoemakers', *Past and Present*, 89 (1980), 86–114

Hoerder, D., *Crowd Action in Revolutionary Massachusetts, 1765–1780* (New York, 1977)

Holmes, C., 'Drainers and Fenmen: the Problem of Popular Political Consciousness in the Seventeenth Century', in Fletcher and Stevenson, eds., *Order and Disorder*, pp. 166–95

Holmes, G. and W. A. Speck, eds., *The Divided Society: Parties and Politics in England, 1694–1716* (1967)

Holmes, G., *The Trial of Doctor Sacheverell* (1973)

Holmes, G., *Religion and Party in Late Stuart England* (1975)

Holmes, G., 'The Achievement of Stability: The Social Context of Politics from the 1680s to the Age of Walpole', in J. Cannon, ed., *The Whig Ascendancy: Colloquies on Hanoverian England* (1981), pp. 1–27

Holmes, G., 'The Sacheverell Riots: The Crowd and the Church in Early Eighteenth Century London', in Slack, ed., *Rebellion*, pp. 232–62

Holton, R. J., 'The Crowd in History: Some Problems of Theory and Method', *Social History*, 3 (1978), 219–33

Horwitz, H., 'Protestant Reconciliation in the Exclusion Crisis', *Journal of Ecclesiastical History*, 15 (1964), 201–17

Humpherus, H., *History of the Origin and Progress of the Company of Watermen and Lightermen, 1514–1859*, 3 vols. (1887)

Hutton, R., *The Restoration: A Political and Religious History of England and Wales, 1658–1667* (Oxford, 1985)

Ingram, M., 'Ridings, Rough Music and the "Reform of Popular Culture" in Early Modern England', *Past and Present*, 105 (1984), 79–113

Johnson, D. J., *Southwark and the City* (Oxford, 1969)

Jones, D. J. V., *Before Rebecca: Popular Protests in Wales, 1793–1835* (1973)

Jones, J. R., 'The Green Ribbon Club', *Durham University Journal*, 49, NS 18 (1956), 17–20

Jones, J. R., 'James II's Whig Collaborators', *Historical Journal*, 3 (1960), 65–73

Jones, J. R., *The First Whigs: The Politics of the Exclusion Crisis, 1678–83* (Oxford, 1961)

Jones, J. R., *The Revolution of 1688 in England* (1972)

Jones, J. R., *Country and Court: England 1658–1714* (1978)

Jones, P. E. and A. V. Judges, 'London Population in the Late Seventeenth Century', *Economic History Review*, 6 (1935), 45–63

Kennedy, W., *English Taxation, 1640–1799: An Essay on Policy and Opinion* (1913)

Kenyon, J. P., *The Popish Plot* (1972)

King, P., 'Decision-Makers and Decision-Making in the English Criminal Law, 1750–1800', *Historical Journal*, 24 (1984), 25–58

Kitchin, G., *Sir Roger L'Estrange: A Contribution to the History of the Press in the Seventeenth Century* (1913)

Korshin, P. J., ed., *Studies in Change and Revolution: Aspects of English Intellectual History, 1640–1800* (Menston, 1972)

Lacey, D. R., *Dissent and Parliamentary Politics in England, 1661–1689* (Rutgers, 1969)

Lamont, W. M., *Godly Rule: Politics and Religion, 1603–60* (1969)

Lamont, W. M., *Richard Baxter and the Millenium: Protestant Imperialism and the English Revolution* (1979)

Landau, N., *The Justices of the Peace, 1679–1760* (Los Angeles, 1984)

Le Bon, G., *The Crowd: A Study of the Popular Mind* (1896)

Lefebvre, G., 'Foules révolutionaires', *Annales historiques de la Révolution française*, 11 (1934), 1–26

Levin, J., *The Charter Controversy in the City of London* (1969)

Lillywhite, B., *London Coffee Houses* (1963)

Lindley, K. J., *Fenland Riots and the English Revolution* (1982)

Lindley, K. J., 'Riot Prevention and Control in Early Stuart London', *Transactions of the Royal Historical Society*, 5th Series, 33 (1983), 109–26

Linebaugh, P., 'The Tyburn Riot against the Surgeons', in D. Hay *et al.*, eds., *Albion's Fatal Tree: Crime and Society in Eighteenth-Century England* (Harmondsworth, 1977), pp. 65–117

Lipson, E., *The Economic History of England*, III (1931)

Logue, K. J., *Popular Disturbances in Scotland, 1780–1815* (Edinburgh, 1979)

'London Conventicles in 1683', *Transactions of the Congregational Historical Society*, III (1907–8), 364–6

Lukes, S., 'Political Ritual and Social Integration', *Sociology*, 9 (1975), 289–308

McCampbell, A. E., 'The London Parish and the London Precinct, 1640-1660', *Guildhall Studies in London History*, II, no. 3 (October, 1976), 107–24

Macfarlane, S., 'Social Policy and the Poor in the Later Seventeenth Century', in Beier and Finlay, eds., *Making of the Metropolis*, pp. 252–77

Maitland, W., *The History of London, from its Foundation to the Present Time*, 2 vols. (1756)

Malament, B. C., ed., *After the Reformation: Essays in Honour of J. H. Hexter* (Manchester, 1980)

Manning, B. S., 'The Nobles, the People, and the Constitution', *Past and Present*, 9 (1956), 42–64

Manning, B. S., 'Religion and Politics: The Godly People', in B. S. Manning, ed., *Politics, Religion, and the English Civil War* (1973), pp. 81–123

Manning, B. S., 'The Peasantry and the English Revolution', *Journal of Peasant Studies*, 2 (1975), 133–58

Manning, B. S., *The English People and the English Revolution* (Harmondsworth, 1978)

Marsh, P., E. Rosser and R. Harré, *The Rules of Disorder* (1978)

Marshall, L. M., 'The Levying of the Hearth Tax, 1662–88', *English Historical Review*, 51 (1936), 628–46

Milgram, S. and H. Toch, 'Collective Behaviour: Crowds and Social Movements', in G. Lindzey and E. Aronson, eds., *The Handbook of Social Psychology*, IV (Reading, Massachusetts, 1969), 507–610

Miller, J., *Popery and Politics in England, 1660–1688* (Cambridge, 1973)

Miller, J., *The Glorious Revolution* (1983)

Milne, D. J., 'The Results of the Rye House Plot and their Influences upon the Revolution of 1688', *Transactions of the Royal Historical Society*, 5th Series, 1 (1951), 91–108

Morrill, J. S., *Cheshire, 1630–1660: County Government and Society during the English Revolution* (Oxford, 1974)

Morrill, J. S., *Seventeenth-Century Britain, 1603–1714* (1980)

Morrill, J. S., 'The Church in England, 1642–9', in J. S. Morrill, ed., *Reactions to the English Civil War, 1642–1649* (1982), pp. 89–114

Muddiman, J. G., *The King's Journalist, 1659–89* (1923)

Muddiman, J. G. 'Benjamin Harris, the First American Journalist', *Notes and Queries*, 163 (1932), 129–33, 147–50, 166–70

Muddiman, J. G., 'Francis Smith, "The Elder"', *Notes and Queries*, 163 (1932), 57–62

Mullett, C. F., 'Toleration and Persecution in England, 1660–89', *Church History*, 16 (1949), 18–43

Neale, J. E., 'November 17th', in his *Essays in Elizabethan History* (1958), pp. 9–20

Newton, T. F. M., 'The Mask Heraclitus: A Problem in Restoration Journalism', *Harvard Studies and Notes in Philology and Literature*, 16 (1934), 145–60

Nye, R. A., *The Origins of Crowd Psychology: Gustave LeBon and the Crisis of Mass Democracy in the Third Republic* (1975)

Pearl, V., *London and the Outbreak of the Puritan Revolution: City Government and National Politics, 1625–43* (Oxford, 1961)

Pearl, V., 'London's Counter-Revolution', in Aylmer, ed., *Interregnum*, pp. 29–56

Pearl, V., 'Change and Stability in Seventeenth-Century London', *London Journal*, 5 (1979), 3–34

Pearl, V., 'Social Policy in Early Modern London', in H. Lloyd-Jones, V. Pearl and B. Worden, eds., *History and Imagination: Essays in Honour of H. R. Trevor-Roper* (1981), pp. 115–31

'Picture Cards of the Popish Plot', *Gentleman's Magazine*, NS 32 (1849), 265–9

Pillorget, R., *Mouvements insurrectionnels en Provence entre 1596 et 1715* (Paris, 1975)

Plumb, J. H., 'Political Man', in J. L. Clifford, ed., *Man Versus Society in Early Eighteenth-Century Britain: Six Points of View* (Cambridge, 1968), pp. 1–21

Plumb, J. H., 'The Growth of the Electorate in England, 1600–1715', *Past and Present*, 45 (1969), 90–116

Plumb, J. H., *The Growth of Political Stability in England, 1675–1725* (1967)

Plummer, A., *The London Weavers' Company, 1600–1970* (1972)

Pocock, J. G. A., *The Machiavellian Moment: Florentine Political Thought and the Atlantic Republic Tradition* (Princeton, 1975)

Pocock, J. G. A., ed., *The Political Works of James Harrington* (Cambridge, 1977)

Porter, R., *English Society in the Eighteenth Century* (Harmondsworth, 1982)

Power, M. J., 'Shadwell: The Development of London Suburban Community in the Seventeenth Century', *London Journal*, 4 (1978), 29–48

Power, M. J., 'The Social Topography of Restoration London', in Beier and Finlay, eds., *Making of the Metropolis*, pp. 199–223

'Present State of the Nonconformists, 1672', *Journal of the Friends Historical Society*, 4 (1907), 122–4

Rahn, B. J., 'A Ra-ree Show – A Rare Cartoon: Revolutionary Propaganda in the Treason Trial of Stephen College', in Korshin, ed., *Studies*, pp. 77–98

Raistrick, A., *Quakers in Science and Industry. Being an Account of the Quaker Contribution to Science and Industry during the Seventeenth and Eighteenth Centuries* (1950)

Reay, B., 'The Quakers, 1659, and the Restoration of the Monarchy', *History*, 63 (1978), 193–213

Reay, B., 'Popular Hostility towards Quakers in Mid-Seventeenth-Century England', *Social History*, 5 (1980), 387–407

Reay, B., *The Quakers and the English Revolution* (1985)

Reay, B., ed., *Popular Culture in Seventeenth-Century England* (1985)

Reddy, W. R., 'The Textile Trade and the Language of the Crowd at Rouen, 1752–1871', *Past and Present*, 74 (1977), 62–89

Reedy, G. S. J., 'Mystical Politics: The Imagery of Charles II's Coronation', in Korshin, ed., *Studies*, pp. 20–42

Roberts, C., *The Growth of Responsible Government in Stuart England* (Cambridge, 1966)

Rodriguez, L., 'The Spanish Riots of 1766', *Past and Present*, 59 (1973), 117–46

Rogers, N., 'Aristocratic Clientage, Trade and Independency: Popular Politics in Pre-Radical Westminster', *Past and Present*, 61 (1973), 70–106

Rogers, N., 'Popular Disaffection in London during the Forty-Five', *London Journal*, 1 (1975), 5–27

Rogers, N., 'Popular Protest in Early Hanoverian London', in Slack, ed., *Rebellion*, pp. 263–93

Ronalds, F. S., *The Attempted Whig Revolution of 1678–81* (Urbana, 1937)

Rostenburg, L., 'Nathaniel Thompson, Catholic Printer and Publisher of the Restoration', *Transactions of the Bibliographical Society*, 3rd Series, 10 (1955), 186–202

Rudé, G., *Wilkes and Liberty: A Social Study of 1763–1774* (Oxford, 1962)

Rudé, G., *The Crowd in History. A Study of Popular Disturbances in France and England, 1730–1848* (New York, 1964)

Rudé, G., 'The London "Mob" of the Eighteenth Century', in his *Paris and London*, pp. 293–318

Rudé, G., '"Mother Gin" and the London Riots of 1736', in his *Paris and London*, pp. 201–21

Rudé, G., *Paris and London in the Eighteenth Century: Studies in Popular Protest* (1970)

Rudé, G., *Hanoverian London, 1714–1808* (1971)

Rudé, G., *Ideology and Popular Protest* (1980)

Rule, J., *The Experience of Labour in Eighteenth-Century Industry* (1981)

Russell, C., ed., *The Origins of the English Civil War* (1975)

Sachse, W. L., 'The Mob and the Revolution of 1688', *Journal of British Studies*, 4 (1964), 23–41

Salmon, J. H. M., 'Algernon Sydney and the Rye House Plot', *History Today*, 4 (1954), 698–705

Schofield, R. S., 'The Measurement of Literacy in Pre-Industrial England', in J. Goody, ed., *Literacy in Traditional Societies* (Cambridge, 1968), pp. 311–25

Scott, J. C., *The Moral Economy of the Peasant: Rebellion and Subsistence in South-East Asia* (New Haven, 1976)

Scribner, R. W., 'Reformation, Carnival and the World Turned Upside-Down', *Social History*, 3 (1978), 303–29

Scribner, R. W., *For the Sake of Simple Folk: Popular Propaganda for the German Reformation* (Cambridge, 1981)

Sharp, B., *In Contempt of All Authority: Rural Artisans and Riot in the West of England, 1586–1660* (1980)

Sharpe, J. A., 'Enforcing the Law in the Seventeenth-Century English Village', in V. A. C. Gattrell *et al.*, eds., *Crime and the Law: the Social History of Crime in Western Europe since 1300* (1980), pp. 97–119

Sharpe, J. A., '"Last Dying Speeches": Religion, Ideology and Public Execution in Seventeenth-Century England', *Past and Present*, 107 (1985), 144–67

Sharpe, J. A., 'The People and the Law', in Reay, ed., *Popular Culture*, pp. 244–70

Sharpe, R. R., *London and the Kingdom*, 3 vols. (1895)

Shaw, P., *American Patriots and the Rituals of Revolution* (Cambridge, Massachusetts, 1981)

Shelton, W. J., *English Hunger and Industrial Disorders: A Study of Social Conflict During the First Decade of George III's Reign* (1973)

Shils, E. and M. Young, 'The Meaning of the Coronation', *Sociological Review*, NS I, no. 2 (December, 1953), 63–81

Simon, W. G., 'Comprehension in the Age of Charles II', *Church History*, 31 (1962), 440–8

Sitwell, Sir G. R., *The First Whig* (Scarborough, 1894)

Skinner, Q., *The Foundations of Modern Political Thought*, 2 vols. (Cambridge, 1978)

Skinner, Q., 'The Origins of the Calvinist Theory of Revolution', in Malament, ed., *After the Reformation*, pp. 309–30

Slack, P., ed., *Rebellion, Popular Protest and the Social Order in Early Modern England* (Cambridge, 1984)

Smith, S. R., 'The Apprentices' Parliament of 1647', *History Today*, 22 (1972), 576–82

Smith, S. R., 'The Social and Geographical Origins of the London Apprentices, 1630–60', *Guildhall Miscellany*, IV, no. 4 (April, 1973), 195–206

Smith, S. R., 'Almost Revolutionaries: The London Apprentices during the Civil Wars', *Huntington Library Quarterly*, 42 (1978–9), 313–28

Smith, S. R., 'The London Apprentices as Seventeenth Century Adolescents', in Slack, ed., *Rebellion*, pp. 219–31

Speck, W. A., 'Political Propaganda in Augustan England', *Transactions of the Royal Historical Society*, 5th Series, 22 (1972)

Spufford, M., *Contrasting Communities: English Villagers in the Sixteenth and Seventeenth Centuries* (Cambridge, 1974)

Stern, W. M., *The Porters of London* (1960)

Stevenson, J., ed., *London in the Age of Reform* (Oxford, 1977)

Stevenson, J., *Popular Disturbances in England, 1700–1870* (1979)

Stone, L., 'The Residential Development of the West End of London in the Seventeenth Century', in Malament, ed., *After the Reformation*, pp. 167–212

Stoughton, J., *History of Religion in England from the Opening of the Long Parliament to the End of the Eighteenth Century*, 6 vols. (1881)

Strong, R. C., 'The Popular Celebration of the Accession Day of Elizabeth I', *Journal of the Warburg and Courtauld Institutes*, 21 (1958), 86–103

Sutherland, L., 'The City of London in Eighteenth Century Politics', in R. Pares and A. J. P. Taylor, eds., *Essays Presented to Sir Lewis Namier* (Oxford, 1956), pp. 49–74

Sykes, N., *From Sheldon to Secker: Aspects of English Church History, 1660-1768* (Cambridge, 1959)

Taylor, S., 'The Scarman Report and the Explanation of Riots', in J. Benyon, ed., *Scarman and After: Essays Reflecting on Lord Scarman's Report, the Riots, and their Aftermath* (Leicester, 1984), pp. 20–34

Thirsk, J., ed., *The Restoration* (1976)

Thomas, K. V., 'Age and Authority in Early Modern England', *Proceedings of the British Academy*, 62 (1976), 205–48

Thomas, K. V., *Rule and Misrule in the Schools of Early Modern England* (Reading, 1976)

Thomas, R., 'Comprehension and Indulgence', in G. F. Nuttall and O. Chadwick, eds., *From Uniformity to Unity, 1662–1962* (1962), pp. 189–253

Thompson, E. P., *The Making of the English Working Class* (Harmondsworth, 1968)

Thompson, E. P., 'The Moral Economy of the English Crowd in the Eighteenth Century', *Past and Present*, 50 (1971), 76–136

Thompson, E. P., '"Rough Music": le charivari anglais', *Annales: économies, sociétés, civilisations*, 27 (1972), 285–312

Tilly, C., 'Collective Action in England and America, 1765–1775', in R. M. Brown and D. E. Fehrenbacker, eds., *Tradition, Conflict, and Modernization: Perspectives on the American Revolution* (New York, 1977), pp. 45–72

Toon, P., *God's Statesman: The Life and Work of John Owen, Pastor, Educator, Theologian* (Exeter, 1971)

Turner, G. Lyon, 'The Religious Condition of London in 1672 as Reported to King and Court by an Impartial Outsider', *Transactions of the Congregational Historical Society*, 3 (1907–8), 192–205

Tyacke, N., 'Puritanism, Arminianism, and Counter-Revolution', in Russell, ed., *Origins*, pp. 119–43

Underdown, D., *Revel, Riot and Rebellion: Popular Politics and Culture in England, 1603–1660* (Oxford, 1985)

Victoria County History of London, vol. I

Wada, G. and J. C. Davies, 'Riots and Rioters', *Western Political Quarterly*, 10 (1957), 864–74

Walker, J., 'The Censorship of the Press during the Reign of Charles II', *History*, 35 (1950), 219–38

Walter, J., 'Grain Riots and Popular Attitudes to the Law: Maldon and the Crisis of 1629', in J. Brewer and J. Styles, eds., *An Ungovernable People: The English and their Law in the Seventeenth and Eighteenth Centuries* (1980), pp. 47–84

Walter, J., 'A "Rising of the People"? The Oxfordshire Rising of 1596', *Past and Present*, 107 (1985), 90–143

Walter, J. and K. Wrightson, 'Dearth and the Social Order in Early Modern England', in Slack, ed., *Rebellion*, pp. 108–28

Watts, M. R., *The Dissenters: From the Reformation to the French Revolution* (Oxford, 1978)

Weekley, C. M., 'The Spitalfields Silkweavers', *Proceedings of the Huguenot Society*, 18 (1947–52), 284–91

Western, J. R., *Monarchy and Revolution: The English State in the 1680s* (1972)

Whiteman, A., 'The Re-Establishment of the Church of England, 1660–1663', *Transactions of the Royal Historical Society*, 5th Series, 5 (1955), 120–35

Whiting, C. E., *Studies in English Puritanism from the Restoration to the Revolution, 1660–1688* (1931, repr. 1968)

Whitley, W. T., 'Militant Baptists, 1660–1672', *Transactions of the Baptist Historical Society*, 1 (1908–9), 148–55

Whitley, W. T., 'Thompson's List of Conventicles in 1683', *Transactions of the Congregational Historical Society*, IV (1909–10), 49–53

Whitley, W. T., 'London Churches in 1682', *Baptist Quarterly*, NS 1 (1922–3), 82–7

Whitley, W. T., *The Baptists of London, 1612–1928* (1928)

Willcock, J., 'List Taken from the Official Narrative – Places which were Haunts for the Conspirators', *Notes and Queries*, 10th Series, 11 (1909), 102

Williams, J. B., 'Nathaniel Thompson and the "Popish Plot"', *The Month*, 138 (1921), 31–7

Williams, J. D., *Memoirs of the Life, Character and Writings of Sir Matthew Hale* (1835)

Williams, S., 'The Pope-Burning Processions of 1679–81', *Journal of the Warburg and Courtauld Institutes*, 21 (1958), 104–18

Williams, S., 'The Lord Mayor's Show in Tudor and Stuart Times', *Guildhall Miscellany*, I, no. 10 (September, 1959), 3–18

Wilson, J. H., *The Court Wits of the Restoration* (1948)

Wilson, W., *The History and Antiquities of Dissenting Churches and Meeting Houses in London, Westminster and Southwark*, 4 vols. (1808–14)

Woolrych, A., 'The Good Old Cause and the Fall of the Protectorate', *Cambridge Historical Journal*, 13 (1957), 133–67

Woolrych, A., 'Historical Introduction', to *Complete Prose Works of John Milton*, 8 vols. (New Haven, 1953–82), VII, 1–228

Worden, B., 'Toleration and the Cromwellian Protectorate', in W. J. Sheils, ed., *Persecution and Toleration* (Studies in Church History, 21, Oxford, 1984), pp. 199–233

Wright, S., *Crowds and Riots: A Study in Social Organization* (1978)

Wrigley, E. A., 'A Simple Model of London's Importance in Changing English Society and Economy, 1650–1750', *Past and Present*, 37 (1967), 44–70

Wrigley, E. A., 'Marriage, Fertility, and Population Growth in Eighteenth-Century England', in R. B. Outhwaite, ed., *Marriage and Society: Studies in the Social History of Marriage* (1981), pp. 737–85

UNPUBLISHED WORKS

Allen, D. F., 'The Crown and the Corporation of London in the Exclusion Crisis, 1678–1681', Cambridge PhD thesis (1977)

Boulton, J. P., 'The Social and Economic Structure of Southwark in the Early Seventeenth Century', Cambridge PhD thesis (1983)

Chivers, G. V., 'The City of London and the State, 1658–1664. A Study in Political and Financial Relations', Manchester PhD thesis (1961)

Clifton, R., 'The Fear of Catholics in England 1637 to 1645. Principally from Central Source', Oxford DPhil thesis (1967)

Crist, T. J., 'Francis Smith and the Opposition Press in England, 1660–1688', Cambridge PhD thesis (1977)

Elliott, V. B., 'Mobility and Marriage in Pre-Industrial England', Cambridge PhD thesis (1978)

Harris, T. J. G., 'Politics of the London Crowd in the Reign of Charles II', Cambridge PhD thesis (1985)

Harrison, J. M., 'The Crowd in Bristol, 1790–1835', Cambridge PhD thesis (1983)

Johnson, W. G., 'Post Restoration Nonconformity and Plotting, 1660–1675', Manchester MA thesis (1967)

Macfarlane, S. M., 'Studies in Poverty and Poor Relief in London at the End of the Seventeenth Century', Oxford DPhil thesis (1982)

Marshall, P. N., 'Protestant Dissent in England in the Reign of James II', Hull PhD thesis (1976)

Pickavance, R. E., 'The English Boroughs and the King's Government: A Study of the Tory Reaction, 1681–85', Oxford DPhil thesis (1976)

Reay, B. G., 'Early Quaker Activity and Reactions to It, 1652–1664', Oxford DPhil thesis (1979)

Reece, H. M., 'The Military Presence in England, 1649–1660', Oxford DPhil thesis (1981)

Shoemaker, R. B., 'Crime, Courts and Community: The Prosecution of Misdemeanour in Middlesex County, 1663–1723', Stanford PhD thesis (1985)

Smith, A. G., 'London and the Crown, 1681–1685', Wisconsin PhD thesis (1967)

INDEX

abhorrers, 173–4, 176, 214
  burnt in effigy, 113
Act of Uniformity (1662), 63, 87
Adis, Henry, 76
Albemarle, Christopher, duke of, 160, 167, 177
Alder, John, 38
aldermen, court of, 3, 18, 29, 41, 48, 183, 195, 203
  veto, 32, 184
Aldersgate Street, 102, 179, 180, 181, 220
Aldgate, 120
Alford, Thomas, 166, 167
Allen, David (historian), 213
almanacs, 106, 110, 133
Alsop, Vincent, burnt in effigy, 169 n. 63
anglicans, 34–5, 37, 40, 68, 86, 92, 95, 211, 224
  critical of royal prerogative, 78
  defend parliament, 78
  poor, 210
  and Restoration, 55–9
Anne Hyde, 91
Anne Stuart, 4, 151
Annesley, Elizabeth, 178
Annesley, Samuel, 59, 222
anti-catholicism, 2–3, 30, 91–2, 95, 109–13, 164, 177–8, 179, 198, 204, 227
  ambiguities of, 32–4, 156–7
  anti-anglican, 32, 73–4, 85, 128
  anti-nonconformist, 32–3, 97, 131, 134, 139–44, 166, 169
  anti-sectarian, 33, 53
anti-populism, 57, 136–9, 152–3
apprentices, 13, 17–18, 23–4, 27, 122, 200, 203
  brothel riots, 22, 24, 82–4, 88, 90
  feasts for, 177–8
  and Restoration, 36, 39, 41–6, 48–50, 53, 59
  tory, 125, 153, 166–8, 174–80, 186, 212–13, 217, 219, 220, 222
  whig, 26, 175–80, 182–3, 186–8, 204,

212–13, 217
army (republican)
  hostility to, 30, 36, 41–7, 136, 139
  mutiny, 48
army (restored monarchy), 82, 83, 112, 158, 160, 171, 173, 194
Artillery Company, 107, 158, 171
Association, 132, 135, 149, 174, 176, 214
  burnt, 168, 170
Ayloffe, John, 92, 93, 101, 118

ballad singers, 102, 133
Baltic Wars, 41
baptists, 69, 70, 74, 77, 119–20, 188
  meeting house demolished, 52
  petition to house of lords, 60
Barebone, Praise-God, 49–50, 53
Bartholomew Hospital, 148
Bateman, Dr, 188
Bates, William, 69, 86
Batty, Jerome, 186
Baxter, Richard, 33, 69, 70, 86, 147, 210
Bedloe, William, 103, 147
Beloff, Max (historian), 1
Bethell, Slingsby, 119, 130, 149, 185
Billing, Edward, 52, 186–7
bishop of London, 77–8
bishops
  hostility to, 47, 61, 74, 75, 76, 81–2, 85, 87, 93–4, 123–9
  presbyterian attitude towards, 54, 74
  support for, 35, 55–6, 58–9, 134, 139, 141, 165
  See also anti-catholicism
black box, 115
Blackfriars, 193
Bloomsbury, 180, 220
Blount, Charles, 101
Bohun, Edmund, 99, 140
Booth, Henry, 101, 119
Booth, Sir George, 41, 45
Boulton, Jeremy (historian), 19, 35
Box, Ralph, 186

Bradshaw, John, 39
Bread Street, 28
Bridgeman, Sir Orlando, 85–6, 87
Brome, Henry, 125, 133
Brome, Joanna, 133, 154
brothels, 80–1
  riots against, 22, 23–4, 25, 82–91, 166, 168, 217, 220, 221
Buckingham, George Villiers, duke of, 86, 93, 100, 103, 115, 119, 182
Bull Feather Court, 32
Burke, Peter (historian), 15, 106
Burnet, Gilbert, 45, 51, 87
Butchers' Hall Lane, 186

Cabal, 86, 91
Calvin, John, 123
Cannon Street, 43, 53
Care, Henry, 100, 106, 107, 120, 121–2, 130, 134, 147, 154
carpenters, 67, 202, 215
Carpenters' Company, 202
Caryll, Joseph, 74
Castlemaine, Barbara Palmer, countess of, 79, 80, 81, 84–5, 87
Catherine of Braganza, 78, 162, 168
catholic lords, 108, 112
catholic relics, burning of, 104
catholics, 33, 71, 76, 77, 87, 108, 140, 141, 165
  attacks on, 183
cavalier parliament, 76–8, 86, 96
cavaliers, 47
Cellier, Elizabeth, 108, 119, 148, 166
censorship, 27–8, 92, 96, 130–1, 154–5
Chancery Lane, 38, 121, 166
Charing Cross, 39, 160, 179
charivari, 25, 32
Charles I, 2, 22, 33, 40, 53, 56, 59, 97, 135, 139, 150, 163, 195
Charles II, 130, 184, 204
  and catholics, 77
  coronation of, 8, 39, 54, 57
  dines with lord mayor, 170
  and France, 91, 140
  illness of, 159
  and King's Evil, 57
  restored to throne, 38–9
  and toleration, 62–3, 65, 76–7, 86, 87
  whores of, 79–80
  See also apprentices, monarchy, Restoration, seditious words
Charterhouse Yard, 180
Chatham, Kent, 80
Cheapside, 38, 45, 104, 120, 168, 174, 186, 220

  pillory in, 24, 187–8
Cheshire, 41, 225
Chichester, Sussex, 159
Christmas, riots at, 22, 54
Church of England, 32, 58, 63, 73, 85
  tories and, 134, 139–41, 153
  whigs and, 118, 121–2, 123–9, 163
  See also anglicans, anti-catholicism, bishops, common prayer book
churchwardens, 59, 71, 121, 159, 160, 210
Civil War, 34, 97, 134, 190, 195
Clarendon, Edward Hyde, earl of, 17, 55, 64, 79, 81, 85, 91
class antagonism, 161, 192
Claypoole, Benjamin, 107
Clayton, Sir Robert, 184
Clerkenwell, 206
Cloth Fair, 193
clubs
  tory, 132–3
  whig, 100–1, 119–20, 172
  See also Green Ribbon Club
coffee-houses, 27, 28–9, 92–3, 99, 101–2, 111, 114, 182
Colchester, Essex, 194
Colchester, Lord, 178
Coleman, Edward, 108
collective action, organization of, 14, 16–17, 22, 25–7, 38, 42, 43, 45, 82, 89, 159–60, 166, 171–3, 176–8, 186, 195–6
collective rescue, 24, 82–3, 182
College, Stephen, 101, 106, 118, 121, 149, 225
  sister of, 185
colours, 25, 84, 89–90, 197, 198
committee of safety, 41, 43, 45, 49
common council, 3, 18, 46, 164–5, 173, 183–4
  petitions to, 29, 49, 175, 183, 195, 202, 203
common hall, 18, 183, 184, 185
common prayer book, 35, 55, 56, 59, 63, 73, 139, 153
commonwealth, 34, 39, 40, 92, 135–6, 153, 195, 208
comprehension, 28, 54, 69, 86–7, 88, 92
Compton census (1676), 65, 68–9
constables, 20, 21, 120, 173, 187, 194
  hostile to nonconformists, 72, 225
  sympathetic to nonconformists, 71–2, 183, 211
Conventicle Act (1664), 63–4, 76, 189
Conventicle Act (1670), 20, 64, 70, 71, 75, 77, 80, 225
Convention Parliament, 55
Cornhill, 120, 170, 220

Cornish, Henry, 130, 185
Corporation Act (1661), 64
country party, 91–4
court of assistants, 154, 164, 183
Court, royal
  catholics at, 2, 78, 80, 84, 87, 94
  libertinism of, 78–81, 94
  organization of demonstrations by, 31–2
  riot against, 82–91
Covent Garden, 38, 59, 168, 170, 179, 219
Crodacot, John, 54
Cromwell, Oliver, 9, 40, 92, 136, 208
  burnt in effigy, 39, 166, 169
crowds
  composition of, 17–18, 90, 193–4 and
    n. 26, 213–14
  elite attitudes towards, 16–17, 21–2, 23–4
Crown Tavern, Ivy Lane, 177
Crutched Friars, 180, 220
Curtis, Jane, 130
Curtis, Langley, 102, 106, 107, 112, 113,
  118, 120, 171, 181

Danby, Thomas Osborne, earl of, 2, 65, 75,
  76, 91, 93, 112, 122, 132, 140
Darby, John, 120
Davis, Natalie Zemon (historian), 189
De Krey, Gary (historian), 68
debtors, mock address from, 118
Declaration of Breda (1660), 60, 65, 76, 86
Declaration of Indulgence (1662), 76, 140
Declaration of Indulgence (1672), 65, 69, 70,
  76, 77, 92, 140
Delaune, Thomas, 65
demonstration, origin of word, 5 and n. 26
Dering, Sir Edward, 150
Desborough, John, 42
Dog Tavern, Drury Lane, 170
Dog-Wonder Tavern, Ludgate, 170, 171, 187
Drury Lane, 170, 219
Dubois, John, 186
Dugdale, Stephen, 181
Duke's Place, 29
Dunn, Richard (historian), 197
Dunton, John, 177, 178
Durkheim, Emile (sociologist), 8
Dutch, 31, 79, 198, 201
Dutch ambassador, coach besieged, 31
Dutch Wars, 2, 32, 41, 79–80, 83, 91, 152

East Smithfield, 82
Easter, riots at, 22, 25, 82–91
economic crisis, 41, 44, 57–8, 189–90, 194,
  207
Elizabeth I, 30, 113, 145
Evans, Joshua, 177

excise, 36, 42, 58, 61, 139, 190, 205, 206,
  208, 216
exclusion bills, 96, 115, 130, 132
  burnt, 170
exclusion parliament, first, 172
exclusion parliament, second, 163, 174

Farringdon without, 12, 219, 222
feltmakers, 202
Feltmakers' Company, 202
Ferguson, Robert, 226
fifth monarchists, 40, 60, 69, 78, 79, 88, 97,
  119, 130, 162, 197
Finsbury gaol, 83, 89
Firth, Sir Charles (historian), 2, 36
fishmongers, 202
Five Mile Act (1665), 64
Flatman, Thomas, 133
Fleet Street, 45, 104, 159, 183, 219
Fleetwood, Charles, 42, 45
Fletcher, Anthony (historian), 34–5
food riots, 190, 191 n. 12
foreign artisans, 13, 199–204
  See also xenophobia
Fountain Tavern, 180
Fowler, Edward, 222–3, 225
Foxe, John, 30
France, 2, 30, 91, 112, 140
  persecutions in, 110, 200, 204
free parliament, 36, 42–3, 44, 45, 48
  opposition to, 46
freemen, 18, 44, 49, 164–5, 202
French, hostility towards, 26, 31, 79–80, 93,
  140, 191, 198, 200–4
Freud, Sigmund (psychologist), 6
Furley, O. W. (historian), 103

Gadbury, John, 133, 148
Gatehouse, 76, 167
George, prince of Denmark, 151
Gerard, Sir Gilbert, 172
Globe Tavern, Cornhill, 170
Glorious Revolution, 3, 205, 227
Godfrey, Sir Edmundbury, 108, 109, 112,
  145, 154, 166
Gold, Sir Thomas, 184, 185, 186
Goldsmith's Court, 183
good old cause, 40, 49, 58, 75, 76, 134
Goodenough, Richard, 207
Gotham, mock address from inhabitants of,
  117
Gracechurch Street, 187, 220
graffiti, 107
Gray's Inn, 214
Green Ribbon Club, 92–3, 94, 100–1, 104,
  107, 111, 118, 119, 148–9, 150, 207

Green Ribbon Club (*cont.*)
  attack on, 179–80, 214
Griffith, Captain, 182
Griffith, Matthew, 55
Guildhall, disturbance in, 183–4
Guilford, Francis North, Lord, 100, 132
Gurney, Sir Richard, 139
Guy Fawkes' Plot (1605), 30

Haberdashers' Hall, 178
Hackney, 65, 206
hackney coaches, 47
Hale, Sir Matthew, 86, 88
Haley, K. H. D. (historian), 100
Halifax, George Savile, earl of, 177
Hampton Court, 174
Harrington, James, 22
Harrington, John, 181
Harris, Benjamin, 107, 110, 117, 119, 120,
  128, 130, 139, 147, 148, 167
  stands in the pillory, 130
Harris, Samuel, 102, 172
Harrison, Thomas, 39
Hatton, Charles, 160
hearth tax, 61, 190, 205, 206, 207
Henrietta Maria, 39, 78
Hesilrige, Sir Arthur, 189
Hewson, John, 43, 44
  mock execution of, 45
Hickeringill, Edmund, 124
high treason, 85, 88, 166, 168, 197
Hill, Christopher (historian), 1, 14, 28, 30,
  34, 36, 37, 61
Hobsbawm, Eric (historian), 1, 7, 90, 199
Hoffman, Benjamin, 225
Holborn, 52, 82, 111, 121
Holland, 223
Holmes, Geoffrey (historian), 4, 6, 189
Hounsditch, 120
house of lords, 47, 58, 60, 118
Howard of Escrick, Lord, 103, 150
Hubert, Robert, 79
huguenots, 200–1, 204
Hutton, Ronald (historian), 62
Hyde, Sir Lawrence, 18

ignoramus juries, 130–1, 149, 181, 182
independents, 33, 34, 40, 55, 69, 70, 74, 77
informers, 72–3, 76, 80–1, 182–3, 212
Ireton, Henry, 39
Irish Rebellion (1641), 30
Isle of Wight terms (1648), 40, 54, 55

James I, 23
Janeway, Richard, 107, 110, 120, 122, 154,
  171, 175, 212

Jessey, Henry, 52
jesuits, 33, 53, 97, 110, 111, 112, 115, 119,
  125, 134, 141, 144, 151, 175
Jones, J. R. (historian), 14, 30, 100, 190
Jonson, Ben, 54
journeymen, 32, 191–2, 200, 202, 203, 204

Keeling, Sir John, 88–9
Kidder, Richard, 68
Kiffin, William, 52
Killingworth, 179
King Street, 49, 180, 220

L'Estrange, Sir Roger, 113, 131, 132, 133,
  139–40, 150, 153, 164, 208
  burnt in effigy, 125, 179
  house attacked, 187
Lambert, John, 41, 50, 97
Langham, John, 186
Larkin, George, 120
Laud, William, 32, 35, 55, 56, 139, 150, 153
law enforcement, popular participation in,
  19–21, 24, 25, 224–5
Lawrence, Sir John, 178
Le Bon, Gustave (social psychologist), 6
Leadenhall Street, 48, 120
Leadenhall market, 206
levellers, 34, 37, 40, 42, 84, 89, 197, 208
liberty of conscience, 75, 83, 85, 217
Licensing Act (1662), 28, 96, 130
lieutenancy, 82, 165, 174, 183, 223
Lilburne, John, 197
Lilley, John, 89, 90
Lincoln's Inn, 214
Lindley, Keith (historian), 190
literacy, 27, 98, 215
Little Britain, 170, 219
liverymen, 18, 164, 183, 213
Lobb, Stephen, 69
Loder, John, 40
London, 225
  fires in, 111, 149, 157
  Great Fire of, 79, 81, 97, 111, 112, 175
  high-church areas, 121
  population, 11
  social topography, 12–13
London, City of, 2, 38, 51, 170, 172, 199,
  210, 221
  attachment to independence of, 29–30, 31,
  32, 41, 44
  attack on whig influence in, 132, 138, 154,
  183–6, 206, 223
  gates destroyed, 49, 58
  government, 11, 18
  petitions from, 48, 49, 174
Long Parliament, 58

lord mayor, 3, 18, 25, 71, 76, 82, 83, 167, 170, 174, 183, 195
  elections, 184, 185
  petitions to, 29, 44, 175
lord mayor's shows, 8, 31, 106, 123, 133
Louis XIV, 2, 94, 140
lower classes, tories and, 136–9, 152–3, 208–10
Loyola, Ignatius, 53, 123
Ludgate, 170, 171, 179, 187, 219
Luttrell, Narcissus, 207

Magna Carta, 113, 114, 136, 151
Manning, Brian (historian), 1
Mansell, Roderick, 148
Manton, Thomas, 59, 69, 86
Marvell, Andrew, 81, 92, 93, 205
Mary I, 30, 110, 158
Mary Stuart, princess of Orange, 96
Mary of Modena, 92, 151
Mason, John, 197
May Day, 22, 26, 27, 83, 89, 90
29 May, 38, 39, 59, 121, 166, 167, 168, 179, 181, 213, 219
maypoles, 54
Meal Tub Plot, 108, 119, 132, 148, 166, 170
meeting houses, attacks on, 52, 166, 217
Mercers' Chapel, 55
Mercers' Company, 185
Merchant-Tailors' Hall, 107, 177, 212
Middlesex
  bench, petitions from, 173, 174
  jurisdiction of, 12
Miller, John (historian), 14
Misopappas, Philanax, 124
Misson, Henri, 20
mob, origin of word, 3 and n. 16
monarchy
  god-like nature of, 57
  hostility towards, 37, 50–1, 61, 74–5
  support for, 34
  whigs and, 112–13, 117–18, 161–3, 178
Monck, George, duke of Albemarle, 16, 48, 49, 50, 52, 61
Monmouth's rebellion (1685), 223, 225
Monmouth, James Scott, duke of, 29, 178, 194, 198
  hostility to, 165, 179, 186
  support for, 130, 157, 158–61, 179, 186–8, 213
  tories and, 145–6, 149
  whigs and, 115–17, 156
monthly assessment, 42
Monument, 93, 111
Moore, Sir John, 135, 138, 186
  house attacked, 187

Moorfields, 82, 120, 148, 193, 204
Morley, George, 80
Morrill, John (historian), 35
Mullins, William, 52

Nalson, James, 141
Nantes, Edict of, 200
neo-Harringtonianism, 91, 93
New Palace Yard, 52, 104
New Prison, Clerkenwell, 83
New World, 110, 223
Newcastle, Thomas Pelham, duke of, 17
Newgate, 65, 121, 167, 196
Newington Butts, 194, 196, 197
Newmarket, Suffolk, 170, 225
newspapers, 106–7, 133, 171
nonconformists
  critical of Court, 80–1
  diversity amongst, 69–70
  geographical distribution of, 66–7, 121, 222
  hostility towards, 72–3, 166, 174, 225
  numbers of, 65–6
  and parliament, 76–8
  persecution of, 4, 63–5, 70–3, 85–7, 92, 182, 224–5
  and poor relief, 210
  and restored monarchy, 74–6
  social composition of, 67–8
  sympathy for, 68, 71–2, 182–3, 217
  tories and, 134, 138–44
  whigs and, 119–23, 165, 175, 178–9
  See also baptists, comprehension, fifth monarchists, independents, meeting houses, occasional conformity, presbyter-burnings, presbyterians, quakers, toleration
North, Dudley, 186, 187
North, Sir Roger, 3
5 November, 26, 30, 31, 93, 104, 140, 157, 169, 180, 186, 219, 220
17 November, 3, 31, 93, 103, 104, 110, 112, 120–1, 123, 157, 159, 163, 169, 180, 214, 219

Oates, Constant, 162
Oates, Titus, 96, 97, 102, 108, 111, 114, 119, 120, 125, 145, 147, 148, 172, 180
  burnt in effigy, 168
oaths of allegiance, 28, 70
occasional conformity, 68–9, 70
Old Exchange, 43
Ormonde, James Butler, duke of, 177, 207
Ossory, Thomas Butler, earl of, 167
Ossulston, petition from grand jury of, 141–2
Owen, John, 86

Oxford parliament, 113, 121, 130, 132, 135, 149, 150, 157, 161, 162, 174, 180, 214

Page, Damaris, 83, 84
Papillon, Thomas, 186
Parker, Dr, 182
Parkhurst, Thomas, 177
parliament
    hostility towards, 76–8, 165
    tories and, 150–1
    whigs and, 113–14, 163, 172–3, 175, 177
    See also exclusion parliament, free parliament, Long Parliament, Oxford parliament, Rump
Partridge, John, 106
Pearl, Valerie (historian), 18, 19, 209, 222
Pelling, Edward, 144
Pennington, Isaac, 139
Pepys, Samuel, 43, 45, 49, 74, 78, 80, 83, 84, 86, 205
Peters, Hugh, 55–6
petitions, 29, 35, 36, 42–4, 46–8, 49, 59, 172–7, 183, 195–6, 199–203, 214, 220, 221
Peyton, Sir Robert, 148
Pilkington, Sir Thomas, 130, 185
pillory, 20, 24, 130, 187, 194
Player, Sir Thomas, 147
playing cards, 102, 108, 110, 111, 112, 119, 133
plays, 54, 103, 109, 110, 133
plots, 75, 121, 132, 148–50, 207, 225
    See also Meal Tub Plot, Monmouth's rebellion, Rye House Plot, Venner's rising
Plumb, J. H. (historian), 91
Plunkett, Oliver, 108
Pocock, John (historian), 91, 93
poll tax, 205
poor relief, 209–11
pope-burnings, 3, 5, 8, 26, 93, 101, 103–6, 109, 110, 112, 113, 123–4, 125, 157, 159, 163, 178, 179, 180, 219, 226
    routes of, 120–1
Popish Plot, 3, 94, 96, 97, 108, 164
Poplar, 82
porters, 29, 202, 208
Portsmouth, Louise de la Querouaille, duchess of, 79, 94
Prance, Miles, 182
presbyter-burnings, 121, 133, 169, 170, 219
presbyterians
    attitude towards episcopacy, 54, 74
    Civil War politics, 33, 34, 35, 40
    comprehension and, 54, 69, 86
    dons and ducklings, 69–70

hostility towards, 54–5, 59, 166
    Indulgences and, 70, 77
    persecution, 63, 70
    and Restoration, 37, 46, 53–4, 217
    whigs and, 119, 120, 122, 134, 163, 178
    See also anti-catholicism, Meal Tub Plot, nonconformists, presbyter-burnings
Price, John, 188
Pride's Purge, 40
Pritchard, Sir William, 138, 185
    house attacked, 187
propagandists
    assaults on, 101–2, 154
    tory, 132–3
    whig, 101–2, 103, 106–7, 119–20
Protectorate, 36, 37, 40, 41
protestants in masquerade, 112, 128
Prynne, William, 33, 97
puritans, 32–3, 122, 141
Pym, John, 33

Quaker Act (1662), 63
quakers, 33, 40, 69, 70, 72, 75, 76, 77, 119, 186, 197
    collective assaults on, 52
Queen's Head Tavern, 179

radicalism, 34, 74–8, 92, 117–18, 161–3
    See also seditious words
Rawlins, Edward, 133
recusancy laws (35 Elizabeth), 64, 122, 145
Reformation, 109, 123
republican literature, 92
Restoration
    hostility towards, 47, 49, 50–1
    support for, 2, 36–7, 38–9, 45–6, 47, 49, 51
Rich, Sir Peter, 186, 187
Robinson, Sir John, 194
Rochester, John Wilmot, earl of, 94
Rochester, Kent, 38
Rogers, Nicholas (historian), 6, 14
Rouse, Sir John, 149
Royal Exchange, 187–8, 202
royal prerogative
    attacks on, 78
Rudé, George (historian), 1, 5, 6, 7, 8, 9, 13, 15, 68, 189, 199, 211
Rugge, Thomas, 38, 41, 42, 45, 46, 49
Rump, 36, 41, 42, 45, 48, 57, 58
    defended, 47
    dissolution of, 49
rump-burnings, 49, 166, 170, 213, 217, 219, 222
Russell, Mr, 178
Russell, William Lord, 223

Rutland, Mr, 168, 169
Rye House Plot, 132, 141, 145, 150, 162, 207, 223, 225, 226

Sacheverell, Henry, 16, 17, 153
Sadlers' Hall, 177
St Albans, Hertfordshire, 48
St Alphage, 160
St Bartholomew Exchange, 40
St Botolph-without-Aldersgate, 66–7 and n. 17
St Botolph-without-Bishopsgate, 66–7 and n. 17, 120
St Bride, 210
St Clement Dane, 55
St Dunstan's Hill, 52
St Dunstan-in-the-West, 49, 121, 210
St George, Botolph Lane, 225
St Giles-in-the-Fields, 65, 71, 160
St Giles-without-Cripplegate, 35, 59, 66–7 and n. 17, 75, 206, 222–3, 225
St Helen Bishopsgate, 68
St James's Fields, 48
St John, Pawlet, 119
St Margaret Westminster, 209
St Martin's Lane, 38
St Martin-in-the Fields, 121, 154, 159, 166, 222
   Society of Young Men of, 211
St Paul's, 170, 181
St Peter's College, Westminster, 169
St Sepulchre, 59
Salutation Tavern, Lombard Street, 100, 119
Savoy, 25
Scottish covenanters, 33, 97, 119, 134
Scroggs, Sir William, 130
seamen, 29, 44, 83, 207, 214
sects, 35, 37, 40–1, 55, 63, 70, 132, 217
   and Restoration, 59–60
   hostility towards, 52–3, 70
   See also anti-catholicism, baptists, fifth monarchists, quakers
seditious libel, 28, 130, 154–5
seditious words, 37, 50–1, 61, 74, 75, 79, 158, 161–3, 165–6, 205, 213, 220–1
sermons, 55, 102, 133, 138, 140, 141, 148, 150, 209, 226
Settle, Elkannah, 101
Shadwell, Thomas, 101
Shaftesbury, Anthony Ashley Cooper, earl of, 93, 100, 101, 103, 115, 120, 145, 149, 161, 221, 223
   Association, 132, 134–5, 149, 174, 176, 214
   attacked in tory press, 146–7
   brisk boys, 207, 225, 226

burnt in effigy, 170
   demonstrations in support of, 159, 188
   trial of, 149, 180–2, 219, 220
Sharp, Buchanan (historian), 190
Sheldon, Gilbert, 80, 85, 86, 87
sheriffs, 3, 18, 23
   disputed election of, 186
   whig, 130, 164, 181, 185
Sherlock, William, 141
Shils, E. and M. Young (sociologists), 8
shoemakers, 67, 215
Shoreditch, 82, 194
Shorter, Sir John, 184
Shrove Tuesday, 22, 23, 24, 83, 85, 87, 91
Shute, Samuel, 130, 181, 185
Sidney, Algernon, 145, 223
Simons, Captain, 170, 179, 187
Six Weeks Meeting of London Quakers, 211
Smith, Arthur (historian), 156, 190, 213
Smith, Francis, 101, 107, 110, 120, 130, 147, 148, 149
Smith, Steven (historian), 17, 23
Smithfield, 103, 121, 159
soldiers, ex-Cromwellian, 88–9, 162–3
solemn league and covenant, 53, 63
   burnings of, 59, 168, 169
Somerset House, 48, 183
Southwark, 11, 19, 21, 29, 31, 51, 59, 74, 82, 199, 202, 221–2
   demonstrations in, 38, 93
   fires in, 111
   nonconformists in, 65
   petitions from, 35, 172, 174
   regicides in, 21
   riots in, 54, 182, 193, 194, 195, 196
Spain, 30, 36, 112
Spanish ambassador, coach besieged, 30
Spanish Armada (1588), 30, 112
Spanish Wars, 41
Spitalfields, 13, 189, 193, 197, 204, 207
Stafford, William Howard, Viscount, 108, 112, 165
Stationers' Company, 154
Stepney, 11, 12, 193, 209, 210, 211
Stillingfleet, Edward, 144
Stillingfleet, Mr, 177, 178, 179, 182, 204
Stocks Market, 186
Strafford, Thomas Wentworth, earl of, 55, 139, 150
Strand, 49, 159, 160, 166, 167, 173, 219, 220
Stratford le Bow, 193
succession
   tories and, 151–2
   whigs and, 114
Sunderland, Robert Spencer, earl of, 177

Surrey
  jurisdiction of, 12
  riots in, 193
Sussoins, countess of, 183
Sutherland, Dame Lucy (historian), 9
Swan Tavern, Fish Street, 100, 172

tailors, 26, 67, 90, 203, 215
tavern signs, destroyed by whig crowds, 186
tax strike, 49
Templars, 25, 121, 179, 180, 214
Temple, 25, 111, 157, 168, 174, 214
Temple Bar, 49, 93, 103, 104, 105, 113, 120,
  121, 160, 179, 181, 219
Test Act (1673), 92, 120, 158
Thames Street, 52
Thames, freezes over, 190, 207
Thirty Years' War, 30
Thomas, Keith (historian), 23
Thompson, Edward (historian), 1, 7
Thompson, Nathaniel, 118, 131, 133, 134,
  140, 147, 148, 151, 152, 161, 181, 212,
  214, 223
  assaulted or threatened, 154, 179
  house attacked, 187
  suspected leader of tory apprentices, 167–8
Threadneedle Street, 202
tithe strike, 40
toleration, 28, 40, 60, 69, 77, 86–7, 92, 140,
  141
Tonge, Israel, 147
Tooke, Benjamin, 133, 154
tory reaction, 3, 64, 76, 182–6, 211, 223–7
Tower, 112, 181
Tower Hamlets, 21, 210, 211, 214, 221
Tower Street, 52, 181
trained bands, 21, 73, 82, 165, 187, 194,
  213, 223, 224
  model for crowds, 25, 89
Trenchard, family, 119
Trinity Minories, 221

Venner's Rising (1661), 60, 88
Verney, John, 151, 160
Verney, Sir Edmund, 151

Waller, Sir William, 104, 166
Wapping, 221
war victories, celebration of, 31–2
Ward, Sir Patience, 111, 123, 175, 178, 184,
  185
wardmote, 18–19, 222
Warwick Lane, 182
Warwickshire, 89, 90
watchmen, 20, 21, 26, 82, 187, 195
watermen, 29, 44, 53, 89, 207, 208, 209,
  210, 214, 221–2

petition of, fraudulently obtained, 47
weavers, 67, 189, 204, 207, 215
  foreign competition, 199–201
  poverty of, 191–2
  riots, 89, 192–8, 201, 215–16, 221, 224
Weavers' Company, 195, 196, 197, 199, 200,
  201
West Country, 225
West, Robert, 111
Westminster, 11, 19, 21, 185, 199, 210, 214,
  220, 221
  demonstrations in, 38, 39, 47, 48–9, 170,
  219–20
  jurisdiction of, 12
  nonconformists in, 222
  petitions from, 172, 173, 174
  riots in, 52, 193
Westminster Confession(1648), 53
Westminster Hall, 11
whigs and tories
  geographical distribution of support, 218–
  23
  social composition of supporters, 212–15
  See also apprentices, clubs, Monmouth
White's Alley Baptist Church, 211
Whitebread, Thomas, 119
Whitechapel, 12, 120, 121, 193
Whitefriars, 168
Whitelocke, Bulstrode, 42
Whitsun, riots at, 22
Whittan, Colonel, 47
Wildman, John, 226
Wilkins, John, 86
Will's Coffee-House, Covent Garden, 170
William of Orange, 4, 96
Williams, Sheila (historian), 103
Williamson, Sir Joseph, 197
women, 46, 72, 193 and n. 24, 196
Worcester House Declaration (1660), 54

xenophobia, 26, 30–1, 32, 152, 191, 198–
  204, 215, 216

Yarmouth, Norfolk, 170
York, James, duke of, 39, 132, 225, 226
  catholicism of, 78, 91–2
  dines with Artillery Company, 107, 158,
  171
  Great Fire, suspected complicity in, 79
  hostility to, 83–4, 93, 157–8, 161, 186
  reconversion rumoured, 170
  support for, 156, 165, 169–71, 173, 174,
  179, 186, 198, 219
  tories and, 151–2
  whigs and, 96, 114–15